MAN
and the
Biosphere
Toward A Coevolutionary Political Economy

Kenneth M. Stokes

D0081984

M.E. Sharpe

Armonk, New York
London, England

Copyright © 1992 by M.E. Sharpe, Inc.

All rights reserved. No part of this book may be reproduced in any
form without written permission from the publisher, M.E. Sharpe, Inc.,
80 Business Park Drive, Armonk, New York 10504.

Available in the United Kingdom and Europe from M.E. Sharpe,
Publishers, 3 Henrietta Street, London WC2E 8LU.

Library of Congress Cataloging-in-Publication Data

Stokes, Kenneth M.
Man and the biosphere: toward a coevolutionary political economy
/ by Kenneth M. Stokes
p. cm.

Includes bibliographical references and index.
ISBN 1–56324–023–8
1. Communism and ecology. 2. Marxian economics.
3. Human ecology.
I. Title
HX550.E25S76 1992
306.3'45—dc20
91–31580
CIP

Printed in the United States of America

The paper used in this publication meets the minimum requirements
of American National Standard for Information Sciences—
Permanence of Paper for Printed Library Materials, ANSI Z39.48–1984.

∞

BB   10   9   8   7   6   5   4   3   2   1

Contents

FIGURES   vii

PREFACE   ix

1. PHILOSOPHICAL ORIGINS OF OPEN-SYSTEMS ECONOMIC ANALYSIS

Introduction	3
Historical Background to the Development of Economic Thought	9
The Origins of Political Economy	13
The Concept of Nature in the Totality Theory of Marx and Engels	31
Conclusion	64

2. BROADENING ECONOMIC ANALYSIS: THE EARLY CONTRIBUTION OF THE GENERAL THEORY OF ORGANIZATION

Introduction	66
Discovery of Thermodynamics and the Collapse of the Laplacean Prototype	67
Unity of Scientific Knowledge	69
Contributions of N.I. Bukharin	84
Heretical Philosophers of Social Energetics	89
The Physiocracy of Frederick Soddy	90
Conclusion	93

3. NEO-PHYSIOCRATIC AND BIOPHYSICAL MODELS OF THE ECONOMIC PROCESS

Introduction   95

Generational Concerns   95

General Systems, Open Systems, and Living Systems   99

Living Systems and Economic Systems: Political Economy   122
  in the Broad Sense

Models of the Biophysical Approach to the Economic Process   132

Conclusions   159

4. BEYOND ENTROPY AND THE ECONOMIC PROCESS: BROADENING ECONOMIC ANALYSIS FROM A SYSTEMS THEORETICAL APPROACH

Introduction   162

Complexification through Differentiation   164

Living Systems, Organizational Dissonance, and Cybernetics   171

The Problem of Wholes and Their Complexity   182

Living Systems, Autopoietic and Allopoietic Systems   187

Hierarchy of Finalities and the General Principle of   200
  Descending Constraints

Political Economy for the Epoch of the Noösphere   206

Conclusions   223

5. GENERAL CONCLUSIONS   227

NOTES   231

GLOSSARY   279

BIBLIOGRAPHY   285

INDEX   317

Figures

3.1. Model of the Circular Flow   107

3.2. Metabolic Model of the Economic Process   125

3.3. Integrated Biospheric–Socioeconomic Models   134

3.4. Koenig's Socio-Cybernetic and Bioeconomic Model   137

3.5. Nijkamp's Open-System Economic Model   143

4.1. Matrix A   174

4.2. Matrix B: Payoff   176

4.3. Cybernetic Dialectics   184

4.4. The Embeddedness of Socioeconomic Relations
      within the Noösphere   204

Preface

The development of modern man is not yet complete, and his creative, but not fully utilized potential is awaiting its further development. Based on this hypothesis, we may refer to the emergence of the Noösphere as a stage in the evolution of the Biosphere; a stage in which man becomes aware of his capacity to influence the further course of evolution. The Noösphere is not merely a portion of space. What is implied is an epoch of Noösphere, an epoch in which the planet's further evolution will be directed by reason. Mankind's entry into the Noösphere epoch means that the earth's evolution has entered a new channel wherein its further flow should ensure the coevolution of man and the Biosphere as an indispensable condition of society's further development. Moreover, it represents a stage in which the power of technological systems is restructured to renounce that form of rationality that has spawned an unthinking destruction of nature, in favor of one that supports the cultivation of the inner aspirations of life.

However, if the epoch of the Noösphere does not crystallize, then the currently existing gap between the real world and its problems, on the one hand, and our understanding of that world, on the other, will increase. In this connection, it is imperative that a synthesis of science emanate from generalized and integral knowledge, and that any progress can be uniquely scientific when it delineates an ethical, moral, social, or political advancement, an improvement in our customs and behavior. In a word, our scientific progress must be cultural in the broadest sense.

By developing material production mankind has in effect incorporated a special artificial organ into the organism of the Biosphere. This activity must be coordinated not only with our aims in terms of both society and production, but also with the functioning of the Biosphere. Material production should be a planned reorganization of the Biosphere which does not transform it into a sick and decaying organism. This theme is maturing due to renewed interest in the works of T. de Chardin and V.I. Vernadsky, however a major obstacle to its development has been the orientation of economic analysis on the narrow conceptualizations of the self-regulating market rather than on multilevel forms of socio-technico-Biospheric planning. It is a view in which the technocratic perspective of the evolution of technological systems opposes itself to socially embedded forms. This development itself is a departure from the humanist sentiments that enlightened classical political economy.

Since its eighteenth-century origins, economic thought has endeavored to make intelligible industrial society. To this end it has elaborated numerous concepts and theories. The thought of the first economists and later that of humanist critics presented an image of the livelihood of man as a subordinate subsystem within the three spheres of society, polity, and nature. And some theorists accommodated themselves to a naturalistic conception. Later analysts understood man's interaction among the three spheres ontologically and situated the economy within an institutional setting; a concept later expunged by the Ricardian tradition. Certainly by the middle of the nineteenth century, if not earlier, economic interpretations of the industrial society were suspected not only of being covertly ideological, but also of being overly disposed to mechanicalism and to the predispositions of the natural philosophy of the Enlightenment.

Today one of the most common criticisms of orthodox economics is that it is grounded on the psychology, moral philosophy, and even the theology of the eighteenth century, all of which, as we know, perpetuated earlier habits of thought that are at variance with present knowledge. Economics is by no means the only science to embody ancient fallacies, but it is perhaps unique among contemporary studies in being the only one in which nineteenth-century (and earlier) habits of thought define the prevailing tradition.

In particular ways the fallacies were succumbing to a paradigm change that was overtaking science, slowly insinuating itself into substantive modes of economic analysis even at the end of the last century. Contiguous to the humanist search for a liberating unity of scientific knowledge, elements of a social energetic theory, together with a general theory of organization and cybernetic concepts of open systems were penetrating economic thought. While the explicit introduction of energy analysis into the social sciences cultivated a reductionist approach, it also led to an appreciation of the concept of open, living systems as a viable alternative to the closed, mechanical model.

While the theoretical traditions of political economy are diverse and interdisciplinary, it is becoming increasingly diversified. A growing contemporary disenchantment with elements of conventional economic thought, as well as a return to substantive categories of analysis are leading to a broader understanding of the biophysical realities of the livelihood of man. We now have a surfeit of possible lines of inquiry including cybernetics, systems theory, information theory, as well as subtle concepts such as self-referentiality and complexity, transcending even relatively recent advances in understanding the economy in the broad sense. In particular, principles underlying the general theory of organization are perceived as relevant to the *problematique* of institution formation and address freedom in technified society.

The contemporary effort to integrate these interdisciplinary lines of inquiry within a socioeconomic context began to emerge as a metascience as early as the beginning of this century. Today these lines of inquiry require us to think at a high level of abstraction and compel us to use formulations that simultaneously point in many directions. Moreover, if we seriously intend to seek an interdisciplinary synthesis, we are compelled to employ a rarefied language of synthesis, a language that compares perhaps unfavorably to that employed in more familiar interpretations.

Technified society is now confronted with novel challenges that must be brought into view and consciousness even when the solutions themselves confound science. Modern society was already relatively far advanced in the eighteenth century when it began to respond to its own structures. At that time this reaction took the form of socioeconomic theories that registered the peculiarities of society's functional domains. Today technified society's impact on social, economic, and Biospheric domains has been altered fundamentally; for it has become evident that the evolution of such a society might threaten the basic preconditions for human life itself. Thus, it has also become clear that the question of how much time we have available is beginning to play a critical role in our thinking about the livelihood of man.

Even while the possibilities for theoretical synthesis have become richer, the socioeconomic need for interpretation has become more urgent and time has become scarce. At this juncture we must avoid the potentially fatal slide toward arcane specialization—even if this means that the background and conceptual framework of our arguments may remain obscure to the uninitiated.

Moreover, insofar as the orthodox tradition endures, we cannot disregard the challenge that now presents itself in terms of a resurgence of fundamentalist market mentality, a resurgence identified with neoconservatism and an archaic rhetoric. For underlying the mentality that informs orthodoxy is a denial of free will, which finds its legitimation in Natural Philosophy. However, as a source of social legitimation, in denying that both free will and power and compulsion are necessary for any functioning social order, it encourages technocratic modes of regulation. Hopefully, it is an errant current in the closing years of twentieth-century drift, a nostalgic response to the complexities of technified society. But history teaches us that sanguine hopes are incongruous. Nor should we take any assurances in believing that the technospheric threat is the author of its own negativity, inevitably leading us to a new appreciative system. The role of the critic of orthodoxy remains that of emancipating economic belief from the sterility of conventional economic thought. The time may yet come when the root of the contemporary confusion and cause of intellectual impotency, which has brought economics into general disrepute, is identified with an obsession with the mechanics of closed systems. The virtual identification of conventional economic thought with closed systems to the near total exclusion of an understanding of the life process of mankind has rendered orthodoxy sterile in addressing in substantive ways the global issues confronting mankind.

The purpose of this work is to further advance the interdisciplinary synthesis of a number of selected and emerging themes in the work of institutionalists and general systems theorists of the livelihood of man.

Kenneth M. Stokes
June 1992

MAN
and the
Biosphere

Philosophical Origins of Open-Systems Economic Analysis

Introduction

From the Age of Reason there emerged an atomistic and naturalistic philosophy of man distinct from the long-held Aristotelian and ethical perspectives. While that philosophy eventually manifested itself in liberal political tendencies, with the transformation of society that attended the Industrial Revolution, it also permeated economic thought. Moreover, two general themes may be identified throughout the development of economic thought—the occasionally suppressed, but nonetheless recurrent, substantive and institutional perspective and the inveterate mechanical paradigm.[1]

From a view of man integrated with nature and embedded within society, at the time of the Industrial Revolution there emerged the theoretical foundations of classical and postclassical economic analysis. The institutional structure of industrial capitalism disembedded the economy from society and polity and abstracted it from nature by turning labor, land, and natural resources into commodities—organizing their supply as though they were items produced for sale and allowing the price mechanism to determine their distribution. In conjunction with this development there emerged a naturalistic and mechanical concept of nature and society.

In pure science, according to Joseph Needham, the concept of mechanical causation, or, to be more accurate, the concentration of interest on the Aristotelian efficient cause, to the exclusion of the Aristotelian final cause, was of enormous importance. So, writes Needham, men were to be thought of as selfish monads or corpuscles, like the atoms of natural science, with the price mechanism imitating the Newtonian laws of motion.[2]

In this connection, while the classical economists incorporated ethical, biological, and demographic dimensions of economic reproduction, the emergence of a concept of value dissociated first from nature and then from man encouraged the detachment of the concept of economic reproduction from its substantive basis. Moreover, the emergence of the self-regulating market demanded nothing less than the institutional separation of society into economic and political spheres.[3]

While no society can exist long without some kind of system that ensures order in the production and distribution of goods, this does not imply the existence of separate institutions; for normally the economic order is merely a function, and a subservient one at that, of the social order in which it is contained. Nineteenth-century society, in which economic activity was imputed to a distinctive economic motive, represented a heroic departure.[4] The narrowing of economic thought led to an atomistic concept of society. A view arose that society and its institutions were organically determined, and, in fact, subservient to the economy.[5] However, both the progressive expulsion of the societal perspective on formalist theoretical grounds, together with the factual social dislocations of the period, sparked a humanist response which coalesced in the historic debate known as the *Methodenstreit*. This debate between the nascent Neoclassical School and the German Historical School, initiated a reevaluation of the substantive issues: of the role of the economy in society, of the axioms and doctrines of market-oriented theory, and later, of the substantive and institutional foundations of the economy itself.

If Newton, Descartes, and Bacon formulated the physics of the mechanical paradigm, then one must search no further than Baruch Spinoza, John Locke, and Adam Smith for the analogy in social relations. These men sought to discover the relationship between the universal laws and the workings of society. Spinoza and Locke brought the workings of government and society in line with the mechanical paradigm; and Adam Smith, together with later luminaries, attempted the same for the economy.[6]

Few social scientists accept, on the whole, the Enlightenment's pristine image of man contracting for his freedoms and bartering his goods to form his society and economy. However, in spite of the accretion of our current understanding of man's social process as a rich interplay of biophysical and social relations, there remains the recalcitrant popularity of atomistic individualism. For at important junctures, social scientists resort to earlier rationalizations of man as a utilitarian atom. Nowhere is this lapse into primitive sociology more apparent than in our ideas concerning the economy. In short, the economist is hampered by the intellectual heritage of the Enlightenment, with its image of man's alleged propensity "to truck, barter, and exchange." This image of "economic man" remains in spite of occasional attempts to provide a social framework and a biophysical foundation for the economy.

In the late nineteenth century, Thorstein Veblen argued that man is not to be comprehended in terms of sophisticated economic laws, in which his innate ferocity and creativity are smothered in a cloak of rationalism. He is better dealt with in the less flattering, but more fundamental vocabulary of the anthropologist or the psychologist: a creature of strong irrational drives, credulous, untutored, and ritualistic. "Leave aside the flattering fictions," Veblen asked of economists, "and find out why he behaves as he does."[7]

It is not with the success or failure of conventional or Marxian economic theory to analyze industrial capitalism that we take issue, but rather with the leading ideas associated with the analytical systems—ideas, that have become fossilized axiomatic notions, as conventional, permanent, and general truths.

Today it is generally recognized that fragmentary and uncoordinated actions of both individual and groups of countries can no longer overcome global contradictions, and that a coevolutionary strategy must be developed for the entire human race regardless of its economic, political, and cultural heterogeneity. In the context of peaceful coexistence of states with different social structures, such a strategy demands international cooperation in solving global problems. The corresponding internationalization will provide a basis for the further development of human civilization.

But in order to correctly evaluate the global processes that are being generated by human activities, to conceive the possible course of future events, and to draft a possible program of research activities that are needed to arrive at a long-term strategy for the human race, it is necessary to develop a general conceptual platform to analyze the present world situation. Many research scientists share the view that such a platform could be based on the Soviet scientist Vladimir I. Vernadsky's general image of the evolution of the earth and his proposition that in the next biogeological age more advanced forms of human consciousness, embodied in a "Noösphere," will increasingly influence all forms of evolution.

It was Vernadsky who first drew attention to the increasing scale of human intervention into planetary biogeochemical cycles. He was one of the first to popularize the notion of the Biosphere, and in concert with the Jesuit paleontologist Pierre Teilhard de Chardin, he developed the notion of the Noösphere—an evolving collective human consciousness on Earth exerting an ever-increasing influence on Biospheric evolutionary processes.[8]

The term Noösphere is composed from two Greek words: "noos," mind, and sphere, in the sense of an envelope of Earth. The emergence of the Noösphere refers to a stage in the evolution of the Biosphere in which man becomes aware of his capacity to influence the further course of evolution. Moreover, it represents a stage in which the power of technological systems is restructured to renounce that form of rationality that has spawned the technological imperative—an unthinking destruction of nature—in favor of a substantive form of rationality that supports the cultivation of the inner aspirations of life. For Vernadsky, this conscious influence itself signaled a new era in the evolution of the Biosphere.

Teilhard de Chardin believed that an evolutionary threshold would emerge with a collective consciousness that would exercise control over the direction of future planetary evolution.[9] For Teilhard, the transition to the epoch of the Noösphere was a movement from biological to psychological and spiritual evolution. Following Hegel, and not unlike Marx (eschatologically interpreted),[10] Teilhard viewed history as the march of the spirit toward freedom. For both Hegel and Teilhard, freedom can be found only in self-consciousness, and absolute self-consciousness is to be found in God.[11] However, unlike Teilhard's idealist and finalistic conception, Vernadsky introduced the materialist concept of the Noösphere.

For Vernadsky the transformation of the Biosphere through human interference was the process of noögenesis—the creation of the Noösphere. He believed that the growth of science and technology would transform inadvertent human interference in global biogeochemistry to more deliberate and purposeful intervention. This change would constitute the transition from Biosphere to Noösphere. According to Vernadsky, human development would be enhanced and sustained in the Noösphere through respect and management of biogeochemical cycles—the limits of planetary life-support systems.[12] He was convinced that this transition was taking place through the influence of scientific achievement and was impatient for humanity to recognize this phenomenon and to direct it consciously. He reasoned that securing the transition to the Noösphere constituted the greatest challenge facing humanity, namely, "the problem of reconstruction of the Biosphere in the interest of freely thinking humanity as a single totality."[13] For Vernadsky, the international pursuit of science was not just the major goal of human intellectual activity, but the best hope for the human species, since only science had a universal binding force.

Above all, Vernadsky believed that the Noösphere was the medium within which humanity could find fulfillment through exercising deliberate and conscious control over its milieu.

The development of the Biosphere into the Noösphere is a natural phenomenon, more profound and powerful in essence than human history. Vernadsky wrote: "This fresh stage in the history of the planet cannot be compared, without modification, to its historical past. This stage creates something that is essentially new in the Earth's history, and not only in the history of mankind."[14]

The socialization of man has greatly accelerated all evolutionary processes within the Biosphere and has brought it to a threshold beyond which its further development can only be secured by human reason. For the activity of men, rational as far as their intentions are concerned, now often proves to be destructive on the scale of the entire Biosphere and limits the possibilities of further development.

> Mankind by developing material production, has in effect, incorporated a special artificial organ into the organism of the Biosphere. This activity must be coordinated not only with our aims in terms of both society and production, but also with the functioning of the Biosphere. Material production should be a

planned reorganization of the Biosphere which does not transform it into a sick and decaying organism.[15]

In this connection, institutional adjustment mechanisms must form a focal point of substantive institutional analysis. Indeed, the political economy in the broad sense pertains to the harmonizing of social relations and to the politicizing and reinstitutionalization of technological relations consistent with the broader imperatives of life and with the Biosphere. The complex forms of analysis that the design and evaluation of institutions require call for an ultimate guiding principle in rejecting some modes of technological evolution while accepting and controlling others. Such a principle is implied in Vernadsky's proposition that in the next biogeological age more advanced forms of human awareness, embodied in a "Noösphere," will increasingly influence all forms of evolution. It requires, however, additional conceptual distinctions in economic science.

While this theme is maturing, due to renewed interest in the work of Teilhard and Vernadsky, a major obstacle to its development has been the orientation of economic analysis on the cybernetics of the self-regulating market rather than on multilevel forms of socio-technico-Biospheric planning. It is a view in which the technocratic perspective of the evolution of technological systems opposes itself to socially embedded forms. This doctrine has cultivated a disregard for socially irresponsible and uncontrolled forms of development of the Technosphere.

In considering specific non-utopian ways in which more advanced forms of human awareness may effectively rival other influences over the evolution of biological and geological entities, one must distinguish explicitly between an institutionally legitimated autonomous Technosphere, on the one hand, and more direct normative embodiments of the human mind and of society on the other.[16]

The general theory of the interaction of society and man (as social phenomena) with the natural environment has been identified with a broadening understanding of political economy. This approach, alternatively identified as the "coevolutionary" or "noöspheric" school, must begin with the notion of "Noösphere." The "coevolutionary" approach is the socio- and technoeconomic approach, which while concentrating on the characterization of societal and technological conditions, also includes biophysical and sociocultural constraints which, both under capitalism and socialism, affect the interrelationship of man and nature. The coevolutionary school represents a new humanism; an appreciation of the inalienable. But "coevolutionary humanism" must be consciously guided toward a planetary political and cultural order. "The total essential unity of man with nature, the true Renaissance of nature, a realized naturalism of man and realized humanism of nature."[17]

In this connection the further development of the substantive classical branch of economic analysis is relevant in ways that transcend marginalist analysis. This branch, which is fundamentally concerned with the social problem of avoiding disharmonies between forms of social organization, together with the analytical categories of cybernetics, identifies specific qualities that must be reincorporated by institutions if they are to effect a "reinversion." It is in the attempt to fashion and adapt institutions appropriate for man in the epoch of the Noösphere that mankind may well meet its ultimate test.

Flourishing at its apogee, mankind is confronting a vital challenge that will be registered as one of the most critical in its history—for it has now reached a period in which man becomes aware of his capacity to influence the further course of evolution. Indeed, mankind has entered a phase in the conscious evolution of the Noösphere whereby mankind will either realize itself or destroy itself. The present period in the history of both the human race and the planet as a whole is marked by an intense acceleration of all evolutionary processes, by the consolidation of a highly interdependent world system, and by an erosion of the boundaries between human evolution and human ecology. It is worth repeating that the epoch of the Noösphere represents a stage in which the power of technological systems must be restructured to renounce that form of rationality that has spawned the unthinking destruction of nature, in favor of a form of rationality that supports the cultivation of the inner aspirations of life.

A central proposition in this work is that in the continuing dialectical development of economic thought there exists a recurrent and ever-elaborated substantive theme—a theme that we shall contend is appropriate in the reformation of economic thought in the epoch of the Noösphere.

Chapter 1 refers to the economic thought of the Physiocrats and later of Marx and Engels, and presents a reference image of the livelihood of man metabolically interacting with the Biosphere. For F. Quesnay, both in his *Maxims* and in *Natural Right*, the economy is analyzed as a subordinate system within society, polity, and nature. With Marx and Engels, following Hegel, this image is once again present, but in an altered context. Whereas the Physiocrats held to a "naturalistic" image, Marx and Engels understood man's metabolic interaction with nature ontologically and situated the economy within an institutional setting. Though their understanding released them from the bonds of naturalism, they were nonetheless carriers of traditional elements of the Enlightenment, a heritage that framed their approach to man's liberation.

Chapter 2 maintains that in the latter years of the elaboration of Marx's and Engels's analysis, developments in the physical and biological sciences were substantially revising the Newtonian model. In particular ways a paradigm change was overtaking these sciences and slowly insinuating itself into substantive modes of economic analysis. Thereafter, several Marxian philosophers sought to revise Marxist thought on the basis of such developments. Contiguous to Marx's and Engels's quest for a liberating unity of scientific knowledge, revisionist Soviet Marxists introduced into the literature elements of a social energetic theory, together with a general theory of organization and cybernetic concepts of open systems. While the explicit introduction of energy analysis into the social sciences cultivated a reductionist approach, it also led to the gradual appreciation of the concept of open and living systems as a viable alternative to the closed, mechanical Newtonian model.

Chapter 3 reviews the recent contributions and observes that the economic reality of man's metabolic interaction with the Biosphere presented itself, in the developed economies, with renewed emphasis in the 1960s. Coincidentally, at that time there was both a growing disenchantment with elements of conventional Marxist and Neoclassical economic thought, as well as a rediscovery of the broad applicability of the general theory of organization. On the one hand, this coincidence led to a broader and substantive understanding of the biophysical realities of the livelihood of man and in particular to a nonreductionist revision of elements of conventional economic analysis according to the theory of open systems. On the other hand, the pervasiveness of market mentality and economistic rationality occasioned the renewal of reductionist social energetics.

Finally, Chapter 4 notes that the relatively recent return to substantive and institutional categories and modes of analysis that attach to an understanding of the economy in the broad sense increasingly focuses on the biophysical and thermodynamic dimensions of the economic process. However, the additional categories of analysis that attach to the general theory of organization, including the cybernetics of autopoietic systems, transcend the earlier open-systems approach. In particular, principles underlying the general theory of organization are relevant to the issue of institutional formations and the issue of freedom in technified society. At this juncture in economic thought the open-systems approach to the economic process marks a further elaboration of the moral and ethical concerns that first imbued the Physiocrats.

Historical Background to the Development of Economic Thought

The evolution of economic thought cannot be divorced from the conception that man has had of his relation to nature, on the one hand, and to society, on the other hand. A society's view of the cosmos is heavily biased in favor of how it is organized. This highly rationalized perspective has been unavoidable. It seems only predictable for conventional philosophers to come to the conclusion that the economic, political, and social reality they experience must, in fact, be reality. It is but a short jump to fashioning a model of nature that is strikingly similar to that world fashioned by society. It is not surprising, then, that man has found comfort in believing that society is organized in accordance with the operating principles of nature. Such a naturalistic contrivance is a simple device by which humanity's behavior is elevated to cosmic importance—a notion by which we convince ourselves that our actions are consistent with the grand operating system of the cosmos.

While cosmologies have long been an essential feature of human society, it is necessary to draw a distinction between the preindustrial and industrial image of nature. In European preindustrial and agricultural societies before the end of the eighteenth century, an attitude prevailed of submission to the state of dependence on natural forces.[18] At this time, man's relationship with nature was more participatory than exploitative. Constrained by its physical capacity to purposively manipulate and redirect nature, society's preoccupation was with coevolving with the forces of nature.[19] In fact, its very survival depended on its ability to conform to the norms of the Biosphere. That the natural order exceeded man's capacity to reason was evident in ancient man's recourse to myth and magic.[20] Nature's laws were interpreted as an expression of divine order imposed on all creatures. The economic sphere, a subsystem of the Biosphere, was constrained by the dynamics of the Biosphere with which it merged and whose laws successive generations learned to respect in empirical ways.[21]

Thus, for millennia, man's productive activities, based on hunting, fishing, and gathering, and later agriculture and animal husbandry, followed the narrow mechanisms of the natural ecosystem. In short, societies were dependent, in all respects, on the varying generosity of the natural environment: in the energy and materials they processed; in the rhythms of their work; and in the archaic techniques which minimally impacted the ecosystems. Economic thinking, as such, was simultaneously thinking about nature.[22] Production could provide for the continuity of man's livelihood only by respecting nature, and the finality of production was self-evident: to meet the organic needs of man.

Prior to the Industrial Revolution in nineteenth-century Europe, economic development rested essentially on the exploitation of various forms of life: cereals, occasionally supplemented by meat, provided nourishment; raw materials consisted principally of flax, wool, leather, and wood. Of the inert materials, only the use of stone for construction purposes was of any importance. Iron was employed primarily for military purposes and played only a minor role in man's livelihood. The motive forces were human labor, animals, the wind and water currents. In all cases, these elements were perfectly adapted to and integrated with nature, governed by its laws, and subordinated to its rhythms.[23] Thus, the livelihood of man necessarily subordinated itself to the requirements of the natural ecosystem. The limited forces of production did not threaten the existence of essentially self-renewing resources. The waste products of production, and of life itself, intimately participated in the cycle of life.[24]

However, as mankind began to develop the mechanical arts, his relationship to nature changed, and so too did his view of nature. With increasing reliance on technology and a corresponding dependence on fossil fuels, humanity began the slow process of breaking away from its dependence on the Biosphere's cycles and flows of solar energy.[25] The power of science and technology encouraged man to believe he could distance himself from nature. Technological developments fundamentally altered man's perceived relationship to the Biosphere. The intimate relationship of man and nature was undermined, and finally ruptured, by the institutionalized and mediating role of technology between society and the living planet. Humanity used science and technology to create an artificial environment cast in its own image. Its view of nature, in turn, came more and more to resemble the newly technified form of civilization.[26] Man in the preindustrial age lived within the norms of the Biosphere. As such, man was indeed *Homo sapiens*, that is, a reasoning creature. With industrialism, man became, at once, *Homo faber*, "man the creator," and, with the institution of the price-making market economy *Homo oeconomicus*.

This transformation implied a change in the motive for action on the part of members of society; for the motive of subsistence had to be replaced by that of gain. All transactions were mediated by money; this required that a medium of exchange enter into every articulation of the livelihood of man. All incomes must derive from the sale of something, and whatever the source of an individual's income, it must be regarded as resulting from a sale. No less is implied by the institutional pattern described in the term "market system." Once established, the peculiarity of the system lies in the fact that it must be allowed to function without interference—prices must be permitted to regulate themselves. Such a self-regulating system of markets is what is meant by a price-making market economy. Moreover, the control of the economic system by the market is of overwhelming consequence to the whole organization of society, for it means no less than the running of society as a mere adjunct to the market. Instead of the economy being embedded in social relations, an inversion causes social relations to become embedded in the economic system. Any other result is precluded. Once the economic system is institutionally differentiated and based on specific material motives, society must be molded in such a manner as to allow that system to function according to its own laws.[27]

Homo Oeconomicus

The logic that underlies the term *Homo oeconomicus* finds expression in the terms "The Age of Reason" and "The Enlightenment," which, when applied to the eighteenth century, underline the fact that a significant alteration had taken place in Western man's image of himself and his environment. In the preceding hundred years, the foundations had been laid, particularly through the Cartesian revolution in philosophy, for a concerted reexamination of the accepted sources of knowledge, standards of authority, and source of legitimation to institutions. By the eighteenth century the break with the Aristotelian spirit of the Middle Ages was complete, and the spokesmen of the new age enthusiastically committed themselves to a belief in human reason, scientific rationality, and natural law. Through reason could be discovered the laws of the natural order, which could then be applied to the improvement of the welfare of man through the reconstruction of his social institutions.

The ancient attitude of submission gave way to one of dominion, which asserted itself following the Industrial Revolution, in the course of which an artificial order created by man sought to impose itself upon that of nature. During the Industrial Revolution, the taming of accumulated energies and of inanimate materials produced a number of consequences. With the harnessing of artificial energies, human rhythms acquired an autonomy, while agriculture, which for a long time remained dependent, was opened up to new possibilities with agro-industrial processes and with the use of artificial fertilizers, herbicides, and pesticides.[28] This reinforced a growing sense of mastery over nature. The surpluses, within the contexts of a new institution, and made possible by a spectacular growth in productivity, permitted a greater satisfaction of material needs, encouraged the financing of new activities, intensified the division of labor, and accelerated urbanization. The economic machine, developing by itself and for itself, created an artificial autojustified ecosystem animated by its own logic, and progressively subjected the natural ecosystem to its laws.[29]

In this respect, the Industrial Revolution represented a rupture. Inanimate materials replaced living forms, and natural energies were successively replaced by artificial energies. The rhythm of exploitation was disassociated from cosmic rhythms. Wastes no longer entered into the cycle of life. From such a perspective, one may view machines, animated by physicochemical energies and dissociated from the dynamics of the Biosphere, as a new type of population possessing its own metabolism, whose effects are added to those of the Biospherically integrated life forms. Whereas everything that is a remnant of a life process can be reconstituted as a life-nourishing element, the wastes of our industrial civilization are not of life but are dismemberments and reconstitutions of inanimate matter for which nature has no mechanism to reverse.

In some respects the consequences of that situation are reinforced by what might be termed the "rupturing of space." For millennia, human populations lived within nature itself. Their places of work and habitation were co-located. The wastes of their activities were absorbed by the environment and by biological agents capable of regenerating them. However, with industrialization, the urban agglomerations of man and machine discharged huge volumes of waste matter into limited ecological spaces. Where their rates of concentration exceed the absorptive capacity of the ecosystem's biological agents, they disrupt the functioning of those mechanisms upon which the natural environment depends.[30] Thus, there emerges the conjoint problematique of accelerating rhythms, depleting resources, and environmental degradation.

Following the upheavals that it brought in its wake, the wave of technical innovations not only shifted the dominant industrial activity toward metallurgy and the exploitation of physicochemical sources of energy, but also made it necessary to reexamine the exclusively agrarian basis upon which the physiological perspective of political economy came to be founded.[31]

As organic needs were progressively met, things became less clear. Production activities serving comfort or well-being came to replace those serving survival. Both through the exploitation of artificial sources of energy and the capitalistic techniques, or else by their final destination, production ceased to emphasize vital organic processes.[32] Moreover, the notion of need itself came to be transformed. Rather than referring to substantive and physiological imperatives, it related to psychological aspirations to which newly institutionalized, monetarized, and productive structures sought to respond.

It was no longer in organic needs, but rather in subjective considerations, that most production activities derived their justification.[33] This caused the problem of value to become the leading problem: goods should be produced only if they are desired, they are desired if they have a value for individuals, and it is these individuals who reveal the measure of that value by offering a certain quantity of money. For the producer, the problem is to establish whether that sum will make it possible for him to meet his costs.

Thus, in two respects, the logic of the economic apparatus fundamentally transformed itself. First, by confusing the instrumental means (Aristotelian efficient cause) with the end (Aristotelian final cause), it ceases to relate to biophysical realities and responds to monetary values on the basis of which a maximizing calculation takes place. In other words, it substituted formal rationality for substantive rationality. Second, it draws away from the dimensions of the Biosphere, whose laws of reproduction it previously sought to respect, to the dynamics of the market, whose equilibrium it sought to assure.[34]

Both in terms of its content and its finality, after assuming an abstract form, economic rationality radically dissociated itself from the logic of the Biosphere.[35] And, for reasons that will be important to consider, that divorce is becoming increasingly acute. For as the impact of economic activities is extended and as the scope of economic analysis paradoxically narrows, a multiplicity of events presents itself as no longer insular, but as the unavoidable consequence of the confrontation of the logic of the Biosphere and that of the price-making market economy.

The Origins of Political Economy

Noöspheric political economy, that is political economy in the broad sense, refers to an analysis of the economic process as an open system. It is in this connection that we turn to the Physiocratic origins of political economy, for it is first with the Physiocrats that the economic phenomenon was not only studied as a discipline apart from philosophy, but comprehended in open-systems terms. Their categories of analysis, model of the economic system, and ethos were formulated during a critical transition in the political economy of France. Though it is not without analytical and philosophical shortcomings, Physiocratic analysis deserves reflection as we enter into the epoch of the Noösphere.

Natural theology—the search for design in the confusion of the cosmos—has been an object of human rationalizing impulse from the earliest times. In his *History of Economic Analysis*, J.A. Schumpeter writes that:

> The philosophers of natural law lived in the heroic age of mathematics and physics. Spectacular discoveries in what for the general public was the "new experimental philosophy" were attended by no less spectacular popularity of physics. Those successes ... were not lost upon the philosophers of natural law. They looked at their tools and wondered whether they did not after all bear some similarity to those victorious physicists. ... Hobbes declared that "civil philosophy"—a term used for the sake of the parallelism to natural philosophy in the sense of physical science—dated from the publication of his own book *De Cive* (1642), and that he was the first to apply to this civil philosophy the methods of Copernicus and Galileo.[36]

In England it was Hobbes who first studied the "laws of civil life" with the explicit purpose of placing political action on the incomparably more certain basis of the scientifically controlled technics that he had come to know in the mechanics of his time. Thus, Hannah Arendt characterized the constructions of rational natural law correctly as the attempt to find a theory "by which one can produce with scientific precision, political institutions which will regulate the affairs of men with the reliability with which a clock regulates the processes of nature."[37]

Under the aegis of Adam Smith's behaviorist approach—the comprehension of the price-making market as a dynamic social artifact—a process of discovery was launched for the hidden mechanisms theorized by Hobbes that governed the lives of men. This was the era of the birth of the social sciences. Thus, it is of no surprise that, like Locke, Adam Smith expounded that natural laws underlay the seeming chaos of society.

While Montesquieu's work provided an important stimulus, the Scottish historians, in general, and Smith, in particular, went well beyond the teaching of their master. In the words of one of their number: "The great Montesquieu pointed out the road. He was the Lord Bacon of this branch of philosophy. Dr. Smith is the Newton." Indeed, Smith was enamored by the mechanical world view and was determined to formulate a theory of the economy that would reflect the universals of the Newtonian paradigm.[38]

In the *Wealth of Nations* Smith argued that just as heavenly bodies in motion conformed to laws of nature, so too did the economy. If these laws are obeyed, economic growth will result. However, government regulation and control of the economy violate these immutable laws by directing economic activities in unnatural ways. Thus, markets did not expand as rapidly as they could and production was stifled. In other words, any attempt by society to guide alleged natural economic forces was inefficient, and for Adam Smith, efficiency in all things was the watchword.

For Adam Smith, and for most of his successors, the discovery of the economy was a celebration of a benign and euphoric social destiny. The "wealth of nations" was fated to accrue by virtue of some "natural law" or a contemporary social equivalent. A feeling of boundless optimism prevailed. Some inherent process within this newly discovered "society" virtually guaranteed abundance and prosperity as long as its norms were not grossly violated by misguided regulation or by other types of shortsighted interference.

An inquiry into the laws of economics, Smith declared, will lead us to the inevitable conclusion that the most efficient method of economic organization is laissez-faire—the notion of leaving things alone and allowing people to act unhindered.[39] Smith's speculation on the efficacy of the depoliticization of the economy, that was after all the operational effect of laissez-faire, was in stark contrast to European traditions. Smith, a behaviorist institutionalist[40] like Locke, believed that the basis of human activity was material self-interest. Since this is natural, he declared, we should not condemn selfishness by erecting social barriers to its pursuit. Rather, we should recognize a person's desire to satisfy himself for what it is—a virtuous activity that, in fact, benefits everyone. It is by each individual working selfishly that scarcity may be overcome by surplus. However, this mandate for social irresponsibility opposed that of the Physiocrats. In terms of both its ethics and aspects of its model of the economic process, Physiocracy is at once a foundation and point of departure for substantive economic thought. It embodies elements of a historic, philosophic, and praxiological basis for coevolutionary economic thought—the political economy of the Noösphere.

The science founded by the Physiocrats was the science of society, not that of economics in the narrow sense. Opposing himself to elements of Locke's and Smith's individualistic argument, François Quesnay, in *The Dialogue on the Work of Artisans*,[41] wrote:

> I know that if I looked to my own self interest I should want to enjoy a great deal with little expense, and that each person as an individual thinks the same. But individual interest is in contradiction with general interest, and is so inconsequent that it would destroy itself if the natural order had not put obstacles in the way of its doing so; that is, if these individual interests themselves, by means of the reciprocity between them, did not resist their own destruction. Men take so short-sighted a view of things, and their greed is so avid, that they would continually go astray if they did not set one another back on the right path through the necessity which forces them all of tending blindly towards the general good.[42]

The Physiocrats referred to themselves as *les économistes*; for in their opinion, the health of the community and the state rested on immutable natural laws similar to those that regulated the household of the animal body. They came to regard their theories as "objectively" scientific and, prior to the Great Revolution of 1789, began to develop a complete view of the French economy.

Their principal essayist, Quesnay, used the term "economy" in the Aristotelian sense, referring to the husbanding or householding of the animal body.[43] Indeed, Quesnay, in surveying the economy of eighteenth-century France, was impressed by its physiological analogy. "We must not lose heart," wrote Quesnay in a letter to Mirabeau, "for the appalling crisis will come, and it will be necessary to have recourse to medical knowledge." To cure a patient suffering from an illness requires a knowledge of the principles of physiology; similarly, to cure a society suffering from grave maladies requires a knowledge of the physiology of the social order. These words ring true today, confronted as we are by the prospects of Biospheric crises.

Natural Order

The Physiocratic school, following Aristotelian and Confucian philosophy,[44] argued for the preeminence of the natural order, whose rules provided for the continuity of human societies. Quesnay endeavored to apply the mores of China to the grave problems confronting France, and to craft general principles of government. His model was one of enlightened despotism, under which the "positive" laws, i.e., statutes, would be drafted especially to give effect to the sublime set of principles that constituted the natural laws. It is appropriate to note at this juncture that the Physiocratic distinctions between positive and natural laws are prototypical of the contemporary concerns with identifying Biospheric thresholds of viability—thresholds within which the economic process may locate itself.

The natural order, an important element in Quesnay's work, was conceptually not unprecedented to European thought. Discussion of the bedrock upon which society was based had existed since the Epicureans of the third century B.C. But speculation on the natural order was given an energizing impulse in seventeenth- and eighteenth-century Europe. The revival of this topic may be ascribed to several causes: to the Protestant reformation, to the movement toward deism and agnosticism, and to the reports on China with her rationalistic Confucian philosophy.

Indeed, although Quesnay's economic philosophy represented an elaboration of Aristotelian thought, there is some speculation on whether it was entirely of European origin. Adolf Reichwein, in discussing Quesnay, notes that he was under the influence of Chinese models from an early period, but that he kept these schemes secret and pretended he was himself inventing that which he proposed. Subsequently, however, with the publication of his *Le despotisme de la Chine*, his secret interest in oriental philosophy became known. Indeed, on Reichwein's authority, Baudeau, Quesnay's editor, referred to him as "the great law-giver, the Confucius of Europe."[45] In 1769 Nicolas-Gabriel Clerc, a Physiocrat, physician, historian, and tutor to Paul I, czar of Russia, credited Quesnay with formalizing what the Chinese philosophers had discovered—the law of the natural order. Clerc's *Yu le Grand et Confucius* (1769) was intended to give Paul I instruction in the essential principles of government. He wrote that the Chinese had long ago discovered the law of the natural order, but had not worked out all its details.[46]

Subject to objective laws, the economic process, according to the Physiocrats, operated independent of human free will. Those forces effective in the direction of the economy were the physical and moral "natural laws." According to Quesnay, it was the observance of these laws that had sustained China in its progressive state.[47]

Assimilating elements of Aristotelian thought, Quesnay expressed views contrary to aspects of the Lockean concept of man and nature. Quesnay wrote in *Natural Right*:

> If we look carefully at the futility of [the] abstract idea of the natural right of everybody to everything, we see that in order to conform to the natural order itself we would have to reduce this natural right of man to a right to the things whose use he can obtain, and this so-called general right would then in actual fact be an extremely limited right.
>
> From this point of view, it will be seen that the arguments just described are nothing but frivolous sophistry, or an intellectual game which is quite out of place in the examination of such an important matter; and we are fully convinced that the natural right of each man is in reality reduced to a right to the share which he can procure for himself through his labor.[48]

Later in *Natural Right*, Quesnay further juxtaposed the principles of physics with that of society. However, unlike later mechanicalists, Quesnay's political economy was grounded in the ethics of the natural order. Moreover, in contrast to the depoliticizing doctrine of the later classical economists, the Physiocrats' mandate embodied a concept of finality with which the "just society" should endeavor to achieve a harmony.[49] In order to gain the essence of that ethical code of conduct it is necessary to quote Quesnay at length.[50]

> In order to understand the order of time and space, and to control navigation and safeguard trade, it has been necessary to observe and calculate precisely the laws of the movement of celestial bodies. Similarly, in order to understand the extent of the natural right of men joined together in society, it is necessary to settle upon the natural laws which form the basis of the best government possible. This government to which men ought to be subject consists in the natural order and the positive order most advantageous to men joined together in society.
>
> Thus men joined together in society ought to be subject to natural laws and positive laws.
>
> Natural laws are either physical or moral.
>
> I am here taking physical law to mean the regular course of all physical events in the natural order which is self-evidently the most advantageous to the human race.
>
> I am here taking moral law to mean the rule of all human action in the moral order conforming to the physical order which is self-evidently the most advantageous to the human race.
>
> These laws taken together constitute what is called natural law.

> The observance of these natural and fundamental laws of the body politic must be maintained through the medium of a tutelary (or guardian) authority established by the nation to govern by positive laws conforming to the natural laws that decisively and unalterably form the constitution of the state.
>
> Positive laws are authentic rules established by a sovereign authority for the purpose of settling the order of the administration of government. . . .
>
> The positive laws are binding laws established by a sovereign authority to fix the manner of the administration of the government; to assure the observance of the natural laws; to maintain or reform the customs prevailing in the nation; to regulate the private rights of the subjects according to their status; to determine finally, the positive order in doubtful cases, along the lines of a preponderance of opinion or propriety; to lay down decisions as to distributive justice.
>
> Thus, a government is the natural and the positive order, the most advantageous to men united into a nation and ruled by a sovereign authority.[51]

Physical laws determined important economic parameters such as rainfall and soil fertility, and as such were embodied within the Newtonian view of the physical world. The Physiocrats argued that natural law operated independent of human free will, and that, if humans accurately deduced the "proper" economic behavior as implied by natural law, social welfare would be secured.[52] In *Rural Philosophy*, Mirabeau and Quesnay argue that

> natural law inspires us and also tells us about duties relative to our needs; the civil laws, which originally are nothing more than rules for the allocation of subsistence; virtues and vices, which are only obedience to or revolt against natural or civil law; agriculture, trade, industry—all are subordinate to the means of subsistence. This is the fundamental force.[53]

With considerable depth of insight into the livelihood of man, Aristotle, in *Politics*, observed that

> the true riches of a household, or of a state, are the necessities of life. . .they are nothing more than the means to an end, and like all means they are intrinsically limited and determined by their ends. In the household, they are the means to life, in the polis, they are the means to the good life.[54]

Expressing a commitment to Aristotelian thought, Quesnay maintained that wealth was a means not an end. For the subsistence of men in society required not only an authority to defend their true interests but the wealth to do so.

Judiciously avoiding ignoble Machiavellian politics, the Physiocrats argued that one of the primary functions of a prince was to make the natural laws known and observed. It was essential that the state make provision for the study of natural law.[55] Authority was not to be left exclusively to "sovereign tribunals." For their distributive justice overemphasized "positive laws" to the point of ignoring those laws of nature that constrain society and secure the property of the nation.

> Neglecting the study of these fundamental laws would favor the introduction of the most destructive forms of taxation, and of positive laws most prejudicial

to the economic and political order. The tribunals, limited to a literal interpretation of the laws of distributive justice, would not base their decisions upon the first principles of natural law, the public law, and the law of nations. It would be more to the advantage of the state if these august companies charged with the verification and the conserving of the positive laws, which are in essence the fundamental laws of society, and the sources of the positive laws; but one must not forget that the primitive laws may be studied only from nature itself.[56]

Cautioning against the "dissension and discontent" that would ensue were the "right of legislation" and the "right of imposing taxes" relinquished to "the confusion of bizarre governments," Quesnay noted that

man can no more create and constitute the natural order than he can create himself. The primitive law of nations is comprised in the general order of the formation of the universe, in which everything has been foreseen and prearranged by the supreme wisdom. Let us not turn from the paths set down for us by the eternal.[57]

The introduction of "positive laws" which militated against the natural order could only serve to corrupt the regular circulation of a nation's wealth. The Physiocrats' conception of the subordination of human laws to those of the natural order reflects Montesquieu's "Principle of Recursion" and is evident such that

The positive legislation, or written legislation, does not provide the motives or reasons upon which it establishes its laws; these reasons existed before the positive laws, and are in essence above the human laws; they are received, then, actually and obviously from the primitive and immutable laws of orderly governments.

The constitutive laws of the Nation are not of Human Origin

The legislative power, often disputed between the sovereign and the nation, did not belong originally either to one or the other; its origin lies in the supreme will of the creator and in the aggregate of the laws of the physical order the most advantageous to the human race. There is a solid basis in the physical order; whereas everything is confused and arbitrary in the order of nations. From this confusion have come all the intemperate and extravagant constitutions of governments, imagined by men too poorly trained by the theocracy, which has always fixed, by weights and measures, the rights and reciprocal duties of men united in nations. The natural laws of nations are the very physical laws of the perpetual reproduction of the goods necessary for the subsistence, for the preservation and for the comfort of men. No, man is not the institutor of these laws, which fix the order of the operations of nature, and of the labor of men, who must cooperate with nature in the reproduction of the goods that they need. All this arrangement is a physical constitution, and this constitution forms the physical order which subjects to its laws men joined together into nations, and who by their intelligence and by mutual association may, through observance of these natural laws, obtain in abundance the goods necessary to them.[58]

The natural order consciousness inherited by the Physiocrats held that the economic sphere was an integral part of nature. Respect for that order represented a precondition for the survival of human societies. It was an awareness that could not envisage the reproduction of the former without the latter. Among the Physiocrats, Le Mercier de la Riviere stated, "We discover an essential order, one from which we may not deviate without betraying our true interests, without ceasing to be societies." He continued, "wealth must be consumed in accordance with one's desires and without impoverishing oneself, and without altering the principle that continuously reproduces it."[59] For the Physiocrats, nature confronted man first as an eternal necessity. Mankind, they argued, has three needs: to subsist, to preserve itself, and to continue the species. These needs constitute, a priori, the essential conditions. On the one hand, the Physiocrats suggested that nature demands respect, for it is the origin of all surpluses. On the other hand, there is also an expression of ethical sentiment.[60]

For instance, Quesnay's Aristotelian economic ethos is apparent in his *Maxims*. He wrote:

> That it should not be believed that cheapness of produce is profitable to the lower classes, for a low price of produce causes a fall in the wages of the lower orders of people, reduces their well-being, makes less work and remunerative occupations available for them, and destroys a nation's revenue.[61]

and

> That the well-being of the latter classes of citizens should not be reduced; for then they would not be able to contribute sufficiently to the consumption of the produce which can be consumed only within the country, which would bring about a reduction in the reproduction and revenue of the nation.[62]

There is in these last two maxims more than a passing similarity to selections from *Nung Cheng Ch'an Shu* [The Complete Treatise on Agriculture], by Hsu' Kuang-ch'i, posthumously published in Peking in 1640; a work available to Quesnay through Jesuit writings.[63]

The Physiocrats, disciples of the rule of nature, were a sect based on physiological tenets. Quesnay expounded on the idea that if natural law were left untrammeled, it would govern economic affairs for the greatest benefit of all. Thus, the doctrine of laissez-faire was introduced as a cornerstone of economic theory and, paradoxically advanced under the tutelage of an absolute monarchy possibly styled on the Chinese model. Moreover, on the basis of reports that in

China agriculture was held in the highest esteem and was given governmental assistance, Quesnay and his associates concluded that the natural order prevailed in simple perfection with a minimum of interference by man-made statutes.

Echoing the French missionaries DuHalde and Poivre in their praise of Chinese agriculture, Quesnay asked,

> [what] is important for the prosperity of a nation? To cultivate the soil with the greatest possible success, and to protect the nation from thieves and evil-doers. The first part is taken care of by self-interest; the second part is entrusted to the civil government. Men of good will need only instruction, which develops from them the illuminating truths which are not distinctly and sharply perceived save through the exercise of reason. The positive laws can only very imperfectly supply this intellectual knowledge. . . . But the positive legislation must not be extended into the province of physical laws, which must be observed with discernment and with extensive knowledge and a thorough and varied understanding, which can be acquired only through the study of the general and enlightening legislation of the supreme wisdom.[64]

From Quesnay's argument for an enlightened despotism, there emerges his Aristotelian understanding and restricted use of the term "economic." Conceptualizing man as a rational being, he wrote that it was only through the "free exercise of reason" that man may advance his understanding of the political economy of nations. In the economical administration of the cultivation of the soil, farmers should be constrained by no other laws. They should be guided by the knowledge they have acquired through training and experience. Those "positive laws," which arbitrarily regulate the administration of the cultivation of the soil, may disrupt the economical administration of the cultivator, and may, thereby, undermine the reproduction of society itself. The farmer, consequently, should not be compelled to observe laws other than those of the Biosphere. "It is, moreover, these laws and these conditions that should regulate the administration of the general government of the nation."[65]

Quesnay's understanding of "economic" achieves an arithmetic precision in the context of the natural order and subservient to the imperatives of that order.

> The physical laws which constitute the natural order the most advantageous to the human race, and which exactly constitute the nature of all men, are eternal laws, unalterable, and decidedly the best possible. The proof of them imperiously compels the adherence of every intellect and all human reason, with a precision that is shown geometrically and arithmetically in detail, and which leaves no margin for error, from imposture, or from illicit pretensions.[66]

Under the banner of laissez-faire, these natural law philosophers were proponents of the rule of nature. Nevertheless, much as a doctor who, believing in the healing forces of nature applies treatments that will harmoniously supplement natural agents, the Physiocrats thought they had discovered those laws according to which nature animated society. It was on the basis of this naturalistic conception that they believed in systematic political intervention; that it was the task of the authorities to remove obstacles to and give support for the working of the forces of nature.

> [The] sovereign authority can and must institute laws against proven disorder, but must not encroach upon the natural order of society. The gardener must remove the moss that injures the tree, but he must avoid cutting into the bark through which this tree receives the sap that makes it grow. If a positive law is necessary to prescribe this duty for the gardener, this law, dictated by nature, should not extend beyond the duty that nature prescribes. The constitution of the tree is the natural order itself, regulated by essential and irrefragable laws which must not be interfered with by extraneous laws. The provinces appropriate to these two legislative systems may be clearly distinguished by the light of reason; the laws on the two sides are established and promulgated by different institutions and means.[67]

In addressing the natural order, Quesnay employed an exaggeration that most likely went even beyond his models. The agricultural and moral principles of government were an outgrowth of the natural laws. These laws had been established and cultivated by the prime mover; they were irrevocable and the best possible. They eclipsed all the powers of human intellect, and there was a geometrical and arithmetical precision to their design. As soon as men would learn about the natural laws, dissension about legislation, about social status, and about taxation would vanish, for each would see that his own best interests would be served by enabling society to harmonize with the natural laws.[68]

> With the exception of predatory nations, which are enemies of the other nations, agriculture is a common feature of all the types. Without agriculture, the societies could form only imperfect nations. Agricultural nations alone can establish fixed and lasting empires under a general and invariable government, subject directly to the immutable order of the natural law. It is agriculture itself, then, that forms the foundation of these empires, and prescribes and establishes the form of their government, because agriculture is the source of the goods that satisfy the needs of the people, and because the success or decadence of agriculture necessarily depends upon the form of government.[69]

The social, for Quesnay, is a part of the natural order, and behind both the social and physical lies a hidden Deism. This is the source of the rules that exist prior to, and outside of, any particular society.

A dual concept of the normative was embedded in Quesnay's vision. The rules for human behavior exist apart from man or any society and these norms themselves define the good. With a Panglossian cast, Quesnay maintained that natural laws not only exist but are possessed of more good than evil. Humans in society, therefore, should attempt to follow the laws of nature, to adapt to them;

self-evidently it is advantageous. Failure to do so brings material cost. For the Physiocrats, nature was rule-governed and moral; it conveyed its own punishment and rewards. "If a government deviated from the natural laws which assure the success of agriculture, would we dare lay the blame on agriculture for the fact that we lacked bread?"[70]

Quesnay's Produit Net

For millennia, economic activity was constrained by the norms of the Biosphere, whose coherent order governed the reproductive activities of its subsystems, notably, the economic system. Within the narrow mechanisms of the natural ecosystem, the continuity of production was ensured by observance of a respect for nature. The economy was seen to relate to the setting in motion of physical flows, the purpose of which was the provision of the livelihood of man. Society and its economic activity could only perpetuate itself through the reproduction of the natural environment. Thus, the circulation among the social classes of the *produit net*: allegedly a surplus born of the inherent fertility of nature, was critically dependent upon the reproduction of what has since been termed the Biosphere.

Mirabeau, an advocate of the principles of Physiocracy, in his correspondence with the encyclopedist Jean-Jacques Rousseau, wrote:

> The discovery of the net product which we owe to the venerable Confucius of Europe, will one day change the face of the world. . . . The whole moral and physical advantage of societies is . . . summed up in one point, an increase in the net product; all damage done to society is determined by this fact, a reduction in the net product.[71]

In Quesnay's *Corn* (published in November 1757), the concept of the net product appears for the first time, as does the doctrine that trade and manufacture are really only branches of agriculture.[72]

The center point of the Physiocratic reliance upon nature as an explanation, however, was that they used it to derive economic value. The agricultural net product was part of an original and real substance, provided by nature. Of a different order from that yielded by other economic activities, this constituted a yearly injection into the livelihood of man. Everything else was a reworking of it. "The crops which the land produces to satisfy the different wants of man cannot serve the purpose, for the most part, in the state in which nature gives them; they must undergo various changes and be prepared by art. Wheat must be converted into flour."[73] Turgot, perhaps the most politically influential member of the Physiocratic school, visualized the entire agricultural process as a cultural shaping of nature. He explained the *produit net* as:

> The produce of the land divides into two parts. The one comprehends the subsistence and the profits of the husbandman, which are the rewards for his labour, and the conditions on which he agrees to cultivate the field of the proprietor; the other which remains is that independent and disposable part, which the earth produces as a free gift to the proprietor over and above what he had disbursed.[74]

The Physiocrats portrayed the economy as a total, circulating system of wealth. But unlike the mercantilists, they identified the source of this wealth as lying in agriculture or production, not in circulation or trade. According to Physiocratic thought, agriculture was almost the only activity that yielded a material output that exceeded its input. The notion that only agriculture is productive was central to Physiocracy. Mirabeau, for example, asserted that "The land is the mother of all goods" and added that "wealth" comes only from the land.[75] Writing with Quesnay, he also spoke of "the spontaneous gifts of nature." Quesnay himself stated the assumption firmly in the *Dialogue on the Work of Artisans*: "The origin, the principle, of all expenditure and all wealth is the fertility of the land, whose products can be increased only through these products themselves." To this he added that only agricultural products represent a "true generation or creation of wealth."[76] Turgot echoed all these notions with his idea that nature is a storehouse that offers a "superfluity" to humans as a "pure gift."[77] The Physiocrats understood nature as not only returning costs but yielding something more.

Maintaining that nature alone produced a net surplus (the *produit net*), they objected to embargoes on the export of grain: prohibitions which were maintained in order to keep wages low in the interest of export trade. Consistent with his natural order criteria, Quesnay sought to reform the complex, corrupt, and harsh French system of taxation. He held that only the net product of agriculture should be taxed. Indeed, the Physiocrat's advocacy of a single tax to be imposed on the *produit net* was based on reports of such practices in China.[78]

In *Despotisme en Chine*, Quesnay wrote:

> The excess of the products of the land, beyond the expenditures for the labour for its cultivation and the necessary amounts advanced to prepare it for cultivation, is a net product, which forms the public revenue and the income of the landowners. The latter have acquired or bought the property, and their money, paid for its acquisition, entitles them to receive from the net product, an income proportionate to the purchase price of the land. But what assures them this income with even more justice, is the fact that all the net product ... is a natural consequence of their ownership and their administration. Without these essential conditions, the land would yield no net profit, but only a product uncertain and hardly worth the outlays made upon it with the most stringent economies, because of the uncertainty of its continued enjoyment, which would not justify expenditures for improvement or maintenance, the profit on which would not be assured to those who undertook these expenditures.[79]

The concept of the *produit net* was intimately associated with class structure. First, there were the landlords or proprietors, who guided, supervised, or otherwise presided over agricultural production, to whom the *produit net* ultimately accrued and to whom fell the responsibilities of the community and state. Second, was the productive class, members of which did the husbandry and worked the soil; it was after they were recompensed that the *produit net* went to the proprietors. Finally, the sterile or unproductive classes were the merchants, manufacturers, and artisans. It was from agriculture that all accretions of wealth came; from other endeavors came nothing.

By "sterile" the Physiocrats did not mean that such activities were not useful or even without honor. These forms of work, to the contrary, were necessary for the social order, but they were not productive in the special Physiocratic sense. "Sterile" was defined not by labor activity, but by the object on which it was performed; those material things that of themselves do not reproduce, alone or under human guidance, are barren. In a positive sense, sterile activities might shape or reform existing materials; but the goods of artisans represent the combination of other, already present wealth forms. Manufacturing can never be productive, for it is not creative of material. To be productive, an activity had to be both "reproductive" and primary.

The Physiocrats thought that labor is a form of consumption, a destruction of produced wealth. Only for the artisan and farmer does labor constitute a wealth conveyor from one depository to another. The farmer alone is productive, because he harnesses nature's powers.

There can be little doubt that the doctrine of the productivity of agriculture was the linchpin of the Physiocratic model. By "productive" the Physiocrats did not mean "capable of creating utility," or "capable of adding value," or being "socially useful." Though a "productive" occupation did contain these characteristics, so too did most "sterile" occupations. The real essence of a "productive" occupation lay in its capacity to yield a disposable surplus over cost; and the real essence of a "sterile" occupation lay in its inherent incapacity to yield such a surplus.

In its unadorned form, the theory of *produit net* held that all wealth originated in agriculture, not in any other industry, trade, or occupation. Merchants bought and sold; it was the same product before as after—nothing was added to it in the process. Somewhat more ambiguously, the case was made that manufacturing merely added labor to the products of the soil; nothing new emerged. Furthermore, manufacturing was limited in extent by its agricultural supply.

In Physiocratic theory, then, labor is the cause but not the source of wealth. The function of labor is to transport wealth from one larder to another. This is a passive labor, a machine for changing inputs rather than outputs.

This same passivity of the human contribution appears in the Physiocratic understanding of productivity changes. The Physiocrats clearly recognized that labor applied to agriculture or artisanry might be done with more or less efficiency, and in a remarkable passage Turgot anticipated Adam Smith's remarks on the division of labor.[80] The source, the fount of the product, they stoutly maintained, was nature, regardless of how well humans were able to control it. Technological processes and their efficiency were of little concern, for wealth was nature manipulated not supplemented. The focus throughout remained upon circulating and increasing material items, not securing them.

In particular, Quesnay argued for the centrality of agriculture, the organizing of the whole economy of the nation around agriculture. This would result in making domestic commerce subservient to and dependent upon the central economic concern—agriculture.[81]

Quesnay's *produit net*, according to Schumpeter, represented a technique for expressing the fact that the rent of land is, or contains, a net return. It holds that the rent of land is the only net return in existence, and that it is coextensive with the whole of society's disposable income, all other returns being balanced by cost items in the sense that they are not more than sufficient to replace what production uses up.[82]

Quesnay's interpretation rested on the concept of the *produit net*; a realistic quantity in terms of the landlord's accounting, but a mere phantom in the process between man and nature—of which the economy is but one aspect. The alleged *produit net*, whose creation Quesnay attributed to the fertility of the soil and the forces of nature, represented a transference to the "order of nature" of the disparity between the selling price and cost. Agriculture happened to occupy the center of the system because the revenues of the ruling feudal class were at issue, and Quesnay was philosophically predisposed to the social coherence and continuity apparent in agricultural societies, i.e., China. The notion of surplus, as addressed by Quesnay, continued to haunt the minds of economists both classical and neoclassical.

In the Physiocratic model economic rent was derived from the un-recompensed work done by nature, since in setting food prices, cultivators take into account their labor and expenses as well as the surplus value contributed by the fertility of the soil.[83] Schumpeter writes that the economy in the Physiocratic sense was seen as "an engine that is fed materials drawn from the womb of nature and that simply works up these materials without adding to them."[84]

The doctrine of the productivity of agriculture was grounded on the not peculiarly Physiocratic idea that agriculture was inherently capable of yielding a disposable surplus over necessary cost. The amount of corn that has to be used as seed and as feed for the men and animals engaged in agricultural production is normally less than the amount of corn that is gathered in at harvest time—a fact allegedly demonstrated by the continued existence of other social groups besides cultivators.[85] Agriculture was inherently capable of yielding a physical surplus, which in a market economy was capable of being transformed into a value surplus. But in the conditions of late eighteenth-century France, certain policy measures were preventing a transformation of the physical surplus into a value surplus. Policies to secure a "proper price" for agriculture were therefore necessary if the productivity of agriculture was to be maximized; and the concept of value productivity was evolved in order to define these policies.

In order to facilitate agriculture properly and to keep agricultural prices high, the many tolls and other barriers to the free domestic passage of goods and to the export of produce should be removed. Contrary to the desires of the landowning aristocracy, the nascent capitalists wanted cheap grain—not, according to Routh, out of humanitarian motivation but because for those who sought profits, it made a vast difference since the price of food was largely determined by the wages of labor. Contrary to the view expressed by Adam Smith, the Aristotelian-oriented Physiocrats insisted that the aim should be a price for grain that would maintain the continuity of society, and particularly, the influence of the aristocratic landlords. Unlike the form of economistic rationality articulated by Ricardo, with its emphasis on capital, Quesnay's concern was with society as a whole. This societal concept was removed from the view that the free price-making market was the best judge of the *bon prix*.[86]

The Tableau Économique

Turgot, a confederate of Quesnay, referred to the circulation of wealth in a manner not unlike Hobbes. The emphasis on a circular-flow model can be traced to Thomas Hobbes's use of William Harvey's 1658 model of the circulation of "nutrients" in the blood as a physiological analogy for the material foundation of the commonwealth.[87] Turgot wrote that the circulation of wealth was one "whose continuity provides for the life of the political body just as the circulation of blood provides for the life of the animal body."[88]

François Quesnay's most "original" contribution, the *Tableau Économique*, which firmly established the physiocratic school, was published in 1758. In this work Quesnay formulated what later became elements of economic liberalism and concluded that all wealth—conceived as a creation of physical products— originates in the then dominant activity of the time, namely, agriculture. In his *Maxims*, Quesnay wrote: "That the sovereign and the nation should never lose sight of the fact that land is the unique source of wealth, and that it is agriculture which causes wealth to increase."[89]

The Physiocrats' main aim was to explain the operation of the basic determinants of the general level of economic activity. For this purpose, they believed that it was useful to conceive economic activity as taking a circular form. In this circle of economic activity, production and consumption appeared as mutually interdependent variables, whose action and interaction in any economic period, proceeding according to socially determined laws, laid the basis for a repetition of the process in the same general form in the next economic period. The Physiocrats then endeavored to discover some key variable within this circular movements that could be regarded as the basic factor causing an expansion or contraction in the "dimensions" of the circle, i.e., in the general level of economic activity. Meek notes that the variable they hit upon was the capacity of agriculture to yield a "net product." Anything that increased this net product would cause an expansion in economic activity; anything that reduced it would cause a contraction of such activity.[90]

Moreover, Quesnay's *Tableau Économique* implied a far-reaching idea: a view of the world as a vast and integrated process of circulation—one that could be schematically presented. It purported to show how products flowed from the cultivator to the landlords or proprietors and on to the merchant, manufacturing, and other sterile classes, and how money flowed back to the cultivator by several routes. The market mechanism of purchase and sale was thus revealed as a complete interlocking system.

In his analysis of the *Tableau Économique*, Schumpeter notes:

> What it depicts is the flow of expenditures and products between social classes, which here become the actors in the economic play. . . . [Quesnay] distinguished land owners (classe des propriétaires, or classe souveraine or what is significant, class distributive), farmers (class productive), and all the people engaged in nonagricultural pursuits, roughly equivalent to the bourgeoisie (class stérile).[91]

The Hippocratic attitude to social ills, with its reliance on the healing powers of nature, as well as Harvey's discovery, were expressed in Quesnay's *Tableau Économique*. However, it is paradoxical that Harvey's original contribution, the study of living organisms, was described in mechanical terms. He described the heart as a pump with pipes called veins and arteries, whose blood flow was regulated by valves, while Quesnay's noteworthy achievement modeled the human economy as a *biosocial* cyclic process. Here, distinct from Aristotle's musings, the economy was presented as a cyclical reproductive process. The conception of the economy that followed from the *Tableau* was that of an activity that set physical flows into motion; an activity whose reproduction was fundamentally constrained by the natural environment without which it could not be analyzed.

According to Meek, this was the first representation of the economic concept of "general equilibrium."[92] Indeed, Quesnay's *Tableau Économique* is considered central to the development of quantitative methods and is hailed as a forerunner of modern numerical techniques, capital theory, and general equilibrium theory. However, unlike the Walrasian system of general equilibrium, Quesnay's *Tableau* depicted a system without inherent forces that would lead to the reestablishment of an equilibrium, were the system destabilized! To the contrary, Quesnay's intent was to demonstrate that a stability could be achieved only as a result of government policies and the direction of private expenditure along prescribed lines, and that once it had been achieved, the slightest relaxation of these conditions would lead to the reestablishment of lower levels of productivity or to a progressive decline in productivity.

As far back as Aristotle, a distinction had been drawn between householding and exchange. A later, but related, division was made between the domains of production and circulation. Still later, the Physiocrats constructed an opposition between (productive) agriculture and (sterile) artisanship. A distinction was made between two kinds of economic activity, with capitalist-like practices found in only one sphere. Meek contends that though neither used the term "capitalist," both Quesnay and Adam Smith were nonetheless concerned with the scientific analysis of nascent capitalist production. Both were interested in securing an increase in national wealth, and both realized that relaxing constraints on trade, internal and external, was a necessary precondition for this. In their theoretical analysis they both tended to concentrate on the issue of the origin and distribution of social surplus, which they regarded as the only source of new wealth.[93]

However, the differences between them were profound and arose essentially from the distinct assumption concerning the form taken by social surplus. The Physiocrats assumed that the surplus took the form of land rent exclusively. The earth is the unique source of wealth; agriculture is productive and manufacture sterile; the net product alone constitutes wealth. According to Meek, such propositions are simply different ways of saying that land rent is the only form that social surplus assumes.[94] Indeed, the case against mercantilism derived from the Physiocrats' perception of natural law; from which it followed that legislation beneficial to the merchants, such as grants of monopoly and the numerous protective restraints on internal trade, were all counterproductive to the true welfare of society.

Fox-Genovese, in her analysis of Quesnay, notes that his moral philosophy derived directly from his own understanding of Confucius, and that like Confucius, Quesnay attempted to "reform the morals of the human race."[95] In *Le Despotisme de la Chine*, he noted that the great Chinese philosopher always worked to reestablish human nature in its original purity, to counteract and eradicate the errors introduced by a history of superstition and false reasoning.[96] "Human nature," he frequently said to his disciples, "came to us from heaven very pure, very perfect: subsequently, ignorance, the passions, the bad examples corrupted it; and to be perfect, it is necessary to reascend to the point from which we are descended."[97] Quesnay's intent was the restoration of the moral integrity of man. This theme, Fox-Genovese notes, ran like a thread through both his medical and economic work. "Quesnay, for all his inventions," she writes, "always says his work is a restoration. New forms might be needed, but their purpose would always be to realize the potential in God's design as manifest in nature."[98] It was, however, perhaps more than merely coincidental that the political import of the Physiocrats' restoration was to: "preserve by reform a society of landed precedence and privilege to which all were committed and to stand off the pretensions and intrusions of merchant capitalism and the unruly, crude and vulgar industrial forces that it had spawned."[99]

Marx credited the Physiocrats with giving expression to a form of materialism and for shifting the focus of attention from circulation to production. His central criticism was that the Physiocrats had failed to see that only labor creates value. Value became confounded with physical substance. He held that although the Physiocrats were the first economists to analyze modern capitalism, they did so through the lens of feudalism. For the Physiocrats, everything appeared through the perspective of land, which is to say landed property, and this was an institutional vestige of feudalism. Thus, notes Marx, surplus value was explained "in a feudal way, as derived from nature and not from society, from man's relation to the soil, not from his social relations."[100]

For the purposes of our analysis, it should be noted that, whereas the Physiocrats' view corresponds to elements of an open systems model in explicitly acknowledging and subscribing to a Taoist harmony between nature and man, later classicals embraced closed mechanical representations. Consequently, there was a detour in political economy obscuring the role of nature in the livelihood of man.[101]

Conclusions

It is evident that the Physiocratic model of the economy was one inspired by biology. However, by the time Alfred Marshall diffidently proclaimed that "Economics is a science of life that adjoins biology rather than mechanics,"[102] the economistic conception of what constitutes economic science had supplanted the substantive sensibilities of Physiocracy.

The *Tableau Économique*, in representing the material flows depicting the circulation of the *produit net*, was a representation of "economic reproduction." Since the *produit net* could arise only within the reproduction of the Biosphere, the Physiocratic model may be considered a partially "open system." For insofar as their model was grounded on Harvey's mechanical representation of the circulation of blood, and not on the characteristics of the digestive system, it displayed elements of a closed system. Unfortunately it was the "closed" portion of the model that was conflated and provided the basis for later similar analysis. This, the Physiocratic faux pas, assumes critical dimensions for later economic analysis. The *Tableau* was a schematic representation of a holistic vision of reproduction of material wealth. It presented a global image of things, whose spirit we find again in emerging modern systemic approaches. The reproduction of the economic sphere within the Biosphere, the Physiocrats' central preoccupation, is an emergent problem of coevolutionary economic analysis in the coming epoch of the Noösphere. The Physiocrats' steadfast belief that nature was the source of wealth became a recurring theme throughout economic thought. In particular, the Physiocrats' ethos, effectively defining the bounds that the economic process must not exceed, not only was echoed in the works of Marx and Engels, but also later by V.I. Vernadsky and by contemporary global ecologists.

The Concept of Nature in the Totality
Theory of Marx and Engels

Nature, as the sole source of wealth and social surplus, was for the Physiocrats the point of departure; but for Ricardo and his contemporaries nature represented the limits of economic development.[103] Harmonious socioeconomic relations came to an alarming end when the limits imposed by nature upon further production became visible.

Economists discerned the limits to economic perfection that nature imposed on population growth in declining fertility of the soil and in the dreaded stationary state. Nature was progressively eliminated from the theory that dealt with the course of economic development, only to enter again by the back door. This perspective did not, however, lead to new theoretical orientations. On the contrary, as nature finally disappeared as a constituent of the normal economic process, it came to be considered as the self-evident basis of economy, as an infinite reservoir beyond the monetary circuit, and thereby was excluded from economics as inessential. The relationship between the individual and nature in the industrial system was henceforth discussed only from the point of view of an instrumental technology. As an object that was tractable and could be worked upon, nature appeared to guarantee material wealth.[104]

Because the elementary relationship of man to nature (i.e., material production) was understood in categories of social relations (i.e., in economic or value categories), the possibility of a productive symbiosis with nature slipped beyond the reach of thought. Nature could be perceived only as an external, refractory presence that had to be mastered. The assaults made upon nature were not comprehended in terms of a totality. Instead, the interconnectedness of production was understood as a nexus of market relations and value abstractions; and with this, the total ensemble of socioeconomic relations disappeared from the theory's field of vision. Economic theory had been so particularized and instrumentalized that economic reality took on an appearance that made industrial progress seem independent of any natural limit and essentially endless. Abetted by its functional rationality "capitalism not only altered the structure of social synthesis in the direction of market integration, but also completely transformed man's relationship to nature."[105]

Through the Middle Ages to the late eighteenth century, the prevailing concept of nature was that of Thomas Aquinas's "great chain of being." In the nineteenth century, the concept took on the notion of strife and of transformation among things. The rapid expansion of large-scale industry and great scientific advances, as well as the technological power of man to purposively intervene in nature, indicated a nature whose orders were subject to man's intervention and change. Technology, above all, stood as proof of this power. Accordingly, the feudal and idealist concept of nature was undermined, and the way was prepared for a dialectic interpretation.[106] The first step in this direction was taken by Feuerbach, the second by Marx.[107] In a systemic manner Marx and Engels attempted to describe the inherent self-destructive instabilities: an essential dialectic which arises between the laws of development of economic systems and the laws of ecology, and specifically between the capitalist relations of production with itself.[108]

Totality Theory and Systems Theory

It was Engels who bequeathed to posterity Marxism's task to renew itself whenever new scientific discoveries emerged. Marxism, as a philosophy-oriented theory of totality, is congruent with open-systems theory that is the hallmark of the Noöspheric approach. While appropriating both the successes and failings of earlier analyses, Marx, in the context of a totality theory and in his critique of the capitalist mode of production, referred to issues and categories of analysis that we find in contemporary discussions of coevolutionary political economy.

However, Marx was not among the first of the German philosophers to propose a totality theory. Kant, opposing the methodology of Descartes in *Critique of Pure Reason*, refers to the "art of systems" in opposition to "technical unity."[109] While the mechanical system, says Kant, starts from single elements and particles (the whole, however, depending on indifferent unchanged elements, is a motionless, stationary system), the organic system starts from the concept of the whole and then sees in the elements, which interact according to their quality, an organic structure which determines the dynamics of the system. The Kantian principle of the organic system provided a definition of the theory of totality. It was, however, limited in scope, for it contained no clear distinction between material and theoretical systems. It was particularly theoretical and constituted "the architectonic plan of all scientific concepts deriving from pure reason."[110]

Kant, in the theory of cognition and thus in his reflections on the conditions of the possibilities of science, sought the road to moral law and systematic organizations. In this way he achieved an unparalleled influence on movements seeking profound social reform. The Physiocrats, too, saw in their economic philosophy a political theory and a theory of law. However, their concept of society is more or less limited to economic relations, so that reflection on the economy could not then serve as a theory of society. Marx was perhaps the last to have followed this approach in the grand style.

Hegel's introduction to the *Phenomenology of the Mind* inaugurated a methodological revolution and the emergence of the theory of totality. He discussed Kantian dynamics of organic systems and expounded the theory of totality as the doctrine of history and self-evolving systems. A system that is self-contained conceives of substance subjectively. For Hegel, it defines the principle of its dialectical identity. The subject moves in a world created by itself which assumes full objectivity; in this way, Hegel, on the basis of objective idealism, established a philosophical dualism between objectivity and subjectivity.[111]

It has been contended that the whole structure of the Hegelian system is integral in the framework of a "general system theory," where different ontological levels emerge as totalities or systems according to the measure of their development. Parenthetically, it was this dualism that was to later become the focal point of Lenin's *Materialism and Empiriomonism*.

Hegel's "totality theory," though displaying modern theoretical value, was doubly faulted. On the one hand, a contradiction lies in the fact that due to its objective idealist conception, it was unaware of the essential difference between material and theoretical systems. Hegel even insisted on their conceptual unity.[112] On the other hand, Hegel, following Aristotle, expressed the allegedly totalitarian view that priority attaches to the whole rather than to its parts. The whole (state) is prior because it possesses or is endowed with an arch which alone forms the basis of its unity, just as the heart is the arch of the living organism (whole system), according to Aristotle. It was Marx who referred to Hegel's "totality theory" of which Ricardo's views on political economy were merely a "special system."[113]

In his review of Marx's *Critique of Political Economy* for the newspaper *Das Volk*, Engels insisted that the latter's intention was not to merely discuss "some" noteworthy economic problems of capitalist society. "His aim," wrote Engels, "has ever been to give a systemic survey of the whole complex of economic science."[114] This means that a new theoretical system was emerging which, recognizing the contradiction arising from the relation of the whole and its parts in capitalism, sought to overcome the paradox of bourgeois philosophy.

Marx said: "We are concerned with bourgeois society as it emerged and is moving along on its own pedestal" and in a systematic exposition we must follow its "definitions" up to their "totality."[115] He explains the emergence of totality as the homogeneous development of society on a new and higher level.

> If in a fully developed bourgeois system each economic relation takes the other for granted in a bourgeois-economic form, so that each requisite is at the same time a precondition, the same is true as far as organic systems are concerned. An organic system as totality has its own prerequisites and its emergence as totality is due to the fact that it can place under its influence all the elements of society, i.e., it can produce from them the previously missing organs. In this way it becomes a historical totality.[116]

Marx's system, as he himself states, points beyond the existing capitalist society, on the one hand, to earlier social formations, and on the other hand, to future social formations. For Marx, capitalist society was a self-evolving system, a historically given totality, achieving process-like existence, in the dual nega-

tion of its emergence and dissolution. Expounding the system of capitalist society: "leads to first equations ... which refer back to the part behind the system ...
on the other hand, to points which move in the direction of changing the present
form of production relations—and consequently project the outlines of future
relations."[117]

Marx believed that the world of abstract one-sided man gave expression to
partial-rationalism and, eventually, irrationalism; similarly the world of concrete
universal man, with his production hinging on a total approach with the correlation of all the functions, placed in the center of research the interaction-structure
between human and social functions. Consequently, Marxist totality theory as a
system theory is juxtaposed to the Marxist theory of socialism, denoting simultaneously a new type of logic of scientific systems and the resolution of segregated
sciences into a unified science.

Indeed, major elements of Marx's theoretical analysis can be read as a fruitful
anticipation of the open-systems theory that was to emerge with Marxist revisionism.[118] In this connection one might refer to:

(1) Marx's conceptualization of the mode of production as a theoretical system
     composed of interdependent elements;
(2) his analysis of the cycles of interdependence of these elements within the
     system; and
(3) his analysis of social change through an endogenous process of immanent
     systemic contradiction.

Marx's social theory can be categorized into two levels, the nature of which
can be found in the first two themes of his proposed plan of study published in
Neue Zeit by Kautsky in 1903.[119] The first theme was to identify those qualities
common to all forms of society, taking into account their historical aspect. The
second was to identify the constituent elements of the internal structure of bourgeois society as a particular form.

The primary subsystem of the model, the economic system, is comprised of
two secondary subsystems: the forces of production and the relations of production. Under the rubric "forces of production" Marx includes: (1) the organization
of labor under a particular social division of labor and form of cooperation, the
skills of labor, and the status of labor in the social context; (2) man's appropriation from the environment and the knowledge of the use of resources and materials; and (3) technical means and processes and the state of science generally.[120]
Item two suggests that Marx considered natural resources as instrumental forces
of production. Marx, however, failed to identify natural resources (and ecology
more generally) as a constraint on capitalist relations of production. The Marxian
dynamic pertains exclusively to the relations of production (class and labor)
vis-à-vis forces of production typically defined as technology. The relations of
production may be narrowly specified as the socially defined rights of access of

individuals to the productive resources or legal property relations and the concomitant system of class stratification created by those formal-legal property relations.

The largely exogenous element in Marx's schema, the concept of nature, is intimately connected within his theory. As Marx wrote: "The first premise of all human history is, of course, the existence of living human beings. The first fact to be established, therefore, is the physical constitution of these individuals and their consequent relation to the rest of nature."[121]

The Open-System Concept in Marx's Analytical Model

Marx's theory meets the basic requirement of "system" on the concrete level. He states, "Society is not merely an aggregate of individuals; it is the sum of the relations in which these individuals stand to one another."[122] Marx's alleged "predeterminism,"[123] that there is unidirectional causality leading from the economic forces of production to all other elements of society, would invalidate the claim that his is a systems-theoretical approach. Yet this is a distortion to which Marx himself contributed.[124]

At various places technology and the economy seem to develop independently of any social coordinates and take on an almost autonomous existence, towing the rest of the social system in their wake. In the preface to *Critique of Political Economy*, the relationship between the economic factor and the rest of the social system even takes on the appearance of unilinear causality, with the economic function determining the entire social structure. On the one hand, Marx wrote that: "The economic structure of society is the real basis on which the juridical and political superstructure is raised, and to which definite social forms of thought correspond."[125] On the other hand, he explicitly stated:

> Man himself is the basis of his material production, as of all production which he accomplishes. All circumstances, therefore, which affect man, the subject of production, have a greater or lesser influence upon all his functions and activities as the creator of material wealth, of commodities. In this sense it can truly be asserted that all human relations and functions, however, and whenever they manifest themselves, influence material production and have a more or less determining effect upon it.[126]

The economic factor plays a leading role, but superstructural elements, maturing from and contingent with changing economic conditions and the various material factors determining these conditions, in their turn react on and exert a decisive influence on the structure of economic life. Nor is there doubt of a simultaneous reverse process at work: a constant process of mutual cause and effect among various categories of social phenomena. Marx referred to such in both *Capital* and *Grundrisse*.

Like all its predecessors, the capitalist mode of production proceeds under definite material conditions, which are, however, simultaneously the bearers of definite social relations entered into by individuals in the process of reproducing their life. Those conditions, like these relations, are, on the one hand, prerequisites, and on the other hand, results and creations of the capitalist process of production; they are produced and reproduced by it.

Marx wrote:

> The result we arrive at is not that production, distribution, exchange and consumption are identical, but that they are all elements of a totality, distinctions within a unity. Production predominates ... from it, the process continually recommences ... but there is interaction between the various elements. This is the case in every organic whole.[127]

Moreover, the effect of the economic factor on the other elements in the system seems to be more of a "boundary effect" than a determination or simple causality. That is, it is the determination of the limits within which the system may function. In *Critique of the Gotha Program*, Marx writes:

> It is always the direct relationship of the owners of the conditions of production to the direct producers—a relation always corresponding to a definite stage in the development of the methods of labour and thereby its social productivity—which reveals the innermost secret, the hidden basis of the entire social structure, and with it the political form of that relation of sovereignty and dependence, in short, the corresponding specific form of the state. This does not prevent the same economic basis, the standpoint of its main conditions ... from showing infinite variations and gradations in appearance which can be ascertained only by analysis of the empirically given circumstances.[128]

The particular causality that Marx attributed to the economic factor in the interacting system that formed his working model of society can be seen to be more complex than has been assumed previously. The complexity of this relationship is attributable to Marx's use of a systems model. This was a breakthrough in nineteenth-century social thought and a sharp contrast to the causal monism of Comtean positivism and Social Darwinism. The elements of Marx's model are neither cause nor effect; rather, they engage in a complex interaction in which the economic factor is the dominant, though not exclusive, determining factor.[129]

The various coexisting elements of Marx's theoretical model are ultimately irreducible structures. The noneconomic elements cannot simply grow out of the economic structures as epiphenomenal relations. Nor can the effect on the economic factor be interpreted as simple causality.[130] There is an interaction of independent, though unequal, forces. In his correspondence with Bloch, Engels noted that

> according to the materialist conception of history, the ultimately determining element in history is the production and reproduction of real life. More than

this neither Marx nor I have ever asserted. Hence, if somebody twists this into saying that the economic element is the only determining one, he transforms that proposition into a meaningless, abstract, senseless phrase.[131]

In Marx's schema the linkage from nature to society has a dual function. Nature provides the "maintenance inputs" necessary for society's continuation. In *German Ideology*, Marx began by stating the ontological presupposition that man must be in a position to live in order to be able to "make history." Before all else life requires the satisfaction of organic needs: eating, drinking, habitation, clothing, etc. Production, the providing of material life itself, consequently is a "historical act" whose reproduction must be assured in order to sustain human life.[132] In addition to providing the raw materials from which mankind achieves sustenance, aspects of the environment influence the form of this productive process.

> The form of this relation between masters and producers always necessarily corresponds to a definite stage in the development of the method of work and consequently of the social productivity of labour. This does not prevent an economic basis which in its principal characteristics is the same, from manifesting infinite variations and gradations owing to the effect of innumerable external circumstances, climatic and geographical influences, racial peculiarities, historical influences from the outside, etc.[133]

The nature-society nexus is reciprocal; not only does nature influence society but society influences nature in an unremitting process.

> In the process of production, human beings do not only enter into a relation with nature. They produce only by working together in a specific manner and by reciprocally exchanging their activities. In order to produce they enter into definite connections and relations with one another and only within these social connections and relations does their connection with nature, i.e., production take place.[134]

In other words, the linkage between the Biosphere and society is mediated by the relations of production and a mode of cooperation. This interaction with nature, rather than being an arbitrary interjection, is a consistent theme throughout Marx's analysis.

The utilization of an analytical model (the mode of production), the conceptualization of society as a system composed of interdependent parts, and the differentiation of endogenous and exogenous sources of change—these crucial theoretical accomplishments fully confirm the view of Marx as a forerunner of the modern open-systems approach.

Nature and the Species-Being of Man

A central issue in Vernadsky's materialist formulation of the concept of the Noösphere was that technified society, that is society that relinquishes control over the development and implementation of science and technology (forces of production), may well inadvertently and critically interfere with the natural rhythms of the Biosphere, restructuring it in ways inconsistent with the continued viability of man himself. Concentrating on the dialectics of society, Marx and Engels, according to Martinez-Alier and Naredo, did not extensively discuss the contradictory relations of man and nature.[135] Yet, Howard Parsons and Alfred Schmidt maintain that they had the latter in mind, as their criticism of capitalism's exploitation of nature demonstrates. Marx's model relied upon a restructuring dynamic that attaches to contradictions between relations of production and forces of production. But, insofar as relations of production exclude Biospheric elements, the ecological dialectic is missing! Nonetheless, rather than assuming a peripheral significance, Schmidt maintains that though Marx rarely referred to nature "in itself" one should not misinterpret this as meaning that nature had little importance from Marx's theory of society. It is rather a product of his particular approach. It is precisely in the articulation of this new phase of technified social development and its present predicament—the global ecological crisis—that Marx's *Grundrisse* is most useful.

Nature and economy for Marx was a totality. It included a conscious, active, sensate modifying part—the human species; and an unconscious, inorganic, insensate inactive part—that part of nature external to man. The two could not be separated. They were both parts of an encompassing unity and process. To speak of man was, by definition, to speak of man's productive praxis, his modification and influence on insensate nature. To speak of insensate nature was, by definition, to reflect on how and in what fashion this passive material was altered and humanized by the activity of man. The stress was always on the active, practical activity of men, the changes wrought by them in their environment, or their attempts to extract from their surroundings objects that fulfilled their needs.

Species-being consisted of a group of anthropological characteristics including not only consciousness but also a system of needs. Men required water, food, and shelter to perpetuate their physical existence. The species had an objective nature because it could only gratify its physical and psychological needs through objects outside itself. By objectifying himself, by making objects, man had also further humanized himself; that is, added to his enjoyment and appreciation of experience.

Insensate nature was both the condition of human labor and the source of human affirmation. As the condition of human labor, insensate nature supplied man with materiality. It was the substance in which human objectification assumed form. Labor could only be fulfilled, could only realize itself in an object. Insensate nature was the basis of mediation, the materiality that afforded labor the possibility to be objectified.[136] It was the source of human affirmation because it possessed qualities that activated and confirmed the species-being of men.

> If man's feelings, passions, etc. are not merely anthropological characteristics in the narrower sense, but are true ontological affirmations of being (nature),

and if they are only really affirmed in so far as their object exists as an object of sense, then it is evident . . . that their mode of affirmation is not one and unchanging, but rather that the diverse modes of affirmation constitute the distinctive character of their existence, of their life. The manner in which the object exists for them is the distinctive mode of their gratification.[137]

In the *Paris Manuscripts* and later in *Capital*, Marx presented an objective viewpoint in which nature is defined in a Hegelian manner.

The fact that man is a corporeal, living, real, sensuous, objective being and a force of nature, means that he has real, sensuous objects as the object of his being and the expression of his life, or that he can only express his life through real, sensuous objects. . . . A being which does not have its nature outside itself is not a natural being and does not share in the being of nature.[138]

In relation to the history of insensate nature, Marx wrote: "Nature, as it develops in human history, in the act of genesis of human society, is the actual nature of man; thus nature, as it develops through industry, though in an alienated form, is truly anthropological."[139]

Industrial production, the change of material forms, had altered the condition of insensate nature itself. In this sense, insensate nature had become anthropological; that is, it bore the stamp of human praxis. That part of insensate nature that became involved in human activity and production was historicized, for it was continuously modified by human praxis in the course of time.

Insensate nature had two sides, the historical and the nonhistorical. History for Marx was synonymous with the autogenesis of the species through its own activity—its autopoiesis. Therefore, only that part of insensate nature that was humanized could also be historicized. Laws of chemistry and physics could produce change and process, but history could not because it lacked a conscious human agent or purposeful praxis. Marx's view of nature led him to an ontological view of human nature. Being was process.

Labour is, in the first place, a process in which both man and Nature participate, and in which man of his own accord starts, regulates and controls the material reactions between himself and Nature. He opposed himself to Nature as one of her own forces, setting in motion arms and legs, head and hands, the natural forces of his body, in order to appropriate Nature's productions in a form adapted to his own wants. But thus acting on the external world and changing it, he at the same time changes his own nature.[140]

The advancement of knowledge implied the ever-increasing humanization of external nature. The more man intervened in nature, assumed control of natural laws, the more nature became anthropological and the more it was put to special purposes. The objects that man produced not only cultivated his species-being, but also altered his mode of consciousness and thus his rational behavior. The

different technology that praxis brought forth, the different socioeconomic structures produced by human labor, also brought forth different modes of consciousness and different forms of relating to the world. Man thus created his own
consciousness, his self. Man was a being in process.

If ontologically man was process, then history could be nothing but the manifestation of that process, the continuous self-creation of man by man. When
Marx wrote: "man has his own process of genesis, history,"[141] he meant that
since the essence of man was process, history itself could only be the autogenesis
of man. Of course the problem of technified society is that the ontogenesis of
man is determined by an institutionally legitimated autonomous technosphere.

Marx's Doctrine of Nature

According to Schmidt, Marx initially shared Bacon's view, inherited and developed by the Enlightenment, that nature should be seen essentially from the point
of view of its usefulness to man. At issue is whether Marx sought recourse to
substantive rationality rather than functional rationality. However, when he was
engaged in his analysis of the social life-process, concretizing the concept of
appropriation, Marx reached beyond the bourgeois theories of nature presented
by the Enlightenment.[142]

Marx's doctrine of nature (that nature is man's body, his creation, and his
expression), can be seen as the product of Marx's transposition of features and
roles in the Hegelian system of thought onto man. Following the thought of St.
Thomas Aquinas, in the Hegelian system nature is God's body, His creation and
necessary self-expression, that in which He recognizes Himself and, through
shaping, creates Himself. In Marx's demystification of Hegel's system all these
properties are attributed to man. Thus, Marx's theory represents the placing of
man in the role previously attributed to God, a transposition characteristic of
eschatological dimensions of Enlightenment thought. But this Enlightenment-
inspired transposition has been and is an environmental disaster under capitalism. The result of the transposition appears to warrant unlimited and
unconstrained human transformation of the natural world—now in the name of
human expression rather than spiritual domination.

The Marxist project revolves around the humanization of nature understood
as man's "inorganic body."[143] In this context a central doctrine for the Marxian
thesis of unity between man and nature (the doctrine that "man creates nature")
should be understood not in some mystical sense, but rather in the obvious and
literal way (man creates nature because man transforms it and molds it to his
will). It is thus through humanizing and transforming nature that man makes
nature his body, his creation, and his self-expression.

The "nature-speculation" in Marx is an attempt, which runs through the whole
of his work, to provide an appropriate concept for the mutual interpenetration of
nature and society within the natural whole. Nature appears in the *Paris Manu-*

scripts as "the inorganic body of man; that is to say, nature, excluding the human body itself." It is his body "with which he must remain in continuous interaction in order not to die."[144] Marx wrote that man's relation to nature cannot as such be fixed abstractly, that it is not initially theoretical and reflective but practical and transforming. Just as in living nature assimilation changes the inorganic into the organic, so man assimilates that "inorganic body" in his work and converts it in an ever-increasing measure into an "organic" part of himself. Man can do this only, however, because he himself belongs directly to nature, which is by no means a purely external world entirely separated from his internal characteristics: "This interdependence of the physical and mental life of man with nature has the meaning that nature is interdependent with itself, for man is part of nature."[145]

The theme in the *Paris Manuscripts*, that nature is the inorganic body of man, appears again in the *Grundrisse*. Therein Marx claims that before the advent of capitalism, although nature is split into two parts, the working Subject and the Object to be modified, it remains an undifferentiated unity—"present to itself" in this division. Man appears as a mode of nature's organic existence; nature appears from the very outset as the "inorganic existence of man himself."[146]

Insofar as the unity of man and the stuff of nature is retained in the shape of use-values, Marx does not require any explanation since it is "common to the most disparate epochs of production."[147] In other words, the substantive biophysical dimension of the economy in its patent universality requires no explanation. What the critique of political economy is interested in and wishes to explain is something typical only of bourgeois society: namely the division between these inorganic conditions of human existence and this active existence itself, a division posited in its completeness in the relation between wage-labor and capital.

Insensate nature, which embodied elements of his epistemological dimensions, was never discussed in isolation in Marx's writings; was never referred to as an agency that had laws and mechanisms peculiar to itself. Marx sensibly retreated from analyzing the inorganic world as having a separate and distinct existence apart from man, as having an essence and metaphysics of its own. The Marxian analysis was always on those areas where the sensate and insensate parts of nature interchanged. In other words, Marx was not an ecologist!

> Physically man lives only on . . . products of Nature, whether they appear in the form of food, heating, clothing, a dwelling, etc. The universality of man appears in practice precisely in the universality which makes all Nature his *inorganic* body—both inasmuch as Nature is (1) his direct means of life, and (2) the material, the object, and the instrument of his life activity. Nature is man's inorganic body—Nature, that is, in so far as it is not itself the human body. Man *lives* on Nature—means that Nature is his *body*, with which he must remain in continuous interchange if he is not to die. That man's physical and spiritual life is linked to Nature means simply that Nature is linked to itself, for man is a part of Nature.[148]

For the essentialist Marx, substantive needs form the basis of social existence. In order to meet these needs, man had to organize or socialize his activities; that is, social existence already was an attribute of these needs; for it was only in society that these needs could be gratified. Substantive need was thus a motivating force in history. Therefore, all history was in part the organization of social and economic structures, which man imposed on the species in order to better answer his needs.[149]

Man must produce the conditions necessary for his continued existence. Man's activity, i.e., his productive labor, not only modified the world external to him, but also in turn modified man. By constantly changing the socioeconomic forms, men changed not their species-being, since that was inherent in their being a living being, but their social consciousness and their behavior.

Human labor-power is "only the manifestation of a force of nature," as "the material of nature transferred into the human organism."[150] Labor itself is only the manifestation of a natural force, it is always a substratum that cannot be reduced to labor alone. In his work man "opposes himself to nature as one of her own forces."[151] "By acting on the external world and changing it, he, at the same time, changes his own nature."[152] Similar sentiments were expressed in Marx's "Marginal Notes to the Programme of the German Worker's Party": "Labour is not the source of all wealth. Nature is just as much the source of use-values (and it is surely of such that material wealth consists!) as labour, which itself is only the manifestation of a force of nature."[153]

In his *Critique of the Gotha Programme*, Marx reaffirms the notion that man does not produce nature; rather, nature was here first, but he adds that: "insofar as man from the beginning behaves toward nature, the primary source of all instruments and subjects of nature, as an owner, treats her as belonging to him, his labour becomes the source of use values, therefore also of wealth."[154]

Marx considered nature to be "the primary source of all instruments and objects of labour,"[155] i.e., he saw nature from the beginning in relation to human activity. The major thrust of Marx's message is to show that the development of capital has freed human beings from the bondage of nature (although enslaving them to the bondage of their own economic system). In *Grundrisse* he says that "the great foundation-stone of production and wealth" is, among other things, man's "understanding of nature and his mastery over it."[156]

Moreover, Marx indicated that society itself was a natural environment. This was meant not only in the immediately critical sense that man is still not in control of his own productive forces vis-à-vis nature, that these forces confront him as the organized, rigid form of an opaque society, as a "second nature" which sets its own essence against its creators, but also in the "metaphysical" sense that Marx's theory is a theory of the world as a whole. It is a form of "totality theory" in the tradition of Hegel.

Marx thus pictured an essentially complementary and interdependent relationship between man and external nature. In fact, this relationship was exactly what Marx referred to as the "Being of nature."[157] "Since this relationship between man and nature is the precondition for the relationship between man and man, the dialectic of the labour-process as a natural process broadens out to become the dialectic of human history in general."[158]

Man forms the connecting link between the instrument of labor and the object of labor. Nature is the subject-object of labor. Its dialectic consists in this: that man changes his own nature as he progressively deprives external nature of its mystery and externality, as he mediates nature through himself, he makes nature itself work for his own purposes.

Nature becomes dialectical. Ontologically, man, as a transforming consciously acting subject confronting nature, expresses himself as a force of nature. In this connection, Frederick Engels had some incisive things to say about the exploitative character of technology.

> Let us not, however, flatter ourselves overmuch on account of our human victories over nature. Each victory, it is true, in the first place takes its revenge on us. Each victory, it is true, in the first place brings about the results we expected, but in the second and third places it has quite different, unforeseen effects which only too often cancel the first.[159]

He cited the destruction of the forests in Mesopotamia, Greece, and Asia Minor, and the consequent and unplanned removal of water reservoirs; the exhaustion of fir forests by Alpine Italians and the consequent impairment of the dairy industry and mountain springs; the creation of furious floods, and so on.[160] We might add that grazing and overgrazing on the steppes of Central Asia by sheep-raising nomads led to the impoverishment of the soil that triggered the Great Migration, which lasted one thousand years and completely changed the economic, social, cultural, and political face of Europe.

Describing the emergence of capitalism as "a total revolution in, and development of, material production," Marx considered that the price to be paid for this is that nature becomes, like man, not merely objectified but alienated. It ceases to be recognized "as a power for itself," and it becomes a "mere object for men, a mere thing of utility."[161] Capitalist relations of production were historically entered into as a means of developing the forces of production, man's mastery of nature, and thus of advancing the richness of human existence, human nature itself. But the forces of production become subordinated to the priorities of capital. As contemporary-sounding as these comments are, something is absent from the analysis.

The patent fact that between the economic process as an open system with respect to the Biosphere, i.e., that there exists a continuous material influence that is history-making, seems to have been obscured at a certain level of analysis. Though it was integral to Marx, the open-systems model was not fully elaborated. Consequently there is a certain level of confusion. On the one hand, in Volume III of *Capital*, Marx wrote that natural elements entering as agents into production, and which cost nothing, no matter what role they play in production, do not enter as components of capital, but as a free gift of Nature to capital, that is, as a free gift of Nature's productive power to labor, which, however, appears as the productiveness of capital, as all other productivity under the capitalist mode of production.[162]

On the other hand, in Volume I he noted that "raw materials form no part of the capital advanced. The subject of labour is in this case not a product of previous labour, but is furnished by Nature gratis, as in the case of metals, minerals, coal, stone, etc."[163] Elsewhere in *Capital* Marx referred to nature as the basis of "the material forms of existence of constant capital,"[164] the provider of the means of production, and this includes also living labor, i.e., man himself.

Subjectively, the radical destruction of nature's qualitative characteristics corresponds to the reduction of the worker to existence as a producer of exchange-values, which involves "the complete negation of his natural existence," i.e., the fact that he "is entirely determined by society."[165] If the earlier modes of human intervention in nature were fundamentally modes of nature's "self-mediation" (since the mediating subject [individual or community] remained a part of immediately natural existence), under capitalism the mediation of nature became something strictly historical, i.e., the economy was disembedded.

In a passage in *Grundrisse* Marx writes:

> Nature becomes . . . pure Object for man, a pure thing of utility; it ceases to be recognized as a power for itself; and the theoretical knowledge of its autonomous laws itself appears only as a stratagem for subjecting it to human needs, be it as object of consumption, or means of production.[166]

The mastery over nature created by the workers becomes the mastery of capital over them. Alienation now can be seen clearly not as the cause of private property or capitalist crisis, but the result, the suffering that accompanies the pathology of capitalist relations of production.

Marx's recommendations regarding the historical cure for this pathology follow clearly from the materialism that underlies and informs his entire analysis.

> The liberation of man is not advanced a single step by reducing philosophy, theology substance and all that trash to "self-consciousness" and by liberating man from the domination of these phrases, which have never held him in thrall . . . in reality and for the practical materialist, i.e., the communist, it is a question of revolutionizing the existing world, of practically attacking and changing existing things.[167]

The problem is that capitalism has not merely objectified, but alienated nature. It has set nature off as the "other." Nature is viewed as an adversary to human development, with laws of its own which may lead to our destruction. The cries of "doomsday" seem to take the responsibility and capacity for determining our direction out of human hands. This is because nature is seen as an objective obstacle over and against human subjective ends. But the split between subjective and objective is a manifestation of our own alienation.[168]

Whereas it has been argued that in Marx's early works "alienation" was clearly distinguished from "objectification," in *Grundrisse*, "objectification" is defined as universally necessary at all stages of history because man creates himself in his labor and crystallizes himself in the objects on which he labors. Objectification, in other words, assumes an ontological dimension. Man interacts with nature, puts his labor into nature, and in the process transforms both himself and nature. But all labor objectifies. It is the very essence of labor. It is only when the finality of objectification is governed by needs and priorities other than the producer's that one can speak of alienated labor. On the one hand, the "objectification" of nature smacks of a homocentric piety. On the other hand, to equate alienation and objectification is to mystify both labor and its relations.[169]

The fictitious commodification of nature as an alien "other," just as the treatment of a human being as an alien "other," sets up the possibility for exploitation. Under the capitalist mode of production, nature is seen as an alien object to be exploited, just as the worker is seen as an alien object to be exploited. In Karl Polanyi's terminology, both nature and labor become fictitious commodities. Thus, the problem of dehumanization and the correlative ecological problems stem from the same root cause—alienation that attaches to commodification.

It is conspicuous, however, that, as nature disappeared from economic theory, it was "discovered" at the same time to be a source of aesthetic experience. In the course of the seventeenth and especially eighteenth century, however, a decisive qualitative change of this specific aesthetic experience took place. This manifested itself in landscape painting, in lyric poetry celebrating nature, and particularly in a new sensitivity toward the natural that informed everyday culture. For instance, in horticulture, plants were no longer set out geometrically, as if to assert the power of mind over matter. Instead, attempts were made to achieve a "natural" simulation of nature. As long as horticulture continued to be governed by a spirit of geometric rationalism, the whole of nature remained merely a potential source of revenue—out of which horticulture endeavored to carve a free space for pleasure and play.[170] This qualitatively new mode of experiencing nature had as ideological prerequisites pantheism and pantheistic nature-religions, i.e., Goethe.

In regard to the essentials that concern us here, Marx saw no inherent flaw or problem between man as creator and the artifacts that he produced. Indeed, in Marx's view it was this very activity that consummates man's humanness. Marx wrote:

> The product of labour is labour which has been embodied in an object, which has become material; it is the objectification of labour. Labour's realization is its objectification. In the sphere of political economy this realization of labour appears as a loss of realization for the workers; objectification as loss of the object and bondage to it, appropriation as estrangement, as alienation.[171]

Marx accepted Hegel's notion of man expressing his life fully and coming-to-be through his own creative activities. He called this man's *Aüsserung*—man's extension or externalization of himself (including his consciousness). Over and against this, Marx contrasted man's *Entaüsserung*.[172] This was the negative connotation given to this activity under capitalism where man was forcibly separated from the fruits of his labor.

But man, living in constant contact with material reality, shapes it to his own purposes. Through his labor, he pours his life into nature and makes it part of himself. In this sense man has two bodies, the one with which he is born and an inorganic body, which is nature. Marx holds that human beings are necessarily involved in sensuous productive activity in a world of material things. Since life and production are virtually equivalents, the mode of production present in a society takes on a supreme significance. Marx spoke of the creative expansion and extension of man into the world through labor as self-activity in community with his fellows.

Alienation is not the automatic outcome of productive labor. It is not the outcome of objectification. Labor's realization is its objectification in any productive activity. It is only in the sphere of political economy, more specifically in commodity production, that alienation occurs. Alienation from production is said to lie in the capitalist's ownership and juridical rights of disposal of that product.

Howard Parsons observes that Marx and Engels viewed capitalism, with its progressing technology and "constantly expanding market," as supplanting the passive barter economy of feudalism.[173] Capitalism effectively subjugated nature, whereas feudalism obeyed and passively acquiesced in it. But the distinction, following Polanyi, is between technified and nontechnified society.

In *Grundrisse*, Marx notes that with the emergence of the price-making market "for the first time, nature becomes purely an object for humankind, purely a matter of utility; ceases to be recognized as a power for itself; and the theoretical discovery of its autonomous laws appears merely as a ruse so as to subjugate it under human needs whether as an object of consumption or as a means of production. In accord with this tendency, capital drives beyond national barriers and prejudices as much as beyond nature worship, as well as all traditional, confined, complacent encrusted satisfactions of present needs, and reproductions of old ways of life."

In the development of the price-making market, Marx and Engels discerned two social movements contradicting each other. One was the "subjection of nature's forces to man," and the expansion of man's productive forces to meet his material needs.[174] Such an "enlarging of the bounds of human empire," as F. Bacon called it, would open the way to true human freedom. The other movement was the inertia and failure of the existing system of social relations with respect to controlling the new power and wealth in the interests of the vast majority.

Though their focus was principally on the dialectic of capitalism, Marx and

Engels did not retreat from attributing to capitalism an unprecedented exploitation of nature. "The mode of perceiving nature, under the rule of private property and money," wrote Marx in 1844, "is a real contempt for, and a practical degradation of, nature."[175]

Marx holds that mankind has developed from nature and in mutual interaction with nature; nature is not an alien "other" but is man's body. The doctrine of the "non-otherness" of nature does not stress the interdependence of two distinct items, man and nature, but rather the destruction of what is genuinely and purely nonhuman and its replacement by a transformed and humanized world. Thus, subjection or exploitation is said to cease and harmony or unity to be realized, but only because nature in effect ceases to be an independent phenomenon.

Debenjak makes the salient point that Engels, in his conception of alienation, understood nature as an alien force, which man has himself placed opposite himself through his productive activities. The more the productive practice is directed at controlling nature and the more man's own action is organized, the more man is threatened by the play of the untamed forces of nature. It is with its very state of being "untamed" that nature represents the limitations and negation of the productive practice. Nature of itself is not an alien force, man being essentially at one with nature. Nature becomes alien only in its relation to the productive practice. However, it is the production process that places itself opposite man as the chief alien force and as the real alien domination over him. The production process represents the elimination of the alien state of nature in that it incorporates and integrates natural agents which then operate as agents of the process, hence in the eliminated form: mechanical, physical, chemical, and biotic processes are through the "understanding of necessity" included in the production process, and in that context lose their spontaneity of "outer nature." They are incorporated in the organism of social development.[176]

Marx had several important insights, but his work in general was not always free of the limitations that are attached to the Enlightenment. In this connection the development of environmental consciousness is to some extent a process of discarding the Enlightenment legacy, of upsetting the human hubris that resulted from it, and of restoring a sense of the limitation of human powers and human ability to understand, interfere with, and manipulate a larger natural order. Marx cannot be taken as the definitive authority on environmental-economic-social issues. For although he had penetrating insights into his historical era, he was also a nineteenth-century thinker who was mainly a critic of nineteenth-century capitalism.

From Marx's view, man's harmony with nature is reached with the accomplishment of a communist society. This played a central role in his theory of history and of the development of human society, and formed a central feature of his overall theory. Thus, the necessity for man to acquire power over nature is used to explain both the development of class society and its final transcending through technological development. In this connection capitalism is only the first step, which itself must be overcome, for man to come into harmony with nature. It is because of the necessity to dominate nature in order to become fully human that capitalism is seen as a necessary stage in human development and mastery of nature.

Capitalism is praised by Marx for taking mankind to a necessary stage of human mastery of nature.

> Hence the great civilizing influence of capital: its production of a stage of society in comparison to which all earlier ones appear as mere local developments of humanity as nature–idolatry. For the first time, nature becomes purely an object for humankind, purely aumter of utility; it ceases to be recognized as a power for itself; and the theoretical discovery of its autonomous laws appears merely as a ruse to subjugate it under human needs, whether as an object of consumption or as a means of production. In accord with this tendency, capital drives beyond national barriers and prejudices as much as beyond nature worship.[177]

Marx approves of the step forward made by capitalism, the creation of the attitude of nature (which according to many ecologists is the very root of our present ecological difficulties); this much of human progress is to be retained by communism. It is only the internal logic and limits of capitalism that make this revolutionary thrust ultimately self-destructive within capitalism.

> But from the fact that capital posits every such limit as a barrier and hence gets ideally beyond it, it does not by any means follow that it has really overcome it, and, since every such barrier contradicts its character, its production moves in contradictions which are constantly overcome but just as constantly posited. Furthermore, the universality towards which it irresistibly strives encounters barriers in its own nature, which will, at a certain stage of its development, allow it to be recognized as being itself the greatest barrier to this tendency, and hence will drive towards its own suspension.[178]

Inherent contradictions within capitalism cause it to fail to master nature. It does so even though it has developed the technological preconditions for such mastery; from this one can predict that capitalism will find itself in ecological difficulties of various sorts which are alleged to be overcome by the revolutionary transition to socialism.

The limit to further capitalist development, notes Groh and Sieferle, lies not in the full realization of the value principle but in another objective barrier to the system. This is the barrier imposed by nature to the continued production of commodities and the useful kinds of labor, or productive activities.[179]

Marx claims that capitalism is "a necessary stage" in the destruction of the fetishism of externalization with respect to nature. Such a fetishism is similar to the fetishism of commodities, which Marx defines as a "social relation between men, that assumes, in their eyes the fantastic form of a relation between things."[180] Thus, nature is falsely seen as an external object to be manipulated. The overcoming of nature's power is a necessary step in the overcoming of human alienation.[181] However, the historical necessity of capitalism appears to environmentalists as an acquiescence to the destructive technology of advanced capitalism.

Marx's critique of capitalism is an effort to get us out of a "prehistory" in which men are enslaved to particular economic conditions, in which they can lay the foundation for a period of liberation in which "real human history" can begin, and in which men are free of their previous exploitation and alienation to express themselves through free and creative and socially productive activity. A further historical development is necessary; the overcoming of the dichotomy between man as subject and nature as object.

Both Marx's doctrine of nature and his bequest that technology serve to enhance the freedom of man, together with Vernadsky's declared interest in scientific and technological advancement are highly nuanced. The facile counter-argument is that science and technology are the villains of the ecological movement. The institutionalist and Noöspheric or coevolutionary theorist argues that it is not science and technology per se but the manner in which they have been institutionalized. Rather than committing ourselves to a Rousseauistic retreat from concrete reality, science and technology must be further developed and institutionalized, not as autonomous phenomena, but embedded within a socially and ecologically responsible social structure.

The distinction between subject and object inherent in capitalism, notes Marx, will be overcome when objectified labor becomes qualitative labor,[182] rather than alienated labor; that is, rather than being a force over and above labor. The abolition of objectified labor as alien will constitute the overcoming of the subject–object distinction when capital becomes the body of labor.[183] Nature is the basis of capital, and man and nature are transformed into and reflected in one another in their interaction.

The overcoming of alienation will be achieved by the "universal development of the individual" through "the grasping of his own history as process, and the recognition of nature (present as practical power over nature) as his real body."[184] This recognition of nature as man's body will constitute the overcoming of the alienation of man from nature, manifested in subject–object dualism. Thus, an identity between external nature and human nature will be established. It has been argued that the view of nature as man's body seems to carry an implication, present in St. Thomas Aquinas and Locke, that nature is man's property—one's body is, after all, one's own, and usually considered to be entirely at one's disposal. However, this rendering stems from a superficial appreciation of Marx's dialectic.

In a fully developed socialist world subject–object dualism would allegedly be overcome. A millennial Marx stipulated in *Grundrisse* that the eventual overcoming of alienation will take place as a result of technological development, the extension of human power over nature.[185] The development of technology, the power over nature, prepares the way for the next stage of development which assumes

> the free development of individualities, and hence not the reduction of necessary labour time so as to posit surplus labour, but rather the general reduction of the necessary labour of society to a minimum, which then corresponds to the artistic, scientific, etc., development of the individuals in the time set free, and with the means created, for all of them.[186]

The more we know and control the natural consequences of our productive activities, Engels argued, "the more will men once more not only feel, but also know, themselves to be one with nature."[187] Nor was Engels immune from seeking solutions in technological advance; for he wrote: "We are reminded that we by no means rule over nature like a conqueror over a foreign people, like someone standing outside nature—but that we, with flesh, blood and brain, belong to nature, and exist in its midst, and that all our mastery of it consists in the fact that we have the advantage over all other creatures of being able to know and correctly apply its laws."[188] Consistent with Hegelian dialectics, Engels emphasized that we are immanent in nature. We do not stand outside and over it, we "belong" to it, in the sense that we have an organic, functional, and qualitative connection to it. In other words, man exists because of metabolic interaction with the Biosphere. To Marx and Engels, man is profoundly dependent on an antecedent nature. Interacting with it to survive and live well, man becomes independent through reason and rational practice, but the independence is always conditioned by its sources, surroundings, and finality within nature.

Such an analysis begs the question, "whether the crises of technified society are phenomena of a particular system of social organization, production, and consumption, which might be overcome by a different more humanistic and embedded mode of social organization?" But crises of technified society, socialist or capitalist, suggest to us that there may be little practical distinction.

Is socialism a sufficient condition for ecological salvation? A convergence theory issue is present in this issue. For instance, Tolman notes that, while alienation may have its origin in the relations of production, environmental problems have their origin more immediately in the developing forces of production.[189] And the solutions to environmental problems are also different from the solution to alienation. Whereas the abolition of alienated labor may lay immediately in a transformation of the relations (organization) of production, environmental problems can be solved only by further advance in the forces of production. This means the further development of technology, but more important, it means the development of a more rigorous theoretical understanding of nature, production, and society so that, to paraphrase Marx, a real coevolution with nature can be attained, one that moves forward fully conscious of the reciprocity and interdependence of nonhuman nature and human needs and aspirations.

With respect to actual achievement of their historical solutions, alienation and environmental problems are alike. Neither, according to Gorz, will be achieved in capitalist society. Environmental problems will remain unsolved not because capitalism is incapable of developing the necessary forces of production, but because its priorities, its relations, will necessarily stifle such development.[190] Capital will support environmental research and will implement environmentally sound procedures only when it is in the interest of the totalizing logic of capital. Here we face the inevitable conflict in capitalism between the forces and relations of production. Reforms, legislation, and protest can yield temporary relief at best insofar as they presuppose the preservation of capitalist priorities, i.e., relations of production. Only revolutionary transformation of these relations, the abolition of capitalism itself, can bring the possibility of genuine relief. "Obviously then, the key to understanding environmental problems for the Marxist . . . is to grasp the significance of the historical concrete relations of production."[191] "Nature," writes Marx, "builds no machine, no locomotives, railways, electric telegraphs, self-acting mules, etc. These are the products of human industry; natural material transformed into organs of the human will over nature, or of human participation in nature."[192]

Marx's Process of Nature—Metabolic Interaction

Though Marx and Engels principally directed their studies to the dialectics of society, Howard Parsons notes that where dialectics touches on nature it pertains to the "metabolism" or "exchange" of matter–energy between man and nature, and between the industrial city and the countryside.[193] Indeed, it is important to note that the concept of man's metabolic interaction with nature, that is, the essence of his livelihood, buttresses the open-systems view and forms a central part of Marx's totality theory.

The dialectics of Marx and Engels pertained to man's collective and immediate material interaction with nature. It brought man into a dialectical relation and into a dynamic and evolutionary interaction with it. Such a relation, when critically analyzed, reveals nature as matter in continuous motion, interconnection, and transformation. The image is that of the dialectic evolution of nature developing in a ceaseless series of unities of opposites, which are mutually creative, mutually destructive, and mutually transforming.[194]

The concept of life-process, i.e., man's material interaction with the Biosphere, present in Marx's writings from the *German Ideology* onward, embodies the notion of external nature as the inorganic body of man. Even as it appears in the *Paris Manuscripts*, the description of the labor-process is that of the metabolism between man and nature.

The labour-process . . . is human action with a view to production of use-values, appropriation of natural substances to human requirements; it is the general condition for the metabolism between man and nature; it is the everlasting nature-imposed condition of human existence and therefore is independent of every social form of that existence or rather, is common to every such form.[195]

Marx knew the works of the so-called vulgar materialists: Moleschott, Bucher, and Vogt. Jacob Moleschott influenced Marx's use of the expression "metabolism"[196] between man and nature, a concept with which Marx introduced a completely new understanding of man's relation to nature.[197]

The concept of metabolism, which dominates the preliminary studies of *Capital*, belongs to the physiological rather than to the social sphere and attains a qualitatively new character by being applied to social institutions. In the same way as the continued existence of an individual is bound up with the functions of the body, society too must stand in an uninterrupted interactive relationship to nature. Through the hands of men pass the materials of nature in the form of use-values, to be transformed back into nature in degraded form.[198] This surprisingly contemporary thermodynamic vision of the economic process is a clear departure from the circular flow concept; for it is suggestive of the modern open-systems theoretical perspective critical to a political economy of the Noösphere.

From Marx's criticism of the abrupt division between town and country it emerges unmistakably that he understood the concept of metabolism not only metaphorically but also in an immediately physiological sense. This division, Marx said, severely disturbed "the metabolism between man and the earth, i.e., the return to the soil of its elements consumed by man in the form of food and clothing, and therefore violated the eternal natural condition for the lasting fertility of the soil."[199]

Marx showed himself in favor of Justus Liebig's argument for small-scale agriculture in terms of its greater capacity to return fertilizing elements to the ground, as compared with large-scale agriculture producing for large and distant cities. Marx, like Moleschott, whose conception of nature as a process of circulation lent the concept of metabolism a somewhat "ontological" dignity, described it as "an eternal nature-imposed necessity."[200] Marx tried to establish the "chemical" linkage between nature and the life of laboring man and argued that the laws of economics were not analogous to the physical laws. He asserted that "economic life offers us a phenomenon analogous to the history of evolution in other branches of biology."[201] Alfred Schmidt was therefore right in pointing out that Marx's use of the expression "metabolism between man and earth" was not metaphorical; it referred specifically to the cycles of plant nutrients.[202]

An important example of Marx's interest in scientific developments of his day is evident in the theory of the "normal working day," which is an essential element in the theory of surplus value. Marx states that the value of a day's labor power is estimated by the normal or average duration of labor and from corresponding normal transformations of organized bodily matter into motion in conformity with the nature of man.[203] Marx supports this idea with a quotation from William Grove's *On the Correlation of Physical Forces*, in which Grove says that "the amount of labour which a man had undergone in the course of 24 hours might be approximately arrived at by an examination of the chemical changes which had taken place in his body, changed forms in matter indicating the anterior exercise of dynamic force."[204]

The notion of a natural scientific determination of labor gives powerful support to Marx's idea that as a whole the material transformation of economic conditions of production "can be determined with the precision of a natural science";[205] or that we can speak of value appearing as the "law of the motions which prices run through."[206]

In the *Paris Manuscripts*, Marx portrayed labor as a process of progressive humanization of nature, a process that coincided with the naturalization of man. This corresponded to a higher form of metabolism between man and nature which "liberates anew the creative powers of a frozen nature."[207] Later Marx took the view that the struggle of man with nature could be transformed but not abolished. In this connection he made particular use of the concept of metabolism. This "metabolism" is subject to laws of nature anterior to man. Any attempt to form the stuff of nature must take heed of the regularities proper to matter. The metabolism between man and nature is thus independent of any historical context for Marx.

He repeatedly used the term metabolism when he had in mind the labor process which takes place solely between man and nature, and he applied this characterization equally to all forms of development. As he wrote in *German Ideology*, there will always exist the "materialist connection of men with each other, which is conditioned by men's needs and their mode of production, and is as old as mankind."[208] In short, the material exchange of man and nature is, for Marx, an ontological category.[209]

In a letter to Kugelmann, Marx wrote: "It is absolutely impossible to transcribe the laws of nature. What can change in historically different circumstances is only the form in which these laws express themselves."[210] "Man can only proceed in his production in the same way as nature itself, that is, he can only alter forms of the material."[211] In other words, the whole of the production process is a shuffling and sorting activity—a view expressed by Quesnay. Beginning with his metabolic understanding and reference to the "sorting" and "shuffling" of material that is the basis of production, Marx equipped himself with nearly all the tools necessary for the contemporary critique of the economic process as an open thermodynamic process.

Engels described human labor as the alteration of the form of matter in accordance with its natural laws. Marx agreed with Engels on this point, at least *in abstracto*,[212] as is apparent from his selecting the following quotation from Pietro Verri's 1773 work *Meditazioni sulla Economica Politica* as corroboration of his own view that man can only proceed in his production in the same way as nature itself:

> All the phenomena of the universe, whether produced by the hand of man or by the general laws of physics, are not in fact newly-created but result solely from a transformation of existing material. Composition and division are the only elements, which the human spirit finds again and again when analyzing the notion of reproduction; and this is equally the case with the reproduction of value ... and of riches, when earth, air, and water become transformed into corn in the fields, or when through the hand of man the secretions of an insect turn into silk, or certain metal parts are arranged to construct a repeating watch.[213]

Natural processes independent of man are essentially transformations of material and energy, and human production itself does not fall outside the sphere of nature. The socially active man, notes Marx,

> confronts the material of nature as one of her own. He sets in motion arms and legs, head and hands, the natural forces of his body, in order to appropriate the material of nature in a form suitable for his own needs. By thus acting through this motion on the nature which is outside him and changing it, he at the same time changes his own nature.[214]

Marx described labor-power as "the material of nature transferred into the human organism."[215] Labor, itself only the manifestation of a natural force, is always dependent on a substratum which cannot be reduced to labor alone. "As labour is a creator of use-values, i.e., is useful labour, it is a necessary condition, independent of all forms of society, for the existence of human beings; it is an eternal nature-imposed necessity, through which is mediated the metabolic interaction between man and nature, i.e., human life itself."[216] Marx had in view for the society of the future a: "higher synthesis ... of agriculture and industry, which of course presupposes that the metabolism between man and nature comes about systematically, as a regulating law of social production, and in a form appropriate to the full development of the human race."[217]

If the possibilities inherent in a use-value are realized neither by the individual nor in productive consumption, it is not put to the service of human purposes. Instead, it reverts to the sphere of the "metabolism of nature."[218] The artificial, humanized, "second" nature, which was erected on the basis of the first nature, is transformed back into the latter. "Thus society is the unity of being of man and nature—the true resurrection of nature—the naturalism of man and the humanism of nature both brought forth to fulfillment."[219] The "transformation" of the materials of nature by man is undone by the destructive force of the extra-human influences exerted by nature.

In referring to "the motion of man on nature," Marx was seeking to express the view that the things that serve to satisfy human needs undergo a qualitative change. As long as nature is appropriated through agriculture and is, therefore, absolutely independent of men, men are abstractly identical with nature. They lapse, so to speak, into natural existence. However, where men succeed in universally mastering nature technically, economically, and scientifically by transforming it into a world of machines, nature congeals into an abstract, in itself external to man. This comment transcends Marx's critique of capitalism and addresses itself to the organization of technified society.

Wherever Marx described the labor-process as a metabolic interaction between man and nature, he confined himself to an enumeration of its moments— "purposive activity of labour," "object" and "instrument" moments which are abstract because they are valid for all stages of production—and he disregarded their specific historical determinations.

With the concept of metabolism Marx presented a picture of the social labor-process as a process of nature. The metabolic interaction of man and the Biosphere is but a particular instance of the metabolism of open living systems. But Marx located it in the category of exchange, and he referred inversely to the concept of metabolism when characterizing the process of exchange. In the direct labor-process, that is, the metabolism between man and nature, "the material side triumphs over the historically determined form; in the process of exchange, which depends on the labour-process, the historically determined form triumphs over the material side."[220]

In the process of exchange, use-value, which is a product of the direct exchange between man and nature, takes on an "existence as an exchange-value or general equivalent, cut loose from any connection with its natural existence."[221] In other words, the price-making market disembeds use-values. Then, through the mediation of this social metabolism, the exchange-value returns to its former immediacy, and again becomes a use-value. With the transition from circulation to consumption, the commodity's social determination becomes extinguished and is replaced with its natural determination. But the natural form of the commodity, its use-value, only appears in the analysis of the process of creating value insofar as it is "the material substratum, the depositary of exchange-value."[222] For Marx, use-values are combinations of two elements: the stuff of nature and the labor that shapes it. Marx's critique of political economy presents the process of production of material goods as a "labour-process" and, at the same time, a process of creating exchange-value which is the main focus of the theory. As such, the commodity as the embodiment of abstract human labor, expressed in terms of necessary labor-time, is independent of any determination from nature. It bears repeating—natural resources are *gratis!* Despite laying elements of a foundation for introducing key analytical elements for a rigorous biophysical understanding, Marx balked at explicitly introducing nature into the analysis of the dyalectic of capital. Indeed, though Marx wrote that capitalism misused natural resources, it did not seem relevant to him in explaining capitalist dynamics. His categories of analysis were labor exploitation (based on the labor theory of value), class struggle, and crises which were a sign that the relations of *pro*duction were blocking the development of the forces of production. On these bases it may be argued that Marx's totality theory was an apprehended one.

In Marx's view, the general nature of the production of use-values was not altered by the fact that it took place in the service of the capitalist, and he therefore considered the labor-process "independently of the particular form it assumes under given social conditions"—a process "in which man through his own acts mediates, regulates and controls the metabolism between himself and nature."[223] Indeed, in *Capital* he dealt with the question of how far the labor process is bound to man's physiology: "However varied the useful kinds of labour, or productive activities may be, it is a physiological fact, that they are functions of the human organism, and that each such function, whatever its form or content, is essentially the expenditure of human brain, nerves, muscles, sense organs, etc."[224]

Marx's understanding of the production process was situated within his totality theory. For the livelihood of man, as with any other organism, survives by a metabolic interaction with nature. From this position there emerge particular aspects of an open-system theory of the economy. Importantly, in situating his analysis within institutional contexts, Marx avoided the naturalist reductionism that later was to plague social energetics.[225]

The regularities allegedly uncovered by Marxist theory (for instance, the economic laws of motion of capitalism) differ from natural laws insofar as they are historically specific and contingent. Marx's effort was to show that these laws— misconstrued by the natural philosophers—are really attributes of a specific social formation. The existence of economic laws of motion testifies to a situation in which the producers forfeited the conditions of life, and their own mutual relations have taken on an autonomous existence which confronts them as a coercive power. Thus, the subjection of human history to quasi-natural laws operating "behind the backs" of actors is a token of the inhuman character of that history—the fact that it is not truly made with free will and consciousness.

Engels and the Natural Unity of Science

The imagination of philosophers and social scientists was captured by the upward sweep of time first with Hegel and then in Darwinian theory. Impressed by Darwin's theory, Marx and Engels followed Hegel's evolutionary optimism in their encompassing theory of evolution in nature and society, which was known as dialectical and historical materialism.

Marx and Engels aimed at a comprehensive view of political economy.[226] They welcomed the method of Darwin in biology and attempted to apply an evolutionary method in political economy, penetrating beneath the particular surface forms to the underlying dialectics. Marx affirmed that "current society, seen economically, becomes pregnant with the new higher form [and] thereby shows socially the same gradual process of transformation that Darwin provided in natural sciences."[227] The logic of this method led Marx and Engels to investigate the economic relations of man and societies to their natural environments, and to pose questions about the foremost of the man–nature relations. However, they never fully formulated the logic of this method; for the demands for a rigorous science of political economy were so monumental as to call for concentration on the intrasocial relations, political concern, and theory and for a resignation from the more intensive study of the exhaustive man–nature relations.[228] Engels, however, undertook the project.

Joravsky comments that the preface to the second edition of *Anti-Dühring* was, in effect, the synthesis of Engels's philosophy of natural science.[229] Schmidt came to the same conclusion: "Engels, by introducing dialectics into the natural sciences, was inventing a philosophy of nature."[230] As such, it was an attempt to apply dialectics to physical processes.[231]

Engels claimed that Hegel's dialectic method could be extracted from its idealist framework and formulated in terms of three fundamental dialectics laws: (1) the principle of contradiction; (2) the interpenetration of opposites; and (3) the negation of the negation. Thus, he took over several categories and principles from Hegel's *Logic*, purged their idealist meaning, and claimed they constituted a "method" that could be applied to reality. Hegel's idealist philosophy of nature gained its bad reputation precisely through the alleged artificialities, empty constructs, and curiosities contained in it. In the case of Engels, the same constructions had a still more repellent effect. This separates his position from Marx, who never tried to codify dialectics as a formal methodological schema, but instead tried to reveal the dialectical character of history by unfolding its alleged conflict-ridden course of development.

(1) Dialectic systems required a motivation or propelling force. For Hegel, the "energizing principle" in the dialectics of logic was desire.[232] For Marx, the "energizing principle" in the dialectics of history was human activity. Motion, for Engels, was the "energizing principle" in materialistic dialectics.[233] Motion then, corresponded to the first dialectical law: the transformation of quantity into quality.

(2) Even though the universe and everything in it could be reduced to the mono-substance "motion," contradiction was still a basic part of organic and inorganic existence. For Engels, the second law of dialectics, the law of interpenetration of opposites, demonstrated that reality was constituted of contending and contradictory forces.[234] Moreover, the law of interpenetration of opposites implied the mutual balancing of contradictory forces. In the scientific law of the conservation of force, Engels assumed that physicists had discovered empirical proof of the dialectical thesis of the interpenetration of opposites: negative forces must be equal to positive forces.[235]

(3) The dialectical law of the negation of the negation required that nature be in continual motion. Negation of the negation meant growth, that the contradiction would be moved to a higher level of opposition. Growth involved disjunction as well as reestablishment of equilibrium.

Insofar as such a philosophy expresses a metaphysical point of view, Schmidt notes that it consists of the following theses, as developed in *Anti-Dühring*:

> (1) The unity . . . of the world consists in its materiality.
> (2) The basic forms of all being are space and time, and a being outside time is just as nonsensical as a being outside space.
> (3) Motion is the mode of existence of matter. Never and nowhere has there existed, or can there exist, matter without motion. The statement that all rest, all equilibrium is only relative, only has meaning in relation to this or that definite form of motion.[236]

Engels's theory understood man as having entered into a dialectical relation with nature, into a dynamic and evolutionary interaction with it. Such a relation, when critically analyzed, reveals nature in continuous motion, interconnected and constantly transforming.[237]

> When we reflect on Nature, or the history of mankind, or our own intellectual activity, the first picture presented to us is of an endless maze of relations and interactions, in which nothing remains what, where and as it was, but everything moves, changes, comes into being and passes out of existence. This primitive, naive yet intrinsically correct conception of the world was that of ancient Greek philosophy, and was first clearly formulated by Heraclitus: everything is and also is not, for everything is in *flux*, is constantly changing, constantly coming into being and passing away.[238]

Engels transformed the historical dialectic of subject and object into a course of development operating deterministically within objects driven by necessary and universal laws of motion. He was prompted to write that "dialectics is nothing more than the science of universal laws of motion and evolution in nature, human society and thought."[239] In other words, Engels's dialectics is the unifying "metascience." Only because he allegedly lost sight of the constitutive role of the active subject in the Marxian dialectic could Engels seek to develop a purely objective dialectics of nature. At the same time, he was led to argue that the same dialectical laws were operative in nature and history, thereby again obscuring the role of the subject in history. Although he admitted that the laws that operate as blind unconscious forces in nature are mediated in history through the will and consciousness of men, he denied that this difference undermined the fundamental parallelism between the two realms. In Engels's view, social laws do not differ from scientific law by dint of their historicity. Rather, "the eternal laws of nature also become transformed more and more into historical ones."[240] This "historicization of nature" is similar to that of the younger Marx, who argued: "History itself is a real part of natural history—of nature's coming to man."[241]

In *Ludwig Feuerbach and the End of Classical German Philosophy*, Engels argued that the laws that operate in nature and history are "identical in substance."[242] Historical evolution is, therefore, simply an aspect of the more general processes of development, just as historical materialism is but one branch of a more general theory of evolution. In this conception, history becomes reified as a second nature governed deterministically by objective laws like first nature. This infers, according to Mendelson, that Engels had lost hold of the critical meaning of Marx's concept of historical laws.[243] In this connection, Engels argued that the unity of nature in motion could only be achieved, in any meaningful sense, by dialectics. "Dialectics divested of mysticism becomes an absolute necessity for natural science, which has forsaken the field where rigid categories sufficed."[244]

For dialectical materialism, as opposed to mechanical materialism, motion, that essential category, is "not merely a change of place, but also, in fields higher than mechanics, a change of quality."[245] One of the limits of mechanical materialism for Engels was "its inability to comprehend the universe as a process, as matter undergoing uninterrupted historical development [that is] eternal motion."[246] In other words, mechanical materialism was a nonevolutionary paradigm. Critical to Engels's view is that this motion can never be created, only transferred, while for Eugen Dühring, "the restoration of the uniformity of matter to mechanical force has the further advantage that a force can be conceived at rest, as tied up, and, therefore, inoperative."[247] But, asks Engels, how could matter pass from this motionless state to movement? "An initial impulse must, therefore, have come from outside, from the outside the universe, an impulse that sets it in motion. But as everyone knows the 'initial impulse' is only another expression for God."[248]

Engels spoke of "the world" and "everything." He believed that the dialectical laws were laws of development of the whole of reality. "Dialectics is nothing more than the science of the general laws of motion and development of Nature, human society and thought."[249] In this conception the dialectic, given its proper materialist foundation, becomes a *Weltanschaung*. Marxism was allegedly transformed from a critical theory into a materialist metaphysics comprised of a theory of nature, a theory of history, and an epistemological theory of the "laws" of the development of mind (logic represented in reflection theory). Engels, assuming a Comtean posture, admitted that each domain had laws peculiar to it, but he believed that the dialectic grasped the overarching laws of motion which asserted themselves in the movement of nature and history. In accord with this conception, Engels attempted to complement Marx's dialectic of history with his own dialectics of nature.

Engels believed he was consistent with Marx's insight, and wrote that dialectical materialism: "constitutes the most important form of thinking for present-day natural science, for it alone offers the analogue for, and thereby the method of explaining, the evolutionary processes occurring in nature, inter-connections in general and transitions from one field of investigation into another."[250]

But the notion that the dialectic of Marxism was a general *Weltanschaung*, which included an independent science of nature, was at variance with Marx's own views. In his historical materialism and critique of political economy, dialectics referred specifically to human history, and nature had a history only in relation to social processes. Marx focused on the interaction of man and nature as mediated by processes of social labor aided by technology. Nature entered into human history both internally, in the form of needs, and externally, as that environment in which men were situated and upon which they labor in order to appropriate the means of subsistence. In both realms nature exhibited historical variation, but this was by virtue of its relatedness to human activity. For Marx, "nature, taken abstractly for itself, rigidly separated from man, is nothing for man."[251] He seemed not to have thought he was developing a *Weltanschaung* which contained a theory of nature alongside a theory of history. However, for Engels the dialectic of history is merely one discipline alongside nature and logic.

Lukács expressed the opinion that there can be no question of a dialectic of external nature, independent of man, because all the essential moments of a dialectic would in that case be absent. Expressing these views in *History and Class Consciousness*, Lukács wrote: "The misunderstandings that arise from Engels' dialectics can in the main be put down to the fact that Engels—following Hegel's mistaken lead—extended the method to apply also to nature. However, the crucial determinants of dialectics—the interaction of subject and object, the unity of theory and practice, the historical changes in the reality underlying the categories as the root cause of changes in thought, etc.—are absent from our knowledge of nature."[252]

After mentioning his projected treatise on the dialectics of nature, Engels remarked:

> [To] me there could be no question of building the laws of dialectics into nature, but of discovering them in it and evolving them from it. . . . To do this systematically and in each separate department is a gigantic task. . . . It may be, however, that the advance of theoretical natural science will make my work to a great extent or even altogether superfluous.[253]

In Engels's conception of the unification of science, the moments of the dialectic are divorced from the concrete historical situation and collapse into the three hypostatized "fundamental laws" laid down in *Dialectics of Nature*. These categories conform to laws that force their way through natural transformations. Supposedly, for Marx, however, "there is no general law formulated by abstraction from the principle of interaction itself," for nature itself is devoid of negativity and emerges only with man's transformation of it. Hence, Engels's dialectic becomes, according to Schmidt, a *Weltanschaung*.[254] Carver, for instance, claims that "there is no evidence that Marx was working towards a unification of all scientific laws on some 'dialectical' basis."[255] Schmidt, arguing to the contrary, notes that "Marxist theory itself already contains the dialectic of nature with which Engels believed it had to be supplemented," and that

Engels' historicization of nature led to a naturalization of human history. This did not occur in the manner of Social Darwinism, whose social function and origin were spotted by both Marx and Engels. Here the naturalization of history means that Engels reduced history to the special area of application of nature's general laws of motion and development.[256]

Indeed, Engels's search for the unification of scientific knowledge led him to the French Encyclopedists. He wrote: "The idea of the Encyclopedia was characteristic of the eighteenth century; it rested on the awareness that all these sciences were interconnected, yet no one was capable of making the transitions, and hence, the sciences could only be placed side by side."[257]

On the empirical level, Engels believed that the actual data for such a unified or totality theory of the natural universe already existed.

If we wish to speak of general laws of nature that are uniformly applicable to all bodies—from the nebula to man—we are left only with gravity and perhaps the most general form of the theory of transformation of energy into heat. [First law of thermodynamics.] But on its general consistent application to all phenomena of nature this theory itself becomes converted into a historical presentation of the successive changes occurring in a system of the universe from its origin to its passing away, hence into a history in which at each stage different laws, i.e., different forms of the same universal motion, predominate and so nothing remains absolutely universally valid except motion.[258]

The older mechanical materialism and corresponding natural science had seen only cyclical or mechanical movement in nature while missing its processes of development. However, the total comprehension of the natural world was heralded by three fundamental scientific laws:

(1) The Darwinian theory of the evolution of species;
(2) The discovery of the cell as the generative source of all plant and animal life gave man the opportunity to systematize the growth of all organisms into a single general law. The theory of transformation of energy meant that heat, radiation, electricity, magnetism, and chemical energy were diferent forms of the same basic energy supply, that is, all were reducible to motion. This law was equated to the first law of dialectics, that quantitative changes made for qualitative changes; and
(3) The theory of evolution allowed us to see that the entire range of organic life was the result of germ plasmas which had gone through a long process of evolution.[259] Natural science, through its own immanent development, seems to be becoming a science of processes and interconnections in which cause and effect are being replaced by relations, interaction, and development.[260]

Beginning with motion, we could derive every form of matter, and, therefore, every form of inorganic life. Moreover, beginning with motion we could derive the cell and from the cell every form of organic existence. Indeed, Engels felt he had discovered the metaphysical nature of the cosmos. In fact, what he had formed was a metaphysical monistic view of nature. He tried to explain the total function of the universe in 1888 in *Ludwig Feuerbach*. He was a materialistic monist, and said as much in his own words.

> Thanks to three great discoveries and other immense advances in natural science, we have now arrived at the point where we can demonstrate the interconnection between the processes in nature not only in particular spheres but also the interconnection of these particular spheres on the whole, and so can present in an approximately systematic form a comprehensive view of the interconnection in nature by means of the facts provided by empirical natural science itself.[261]

Employing the concept of metabolism present in much of Marx's work, Engels referred to life as the conversion of matter from one form into another. Matter was conceptualized as congealed motion or energy. Thus, life itself was reducible to the dialectic laws of motion. The same was true of the mind, which for Engels was simply another "mode of energy."[262]

A central idea that distinguished Marx's interpretation of nature from Engels's was the notion of praxis. Whereas Marx spoke of a pregiven natural and social environment in which man coexisted with insensate nature, Engels described a micro-macrocosmic determinism, in which thought was merely the epiphenomenon of physical forces. Marxism referred to humanistic and programmatic naturalism, that belief that man modified the inorganic world; while Engels referred to a metaphysical monism, that belief that organic and inorganic existence were all reducible to a universal monosubstance.[263] The Marxian vision was always on man who acts, while the Engelian vision tended to cosmological monism.[264]

Marx aimed to keep physical science and its laws within a human, social perspective, alerting us to the enormous importance of scientific discoveries in improving the productivity of human labor and, in certain cases, such as the physiology of labor, assisting us in our understanding of socially productive activity itself. Engels's focus as a systematizer asserted that human thought and behavior could not be other than emanations of matter and thus subject to the same dialectical laws.[265]

In postulating that the laws of nature themselves were dialectic, Engels was attempting something that Marx himself did not attempt. For Marx the dialectic was not in nature itself, but in the ontological metabolic interaction between man and nature. The dialectic process for Marx was the motion of form and content; species-being was the content while nature was the form. When Marx said that he stood Hegel on his head, he did not mean that he had erased the subjectivity of history. What Marx did was to keep the subjective element: man who modifies—*Homo faber*. But, instead of modifying in a strictly logical form, as Hegel believed, man modified because he had to labor to produce use-values to provide for his livelihood. Engels, therefore, lessened the subjectivist dimension. For Engels the essence of nature was dialectical and all other existence proceeded from these laws.[266]

The claim may be made that Engels's metaphysical monism shaped his view of social history, that Engels's monism projected a deterministic philosophy of history. In the grand style, Engels can be compared with Augustine, Comte, and Hegel. Indeed, in *The Origin of the Family, Private Property and the State*, Engels adopted a modified Comtean thesis. Borrowing the Comtean formula of a three-stage development sequence (theological, metaphysical, positive), Engels fit it into a nineteenth-century anthropological frame of reference. In this thesis, history was linear: all societies must pass through certain fixed stages. It was a universally deterministic scheme of historical development. Engels declared his faith in this proposition, saying it introduced "a definite order in the prehistory of man" and, consequently, capitulated to macroscopic determinism.[267] Such a concept corresponded to his monistic view expressed in the *Dialectics of Nature*. The physical and the historic processes were of the same order. It may be argued that Engels set the course that German Social Democrats in the 1890s and vulgar Marxists later followed. Indeed, some Marxists declared that "history" had been determined—independently of free will; that socialism is inevitable because of the march of economic forces. Such a view had, of course, particular propagandistic value for Stalinists.[268]

"Men make their own history," wrote Marx, "but, they do not make it as they please; they do not make it under circumstances chosen by themselves, but under circumstances directly encountered, given and transmitted from the past."[269] Beginning with the assumption that man is a conscious change-inducing agent, Marx could easily move to a praxiological multilinear concept of history. He could understand in Promethean terms that *Homo faber* could give rise to different societies, could so act on similar material as to fashion alternative paths of evolution. Deemphasizing the creative activity of man, subjectivity, and consciousness and referring to a metaphysical monism, Engels logically contrived an "automatic" Marxism; that history was controlled by universal law. Thus, it was Engels who was the economic determinist. It is alleged that he found in economic laws the determinate causal law of history in the same way that he found in motion the determinate causal law of the physical universe. However, in fact, Engels's work is replete with statements qualifying such a determinism as asserting the historicity of social laws.[270]

Marx's and Engels's observations on society and the economy were comprehensive in many respects. Their totality theory foreshadowed and provided the impetus for the later appearance of a general theory of organization and a formative open-systems or metabolic understanding. And in some respects their efforts also enabled later ecological and biophysical contributions to economic thought. However, in some cases they failed to go beyond the mechanical concepts. In this connection, unlike Engels's albeit confused understanding,[271] Marx was unaware of the economic-ecological-social significance of the second law of thermodynamics that had been formulated in France and Germany; and no wonder—Marx lived in the age of unprecedented expansion of industrial production due to coal and iron.[272] Thus, economics and political economy have continued to posit that production and reproduction are carried out perpetually without constraint and that spiraling technological advances may eventually lift the burden of man.

Conclusion

Contiguous to elements of Hegel's methodological revolution, Marx sought to give a systematic survey of the whole of economic science, the scope of which extended beyond the analysis of Ricardo. In the context of his open-systems model, he departed from the linear causality present in Ricardo's work. Anticipating elements of the theory of open systems, Marx referred to the species-being of man in connection with the production process as composed of interdependent elements, including nature. In this context social change is an endogenous dialectic process in which the nature–society nexus displays reciprocal and complex interpenetrations. Nature itself becomes dialectical only in the context of that interpenetration.

The noteworthy attempt of Marx and Engels to formulate a grand synthesis— a totality theory—was to some extent premature. The puzzle of the two arrows of time could not be resolved by nineteenth-century science. For the grand syntheses based on nineteenth-century science had to opt for either the Boltzmann's downward-pointing arrow of the second law of thermodynamics, or the biologist's upward-sweeping spiral of life. Marx and Engels elected to follow a dialectical materialist and evolutionist line that was present in V.I. Vernadsky's formulation of the Noösphere. Though Marx and Engels only casually referred to the persistent and accelerating dissipation of energy effected by production processes, their model explicitly embodied the open-systems notion of the metabolic interaction of man and nature; the notion that the economic process is embedded in the Biosphere. The explicit insertion of energetics into Marxian thought, together with the elaboration of totality theory, was to become the project of a number of dissident Soviet theorists in the twentieth century.

While efforts to cultivate a rigorous understanding of the complex relationship between technological production activities and nature are becoming more numerous and achieving a new level of sophistication, it nevertheless remains clear that the greater portion of the work on this crucial problem has yet to be ventured. Of the diversity of approaches to this issue considerable promise is held in the ascendance of substantive modes of thought on the relationship between social production and the Biosphere. In Vernadsky's materialist formulation, Noögenesis—the creation of the Noösphere—corresponded to the further development of science and technology. Science, in particular, would transform inadvertent human interference in the Biosphere to more deliberate and purposeful intercession. To argue that man-equipped science and technology "remakes" nature is not to argue that certain natural laws do not lie beyond man's control. The mere assertion of the historicity of science is not sufficient to permit man to make the sun rise in the West. Some more precise formulation is needed if the gap between immutable natural laws and "historical" man-made laws is to be overcome. Marx and Engels were well aware of this problem, one that they regarded as crucial to the development of a universal science, a science that was absolutely essential for their own theory. Accordingly, man's further development would be enhanced and sustained in the Noösphere consistent with an ethos that respected the natural rhythms of the Biosphere. The problematique that Vernadsky addressed was "the reconstruction of the Biosphere in the interest of freely thinking humanity as a single unity."[273] In this connection the earlier and holistic contributions of Marx and Engels cannot be dismissed out of hand.

Broadening Economic Analysis: The Early Contribution of the General Theory of Organization

Introduction

Chapter 2 of this work initially concerns itself with a background review of the theoretical and epistemological difficulties encountered at the end of the last century. The crisis of physics, the appreciation of principles of thermodynamics, together with elements of phenomenological epistemology and the concept of open systems were formative elements in the emergence of an alternative paradigm for economic analysis. In particular, it is argued that the discovery of the fact and principles of thermodynamics together with controversial speculations in the physical sciences presented philosophical materialism with a challenge to renew itself. It shall be argued that this challenge was first countered sociologically by Ostwaldian "social energetics" and philosophically by phenomenology. A growing appreciation of the role of energy in the economy provided an impetus for a reevaluation of economic analysis along Physiocratic lines. It tendered a biophysical basis of the economy. This train of thought, in some cases, however, substituted the reductionism of mechanical materialism for a form of energy reductionism known as "social energetics." Moreover, seeking to meet Engels's bequest that Marxism renew itself and seek a unity of scientific knowledge, a number of Soviet Marxists, inspired by Mach's phenomenological perspective, sought the unity of science in a general theory of organization. In the explication of the open-systems coevolutionary model it is necessary to review briefly the methodological and epistemological predisposition that had infused conventional economic thought—the crisis that is bringing about a substantive reformulation of a political economy in the broad sense; a political economy for the epoch of the Noösphere. In the following pages I shall endeavor to summarize the discoveries that coincided with this development and argue that these seminal contributions provide the substantive basis for a contemporary broadening of economic analysis.

Discovery of Thermodynamics and the
Collapse of the Laplacean Prototype

In the age of clocks, the Newtonian universe was represented by man as a huge mechanism that had been wound up once and for all time. Theorists saw mechanical motion (the displacement of bodies in space) as the basis of all existence, taking place according to Newton's laws of motion. From this point of view, life was discussed as being merely a special kind of mechanical motion.

At the peak of its glory, the Laplacean dream met with its first setback. As Max Planck noted, the irreversibility of the second law of thermodynamics upset the Laplacean ideal.[1] A physical theory had been discovered—one every bit as mathematically rigorous as the mechanical laws of motion, but with a character alien to the Newtonian world. It became apparent that natural open systems, characterized by irreversible thermodynamic processes, were recognized as the norm, and the closed, mechanical, and reversible processes of Laplace were identified as the exception.

Carnot's memoir on thermodynamics was ultimately to force the realization upon physicists that, after all, Laplacean mechanics can not account for every phenomenon in the universe.[2] It is unable to explain faithfully the phenomenon of heat always passing by itself from a hotter to a cooler body, never in the reverse. Moreover, Carnot discovered irreversible time, heterogeneous to Newtonian time. This was the origin of the entropy law and, parenthetically, by the same token, the negation of the perpetual engine hypothesis of the economy.

The principle of conservation of energy was very important to the nineteenth-century scientists. For many of them it meant the unification of the whole of nature. Moreover, it fostered a belief in a new golden age, one that would lead to the ultimate generalization of mechanics. The cultural implications were far reaching, and they included a conception of society and man as energy-transforming engines. The role of mechanics in the study of life was taken over in many sciences by what was known as energetics. But thermodynamics also presented problems.

Paradox of Life

The great arrow of evolution points not toward increasingly differentiated and complex unities, but toward progressively disorganized, simple, and random aggregates. The effect of the thermodynamic laws on the thinking about evolution in the universe was profound. The optimism expressed in Spencer's Law of Persistence of Force concerning evolution leading to perfection and happiness, which was included in the first edition of Spencer's *First Principles*, was excluded from the sixth.

In classical thermodynamics Eddington's "arrow of time" points downward, toward Boltzmann's state of *warmtod*,[3] to disorganization and randomness, while in Darwinian biology it points upward, toward higher levels and differentiated forms of organization.[4] Since Newton's classical mechanics was not challenged until the beginning of the present century, nineteenth-century natural science found itself confronted with two arrows of time—and a framework of classical physics that knew nothing of either. This was the general paradox of living systems and of the livelihood of man in particular.[5]

Entropy Law and Philosophy of Materialism

The well-defined boundaries between individual disciplines disappeared, and doubts arose concerning many of the integrating ideas. The crisis of physics emerged, a product of both the discovery of thermodynamics and of the revision of the theory of matter according to particle physics. It led to a number of attempts to revise classical mechanics.[6]

Around 1870, patent signs of crisis began to appear, connected both with the internal development of thermodynamics and with the obscurities that had been found in classical (Newtonian) mechanics. This crisis grew broader and deeper, leading to the rapid decline of the image of the world that science had constructed from the time of Galileo.[7]

Two thinkers who had the clearest realization of the depth and seriousness of the change were Ernst Mach and Frederick Engels. However, the ways in which they proposed to work out a new and more satisfactory world view differed radically.

Mach, on the one hand, asserted he could give up materialism and replace it with a phenomenalistic view of reality, maintaining, in the elaboration of this vision, a link with the great tradition of philosophical empiricism. Engels, on the other hand, thought that he could sustain materialism by transforming it from its mechanistic kernel to one grounded on Hegelian "dialectics." Dialectical materialism (diamat) emerged. Despite the fact that for half a century Hegelianism had been completely outside the major currents of modern science, Engels was not deterred from reviving Hegelian philosophy.[8]

Whereas, Engels's diamat was not taken seriously by scientists of his day, Mach's phenomenalism found favor with a large number of the avant garde. In particular, it cultivated the rise of "phenomenological physics," which undertook to expunge from science all the intrinsically unobservable entities that the mechanists were in the habit of introducing to explain natural processes, i.e., ether to explain the wave theory of light. Phenomenological physics became the ally of the doctrine of energetics, which was strongly advocated by Wilhelm Ostwald. Energetics aimed at unifying science on the basis of thermodynamics rather than mechanics.[9]

Whereas Comte had contended that the passage from the metaphysical to the scientific stage meant that disciplines would have to abandon the false metaphysical problems, Mach argued that in some cases disciplines concealed within themselves obscurities that seriously hindered the advance of knowledge. To escape being trapped forever, the scientist was obligated to make a meticulous survey of the epistemology and methodology of science so as to free it from the yoke of dogmatism.[10] It was in the spirit of this ablution of science that Ostwald, among others, advanced his principles of energetics.

At the turn of the century, experimental discoveries showed that the atom could no longer be taken to be the irreducible unit of matter that mechanists had imagined it to be. The discovery prompted the replacement of the mechanical model with a more complex and elaborately structured one. However, with the advance of such models it was realized that laws valid for the macrophysical world could not be transferred to the microphysical. This ended the pretension that models must be "evident," as it became clear that "evidence" is a vague and equivocal notion derived from equating all knowledge with the particular type of knowledge obtainable from everyday experience.[11]

Nineteenth-century positivism usually presented scientific activity as a progressive discovery of laws, each of which had absolute validity insofar as it was founded on rigorously controlled observations. Theories had no function beyond systematizing a larger or smaller number of such laws, linking them to one another by means of principles that generalized their content. Modern positivist methodology has vigorously opposed this interpretation, asserting to the contrary that all scientific laws are substantially hypothetical in character, since no observation is able to provide an absolute guarantee of the "universal" assertion contained in the statement of the law.[12]

While it may be claimed that a dialectical materialist cannot accept the phenomenalist integration of modern scientific methodology, in view of the incompatibility between philosophical principles of phenomenalism and those of materialist realism, one of the canons of the Engels–Lenin theory of knowledge is the unequivocal acceptance of the dynamic (dialectic) nature of all knowledge. Hence, they refused to admit that there existed absolute truths or absolute unknowables, either of which would preclude the possibility of pursuing the cognitive process in every direction without interruption.

Dialectical materialism argues that the progress of science, while never giving us absolute truths, nonetheless represents genuine conquests that can enrich our sum of knowledge. It is alleged that this is the sense in which Lenin referred to "human science, advancing." Diamat argues that the cognitive process enables us to arrive at knowledge that is authentic, even though it is neither absolute nor definitive.

Unity of Scientific Knowledge

The search for unifying principles in physics was confounded by the second law of thermodynamics. The attempt to reconcile thermodynamics with classical mechanics and hence resolve that paradox of life became science's new quest. However, the determinism of classical mechanics was not fated to endure. Concrete reality, as physical objective data, completely disappeared. What remained was only a formal representation of relations in terms of differential equations. The concept has replaced the real element everywhere. Thus, historically, by virtue of the mathematical form assumed by theoretical physics, the crisis of physics was an apparent withdrawal from objective facts. In probing the depths of matter, physicists moved one step beyond Galileo and sought a purely mathematically descriptive science. The strict interpretation of determinism yielded to *statistical laws*. Modern positivist science is gradually removing intuitive and physical content, both of which appeal to the senses. It is utilizing purely synthetic and ideal concepts about which all we know are mathematical laws. This is particularly true of Albert Einstein's theory of relativity. Science has become rationalized fiction, rationalized by mathematics.[13]

The model, which has become basic to social science in the mood of applied behavioral science and almost obligatory today in Anglo-American academic environments, resembles a "kinetic gas theory of society."[14]

While the principles of thermodynamics presented a number of difficulties for biologists, the critical role of matter for dialectical materialist philosophers was thought to have been compromised. Particular difficulty emerged in connection with what came to be termed "the disappearance of matter."[15] Marxian materialism was identified with a philosophy that failed to grasp the significance of the achievements of physics.

Energetics

Evidence of the nineteenth century's mechanistic attitude to life and society is conspicuous in the work of Nassau Senior's 1836 *Outline of the Science of Political Economy*, in the "social physics" of H.C. Carey's 1858 publication *Principles of Social Science*, and in W.S. Jevons's 1865 *Coal Question*.

Nassau Senior had borrowed from Babbage a physical theory of production based on an engineering perspective.[16] Though Senior's analysis included a physical classification of production inputs (land and other agents provided by nature, raw materials, labor skills, and instruments of labor), it was seriously faulted insofar as it lacked the appropriate concepts for treating energy. Indeed Senior, like McCulloch, was puzzled about the classification of coal, books, and seeds. Consequently, he assigned coal to instruments of production, since, unlike materials, it was not physically embodied in the final product.

Carey wrote that commerce is "a change of matter in place," whereas "production, mechanical and chemical, are changes in the form of matter."[17] However, even while Carey espoused Newton's physics as the template for economic analysis, he also sought to introduce the first principle of thermodynamics into that analysis.

W.S. Jevons proceeded to hypothesize that the development of England, as a "progressive state," was principally a consequence of its originally ample coal basins in conjunction with the institution of free trade. The first law became a maxim for Jevons, such that he spoke, for instance, of "coal-driven labour."[18]

From Ostwald's general proposition in *Kulturwissenschaften*[19] that any event or social or historical change is nothing but a transformation of energy, he alludes that society is merely an arrangement for the better utilization and more perfect transformation of "crude" into useful energy. The greater the coefficient of useful energy obtained in such a transformation, the greater the progress of culture. Moreover, Ostwald asserts that it is only in this connection that society, in serving this purpose, is justified. When the state or society instead hinders this ultimate purpose, lacking justification, it forfeits its purpose for existence. Insofar as wealth and money are useful forms of energy, their accumulation and circulation are purposeful. When their functionality is impaired, their reason for existence is lost as well. Conceptually, Ostwaldian social energetics is nothing more than a transposition of formal rationality from an emphasis on money or capital-enumerated coordinates to an energy coordinate.

In the closing years of the nineteenth century and the early twentieth century, Ostwald sparked a broad interest in so-called social energetics. This interest encouraged L. Winiarsky to attempt to extend what was perceived as Engels's project of formulating socialism as a natural science. Relying on the first law of thermodynamics, Winiarsky wrote that life is a specific form of physicochemical energy and the human organism is an embodiment of energy and the mechanisms for its transformation. In particular, from the second law he ventured that psycho-social phenomena proceed in accordance to the energy gradient, and cease when the gradient is dissipated. He concluded that insofar as the universe is driven to a thermodynamic equilibrium, so shall the history of mankind.[20]

Epistemology and Dialectical Materialism

In the late nineteenth and early twentieth centuries the synthesis of natural scientific knowledge with dialectical materialism was allegedly confounded by the "disappearance" of matter and by the role of energy.[21]

The efforts of the Vienna Circle stimulated a number of economists to revise their thinking about the economy. However, in some cases the early reconstruction of Marxian economic thought, consistent with biophysical (energy) principles, came to be regarded as a malicious attack on science, materialism, and diamat. Clearly, the most interesting of the contributions to this emerging field arose in prerevolutionary Russia. I refer to the works of the Russian economist, physician, and philosopher, A.A. Bogdanov.

Today, insofar as there is a search for a "meta-science" and an emerging awareness of the role of energy and of an ecological imperative in political economy of the Noösphere, considerable advantage may be gained by an analysis of Bogdanov's early and fundamental contributions.

Marxian materialism was identified with a philosophy that failed to grasp the significance of the achievements of physics. Bogdanov, following Engels's bequest that the task of Marxism was to renew itself, attempted a resolution that corresponded to the development of a general science of organization called "Tektology." In his endeavors, therefore, Bogdanov attempted to revise Marxian dialectics.[22]

Empirio-monism to Tektology

The perspective of nature as a unitary and dynamic system of systems arose at the end of the nineteenth century as a result of the convergence of some germinal ideas in the natural sciences: the notion of omnipresent energy (atomic theory, field theory, the conservation of energy), the notion of the creation and evolution of forms of living energy (evolutionary theory), and the notion of the continuity of energy and life. In this perspective every thing or every event is a thermodynamic process or nexus of processes defined by its location in a web of trophic and quasi-trophic interconnections with other natural and artificial ecosystems. The concept of the unity of science was present in the thought of Marx, who wrote: "Natural science will in time incorporate into itself the science of man, just as the science of man will incorporate into itself natural science: there will be one science."[23]

In this connection positivism was an attempt to subordinate philosophy to science.[24] It seemed appropriate to scientists of various specialities and became for them a specific philosophic creed. The positivist pursuit of the unity of scientific knowledge phenomena was widespread in Europe, and in Russia it was strikingly expressed, especially among natural scientists in particular Ernst Mach.

Pushing Ostwald into the background (but never abandoning him), Bogdanov found new inspiration and ample models in the "scientific philosophy" of Ernst Mach and Richard Avenarius, with whom he was united not with common scientific interests but by an epistemology.[25] He named his new philosophical system "empirio-monism" and defined it as a synthesis of Mach's and Avenarius's theory of knowledge and Marx's theory of social history. Empirio-monism rejects the mechanistic orientation in science as an ideology rooted in the custom-bound organization of social labor in the seventeenth century. Empirio-monism, like the neopositivistic philosophies of Mach and Avenarius, demands that both philosophers and scientists abandon their traditional concern with the "explanations" of mechanically intertwined phenomena and instead emphasizes the "description" of pure forms of experience, which are reducible to mathematical description.[26]

Insofar as Engels's theorizing was regarded as a deterministic economic materialist doctrine,[27] it was argued that it was incapable of producing a compelling epistemological system. The Legal Marxists conceded that Marx and Engels had provided an excellent exposition of historical materialism. However, their theory lacked a purely philosophical basis. The resolution of this problem was sought outside Marxism-Engelism.

Lenin notes that Bogdanov was led astray by Wilhelm Ostwald's "energetics" and later by Ernst Mach's "subjective idealism," and that it was under their influence that Bogdanov wrote *Empirio-monism* in 1905. Lenin's specific criticism of Bogdanov was derived from the latter's attempt to "refute materialism from the standpoint of recent and modern positivism and natural science."[28]

Lenin inveighed against those Machian scientists who questioned materialism, arguing that while they may be good physicists they were bad philosophers. When faced with the assertion that in modern physics "matter is disappearing," Lenin retorted that, on the one hand, the philosophical concept of matter is not affected by the historically changing views of physicists about its structure. On the other hand, what was called the "disappearance of matter" had nothing to do with the basic materialist doctrine that matter is prior to mind. Lenin correctly took the view that it was not materialism in general that had become untenable, but only its traditional mechanical form. "The sole property of matter, with whose recognition philosophical materialism is bound up, is the property of being an objective reality, of existing outside our mind."[29]

The Revisionist Marxism of Aleksander A. Bogdanov

Among those who contributed to a neopositivist concept of the unity of nature and the role played by the energy nexus in social thought was Aleksander Bogdanov. He was influenced by the energeticism of Wilhelm Ostwald and sought to formulate a monistic synthesis between economic and social materialism of Marx and the natural sciences.

Undoubtedly influenced by Lavróv and having absorbed the Vienna Circle's (Ostwald, Mach, Avenarius, et al.) concept of social energetics[30] and Le Chatelier's principle, Bogdanov initially attempted to revise Marxism along biophysical lines. For Bogdanov, energy represented the practical relationship of society to nature, of human activity to that which resists it. The transformation of energy, he said in *The Philosophy of Living Experience*, refers to the creation and change wrought by active, human effort on resisting nature: "to see energy in the processes of nature means to look at those processes from the perspective of their possible labour exploitation by man."[31] In 1920 he wrote that "man is able to change the world by systematic and planned transformation of energy."[32] However, with his further understanding and recognition of the analytical limitation of social energetics, he sought a more general theory in Tektology.

The basic trend of human thought, he believed, was toward a "scientific monism." He thought the time had come to construct a monism that could be tested empirically and selected the thermodynamic theories of Le Chatelier, convinced that they furnished the chief hypothesis for such a monism. Moreover, he tried to surmise how the main theories of other sciences—Marxian economics included—might somehow be converted into instances of the "universal law of equilibrium." Since the sources of strife in the livelihood of man, according to Bogdanov, were larger than the merely "economic," the common language must be larger ,than traditional Marxism, although it would include Marxism as a special case.[33]

Bogdanov, consistent with Marx, recognized that social processes were part of a historical development. He thought Darwin's and Spencer's bio-organismic theories suggested general principles of social change, which could be viewed in non-reductionist ways.[34] In nature, the development of animal species was regulated by a struggle for survival; whereas in society, struggle and adaptation reached its highest level in the collective. Moreover, transcending Darwinian modes of selection, the evolution of consciousness and knowledge in society became the motive power of development. Bogdanov advised that society's ability to adapt to nature depended on its ability to obtain, process, and generalize information whereby it might "eliminate internal contradictions and strengthen harmonious relations."[35]

Bogdanov writes that

> social adaptation, an extension of natural adaptation, holds the key for a full understanding of the historical nature of social phenomena. Its basic operative mechanism is social selection, which produces either positive results, when it creates the forms of adaptation that add to the intensity and plasticity of social life; or negative results, when it brings forth the forms of adjustment that reduce both the quality and the intensity of social energy. While positive selection produces social progress, negative selection produces social regress.[36]

Bogdanov's Tektology displayed a continuity with the theoretical postulates of Marx and Engels.[37] Marx developed a logico-methodological means of systems research. The principles he formulated of the study of "organic wholes" were a vital component in the new methodology of scientific knowledge. The classics of Marxism, and the materialist dialectics they created, exerted an influence on the systems approach of Bogdanov.

In his *Essays on Tektology*, Bogdanov considered that Engels's scientific socialism was best expressed by a formula: production of people, production of things, and production of ideas. The concept of organizing action is hidden in the term "production." We shall, therefore, make this formula more precise: *organization of the external forces of nature, organization of human forces, and organization of experience.* Mankind has no other activity except organizational activity, there being no other problems except organizational problems.[38]

Bogdanov felt that Marx and Engels had many perspicacious ideas that could be further developed if their philosophy were superseded by a philosophy more in harmony with the methods and spirit of modern natural science.[39] Disputing

Engels's theory, he claimed that dialectics was neither a universal theory of knowledge nor a universal ontology, but rather a confused version of the commonplace idea that opposing forces can sometimes produce motion and change. Bogdanov's organizational theory marked a departure from Marxist philosophy. Having tried to adapt the empirio-monism of Mach for use within Marxism and presenting it as the further development of Marxism, Bogdanov departed from orthodoxy, asserting that "the concept of dialectic has not yet achieved full clarity and completeness."[40] While in the thought Marx and Engels "diamat" is a universal dynamic in society, in Bogdanov's tektological view it is only a component of a more universal dialectic of organizational processes. According to Bogdanov, the dialectical character of life is not that the "organism contradicts itself, being simultaneously 'the same' and 'not the same'; the organism makes itself 'not the same' in the struggle with the environment."[41] For Bogdanov, "dialectic is not something universal; it is a special case of the process of organization, which may also take other forms."[42] Diamat was, for Bogdanov, a near truth made dogmatic. In his science of organization—Tektology—he emphasized its practical aspect and its function of changing the world. He viewed the synthetic construction of a "universal science of organization" as the science of sciences—a meta-science—demanded by the development of automated production and the rise of the proletariat.

Thus for Bogdanov, Tektology represents a further revision of Marxist thought. It is important to note that from Bogdanov's conceptualization of Tektology there emerged an understanding of the autopoiesis of hierarchical systems, as well as related cybernetic categories of analysis. Implicit in Bogdanov's analysis is an integrative and dynamic model, a model that has only in the last decade come to the attention of theorists of political economy in the broad sense. Bogdanov's contribution is a major advance in the emerging concept of cybernetic economic analysis and modern coevolution theory.

Both Lenin and Bogdanov subscribed to what they termed "philosophical monism." Lenin's monism is essentially ontological: it is based on the axiom of the material unity of the universe, both natural and cultural.[43] Bogdanov's monism is mainly epistemological: it is based on the notion of the unity of knowledge, on the idea of "the continuity in the system of experience" and of the unity of "cognitive materials" or "psychic and physical elements."[44] Ballestrem notes that the irreconcilable differences between Lenin and Bogdanov erupted into an open fractional struggle, splitting the Bolsheviks into two bitterly fighting groups for years to come.[45]

Starting from his allegedly "Machian" empirio-monist epistemological position, according to which the originally chaotic "elements of experience" can be arranged in many different ways, Bogdanov proceeded to a type of "praxiology" which gives the most general rule to organizing the "elements of experience"[46] practically.

According to Bogdanov, what we regard as the material world, as nature, and as the common world, is the product of collectively organized experience, having a social basis. That is to say, in the course of human history, the common world, as experienced, has been progressively formed out of the raw material of sensation. However, in addition to that world which is basically the same for all, there are, so to speak, private worlds. That is, in addition to collectively organized experience there is organization in the form of ideas or concepts which differ from person to person or from group to group.[47] It was with this notion that Lenin took great exception.

Copleston reflects that

> [for] the Marxist, matter is the basic reality, this means that all reality falls within the sphere of experience, actual or possible. In fact, we can say that reality is experience. If, therefore, we accept the empirio-monism of Avenarius and Mach, it follows that reality is reducible to sensations, inasmuch as, according to empirio-monism, sensations are the ultimate data or elements of experience.[48]

Karl Kautsky, the leading German orthodox Marxist theorist of the period before the First World War, was asked by Lenin to express an opinion on the Russian Marxists' quarrel over Machism. Kautsky wrote that he deplored it. He was himself a dialectical materialist, yet speculated that Marxian social theory could be united with Machist philosophy.[49]

The revolutionary events of December 1905 led to Bogdanov's arrest. He was jailed in the summer of 1906 and while in prison wrote volume 3 of *Empiriomonism*. When he left prison, he resumed his collaborations with Lenin and presented him with a copy of this newest literary product. This time Lenin's reaction was even worse than earlier. "I sat down to a careful study of it," Lenin writes in a letter to Gorky of February 25, 1908. "On reading it through I lost my temper and was unusually furious: it became clearer than ever to me that he was moving along an arch-mistaken way, not a Marxist way. I wrote then 'a declaration of love' to him, a short letter on philosophy to the length of three exercise books."[50]

In a retort to Plekhanov, who had rebuked him for becoming a "Machian," Bogdanov wrote: "I do not consider myself a Machian in philosophy. I took only one thing from Mach's general philosophical conception—the idea of the neutrality of the elements of experience with respect to 'physical' and 'psychical' and the exclusive dependence of these characterizations on the interconnection of experience."[51]

Copleston records that if, as Machians, we assume that the ultimate elements of experience are sensations, it is obvious that we customarily think that the world of experience would not have arisen without a process of organization.[52] J.D. White apprises that Bogdanov came to this understanding with the abandonment of his Ostwaldian "energy" perspective. This marked an interesting development in Bogdanov's ideas. He thought in terms of the primacy of individuals over society. He had, therefore, to offer some explanation of why individuals formed societies. The Ostwaldian hypothesis offered by Bogdanov was the conservation of energy; more could be achieved and there was a better chance of survival if individuals acted in concert. Energy, by analogy, was held to play the same unifying role in the rest of the animate and inanimate world. But by 1904 Bogdanov came to the conclusion that Durkheim would later express: human society existed prior to individuals, collectivism was the natural human condition, and individualism was a historical product and the concomitant of the "metaphysical outlook." For "energy" there was substituted "collectivism" (organization), which became a key philosophical concept for Bogdanov.[53]

Jensen observes that in his *Philosophy of Living Experience*, Bogdanov optimistically speculated on human praxis; that the proletariat realizes the active relationship of man to the world in that he sees and acts on the possibility and necessity of changing it. According to Jensen, this realization is at once a reflection of the way in which machine production itself changes the world and a lapse into Ostwaldian thinking. For according to Bogdanov, the outcome and essence of machine production is "the systematic transformation of efforts, or, in scientific and exact terms, the transformation of energy."[54] It is, moreover, a reaffirmation of Bogdanov's Marxian roots.

Expressing a view offered by a number of philosophers who both preceded (i.e., Ostwald), and followed him (i.e., Carver), Bogdanov noted that machine production changes the world by turning the physical, chemical, and electrical forces of nature into one another after the manner in which natural forces are turned into mechanical forces of production. Such a view is not inconsistent with that of Marx, whose concept of forces of production can be understood to comprise all of physical technology. Marx usually employs the term to mean the sum total of tools, instruments, and machines available in a society, plus all sources of energy that move these implements: steam, water, coal, animal, and human power. Under the term "forces of production" he brings together with a single concept, the instruments, energy, and labor involved in the active effort of individuals to change material reality to suit their needs. Jensen reasons that, for Bogdanov, this feature of machine production generated a new perspective on the world and, subsequently, on causality. The new view was that, for the labor collective, "every process in the world is the possible source of every other process. The practical bond of phenomena, the practical unity of nature," he said, "is expressed in this perspective."[55]

Bogdanov wrote that in the social sciences the energy approach is the same as the historical approach: it places the primary emphasis on the interaction of social processes. Social processes are to human society what the transformation of energy is to nature in general: they depict the continuity and measurability of social change. Bogdanov's sociological theory is both historical and monistic. It is historical inasmuch as it places the primary emphasis on the dynamics of social processes; it is monistic inasmuch as it interprets all phenomena of social dynamics as specific adaptations to increases and decreases in social energy and inasmuch as it operates on the assumption that human society manifests a spontaneous tendency to eliminate internal contradictions and to strengthen harmonious relations.[56]

Bogdanov's dispute with orthodox Marxism over the issue of class interests was grounded in his broader rejection of economism.[57] Ever attentive to the higher realms of human interest, including science, philosophy, art, and morals, for Bogdanov the narrow theory of class interests was evidently inadequate. Arguing that man's history is related to every social activity, Tugan-Baranovsky had earlier rejected the alleged economistic attempts of Feuerbach and Marx and Engels to reduce ethics, art, and religion to utilitarianism.[58] He concluded that the class struggle could not be viewed as determining nor coordinating the economic basis of history.

In this sociological tradition Bogdanov was aware that in advanced capitalism Marx's class categories existed for reasons other than purely economic. He recognized the importance of gradations of authority positions and was sensitive to the separation of ownership and control.[59]

Distancing himself from the Marxian position, he further abstracted the concept by replacing the idea of "class" with the functional differentiation of "organization." Rather than merely tendering unconnected adaptations of Marxism, Bogdanov's ideas on ideology, classes, and revolution offered an integrated and singular conceptualization of society and social dynamics. Seeking to combine the alleged "conflict model" of Marxism with his own general theory of organization, he was keenly aware that the labor-process was not the sole integrative force in society.[60]

Bogdanov defines dialectic as the "organizational process, taking the path of the conflict of opposing tendencies."[61] He specifically notes that this notion of the dialectic does not fully agree with that of Marx, who speaks of "development" instead of organizational processes. Instead of dialectics, Bogdanov stressed "moving equilibrium" as the basic process in the development of nature and society. All components of a society are engaged in a constant search for equilibrium in their interaction and their relations to the total natural and social environment.[62]

In a capitalist society, Bogdanov argued, the equilibrium of interacting and contradictory social forces is achieved by the help of "external norms." Institutional norms are generated and enforced by the state, rather than with the aid of "internal norms," that is, norms generated by society itself.[63] Bogdanov conceived social change as proceeding until a state of equilibrium is attained between the various factors involved. Like Hegel or Darwin's contemporary, Claude Bernard, and unlike Lenin, Bogdanov saw synthesis and harmony as more permanent and productive than opposition and conflict. The corresponding equilibrium can be, and is, disturbed by external factors. The process of organization then begins again, until a new equilibrium is attained, which is disturbed in turn.

Bogdanov felt that future society, the society unencumbered by "external norms," will come about as a result of the gradual but inexorable growth of technology rather than by revolutionary political action. He believed that technology alone can create the prerequisite conditions for the growth of social cooperation and for a full elimination of social-class conflict. Vucinich remarks that by placing the main emphasis on technical forms of social adaptation Bogdanov shared the utopian dream of an Athens without slaves and argued that every ideology and every change in social forms ultimately derives from the technical process.[64] The term technology, according to Bogdanov, denotes not the material equipment of a society but the organization and utilization of knowledge related to external nature. Expressing a conviction present in the recent systems perspective of K.E. Boulding and E. Laszlo, Bogdanov, among others, viewed knowledge as the basic tool of human development.[65] And yet science and technology were a source of deep apprehension.

Unlike utopian socialist philosophers, he believed that even after socialism had been successfully created, civilization would be plagued by a whole series of problems, which we would now recognize as problems of "technified societies." In this connection Zenkovsky, among others, speculated that Bogdanov was influenced on these issues by the philosopher N.F. Fyodorov.[66]

Whether or not influenced in this respect by Fyodorov,

> there is little question that Lenin and Bogdanov discerned a nuanced reality. Both looked at the same revolutionary scene in Russia but perceived dissimilar problems and potential. Lenin, with his Marxist perspective, saw class conflict and centers of power that others, to their detriment, neglected. Bogdanov, with his revised Marxism, saw elements of exploitation and alienation to which Lenin was blind. Through an endless stream of publications, Bogdanov at least drew Lenin's attention to other dilemmas and other realities. If Lenin ignored them or refuted them, that was a choice. Out of their dialogue, or, more accurately, debates, came two different attempts at revolutionary breakthroughs and cultural change. Ultimately, two visions of socialism emerged, this alternative vision being the threat and the appeal of Bogdanovism.[67]

Graham and Stites feel that Bogdanov, following Fyodorov, was brilliantly prescient in sketching the issues that now confront all industrialized nations: the dangers of atomic energy, the problems of preserving the environment, the dilemmas of biomedical ethics, and the shortage of natural resources and food.[68] Indeed, according to Bogdanov, mankind would create such a fearful "machinery for the transformation of energy" that in order to avoid destruction people would have to establish a social system based on rational organization.

While Bogdanov intuitively anticipated the dangers of the Technosphere on the Biosphere (a viewpoint since addressed by V.I. Vernadsky and more recently by a variety of international conferences), he contemplated that only after the proletarian revolution had been successful and had eliminated struggles (i.e., organizational distinctions) among human beings would they see that a more daunting battle lay ahead—the struggle of united humanity to avoid being over-whelmed by the by-products of its own technological successes.[69]

Bogdanov chose to express his vision of the future not on the basis of a detailed statistical investigation of available resources and of necessities but in the form of novels. He argued that technical progress was bound to make concrete plans for the organization of the "state of the future" rapidly obsolete.[70]

In a recondite work of science fiction, *Engineer Menni*, Bogdanov shows the "dark" side of modern society.[71] In fact, the problems created by technified culture turn out to be precisely those issues addressed by K. Polanyi, H. Marcuse, and J. Habermas, among others. In this connection, Bogdanov's vision differs little from Polanyi's, whose research in economic anthropology was directly motivated by the problems that he sought to address throughout his life: how to organize the economy of our modern technological society in a manner that would make technified production subordinate to man's societal and cultural needs; how to "reembed" the economy in society; and how to institute a social and political order in which personal responsibility of man for his fellow man, and man for his natural environment can supersede dictates of impersonal market forces and impersonal state technocracies.[72] However, unlike Polanyi's conceptual basis which was grounded in property relations, Bogdanov's organizational perspective lead him to a more disparaging vision of socialism—a vision more akin to the views of Marcuse and Habermas.[73]

> In contrast to Lenin, Bogdanov focused on changes in both private property and authority relations as essential to socialism; together they would make possible new comradely relations as well as genuinely classless society. It was too facile, argued Bogdanov, to consider socialism the negation of capitalism in terms of private ownership; alienation and even exploitation could continue unless there were an additional, and explicit, change in authority relations. Bogdanov in essence not only offered a more dynamic definition of socialism than Lenin but also drew attention to sources of alienation that Marx had not foreseen—namely, those of a political and cultural nature that perpetuated authority relations despite a change in the economic base. Precisely for these reasons, Bogdanov attempted to cast a wide net in social transformation, encompassing collectivist organization of labour, aesthetic creativity or political behaviour.[74]

Although, according to Sochor, both Lenin and Stalin embraced a technocratic trend associated, for instance, with NEP, Bogdanov discerned, albeit somewhat ambiguously, a potentially threatening fusion of technology with authoritarianism. Much of his analysis focused on the elements that recreate a political elite and subordination, whether it be new (i.e., noneconomic) forms of power or a rigid value structure. There was, however, in Bogdanov's analysis, an ironic breach represented by his anticipation of a technocratic, rationalistic, self-regulating socialist society converse to his prescient warnings of a technocratic determinism and authoritarianism. Searching for an understanding of some of the problems that have agitated such neo-Marxists as Marcuse and Habermas, Bogdanov clearly viewed the growth of science and technology as the most potent force of the emerging era. He was convinced it would be brought under control by its incorporation into a new socialist value system. Sochor regards this view as resembling Habermas's solution of accepting technology while proposing to subdue its "negative consequences" through a new "institutional framework" of "symbolic interaction."[75] However, once having thereby "revolutionized rationality," Habermas, unlike Bogdanov, contradicts himself saying: "The structure of scientific-technical progress would be conserved, and only the governing values would be changed."[76]

One may assume that the theory of Tektology, on which Bogdanov worked while writing *Engineer Menni*, was envisioned as a tool not only for the organization of science (as a kind of "metascience"), but also not only for the organization and solution of human problems as raised by rapid scientific, technical, technological, and informational advances. Jensen writes that Bogdanov anticipated that the science of Tektology would facilitate the analysis of divisive problems, but he had not yet reached the point in his thought where he could feel confident that it would.[77] Insofar as the sources of strife were larger than the merely economic, the common language must be larger than traditional Marxism, although it would include Marxism as a special case.

From the Hegelian Dialectics of Organization to Tektology

The bold attempt by Bogdanov "to gather together and harmoniously integrate the fragmented organizational experience of mankind,"[78] has a strong appeal to contemporary theorists who seek to unify scientific thought. The need for a synthesis stems primarily from the growing attempts to tackle problems whose solutions lie within often far-removed fields of specialization. The attempt by Bogdanov to provide just such a synthesis, therefore, should attract more than passing attention from contemporary systems theorists.

The organizational approach is both structural and dynamic. It is structural in that it relies on a holistic view of natural and social systems. It considers a natural or social system irreducible to its component parts. According to Bogdanov, the more a system differs from the sum total of its component parts, the higher the level of its organization.[79] The organizational approach is dynamic inasmuch as it is concerned with continuous changes of an adaptive and selective nature. Tektology studies not only the functional differentiation and convergence of existing forms but also the forces contributing to the maintenance of intra- and inter-system equilibria. Bogdanov stresses "moving equilibrium" as an area of inquiry in which the structural and dynamic aspects of organization are only two sides of the same reality. His mechanism of organization is dominated by "motion" and equilibrium. While orthodox Marxists treat equilibrium as a specific state of motion, Bogdanov views motion as a specific expression of equilibrium.

There is in Tektology a reorientation of thought and world view on the introduction of the concept of "system" as the center of a new scientific paradigm (in contrast to the analytic, mechanistic, linear-causal paradigm of classical science).

Tektology deals with organizational experiences not of this or that specialized field, but of all these fields together. In other words, Tektology transcends particularism and embraces the subject matter of all the sciences and of all the human experience giving rise to these sciences, but only from the aspect of method; that is, it is interested only in the modes of organization of this subject matter.[80]

Tektology and the Regulating Mechanism

The basis of the regulating mechanism is the notion of selection—natural and artificial. The regulative mechanism accounts for the maintenance or preservation of the stability of such systems as a social class or an organism. It also helps maintain the continuity of natural and social development, in attenuating cataclysmic changes that attach to conjunctive and disjunctive crises, i.e., crises that obtain from a breach of tektological boundaries, invalidating the homeostasis.

Commentators on Bogdanov have pointed repeatedly to the apparent prefiguring of the cybernetic concepts of positive and negative feedback.[81] Bogdanov considered the "law of ingression" to have "tremendous practical and theoretical significance." He believed it showed that ideas, norms, and political institutions, all "disingressive complexes for the stable organization of vital activities of society," have a built-in tendency toward ossification.[82] Although internal changes are important for the evolution of a system, Bogdanov maintained the real impetus for change comes from the environment, which affects both the internal structure of the system and the relationship between it and in turn the environment itself. At the same time, each disturbance of the equilibrium creates pressure to establish a new equilibrium. Bogdanov's was a homeostatic open-systems approach with a moving or dynamic equilibrium and a "bi-regulator" to provide for the maintenance of order.

Tektology and Generalized Metabolics

By means of the selection mechanism organizations disassimilate and assimilate variety from the environment and thus, in effect, are regulated by it. This infers that organization, as such, is a response to complexity. In cases where there is a relative equality between the two processes, there is a preservation of an organizational complex in the form of a dynamic equilibrium. For continued preservation of a complex, however, a simple dynamic equilibrium is not sufficient. We must remind ourselves that these startling cybernetic concepts emerged some forty years before W.S. Ashby's theories.[83]

Systemic disorganization culminates in either of two states: the complex in question either disintegrates completely or it changes in such a way that its preservation is assured. The latter is achieved by means of a process that Bogdanov calls "contra-differentiation of parts"—meaning the reverse of systemic differentiation.[84] Contra-differentiation limits or completely removes disorganizing influences of systemic contradictions by creating new linkages through a conjunctive process of affected parts, and thus prevents systemic collapse. The mechanisms of selection again lie at the base of this process. By making a system more complex and increasing its variety, positive selection produces for the system more material from the environment. Negative selection, by simplifying this material, removes from the system that which is volatile, discordant, and antagonistic. Thus, both positive and negative selections play crucial roles in the preservation and development of organizational complexes.

Tektology and Open Systems

Bogdanov's Tektology referred to an open system as a complex that can maintain itself only at the expense of its environment; thus, all living systems are open systems. His two basic modes of interaction—positive progressive selection and negative progressive selection—were more than merely progressive (increasing) and regressive (decreasing) quasi-metabolic processes. These processes were critical elements in Bogdanov's organizational dialectic. Once again, positive selection contributes to the increased complexity and internal heterogeneity through the assimilation of useful ambients from the environment. Negative selection facilitates the removal of all that is volatile, discordant, and antagonistic from the system, resulting in a state of increasing homogeneity, order, and coordination.

Positive selection adds new contradictions and enriches a system's organization while weakening the whole from a structural viewpoint. Negative selection removes the weakest links, simplifies the organization, and leads to a greater structural stability. It progressively destroys the least stable elements, connections, and groupings which hinder the internal organization of the system in question. This results in the system becoming structurally stronger. Consequently, if negative selection is arrested short of the disintegration of a given system and is replaced by positive selection, the whole system may be raised to a higher level of organization.

The more powerful the integration, the more resilient the system becomes, i.e., the more capable of forming new links, regrouping its structure, and adapting to environmental perturbations. The weaker the forces of integration, the more "skeletal" the system becomes, i.e., more durable, less vulnerable, less adaptive, but more autonomous. Negative selection manifests itself more intensively in "diffused" systems; that is, systems whose frontiers expand in various directions. In "fused" systems, both positive and negative selection are less intensive. Under conditions of negative selection, fused structures are more favorable to systemic preservation and development than are diffused structures; and, under conditions of positive selection, diffused structures are better. These concepts assume particular importance in the context of management cybernetics.

Bogdanov recognized quite early that it is the interaction between organization and structure that maintains the necessary autopoiesis. It may be only a slight exaggeration to say that this anticipated not only the recent generalizing of non-equilibrium thermodynamics, but also a comprehension of the economy as a form of autopoiesis.

Contributions of N. I. Bukharin

Marx was convinced that having overthrown Hegel's metaphysical understanding he had rendered dialectics consistently materialistic and consequently confined himself to its application to history. It fell to Engels to extend and systematize an understanding of the dialectic in history, nature, and human thought. In doing so it is claimed that he laid the groundwork for a universal doctrine of dialectical materialism.[85]

Like Bogdanov, Nikolas Bukharin was a "seeking Marxist," refusing to regard Marxism as a closed, immutable system. He was alert both to its inadequacies and to the accomplishments of rival doctrines. Though allegedly influenced by the Vienna Circle, he described himself as a Marxist and a dialectical materialist. Nonetheless, Bukharin attempted to reconcile Marxism with scientific advances of the period. In the preface of his *Historical Materialism*, Bukharin wrote: "It would be strange if Marxist theory eternally stood still."[86]

From Moscow, Bukharin followed the bitter philosophical controversy between the exiled Lenin and Bogdanov. It was not surprising that he leaned toward Bogdanov. Bukharin's work, particularly *Historical Materialism*, showed Bogdanov's enduring influence on his intellectual development. He was not, however, Bogdanov's disciple, as his Party enemies were later to argue. He did not accept unequivocally the older theorist's philosophical arguments, but rather admired and was influenced by Bogdanov's capacity for creative innovation within the framework of Marxist ideas. Nevertheless, there was a similarity of their intellectual temperament. Whereas Bogdanov sought to revise Marxism initially on the basis of social energetics, and later on the basis of Tektology, Bukharin sought to modernize it in light of the achievements of Western sociology. However, "Bukharin's quest for scientific sociology lead him to mechanism." He allegedly subscribed to a "mechanistic understanding of Marxist dialectics" located within the context of his general theory of equilibrium, which was a general "formulation of the laws of motion of material systems."[87] Marxists, he argued, had opposed mechanistic explanation in social science, but this had derived from the discredited conception of the atom as "a detached isolated particle." The electron theory, with its new findings on the structure and movement of matter, disproved this and validated the language of mechanics as a means of expressing organic connections.

Bukharin's General Theory of Equilibrium

In his major work, *Historical Materialism*, Bukharin cautioned his readers that though he intended to "depart from the usual treatment of the subject," he assured the faithful that he, nonetheless, adhered to "the tradition of the most orthodox, materialist, and revolutionary understanding of Marx." Like Bogdanov, Bukharin sought to systematize and to introduce "innovations" into Marxist tenets.

According to Bukharin, Heraclitus in ancient times and Hegel in the modern world not only say that there is constant motion in the world, but also that "changes are produced by constant internal contradictions, internal struggle."[88] And, though Marx and Engels had "liberated the dialectic from its mystic husk in action," it retained "the teleological flavor inevitably connected with the Hegelian formulation, which rests on the self-movement of 'Spirit'."[89] By locating the source of motion in the conflict of forces and not in "self-development," Bukharin believed that he had purged the Hegelian triad of its idealist elements.

Every system, Bukharin argued, is involved in two stages of equilibrium: internal and external. The first refers to the relationship between different components within a system, the second to the entire system in its relationship with its environment. In neither case is there ever an "absolute unchanging equilibrium." It is always "in flux"—a dynamic or moving equilibrium. It is for this reason, parenthetically, that it is more appropriate to describe Bukharin's general theory of equilibrium as a theory of persistent non-equilibrium or quasi-equilibrium.

The internal structure of the system must change together with the relation existing between the system and its environment. The latter relation is the decisive factor. The internal (structure) quasi-equilibrium is a quantity that depends on the external quasi-equilibrium (is a "function" of this external equilibrium).[90]

This theoretical model conveys a selected aspect of Bukharin's historical materialism. It systematizes social development. Social quasi-equilibrium is constantly being disturbed. It can move toward restoration in one of two ways: either by "a gradual adaptation of the various elements in the social whole (evolution)," or by "violent upheaval (revolution)."[91] Evolution occurs as long as the envelope of social quasi-equilibrium, primarily the relations of production as embodied in the classes directly participating in production, is sufficiently broad and durable. In this way, for example, capitalism progressed through its alleged historical stages. But when the forces of production increase to a point where they come into conflict with "the fundamental web of these productive forces, i.e., property relations," the probable result is revolution (i.e., a new and durable envelope of production relations capable of serving as an evolutionary form of productive forces).[92] Consistent with Engels, Bukharin added that the transformation of quantity into quality was one of the fundamental laws in the motion of matter. "[It] may be traced literally at every step both in nature and society."[93]

The fundamental Marxian criticism of Bukharin's sociological theory and its political implications was that equilibrium presupposes social harmony while orthodox Marxism argues for the prevalence of class contradiction. Western sociologists have argued that Bukharin's variant of functionalism, with its concept of homeostasis, is unable to accommodate real endogenous change and therefore puts a premium on harmonious stability. They have suggested that equilibrium implies a normative (conservative) orientation, which looks askance at contradiction and regards disequilibrating elements as abnormal and pathological.[94]

Though without referring to it as such, Bukharin's model described an open system in homeostatic quasi-equilibrium. We say of a system that it is in a state of quasi-equilibrium when the system cannot of itself emerge without an unbalanced communication with its environment. If, let us say, several forces are at work on a body, neutralizing each other, that body is in a state of quasi-equilibrium; an increase or decrease in one of these forces will disturb the quasi-equilibrium.

Bukharin did not pay any attention to Bogdanov's foreboding idea that an increase in energy also meant growth in the potential for destruction.[95] While observing the first law of thermodynamics, Bukharin neglected the second—the entropy law. Nonetheless, he elaborated upon Bogdanov's concept of the open systems prior to Ludwig von Bertalanffy's contribution of 1932. Indeed, Bukharin's elaboration is evident in his theory of quasi-equilibrium.

> It is quite clear that the internal structure of the system (its internal equilibrium) must change together with the relation existing between the system and its environment. The latter relation is the decisive factor; for the entire situation of the system, the fundamental forms of its motion (decline, prosperity, or stagnation) are determined by this relation only. . . . Consequently, the internal (structural) equilibrium is a quantity which depends on the external equilibrium (is a function of this external equilibrium).[96]

Susiluoto notes that this conceptual stance was critical to Bukharin's transition from dialectical to historical materialism and to the *Zweckrational* that underlay his cybernetics of social guidance. "The task which became the central one was that of pinpointing the 'contradiction' between society and nature, and that mediating link through which the interaction between society and nature was channeled."[97]

However, the quasi-equilibrium that endured between the system and its environment determined which relations were feasible and prevailing in the social system itself. Susiluoto senses that in the analysis of social phenomena Bogdanov and Bukharin, though referring to the role of energy as important, regarded technology as the principal dynamic. Without doubt, Bukharin's "external formulation" led to the notion that technology played a definitive role in the evolution of society. The combinations of social technology (capital) of labor were the deciding factor in the combinations and relations between men. Bukharin remarked that

> human society in its technology constitutes an artificial system of organs which also are its direct, immediate and active adaptation to nature (it may be stated parenthetically that this renders superfluous a direct bodily adaptation of man to nature; even as compared with the gorilla, man is a weak creature; in his struggle with nature he does not "interpose" his jaws, but a system of machines). When viewed from this point of view, the question leads us to the same conclusion: the technological system of society serves as a precise material indicator of the relation between man and society. "We may therefore definitely state that the system of social instruments of labour, i.e., the technology of a certain society, is a precise material indicator of the relation between society and nature."[98]

Moreover, Bukharin's concept of quasi-equilibrium also yielded an ideologically desirable bridge in another direction, linking the theory of quasi-equilibrium to dialectics. Bukharin, following Bogdanov's tektological concept of integration, was convinced that conflict and struggle could be treated as an imbalance in the system, that is, as disturbances to its balance.[99] However, it was only the equating of conflict with contradiction that allowed Bukharin to make the claim that Hegel himself could be presented as a theoretician of equilibrium.

> Hegel observed this characteristic of motion and expressed it in the following manner: he called the original condition the thesis, the disturbance of equilibrium the antithesis, the reestablishment of equilibrium on a new basis the synthesis (the unifying proposition reconciling the contradictions).[100]

Bukharin's analysis of growth, equilibrium, and the dissipation of systems was a somewhat one-sided interpretation in which they were presented, as we shall see, as a function of the quantity of energy. Soviet critics accused Bukharin of having a naive understanding of dialectics.[101] In fact, Lenin charged that Bukharin "did not understand dialectics at all," while Stalin pointed out that Bukharin's "theory of equilibrium had nothing to do with Marxism."[102]

Bukharin's Cybernetics

Selecting as his point of departure Rudolf Stammler's distinction between *Naturwissenschaften* (natural science) and *Zweckwissenschaften* (goal-oriented science),[103] Bukharin advised that it would make no sense to speak of a society at all without conscious regulation and guidance. While Stammler envisaged cybernetics in the context of society in abstract, Bukharin referred specifically to the anarchic development of commodity-economy under capitalism. He postulated that the law of value functioned as a cybernetic regulative mechanism in capitalist society. In post-capitalist society, after the anarchic phase of the revolution, the return of society to equilibrium would no longer occur as one of "blind regulation" (i.e., price-making markets), but rather through consciously planned guidance. Bukharin understood regulation to be an omnipresent phenomenon. Consequently, he correctly understood the functioning of the economy as a kind of regulative cybernetic system.[104]

For Bukharin, following Bogdanov, argued that the function of cybernetic feedback mechanisms is to regulate the tendency toward disorganization; in other words, to produce a temporary and local reversal of the normal direction of entropy. This concept figures in Norbert Wiener's later formulation of cybernetics, as well as in Schrödinger's and Bertalanffy's notion of living systems, and was more recently adapted by R. Passet and Y. Tamanoi to the analysis of economic systems as open living systems.[105]

Bukharin's Metabolics

Though not without doctrinal elements, Bukharin's "Theory of Historical Materialism" correctly rendered the livelihood of man as an open thermodynamic system. While maintaining a continuity with Marx's concept of metabolism, Bukharin's contribution constituted a major, though little recognized, advance in substantive economic thought. "[Society] is unthinkable without its environment," that is, nature. Society adapts itself to nature, strives toward equilibrium with it, by extracting energy from it through the process of production.[106]

Having rigorously defined stable and unstable equilibrium and specifically employing energy and ecological analogies in conjunction with the principle of conservation and feedback concepts, Bukharin, like Bogdanov, sought a generalization.[107]

Expressing himself in a manner not unlike Wilhelm Ostwald, the patriarch of social energetics, Bukharin concluded that a growing society is one that extracts from nature more energy than it can consume. However, in following Engels, Bukharin distanced himself from Ostwald's seductive reductionism. "The distinction," he wrote, "between society and nature will be in each case reproduced on a new and higher basis, a basis on which society will increase and develop."[108] Such a society–nature relationship forms a new equilibrium of an unstable character "with a positive indication."[109]

An existing society, he wrote, presumes "a certain equilibrium" between its three major social elements: things, persons, and ideas. This is internal equilibrium. But "society is unthinkable without its environment," which is nature. Society adapts itself to nature and strives toward equilibrium with it by extracting energy from it. The metabolism between man and nature consists in the transfer of material energy from external nature to society; the expenditure of human energy (production) is an extraction of energy from nature, energy that is to be added to society (distribution of products between the members of society) and appropriated by society (consumption). This appropriation is the basis for further expenditure, which is achieved through the process of social production. However, Bukharin argued: "it would be truly monstrous to suppose that, let us say, the law of the conservation of energy makes the law of labour value."[110]

Human society has had to abstract material energy from external nature; without these loans it could not exist. Society best adapts itself to nature by abstracting (and appropriating to itself) more energy from nature. Only by increasing this quantity of energy does society succeed in growing.[111]

In economies of the "stagnant type," Bukharin notes that

> if the relation between society and nature remains the same, i.e., if society extracts from nature, by the process of production, precisely as much energy as it consumes, the contradiction between society and nature will again be reproduced in the former shape; the society will mark time, and there results a state of stable equilibrium.[112]

In the process of adaptation, society develops "an artificial system of organs," which Bukharin calls technology and which constitutes "a precise material indicator of the relation between society and nature."[113] The abstraction of energy from nature is a material process. This material process of "metabolism" between society and nature is the fundamental relation between the environment and the economic system, between "external conditions" and human society.

It is by identifying social technology with productive forces and by making the internal structure a function of the external equilibrium that Bukharin is able, despite his pluralistic analysis of social development, to preserve monistic causality in economic determinism.

The productive forces determine social development because they express the interrelation between society and its environment. And the interrelation between environment and system is that which determines, in the last analysis, the movement of any system.[114]

Although he considered the role of energy to be important, Bukharin regarded technology as the principal dynamic. Without doubt, Bukharin's "external formulation" led to the notion that technology played a definitive role in the evolution of society. The combinations of social technology (capital) of labor were the deciding factor in the combinations and relations between men.

Heretical Philosophers of Social Energetics

Ostwald, Winiarsky, Bogdanov, and Bukharin were not the only philosophers speculating on the relevance of energy and biophysical foundations of economics. Eduard Sacher, Felix Auerbach, Rudolf Clausius, Patrick Geddes, Leopold Pflaunder, Julius Davidson, G. Helm, T.N. Carver, F. Ackerman, F. Henderson, and A.J. Lotka were also among the early analysts. The contributions of these early commentators on the biophysical foundations of the livelihood of man were often fetishistic, reductionist, and technocratic, though occasionally holistic. Nonetheless, they were united by a central, often intuitive theme: the necessity to provide an alternative paradigm for economic thought.[115] Though counted among these amateurs and critics of conventional economic thought, the English radiochemist and Nobel laureate, Frederick Soddy, eclipsed his contemporaries. Even today his work inspires a number of critics seeking to broaden economic thought.

The Physiocracy of Frederick Soddy

Frederick Soddy wrote:

> It is an insult to the human intelligence that the age which has solved the problem of the production of the physical requisites that enable and empower life should be unable to solve the problems of their equitable distribution, and be compelled to destroy our potential abundance periodically by internal sabotage, world wars and monetary inflation.[116]

Whereas orthodox Marxian analysts viewed the collapse of capitalism on the basis of an internal logic which denied the role of nature, and while Soddy was similarly convinced that the economic system contained built-in elements for assuring its destruction, he maintained that the basis of that event was derived from unprincipled functional and scientific rationality. The key problem was to discover and correct the errors in conventional economic thinking and institutions, a task that Soddy tackled with both moral fervor and systematic conviction.

His paper *Transmutation: the Vital Problem of the Future* dramatically demonstrates the catholicity of his Physiocratic thinking on this matter. Soddy predicts that "so far as human affairs go, wealth and available energy are synonyms, and that the poverty or affluence of this planet are primarily measured only by the dearth or abundance of the supply of energy available for its life and work."[117]

In *Science and Life* of 1920, Soddy went one step farther, noting that "the history of man is dominated by, and reflects, the amount of available energy. The energy available for each individual is his income."

Naming his social energetic reformulation of economic science *Ergosophy* (meaning the wisdom of work, energy, or power, in the physical sense),[118] Soddy sought to rehabilitate with a precise meaning the old-fashioned and indispensable word "wealth," which the orthodox economist took too much for granted. Originating somehow through divine agency, the economist came to regard the acquisition of wealth as tantamount to its creation. Obsessed with commerce and mercantile exchange, he neglected the physical principles underlying all production.

Ruskin, Soddy's mentor, had reflected that "there is no wealth but life."[119]

And essential to Soddy's social economic theory was the link between wealth and energy and the distinction between wealth and money. He located the focus of economic science precisely, stating that "if we have available energy, we may sustain life and produce every material requisite necessary. That is why the flow of energy should be the primary concern of economics."[120]

However, strictly speaking, wealth is not merely available energy, but usefully directed available energy, or some embodiment of it. Human "labor" (that is, some form of intelligent human activity which may need only a minimum of physical energy) is usually, though not necessarily, an essential factor in its appropriation. With an adequate supply of energy there is prosperity, expansion, and development. Yet "wealth and available energy are synonyms" and, furthermore, "wealth is the power of purchasing."[121] If a stable source of energy could be provided by science, the desired goal of increasing the amount of purchasing power in the world could be achieved. The hitch was money, which Soddy regarded as a "purely conventional symbol" of wealth. "We must reform the monetary system in accordance with modern knowledge of the physical factors of life, for it is money which, in addition to illegitimate and quite alien functions, effects the distribution of revenue."[122]

Money, he contended, must fulfill its function as a criterion of value. To satisfy this criterion currency must be regulated *pari passu* with the changing revenue. It should be issued as revenue expands and destroyed as revenue contracts.

A cardinal error of economics, according to Soddy, is the confusion of wealth, a magnitude of irreducible dimension, with debt.

> Debts are subject to the laws of mathematics rather than physics. Unlike wealth, which is subject to the laws of thermodynamics, debts do not rot with old age and are not consumed in the process of living. On the contrary they grow at so much per cent per annum, by the well-known mathematical laws of simple and compound interest.[123]

The orthodox economists were alleged to be the victims of this delusion. Soddy took issue with Keynes's view on long-term growth, as set out in *The Economic Consequences of the Peace*. Comprehending capital as a vast accumulation of fixed wealth, Keynes speculated that the law of compound interest was the law for incrementing wealth. "One geometrical ratio," he wrote, "might cancel another and the nineteenth century was able to forget the fertility of the species in a contemplation of the dizzy virtues of compound interest."[124] In a supercilious manner he contemplated that "overcrowding and underfeeding would come to an end, and men secure of the comforts and necessities of the body could proceed to the nobler exercise of their faculties." To this Soddy responded: "Mr. Keynes likens wealth to a cake, which one day, owing to the dizzy virtues of usury, may be large enough to go round."[125]

Since wealth is constrained by the principles of thermodynamics, and its growth is slower than debt, Soddy speculated that the one-to-one relationship between debt and wealth would be repudiated at some point, either through inflation or through bankruptcy.[126] If wealth cannot grow at compound interest for long, then debt should not either. If wealth cannot be created *ex nihilo*, then how can we allow money (debt) to be created *ex nihilo* (and just as easily destroyed)? "You cannot pit an absurd human convention, such as the spontaneous increment of debt [i.e., compound interest], against the natural law of the spontaneous decrement of wealth [i.e., entropy]."[127] According to Soddy, this reveals much that is incontrovertible regarding the threatened collapse of the technified civilization.

For Soddy wealth is "the power of purchasing, as energy is the power of working."[128] He wrote that energy is revealed only in the effects it gives rise to (i.e., wealth), and its purely conventional symbol (i.e., money) similarly manifests itself.

> Money is not wealth to a starving man in a deserted place. It is both a symbol and a measure of wealth earned, as work done is a measure of energy expended. Heat energy, mechanical energy, chemical energy, and so on, are different forms rather than different kinds of energy, just as coins, bank-notes, cheques, and so on, are forms of money.[129]

Soddy argued that the real problem of the analysis of the wealth of society lies not with focusing on the monetized dimensions of that problem, but rather with the prerequisite and substantive biophysical realities. It is not surprising then that central to Soddy's discourse, and distinct from that of neoclassic economic theory, is his insistence on use-value rather than exchange-value. His proposition was not without precedent, for Petty and Marx had written that matter (low-entropy) is a prerequisite to labor.

> It is wrong to speak of labour, insofar, as it is applied to the production of use values as the only source of wealth, namely, the material wealth produced by it. Being an activity intended to adapt materials to this or that purpose, it requires matter as a prerequisite. In different use values the proportion between labour and raw material varies greatly, but use value always has a natural substratum. Labour, as an activity, directed to the adaptation of raw materials in one form or another, is a natural condition of human existence, a condition of exchange of matter between man and nature, independent of all social forms.[130]

Manifestly obvious to Soddy was the fact that the wealth that science was in the process of creating was not filtering properly through society. Soddy deduced that the fault lay with the means of distribution, that is, with the monetary system.[131]

Defining wealth as a flow, which could not be saved, but only spent, Soddy surmised that real wealth, a flow of energy, could only be consumed and could not be stocked. Part of this wealth took the form of so-called capital goods or was measured as financial capital, that is, as credits against the community. Real wealth, in the form of a wheat crop, for instance, would rot if stored for any length of time. Whereas the wealth that took the form of so-called capital goods and was registered as financial capital, was supposed not to rot, but, on the contrary, to grow independently at compound interest, *ad infinitum*. This was an institutional convention, subject to contingent values, which were historically variable, but could not run permanently counter to the principles of thermodynamics.

> Money is now a form of national debt, owned by the individual and owed by the community, exchangeable on demand for wealth by transference to another individual. Its value or purchasing power is not directly determined by any positive or existing quantity of wealth, but by the negative quantity or deficit of wealth, the ownership and enjoyment of which is voluntarily abstained from without payment of interest, by the owners of the money, to suit their individual business and domestic affairs and convenience. The aggregate of this deficit is called virtual wealth of the community, and it measures the value of all the money owned by the community, which is forced by the necessity of exchanging its produce to act as though it possessed this amount of wealth more than it actually does possess. The virtual wealth of a community is not a physical but an imaginary negative wealth quantity. It does not obey the laws of conservation, but is of psychological origin.[132]

The fact that money seems to have escaped the laws of conservation and entropy led Soddy to conclude that the flaw in the system must lie with the "conjuror's trick" of modern bankers. Bankers, notes Soddy, have been allowed to regard themselves as the owners of the virtual wealth which the community does not possess, and to lend it and charge interest upon the loan as though it really existed and they possessed it. The wealth so acquired by the impecunious borrower is not given up by the lenders, who receive interest on the loan but give up nothing, but is given up by the whole community, who consequently suffer the loss through a general reduction in the purchasing power of money.

Conclusion

It has become apparent that there arose out of the crisis of physics a reevaluation of categories of economic analysis in terms of the principle of energy conversion. Furthermore, in the early efforts to resolve the paradox of living systems, there emerged an analysis of the economic process in non-mechanistic, non-vitalist terms, incorporating physical, biological, and eventually ecological perspectives. Indeed, from this non-Newtonian perspective the philosopher, physician, and economist, A.A. Bogdanov, formulated his general theory of systems—Tektology. His functionalist theoretical formulation of the economy in cybernetic terms as an autopoietic system interactive with other dimensions of society, together with his prescient understanding that technified society was threatened by the by-products of its own success, denote A.A. Bogdanov as a major, albeit obscure, contributor to coevolutionary economic thought. Though occasionally steeped in doctrinaire terminology, Bukharin's explicit open-systems model depicting the economy as a quasi-equilibrium system metabolically interactive with the environment, nonetheless constitutes a second major contribution. Finally, addressing himself to the observed inequities of society, Frederick Soddy criticized the distributive system and explicitly focused on the alleged nonscientific basis of money. In defining the economy as a thermodynamic machine, Soddy recognized that the inequities were consonant with a definition of money that bore no relation to the biophysical realities of the economic process. These observations and analyses together constituted a major contribution to coevolutionary economic thought. Unfortunately, despite their seminal contributions to biophysical and thermodynamic concepts of the economic process, those contributions lay dormant. This hiatus lasted some forty years before the issues once again became a focus of concern. And when these issues reemerged, the cybernetic analytical categories adopted were those of Ludwig von Bertalanffy, rather than A.A. Bogdanov.

Since the nascent scholarship of Bogdanov, et al. our understanding of energy flows in biological and socioeconomic systems has advanced in a number of fields. The paradox of life, the contradiction between the evolutionary processes and the entropy law, we now know is a chimera. Living systems can never exist as isolated systems. On the contrary, it is characteristic of living systems that they constantly interact with their environment and they therefore must be regarded as open or "flowing" systems. This concept was explicit in both Bogdanov's Tektology and Bukharin's analysis. Moreover, it is also true that critical dimensions of Bogdanov's Tektology have not been addressed by those analysts seeking to broaden economic thought.

Neo-Physiocratic and Biophysical Models of the Economic Process

Introduction

The mid-nineteenth-century art critic and pundit John Ruskin remarked that

> the real science of political economy, which has yet to be distinguished from the bastard science, as medicine from witchcraft, and astronomy from astrology, is that which teaches nations to desire and labour for the things that lead to life; and which teaches them to scorn and destroy the things that lead to destruction.[1]

And, indeed, threatening technospheric developments have brought forth vital global issues that warrant a Noöspheric or coevolutionary paradigm for economic analysis.

Biospheric and economic coevolutionary interdependence are most evident, at the moment, in considerations of environmental disturbances. What were once local incidents of pollution shared throughout a common watershed or air basin now involve multiple nations—witness the concerns of acid deposition in Europe and in North America. What were once acute episodes of relatively reversible damage now are intergenerational—witness the debates over disposal of radioactive wastes. What were once straightforward questions of conservation versus development now involve complex linkages—witness the global feedbacks among energy and crop production, deforestation, and climate changes that have emerged in studies of the "greenhouse effect."

Generational Concerns

Three generations of environment–development concerns, characterized by successively increasing scale and complexity, can be identified in the post–World War II era.

First-Generation Issues

The first generation entailed small-scale problems of local pollution. The air basins filled by automobile exhaust in such cities as Tokyo and Los Angeles, for example, resulted in hundreds to thousands of square kilometers of land being affected. Even larger-scale water pollution problems have been experienced. The pollution episodes affecting Lake Baikal in the USSR and Lake Erie in North America influenced tens of thousands of square kilometers of water surface.

These first-generation problems have shown themselves to be largely controllable, despite their size and despite the uncertainty expressed at the time concerning the dominant issues. They are of a kind and scale that are relatively reversible given political resolve and financial commitment. Alternative technologies exist; and there is a source for renewal of the air, the water, and even the species that have been affected.

Second-Generation Issues

Today, however, industrialized economies are facing a second generation of environmental problems. These are characterized by increases in the spatial scale of up to two orders of magnitude. For example, one might refer to the now-deceased plan to divert water from rivers flowing north to the Caspian Sea. The plan was to transfer yearly 20 cubic kilometers of water from the Pechora and Sukhona rivers and the Vozhe, Lacha, and Onega lakes (all of which lie to the west of the Urals), into rivers feeding into the Caspian Sea. The plan had been formulated in response to the tremendous pressure of economic development on the Caspian Sea basin. More than one-third of the industrial output and about one-fifth of the agriculture production of European USSR comes from that basin. This diversion was intended to ameliorate the annual water deficit due to reduced inflow from rivers. The water deficit has already led to an economically and ecologically damaging drop in the level of the Caspian Sea and could, without action, lead to a further drop of another 1.4 meters by the year 2000. The area of the basin itself, let alone the area affected by the diversion, amounts to over two million square kilometers.[2]

Air pollution problems also are increasing sharply in scale and complexity. Air pollutants in North America and Europe are now known to travel hundreds and even thousands of kilometers from their origin in power plants, industrial installations, and transport centers. The Ohio River Basin Study found that large amounts of sulfur dioxide concentration in southeastern Canada were estimated to have resulted from sulfur emissions originating in the midwestern United States. The Organization for Economic Cooperation and Development (OECD) has estimated that at least one-half of the sulfur deposition in Nordic countries is due to foreign sources, with some contributions coming from as far as 1,000 kilometers away.[3]

There are some suggestions that in these second-generation problems the increasing scale of perturbations is being accompanied by a change in the qualitative character of the resulting problems. First, in some cases the monetary costs to reverse the trends are enormous. It has been estimated that several billion U.S. dollars would be required for each of twenty years to reduce sulfur emissions by 50 percent in the midwestern states of the United States. The problem is only exasperated by political intransigence during a time of fiscal restraint. Second, traditional control or mitigation policies seem unfeasible because the sources of emission are separated from the major impacts by hundreds to thousands of kilometers. Policies that are mired in a tired market mentality, such as the "polluter pays," internalizing within the market the environmental problem, fail to address broader intergenerational issues and consequently lack equity. Third, these problems can cross so many political jurisdictions that the authority and credibility needed for action often are lacking. Finally, the difficulty of the solutions places an inordinate demand upon certain knowledge of the causes and effects in order to provide a basis for confident action. Moreover, as N.N. Moiseev writes, projects such as these touch upon enormous areas of our planet. While possibly improving the conditions of life in some regions they may at the same time bring life on entire continents to the brink of catastrophe. Even regional projects can no longer be approached in an intuitive manner.

Third-Generation Issues

A third generation of environmental developmental concerns is beginning to emerge, characterized by truly global scales. Biogeochemical evolution has led to a dynamic exchange of chemical constituents among the oceans, the atmosphere, and the terrestrial Biosphere. Natural variations of these exchanges and their environmental consequences can be substantial. However, due to expansion of industrial and agricultural development, the perturbations to those natural exchanges are beginning to reach a magnitude that approaches or exceeds that of natural variation over areas of tens or even hundreds of millions of square kilometers. Perhaps the classic example was that foreseen by Alfred Lotka in 1924— the significant increase in global concentration of atmospheric carbon dioxide that has resulted from the burning of fossil fuels and the permanent clearing of forested land for agriculture. Coupled with the global increase in other "greenhouse" gases, the technologically driven development-induced alterations in the carbon cycle could cause significant changes in regional and global climate in the foreseeable future.[4]

In the first half of this century the accelerating rhythms of industrialization encountered limitations—not on technological development as such, but with the very institutional sources of resilience that contributed to the continuity of the Industrial Revolution.

The liberal utopian approach to the Technosphere manifested itself early and with dramatic force in the military sphere. "War, for all its horrors, was a means of decision in the service of the continuance of life, not a universal death trap."[5] By 1940 even the larger countries of continental Europe were inadequate as military units. Only the USSR could sustain a major military reversal without collapsing. Since 1945, however, "improved" conventional weapon systems alone suffice to make any geopolitical unit inadequate in a military confrontation. Moreover, the advent of modern nuclear weapon systems is such as to stultify all plausible defensive responses (the Strategic Defense Initiative notwithstanding). The unregulated power of the Technosphere and its ability to influence the course of the planet's evolution are becoming significant.[6]

That, in principle, the power of the Technosphere can disrupt the global homeostasis, has already been established by scientists. Greater foresight and planning than anything humanity has ever dealt with before is necessary. As man stretched his conscious mind to absorb this new reality, he also altered his concepts of nature to accommodate the expanded horizon within which he was forced to operate. This basic alteration of time and space revolutionized both the economic environment and paradigm and led to the gradual disintegration of St. Thomas Aquinas's "Great Chain of Being" and its replacement with C. Darwin's theory of evolution.

In the context of the intimate association between the livelihood of man and the Biosphere, the growing awareness of the thermodynamic and biophysical dimensions of the global Technosphere have led to the resurrection of a number of philosophical, epistemological, and analytical issues first identified over a hundred years ago. This reemergence of what shall be variously referred to as the Noöspheric or coevolutionary images is at once a marked departure from psychological and economistic perspectives and symbolizes a return to substantive economic theory insofar as it refers to political economy in the broad sense.

The biophysical dimensions of the livelihood of man have long been obscured by the closed-system mechanical paradigm which forms the basis of neoclassical economic thought. Nevertheless, an alternative paradigm based on the dynamics of open systems has been developing in recent years.

In the following pages, and from the context provided by the concept of open or flowing systems of Bogdanov and Bertalanffy, we shall seek to demonstrate that the traditional analytical framework of economic thought, characterized by the model of the "circular flow," is stigmatized by misplaced concreteness. We shall then turn to an explication of an alternative model, the substantive economy, which is epitomized by the phrase "the economy in the broad sense." This model must be understood as being constituted on two levels: one is the interaction between man and his surroundings; the other is the institutionalization of that process. In this connection we shall examine the metabolic and biophysical dimensions of the economic process and review a select number of corresponding models. It shall become apparent, however, that a number of analysts of the open-system models are mired in market mentality and present reductionist biosociological and neosocial energetic images of the economic process.

General Systems, Open Systems,
and Living Systems

When considered at the level of mankind, life is not, as has been said in the past, a historical accident, but rather, as was established by Christian Huygens in *Cosmotheoros*, "life is a cosmic phenomenon somehow sharply distinct from inert matter." It is the normal continuation, on another level, of universal evolution.

Organization is not a specific feature of the world introduced by the act of the prime mover from the outside. It is, rather, an innate property of the world. Thus, we can not regard organization as originating from chaos as described in Plato's *Timaeus*; nor does Milton's intuition that "first there was Chaos, the vast immeasurable abyss, outrageous as a sea, dark, wasteful, wild" provide any satisfactory explanation. Indeed, in most of the ancient mythologies, people expressed their intuitive awareness of the tension between the ordered universe and the chaos that resulted when organization broke down. In was common for the preservation of order to be attributed to a god who was strong enough to maintain order in the face of chaos. Modern views, though less poetic, are more rigorous.

Traditional science, in the age of the machine, tended to emphasize qualities of stability, order, uniformity, and equilibrium. It concerned itself with closed systems and linear causality. Closed self-equilibrating systems became the unique frame of reference for all propositions of theoretical physics and conventional economic analysis. Whereas, in physics this abstraction made possible the approximation of "real" systems in laboratory settings, other disciplines were less fortunate. In biology, as in economic science, where experimentation with closed and isolated processes was attempted, the isomorphs were far from being miniature simulations of concrete reality. The reductionist isomorph meant the dismissing of all that was disorderly, changeable, and qualitative. It distorted the complex and richly interactive nature of life itself.[7]

However, during the golden age of mechanism, physiologists such as Claude Bernard avowed that organisms were not in a static, but in a dynamic equilibrium.[8] Bertalanffy, consistent with Bogdanov's earlier efforts, realized that the advance of the life sciences needed a different type of model from that which had evolved in the physical sciences.

An important landmark in the development of Bertalanffy's methodology of science and general systems theory is his theory of open systems, the analytical issues of which were addressed in his *Problems of Life*. In *Problems*, Bertalanffy observed that an open system implies that some kind of structure is maintained in the midst of throughput from inputs to outputs. Although the concept of open systems was rooted in the thermodynamics of physical chemistry and biophysics, it transcends these fields and extends to general questions of methodology, philosophy, and epistemology.[9] Indeed, in the West, Ludwig von Bertalanffy's essay *The Theory of Open Systems in Physics and Biology* established systems theory as an interdisciplinary scientific movement.

Bertalanffy asserts that the meaning of dynamic equilibrium was not clearly defined until 1932, when he himself showed that

> true equilibria can occur only in closed systems and that, in open systems, disequilibria called "steady states," or "flow equilibria"[10] are the predominant and characteristic feature. According to the second law of thermodynamics a closed system must eventually attain a time-independent equilibrium state, with maximum entropy and minimum free energy. An open system may, under certain conditions, attain a time-independent state where the system remains constant as a whole and in its phases, though there is a continuous flow of component materials. This is called a steady state. Steady states are irreversible as a whole. . . . A closed system in equilibrium does not need energy for its preservation, nor can energy be obtained from it. In order to perform work, a system must be in disequilibrium, tending toward equilibrium and maintaining a steady state. Therefore the character of an open system is the necessary condition for the continuous working capacity of the organism.[11]

There is some variation in the use of terms among those concerned with general systems theory, and this is particularly true of the terms "closed" and "open." Rubin, for instance, notes that "the final state of a closed system, or any intermediate state is determined by those forces and processes already within it at the moment of closure."[12] In classical mechanical systems, for instance, in the case of an ideal pendulum, the motion and final state is determined by its initial conditions. Such systems are assumed to be linearly deterministic. "The final state of an open system, or any intermediate state is determined by both the forces within it the moment it became open, and the forces of the environment."[13]

Although Boltzmann spoke of thermodynamic potentials whose extrema correspond to states of equilibrium toward which the cosmos irreversibly tends, Bertalanffy wrote that

> in closed systems the trend of events is determined by the increase of entropy, irreversible processes in open systems cannot be characterized by entropy or another thermodynamical potential; rather the steady state which the system approaches is defined by the approach of minimal entropy production. From this arises the revolutionary consequence that in the transition to a steady state within an open system there may be a decrease in entropy and a spontaneous transition to a state of higher heterogeneity and complexity. This fact is possibly of fundamental significance for the increase in complexity and order which is characteristic for organic development and evolution.[14]

The theorem of minimum entropy production does, in fact, show that a system evolves toward a stationary state characterized by the minimum entropy production compatible with the constraints imposed upon the system.

Indeed, Bertalanffy noted that, from the physical perspective, living organisms can be defined as open rather than closed systems with respect to their surroundings. That is, they are enmeshed in a continuous material interaction with their environment. Such a continuous exchange means the system is in a steady state.[15]

The stationary, but not static, state in which open systems exist is maintained constant not because it is in a state of "maximum entropy" or because its free energy is at a minimum (as in the case of thermodynamic equilibrium), but because the open living system is continually receiving free energy from its environment in an amount that compensates for the decrease taking place within the organization itself. This was, according to J.D. White, apparent in Bogdanov's *Tektology* and in Bertalanffy's *Problems of Life*. Bertalanffy wrote: "The organism as a whole is never in a true equilibrium and the relatively slow processes of metabolism lead only to a steady state, maintained at a constant distance from true equilibrium by a continuous inflow and outflow, building up and breaking down of the component materials."[16]

The attempt to grasp life as an entropy-driven process was made by the Vienna-born physicist Erwin Schrödinger, who stated that a living organism attracts "a stream of negative entropy upon itself, to compensate for the entropy increase it produces by living and thus to maintain itself on a stationary and fairly low entropy level."[17]

The first edition of his work, published in 1944, provoked a torrent of objections and reservations from physicists because of this particular condition. To purge any confusion stemming from his proposition, Schrödinger added a footnote in the revised edition, in which, following Bertalanffy, he delineated a new image of life: life must get rid of the excess entropy produced by living activities.[18] This perspective constituted the essence of his celebrated work *What is Life?* and has since been considered the standard description of the life process by natural scientists. Indeed, J. Lovelock, author of the controversial concept of Gaia, expressed a definition of life similar to that of Schrödinger. Lovelock wrote: "Life is a member of the class of phenomena which are open or continuous systems able to decrease their internal entropy at the expense of substances or free energy taken in from the environment and subsequently rejected in a degraded form."[19]

An open system is, however, not sufficient for a system to be a living system. The late Japanese economist Yoshiro Tamanoi maintained that

> in order for an open system to be a living system, it has to be coexistent [i.e., it experiences a continuous material exchange with its environment]. It is the very nature of *becoming* that moves us to think in terms of the coevolution of systems with other open systems. In other words, a living system is an open system that maintains a symbiotic relationship with other open steady systems in its environment.[20]

This caveat was already present in Bertalanffy's remarks of 1952.[21]

Considered as a partially isolated system, any organism must degrade entropically. In the end, it dies if isolated from its life-sustaining environment. What allows an organism to survive in spite of its entropic degradation, according to Schrödinger and Bertalanffy, is the fact that it can extract available matter-energy from the environment and expel its produced unavailable matter-energy—its wastes—into the environment. Here, too, Bertalanffy anticipated Tamanoi's analysis, writing that "until recently physics dealt almost exclusively with closed systems, i.e., with systems which do not exchange matter with their environment. Such an organism continually takes in and excretes matter, it obviously asks for a theory of open systems."[22]

The main concepts, according to Bertalanffy, are:

(1) The characteristic state of the living organism is that of an open system. It is open in the sense that it exchanges material with its environment; by this import and export of materials there is change of components.[23] Previous conceptions of the organism as maintaining a state of equilibrium must yield to the idea of the steady state.

(2) The concept of the open system maintaining itself in a steady state represents a departure from the concepts of classical physics, which has dealt for the most part with closed systems. According to the second law of thermodynamics, a closed system must eventually attain a state of equilibrium with maximum entropy and minimum free energy. But under certain conditions an open system may maintain itself under a steady state.[24]

The characteristics of steady states are exactly those of organic metabolism. First, there is the maintenance of a constant ratio of components in a continuous flow of materials. Second, the composition is independent of, and maintained constant in, a varying assimilation of materials. This corresponds to the fact that even in varying nutrition and at different absolute sizes the composition of the organism remains constant.[25]

(3) Following Claude Bernard, after a disturbance the system seeks to reestablish a steady state. Thus, the basic characteristics of self-regulation are the general properties of open systems.

Ludwig von Bertalanffy and Erwin Schrödinger have described life as a system in a steady-state thermodynamic non-equilibrium which maintains its constant distance from thermal equilibrium (death) by feeding on low entropy from its environment[26] (that is, by exchanging high-entropy outputs for low-entropy inputs).[27]

Living systems are inseparable from complexifying evolution.[28] It follows, according to Passet, that from the thermodynamics of irreversible phenomena:

(1) If a system receives a flow of energy or one that is less than its own production of entropy, it will disorganize itself;

(2) If it receives as much as it eliminates, it finds itself in a stationary state of non-equilibrium and maintains its structure; and

(3) If it receives more than it returns, the surplus that is available to it will permit it not only to maintain its organization but to evolve toward a state of higher complexity.

But, as we shall see in Chapter 4, this Ostwaldian speculation is a necessary but not a sufficient condition for organizational development.

Bertalanffy's application of open-systems theory to a range of biological phenomena is generally acknowledged as his most important contribution to theoretical biology. Moreover, it has influenced the broadening of economic thought in a number of specific ways which we shall address.

Together with the earlier analyses of Bogdanov and Bukharin, Bertalanffy's theory of open steady-state systems suggests an alternative model of the economic process. Such an approach contrasts in significant ways with conventional economic thought. It belies that abstraction known as the "circular flow." It argues that the economic process is thermal, characterized by irrevocable and irreversible phenomena, rather than being a kind of perpetual-motion machine of mythic dimension. Moreover, the emerging open-systems approach characterizes the economy as a living system metabolically interacting with its environment. While there are a growing number of open-system models characterized by socioeconomic biophysical interpenetrations, they are not all free of reductionism. Nor has the enabling myth of market mentality been expunged from such models; for there remain both neosocial energetic reductionism and attempts at the internalization of externalities according to market criteria.

The Misplaced Concreteness of the Circular Flow

Conventional economic thought has been defined as the study of how scarce resources are administered according to *Zweckrationalität* (functional rationality). It is only as one becomes acquainted with the history of economic thought that one discovers that this definition serves to weave a web of obscurities.

Having excluded nature and economic reproduction, Lionel Robbins hastened to discharge technology as well, noting that "the ends as such lie outside [the] objective, this also applies to the technical and social environment." The environment was made to belong to a world of data in relation to which "the economist has no grasp . . . and which the economist must accept as a basis for his analysis."[29] Robbins's comment is more than a mere rejection of the technical; it precisely locates postclassical analysis independent of substantive coordinates. With Robbins the "inversion" is complete, all ethical proportions are expunged from economic analysis. On the basis of an ossified assertion, the Physiocratic perception of a natural and coherent order was supplanted. As we have already seen, Lionel Robbins's formulation of this position is that the scope of economics is confined to the study of how given means are applied to satisfy given ends. In more specific terms: at any given instant of time the means at the disposal of every individual as well as his ends over the future are given; given also, are the technical and social ways in which these means can be used directly or indirectly for the satisfaction of the given ends; and, thereby, the essential object of economics is reduced to determining the rational allocation of the given means toward the optimal satisfaction of the given ends. The formal meaning springs from the logical character of the means–ends relationship, as expressed by the terms "economizing" or "economical." Aristotelian efficient cause coupled with scientific rationality, economism becomes the science of choice, and its typical concern is the deductive exploration of the logic of maximizing under the constraint of scarcity. In this view, calculated choice, oriented toward maximization, becomes the central economic problem, and the economy consists of a series of choices imposed by scarcity situations and informed by relative prices. It is in this context that the scarcity definition of the late Lionel Robbins ("Scarcity of means to satisfy ends of varying importance is an almost ubiquitous condition of human behavior") surely arises. This now-ubiquitous definition has become a source of aggravation to economic historians. Robbins wrote: "The nature of economic analysis should now be plain. It consists of deductions from a series of postulates, the chief of which are almost universal facts of experience present wherever human creativity has an economic aspect."[30] He argues further that four conditions must be met if a phenomenal situation is to provide a problem for economic science. There must be various ends or goals and limited means for achieving these ends. These means must be capable of alternative applications, and the ends must be of varying importance. For Robbins, if these conditions are met, the behavior involved necessarily assumes the form of choice. It follows that economic science may not be concerned with concrete productive and consumptive activities at all if these activities do not meet these conditions. It also follows that any activities that do meet these conditions provide scientific problems for economics whether or not the activities are generally conceived of as economic. Robbins's conception of economic science was that it

> focuses attention on a particular aspect of behavior, the form imposed by the influence of scarcity. It follows from this, therefore, that insofar as it represents this aspect, any kind of human behavior falls within the scope of economic generalization. We do not say that the production of potatoes is economic activity and the production of philosophy is not. We say rather that, insofar as either kind of activity involves the relinquishment of other desired alternatives, it has its economic aspect. There are no limitations on the subject-matter of Economic Science save this.[31]

Semantic disputation aside, the conventional term "economic" is actually the embodiment of two meanings—the formal and the substantive.[32] Moreover, one must also discern what is meant by "resources," which conventional economics understands as only labor, capital, and Ricardian land (i.e., land as mere space). The role played by natural resources in the economic process has been, according to Georgescu-Roegen, assiduously ignored.[33] The omission is highly intriguing and has recently become the cause of some embarrassment. For even a cursory reading of history would have shown that control over mineral resources has been, and remains, one of the most important factors of political struggles among nations. The patent fact that between the economic process and the Biosphere there exists a continuous material influence that is history-making carries no weight with conventional economic knowledge.[34] For instance, although Marx and Engels referred to environment exigencies, "history-making" was the domain of class contradiction.

While the whole Biosphere has evolved as a complex system around the fixed solar flux, humankind has supplemented the "solar income budget" by consuming "terrestrial capital," especially with the advent of the petroleum age.[35] As early as 1912 this was apparent to Frederick Soddy, who wrote:

> As regards energy, and therefore as regards every other commodity, the modern world is undoubtedly living far beyond its income. It has recently come into a legacy from the remote past and it is living on the capital. It cannot now be very long before it wakes up to the appreciation of this fact.[36]

Yet it took more than sixty years before the "energy crisis" made headlines and before nations began to grasp the social and economic implications of energy as a critical use-value. Measured against these recent events, Soddy's comments of 1912 appear far less obtuse and of much greater portent than they did in his own time.[37]

Even at this late hour, the belief persists that all we need in order to produce more energy and solve the ecological crisis is to have correct prices and to have command over sufficient money.[38] The mechanical paradigm together with the dogma of market mentality is all pervasive. Levi-Strauss suggested that the frame of reference offered by neoclassical economics is insufficient to permit a necessary depth of insight into the enigmas of contemporary society. Insofar as neoclassic economics posits an allegedly eternal and a priori market exchange relationship it presumes to be the basic coordinator of social relations.[39]

The production theory of post-classical economic science was reduced to a crude and timeless kind of kinematics resembling the cosmological system of Aristotle with its crystalline spheres and eternal motion of the stars. Indeed, nothing reveals the mechanistic philosophy of the doctrine as that model so familiar to students of economics—a model that purports to show the economic process as an infinitely self-sustaining perpetual motion machine eternally balanced in an equilibrium (see Figure 3.1).

Indeed, for economic analysis the concept of equilibrium assumes critical importance, for it is synonymous with order. Implicitly, the corresponding model embodies two dominant ideas: (1) it is an attempt at a scientific explanation of the interrelated material phenomena; and (2) its object is to demonstrate the existence of a natural order. Consequently, equilibrium analysis has become the central organizing concept of economics. Its effect is to locate the cause of social order in nature and in natural forces instead of in society and human institutions.[40]

The concept has its heritage in the systematic study of society developed out of the speculations of the natural law philosophers (including Quesnay). Their attempt was to analyze society independently of revealed religion, but it was also an effort to develop an objective moral code by which society might be regulated.[41] The view adopted during the Enlightenment was that the social and physical universes were but different aspects of one reality, that both the physical and social universes were ruled by God's natural laws, and that these laws could be discovered by inquiring into nature—which for the social sciences meant human nature. Reason itself was inspired by revelation and was employed to derive positive laws that would support and reinforce God's law of nature. The medieval outlook concentrated on controlling and regulating those aspects of human nature that came into conflict with revealed morality.

It was Adam Smith who synthesized aspects of the intellectual movement of his time, Newtonian Revolution and natural law philosophy. Each constituted essential ingredients in Smith's discovery of the natural order. The Newtonian outlook held that the blueprint of the physical universe was written in nature. Smith stated that the blueprint of the social universe was written in human nature. He then transmuted the passions into interests. In the economic realm, the passions—natural propensities to truck, barter, and exchange thereby bettering one's position—through the invisible hand of competition, led to prosperity. Individual self-interested actions led to order and not to chaos. Moreover, since it was the result of the natural forces God implanted in humans, the resulting order was the natural order.

For the timeless kinematics of the circular flow, Smith's natural order manifests itself in the idea of economic equilibrium. The market and other economic institutions were understood as parts of an orderly system. The source of this order is nature.

Despite its sophistication, there has been no substantial deviation from the natural law outlook as the underpinning of economic theory. The preconceptions are hidden in the calculus, yet they become clear when we see that history, society, and free will are excluded. By abstracting from history and society they have excluded the very factors that provide for the interrelations and regularities they sought to explain; they have abstracted the source of order. For the coherence and comprehension of any social act comes from its social reality, exactly what the equilibrium economists insist upon excluding.

Grounded on the universality of natural laws, history and society could be excluded unceremoniously. Order in society, or at least in the economy, could be provided by natural forces consummating a natural order—an equilibrium—alleged to be the most beneficial.

Implicit in the concentration on equilibrium, and the exclusion of history and society, is the idea of the natural order. The market economy is treated as if it were a

Figure 3.1. **Model of the Circular Flow**

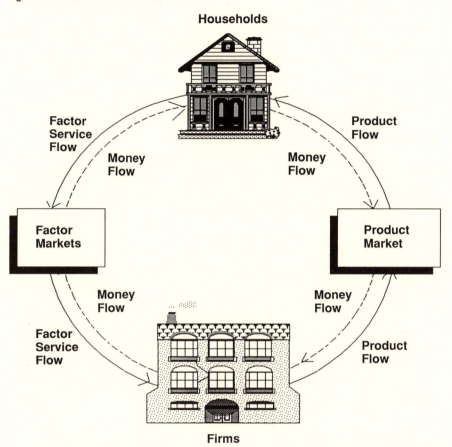

natural phenomenon, resulting from human nature and scarcity, not a particular social formation with institutions and a history. *Homo oeconomicus*, following the "pure logic of choice," acted according to instincts embedded in human nature, not as the result of a socialization process. Moreover, the economics of the circular flow or equilibrium economics achieved dominance because of its role as legitimator of the process by which social knowledge explains and justifies social reality.[42]

The critique of the circular-flow model of the economic process, based on a natural philosophy denial of the reality of society and human free will, is not the only grounds upon which we criticize the model. There remains a second substantive critique which we shall now present.

There is the general practice of representing the material side of the economic process by a closed system, that is, by a mechanical model in which the continuous flow of Biospheric inputs is obscured.[43] In the analyses of production processes, for instance, economists have generally proceeded by the Galilean method, partitioning reality, and selecting out readily quantifiable parameters, thereby creating a partial process. It is, then, upon this mechanical abstraction that analysis of production proceeds. The conceptualizing of economic reproduction in mechanical terms even introduced a special nomenclature: Eugen von Böhm-Bawerk's "roundaboutness," Joseph Schumpeter's "circular flow," and Walrasian "general equilibrium." These expressions were coined in order to adapt economic terminology to the mechanical model. Even this symptom of neoclassical economics has been preceded by a far more common one: the concept that the economic process is wholly circular.

Despite the dominance of neoclassical theory in the twentieth century, there has been a significant revival of classical themes and models. Walsh and Gram note that this approach to the analysis of production gained popularity with the 1960 publication of Piero Sraffa's *Production of Commodities by Means of Commodities*. In that work Quesnay's *Tableau* was presented as "the original picture of the systems of production and consumption as a circular process."[44] According to G. Vaggi, since Karl Marx's praise of Francois Quesnay in the *Theories of Surplus Value*, the *Tableau Économique* has been regarded as the first description of the economy as a physical system of reproduction, in which commodities are produced by labor and other commodities.[45]

Conventional economic theory derives considerable sustenance from the equilibrium model of the circular flow of exchange-value. This is especially the case for macroeconomic and national income accounting. In this all too familiar model, value embodied in goods and services flows from firms to households and is called "national product." An equal value, reincarnated in factors of production, flows back to firms from households and is called "national income." The circular-flow model traces exchange-value around its cycle. Although the physical embodiments differ, the exchange-values in the two loops of the cycle are the same. This is because of the axiom of equality in exchange: that both sides of a transaction have equal exchange-values (though different use-values).

According to the standard vision, the economic process is a self-contained, self-equilibrating, self-sustaining merry-go-round between "consumption" and "production." Since institutionalized general purpose money seems to run in circles, a money fetish characteristic of commercial practice must have constituted still another cause for the circular vision of the economic process. The reference image of the economic process rests on the seemingly vulgar grounds that only money counts.[46]

The fallacy of misplaced concreteness that attaches to the conventional understanding of the circular flow was already a central theme in the work of Frederick Soddy, who stated:

> It is, of course, the linear throughput [of matter-energy] not the circular flow of value that impinges on the environment in the forms of depletion and pollution. It is impossible to study the relation of the economy to the ecosystem in terms of

the circular flow model, because the circular flow is an isolated, self-renewing system with no inlets or outlets, no possible points of contact with anything outside itself. Yet in economic theory circular flow has the spotlight, while the concept of throughput is only dimly visible in the shadows.[47]

But the circular flow of exchange-values is coupled with a physical flow of matter-energy that is not circular. The matter-energy flow is linear and unidirectional, beginning with the depletion of low-entropy resources from the environment and ending up with high-entropy wastes and pollution of the environment. Studying economics in terms of the circular flow without considering the entropic throughput is like studying physiology in terms of the circulatory system without ever mentioning the digestive system. This was the Physiocratic faux pas.[48]

It is impossible to study the relation of the economy to the ecosystem in terms of the circular-flow model. The circular flow is presented as an isolated, self-renewing system with no inflow or outflows and with no possible points of contact with anything outside itself. It is, after all, a closed system. Moreover, when "leakages" and "injections" are discussed, they refer exclusively to monetized elements—to purchasing power, not matter-energy. Furthermore, the whole point of Keynesian policy is to ensure closure, channeling the sum of all leakages (S+T+M) back into an equal sum of injections (I+G+X).

Aside from the Natural Philosophy undergirding, an important cause of the uniquely resilient adherence to the mechanistic epistemology of economists is a lasting appreciation of how human understanding works. It is probably because we can act only by pushing or pulling, in a mechanical fashion, that we feel a strong attraction for mechanical explanations. Even the great physicist Lord Kelvin admitted that "I can never satisfy myself until I can make a mechanical model of a thing."[49] The entire history of not only nineteenth-century physics, but also economic science is very telling in this respect. The mechanistic foundation of standard economics is demonstrated not only in the terminology borrowed from mechanics, but also in the conventional argument of how the economic process itself proceeds. An indiscriminate attachment to the mechanistic dogma conveys the reference image of the economic process as a mechanical analog consisting of a principle of conservation and an optimization rule. And just as in mechanics, shifts and displacements leave no trace of their occurrence. With its emphasis on the conservation of mass, reversible Newtonian mechanics allowed for only a change of location. Without a sense of qualitative transformation there was no room for irrevocably exhaustible resources. The mechanistic dogma ignored these issues and enjoyed an unparalleled prestige until well into the second half of the nineteenth century.

Laplace felt completely justified in maintaining in his famous apotheosis of mechanics that absolutely everything in the universe is determined by a vast system of mechanical equations. The sole concession made was that only an intellectual demon could possibly solve such a system. To the divine understanding, all phenomena are coexisting and are comprehended in one mathematical structure. The senses, however, recognize events one by one and regard some as the causes of others. We can understand now, said Descartes, why mathematical relationships are preexisting. The mathematical relationship is the clearest physical explanation of a relationship. In brief, the real world is the totality of mathematically expressible motions of objects in space and time, and the entire universe is a great harmonious, mathematically designed machine.[50] What Laplace had envisioned now seemed a fact—albeit a fleeting one.

Consistent with St. Thomas Aquinas and the Physiocrats, conceptually man's efforts and sacrifices result in changing the form of, or restructuring, matter to adapt it better for the satisfaction of his wants. His production of use-values is really nothing more than a rearrangement of matter rendering it new utilities. Conversely, consumption of use-values is nothing more than a disarrangement of matter which diminishes or destroys its utilities thereby rendering a service.[51]

Within the context of the circular flow, matter is infinitely rearranged in production, disarranged in consumption, rearranged again in production, etc. Matter consists of homogeneous, indestructible building blocks that just keep recycling and rearranging.[52] For instance, Alfred Marshall retained the classical perspective (also present in Marx's theory of production), viewing production as a process of the "working-up" of materials. From such a perspective, the laboring activity becomes that of "sorting." Man, as an appropriator and the "informing" agent of environmental low entropy is credited with creating use-values within the context of the labor theory of value. But man does not "create" use-values, he merely rearranges preexisting objects of environmental low entropy. Looking at the physical basis of the economic process from the perspective only of the first law of thermodynamics tends to reinforce the circular-flow model and sanction its generalization to levels of abstraction involving physical dimensions in addition to the exchange-value dimension.

Even within the context of closed systems the rearrangement of matter is the central physical fact of the economic process. It behooves us to ask: What determines the capacity to rearrange matter? Is all matter equally capable of being rearranged? Is all energy equally capable of effecting the rearrangement? The second law of thermodynamics provides an answer. There is a qualitative difference between equal quantities of raw materials and waste materials. Raw materials represent low entropy; waste materials, high entropy.

According to a number of authors, the dissipation of available energy imposes a one-way direction on the economic processes. Indeed, the key to understanding the economic system as an open coevolutionary system is precisely this fact.[53]

Thermodynamics and the Nature of the Economic Process

Resurrecting themes that had been formulated in the late nineteenth and early twentieth centuries, in 1965 Nicholas Georgescu-Roegen began a careful analysis of the economic process, not in terms of the mechanical paradigm, but rather in terms of open systems and energy and material transformations. Georgescu-Roegen has reasserted Frederick Soddy's dictum that the entropy law is a principal determinant of all material transformations associated with life. It is a process that advances in an irrevocable way.[54] Accordingly, he sought to reestablish the conceptual basis for economic models with a solid foundation in thermodynamics. His work has focused on the irrevocable transformation that energy and resources undergo as they pass through the economic process, and on the role of thermodynamics as "in essence a physics of economic value."[55] Indeed, Daly observes that if one were to insist on a real-cost theory of value one should focus on entropy, rather than labor or energy.[56]

A long-time advocate of a qualitatively different model of economic activity, Georgescu-Roegen writes: "The economic process, like biological life itself, is unidirectional."[57] Together with a number of other authors,[58] Georgescu-Roegen maintains that the mechanistic epistemology to which analytical economics has clung is principally responsible for the conception of the economic process as a closed system or circular flow. Standard economists have conveniently ignored both Eddington's observation that time's arrow proceeds in one direction and the more obvious and concrete fact of the material and energy entropic verities of the economic process. The identity of this phenomenon with that proposed by the Austrian-born Erwin Schrödinger for the biological processes of living organisms vindicates those economists who followed Alfred Marshall's meek assertion:

> It is true that the forces with which economics deals have one advantage for deductive treatment in the fact that their method of combination is, as Mill observed, that of mechanics rather then chemistry. That is to say, when we know the action of two economic forces separately—as for instance the influences which an increase in the rate of wages and a diminution in the difficulty of work in a trade will severely exert on the supply of labor in it—we can predict fairly well their conjoint action, without waiting for specific experience of it.
>
> But even in mechanics long chains of deductive reasoning are directly applicable only to occurrences of the laboratory. By themselves they are seldom a sufficient guide for dealing with the heterogeneous materials and complex combinations of forces of the real world. Lastly, the matter with which the chemist deals is the same always: but economics, like biology, deals with a matter, of which the inner nature and constitution, as well as the outer form, are constantly changing.[59]

He felt that it was indeed biology, rather than Newtonian mechanics, that should be the model of economic science. For Marshall argued that "economics is a branch of biology broadly interpreted."[60]

While efforts to better understand the very complex relationship between technological activity and nature are becoming more numerous and sophisticated, it nevertheless remains clear that the greater portion of work on this vital question has yet to be attempted. Of the diversity of approaches to this issue great promise is held by the emergence of what might be termed a Neo-Physiocratic perspective which identifies: (1) the concept of the livelihood of man as an open system coevolving within other open systems, and (2) the related issue of the intersystemic relationship between man and the Biosphere. In this connection, Kawamiya claims that Bertalanffy's notion of flowing open systems is a condition applying not only to "individual organisms but to their aggregates at all levels."[61]

Professors Passet, Georgescu-Roegen, and Tamanoi stress that the economic process, like any other life process, is irreversible; hence, it cannot be rigorously explained in accord with mechanical principles. Indeed, Kenneth Boulding, though he cautions against a categorical interpretation, asserts that the thermodynamic perspective represents a new paradigm for economic analysis.[62]

Casual observation, notes Georgescu-Roegen, reveals that our whole economic life feeds on "low entropy." An economy, in real terms, is a thermodynamically open system which extracts low-entropy energy and materials from the environmental systems and uses that energy in appropriately designed structures and processes to upgrade materials into new forms.

It would be absurd to say that the economic process merely taps available environmental resources only to transform them into unavailable waste, for this is only the material side of the story. Paradoxically, the true products of the process, as Fisher and Hobson contended, are not the material flows that result, but the immaterial flux—a kind of service that corresponds to the enjoyment of life itself. Georgescu-Roegen categorically notes that if we do not recognize this fact, we cannot be in the domain of the phenomena of life.[63]

Without doubt, notes Georgescu-Roegen, it is classical thermodynamics that recognizes the qualitative distinction that economists should have made from the outset between the inputs of valuable resources and the final outputs of valueless waste. On the basis of this distinction he then applies the entropy law to the economic process in order to prove in a highly generalized manner that inputs cannot become outputs without producing entropy. The point is that whereas the quantity of matter and energy is given, their form and state changes continuously. In short, matter cannot but lose its shape, thermal energy gradually diffuses, and, in the end, only unavailable energy is left.[64]

Georgescu-Roegen's thinking has developed in a number of articles and books, and along with Kenneth Boulding and Herman Daly, he was at the forefront of the modern economists who drew attention to the physical dimension of the economic process. The issues raised by Georgescu-Roegen, Boulding, and Daly have influenced the development of subsequent thinking in this area, particularly that of P. Christensen, P. Norgaard, and Y. Tamanoi.

The Myth of Perpetual Motion and
the Circular Flow

The late Japanese economist Tamanoi wrote that study of the economy in the broad sense must use the concept of production as its point of departure.

> [Both] in Marxian political economy and in neoclassical economics, production has been interpreted as the process between inputs and outputs, i.e., the process which solely concerns the pricing of products. In other words, production has been viewed as the matter of the effective use of inputs. The environmental issues brought, however, an unexpected question: How can one dispose of the wastes that are generated in accordance with the expansion of production? In a sense, waste is also a sort of output, which has never been focused on in either economics or political economy. This suggests that in actuality production consists of two aspects of which only a half has been dealt with.[65]

From the perspective of open-systems theory the livelihood of man cannot continue without a continuous material exchange between man and the Biosphere. A history-making feedback loop exists such that the economic process is itself influenced by those alterations of our physical environment.

Though there has been a rehabilitation of classical theory it has largely been confined to an exploration of Ricardian and Marxian theories of value and distribution. Very little attention has been given to the development of a theory of physical production. The Sraffa-led rehabilitation, asserts Christensen, has missed the existence and implications of the materials-flow classical models of production theory. These modern classical models (following Marx) are essentially representations of industrial economies reproducing themselves in time and space without any representation of the negentropic material and energy flows from geological and living systems which are the true "basics" of economic activity.

But there is a lesser known dimension of classical models that remains of continuing interest to the development of an open-systems paradigm because it has an essential consistency with thermodynamic principles. This is an inheritance from the physiological origins of the theory which, according to Christensen, implies an implicit energetics perspective, and the formulation of the problem of production in terms of the conservation of mass. To grasp Christensen's argument it is necessary briefly to review the classical dimensions of the problem.

As W.S. Jevons related, Adam Smith was keenly aware of the phases of economic change.[66] Smith's *Wealth of Nations* may be regarded as a sublime evolutionary plan. In *Wealth* society allegedly progresses through a sequence of four organizational modes. The sequence begins with "the lowest and rudest state of society, such as we find it among the native tribes of North America"; it then passes into "a more advanced state of society, such as we find it among the Tartars and Arabs"; and proceeds to a "yet more advanced state of society [comprised of] nations of husbandmen who have little foreign commerce." It terminates in the fourth stage, of which the *Wealth of Nations* virtually in its entirety must be the reference.

But the classical economists were also conscious of the fact that the progressive state could not go on forever, and that there were limits, not only to the growth of population but also to the growth of capital.

There is another central theme with respect to Smith's philosophic and historic "vision" whose merits have failed to garner adequate attention. This is the profound pessimism within Smith's own economic and social evolutionary schema. The distressing message of the *Wealth of Nations* is that of a socioeconomic system whose legitimation is neither to be found in the promise of continuous economic advancement nor in the expectation of general social betterment. Though Smith variously speaks of a "natural progress of things toward improvement," of a "uniform, constant, and uninterrupted effort by every man to better his condition," society is, nonetheless, confronted with the somber prophecy of an evolutionary trend in which material decline and moral decay attend.[67]

> It deserves to be remarked, perhaps, that it is in the progressive state, while society is advancing to the further acquisition, rather than when it has acquired its full complement of riches, that the condition of the labouring poor, of the great body of the people, seems to be the happiest and the most comfortable. It is hard in the stationary and miserable in the declining state. The progressive state is in reality the cheerful and hearty state to all the different members of society. The stationary state; the declining melancholy.[68]

Smith's normative sequence of historical evolution was not "hitchless," to use Schumpeter's term. At the end of the long rising gradient, society is confronted with the spectacle of a nation that has attained "that full complement of riches which the nature of its soil and climate and its situation with respect to other countries allow[s] it to acquire," and discovers to its great consternation that in such a nation "the wages of labour and the profits of stock would probably be very low." Thus, growth has somehow terminated in general poverty, a fact that suggests that some important "hitches" underlay the dynamics of *Wealth of Nations.*[69]

The mechanism by which the "progressive state" may be brought to an end was, in the case of population, the Malthusian one. Smith must have reckoned on population growth that continues to be positive throughout the various stages of real per capita well-being implied in the long trajectory of economic growth and decline. But as the population grew, it would eventually reach a point at which real income would decline, mortality would rise, and births would eventually be equal to deaths. It was Ricardo's analysis that provided an analogous model for capital. "As capital accumulated, the classical economists, especially, believed that the rate of return on it would fall due to the increasing competition among capitalists, and that this would eventually reach a point at which there was no motivation for the further accumulation of capital."[70]

The sociological side of the argument was, even in the early phases of the Industrial Revolution, replete with evidence that the system of liberal individualism leads to a human condition that is inferior, rather than superior, to that of the preceding stages of the historical process.

> In the progress of the division of labour, the employment of the far greater part of those who live by labour, that is of the great body of the people, comes to be confined to a few very simple operations, frequently to one or two. But the understandings of the greater part of men are necessarily formed by their ordinary employments. The man whose life is spent in performing a few simple operations, of which the effects too are perhaps always the same or very nearly the same, has no occasion to exert his understanding, or to exercise his invention in finding expedients for removing difficulties which never occur. He naturally loses, therefore, the habit of such exertion, and generally becomes as stupid and ignorant as it is possible for a human creature to become. The torpor of his mind renders him, not only incapable of relishing or bearing a part in any rational conversation, but of conceiving any general, noble, or tender sentiment, and consequently of forming any just judgment concerning even the ordinary duties of private life.[71]

More telling is Smith's candid contrast of commercial society with the condition of life in previous stages of the historical sequence.[72] For "no society can surely be flourishing and happy of which the far greater part of the members are poor and miserable."[73]

The final judgment passed on the quality of life in commercial society is devastating: "Notwithstanding the great abilities of those few, all the nobler parts of the human character may be, in great measure, obliterated and extinguished in the great body of the people."[74] In *Lectures*, Smith concludes: "These are the disadvantages of a commercial spirit. The minds of men are contracted and rendered incapable of elevation. Education is despised, or at least neglected, and heroic spirit is almost utterly extinguished."[75] Smith relegated the moral qualities of the liberal system to a position inferior to that of a "ruder," though allegedly more wholesome, epoch.

From an inquiry into the wealth of nations there emerged two contrasting, though evolutionary, views of the nature of capitalism. The first, originating with John Stuart Mill, was a response to the pessimism expressed by Adam Smith, and prophetized institutional continuity under varying conditions. Karl Marx, alternatively, subscribed to a second view which allegedly embodied a historical determinism and divined the collapse of capitalist institutions. Mill was somewhat optimistic about the prospects of capitalism and thought that even though population and capital might cease to grow, there would be no hindering human creativity in the arts and expansion of knowledge.[76]

Mill wrote: "I cannot. . . regard the stationary state of capital and wealth with the unaffected aversion so generally manifested towards it by political economists of the old school. I am inclined to believe that it would be, on the whole, a very considerable improvement on our present condition."[77] It remained for Mill to note that a model of the "progressive state" could be constructed without a population increase. He asserted that capitalism need not grow incessantly and could evolve into a balanced, stationary state.[78]

Out of the classical analysis of the stationary state a subsistence theory emerged, which Marx elaborated as the case of simple economic reproduction. But the very essence of capitalism, according to Marx, and contrary to Mill, is expansion—which is to say, the capitalist, as a historical "type" finds his *raison d'être* in the alleged insatiable search for money-wealth gained through the constant growth of the economic system.[79] The idea of a "stationary" capitalism is, in Marxian eyes, a contradiction in terms.

This constitutes the second view. The stationary state was described as one in which there is some per capita income in the case of population, or real rate of return in the case of capital, at which neither population nor capital would grow. As they advance in the progressive state both income and the rate of return decline until they reach their subsistence level, at which no further growth takes place. Both capital and population simply reproduce themselves at "equilibrium" rates. It is a perpetual-motion machine.

The problem of Mill's stationary state and Marx's simple reproduction is that while it explicitly assumes capital and population as constant, it implicitly assumes that there are no exhaustible natural resources. In this connection it is worth recalling that in W.S. Jevons's analysis of "progressive" and "stationary" states in the *Coal Question* of 1865, he flirted with the institutional dimensions of the problem of a growing physical scarcity of coal that attaches to a "stationary state."[80]

Baring Jevons's transient insight no emphasis is given to the constraints imposed on the availability of material inputs or threatening accumulations of dissipated outputs, nor is the motive power of the economic process an issue. This "hitchless" view is also present in the Sraffian "production of commodities by means of commodities."[81] The Marxist vision of the capitalist machine is different from that of the functionalists who describe development as "hitchless." From Marx's image of "expanded reproduction," one part of the machine would grow more than the other part. Though Marx made occasional remarks on how capitalism misused nature, a reference to an integrated economic-ecological model was, of course, outside his purview.[82]

Although Marx agreed with the classical economists that production is the proper starting point of economic analysis, he rightly accused them (Mill is cited as an example) of attempting "to present production ... as encased in eternal natural laws independent of history" and then smuggling bourgeois relations into the matter as "the inviolable natural laws on which society in the abstract is founded."[83] However correct Marx's critique, according to Christensen, he disregards the physical side of classical production theory and its contribution to the classification and analysis of production activities.[84] For Marx's starting point in

Capital is not production as a physical process but the commodity considered from two points of view (as use-value and exchange-value). While this provides his analysis with the potential of interactions between physical and social structures, Christensen argues that he provides no systematic analysis of the underlying physical processes. There is also a systematic subordination of nature and physical artifacts to labor. Labor activity is, for Marx, the starting point of economic activity. Physical, i.e., nature, considerations are taken up only as they bear upon labor. Thus, Marx allegedly foregoes a theory of surplus value based on the dual exploitation of labor and natural resources.

This is not to say that the biophysical perspective is inconsistent with Marx's analysis of industrial capitalism.

> Just as the individual machine retains its dwarfish character, so long as it is worked by the power of man alone, and just as no system of machinery could be properly developed before the steam-engine took the place of earlier motive power, animals, wind and even water; so too Modern Industry was crippled in its complete development.[85]

For Marx, only labor creates surplus value and it is society, not environmental factors, that constrains productive potential.

At the basis of the Marxian analysis of capitalist simple reproduction the idea that a constant material flow, which attaches to the steady state, can arise from an unchanging structure.[86] In the scheme of expanded reproduction he ignored the problem of the primary source of the flow. To the extent that Marxist economics occupied itself with natural resources, the treatment has not been an ecological one (that is, consideration of availability of resources, of waste disposal, and of intergenerational allocations), but a Ricardian one. It refers to how rent paid to the owners of natural resources would alter the pattern of distribution of income and of savings and investment. The Marxist schema of simple and expanded reproduction do not take into account whether the availability of exhaustible resources would place a limit on even simple reproduction.

In the scheme of "simple reproduction" there is no question that the process could be continued indefinitely through advances in technological means. Marx asserted that at some point in history man will develop the productive sources of nature to such an extent that the antagonism between man and nature will be resolved by technological development.[87] At this point "the prehistory of man" will come to a close and truly human history will begin.[88]

Marx dichotomized the relation between humans and their physical environment and stated that the one-way flow of natural resources, outside of the livelihood of man, did not have a historical context. In other words, nature became dialectical only in the context of man's economic strivings.[89] Nonetheless, one might refer to *Grundrisse*, for instance, to locate Marx's broader appreciation of nature and the economic process.[90]

It may be argued that while social factors determine the amount of energy used to subsidize a worker's effort and the rate at which surplus value is produced by labor, the large amounts of net energy available from fossil fuels, solar energy, and uranium are the physical basis for the production of surplus value. This line of argument is consistent with the view that the economic process is not an isolated, self-sustaining mechanical process.

Irrespective of the enigmatic Marx, it nonetheless remains true that the mechanistic epistemology to which analytical economics has clung is responsible in significant ways for the concept of the economic process as a closed system of circular flows. Neoclassical economists chose to ignore the biophysical foundations of the economy. One fundamental idea dominated that school. A.C. Pigou stated it explicitly: "In a stationary state factors of production are stocks, unchanging in amount, out of which emerges a continuous flow, also unchanging in amount or real income."[91] With respect to economic reproduction, both the classical and post-classical schools may be said to accept the Pigouvian myth of a stationary state in which the sustaining material flows emerge from an invariable source. In this lies the germ of economic fallacy.

While the Pigouvian myth is a source of derision, a chronic preoccupation with the general commensurability of monetary flows at the expense of thermodynamic principles misleads Marxians and neoclassicals into believing that technological advance is limitless, and that perpetual economic growth is not only physically possible, but also morally and ethically desirable.

Circular Flow, Money Fetish, and Growth

Exchange-value may be measured in money forms which, according to Soddy, are essentially debt. A unit of currency is a kind of non–interest-bearing debt issued by a government and accepted by the citizenry as a medium of exchange. In owning a unit of currency, an unknown someone is obligated to provide the bearer with a unit of currency's worth of wealth. But, as Soddy compellingly noted, wealth has a physical dimension, debt does not.[92]

A poignant example of misplaced concreteness in economics is "money fetishism"; applying the characteristics of money, the token and measure of wealth, to concrete wealth itself. If money can grow forever at compound interest, then, presumably, so can wealth; if money flows in a circle, then, presumably, so can wealth.[93] The circular-flow theory has taken a characteristic of money and overgeneralized it into a basic coordinate for the economic process. Debt has no physical limit, whereas the repayment of debt in terms of real wealth faces the limits inevitably and irreversibly imposed by the second law of thermodynamics. The open-system coevolutionary economic paradigm demands this conceptualization.

We have unfortunately become addicted to extrapolating the growth of wealth at compound interest into the indefinite future. Add to that the fact that evidence of sociocultural or physical limits to growth are a matter of some debate, occasionally interpreted as mere bottlenecks to be resolved by technical innovation, and the Pigouvian conclusion is reached that the circular flow is unencumbered.

In an expression of market mentality, technified society has accepted the myth that economic growth reduces social divisiveness and brings about happiness. It is viewed as a precondition for social development and the motive force behind psychological aspirations and human self-fulfillment. Thus, the logic of the development of capital reduces to a logic of growth that loops back on itself, finding justification in its own coherence.

It is an autojustified system wherein redistributive justice is judiciously avoided. There is nothing in the price-making market system that can identify the best distribution of juridical rights according to the criterion of justice, for Pareto optimality is "ethics-free"; independent of the distribution of property rights of physical resources, i.e., there is Pareto-efficient allocation for any distribution, including an unjust distribution. Daly notes cautiously that the social goal of distributive justice must be pursued independently of, though not necessarily in conflict with, the price-making market system. Nor is there anything that allows the price-making market system to determine the best scale of throughput according to ecological criteria of sustainability. Just as a Pareto-optimal allocation may coexist with a socially unjust distribution, so may it coexist with an ecologically unsustainable scale.[94] In this connection, "economics has been both too materialistic, and not materialistic enough. In ignoring the ultimate means and the laws of thermodynamics, it has been insufficiently materialist. In ignoring the Ultimate End ethics, it has been too materialistic."[95] To some extent the issue of sustainability pertains to intergenerational distributive justice. To disregard future wealth without referring to the biophysical coordinates of wealth is to disregard the underlying coevolutionary basis of the livelihood of man.

Insofar as redistributive justice is precluded and poverty is a reality, conventional knowledge accords priority to growth. The circular flow must continually expand, not only to make us "richer" but also to keep us fully employed. If, *ceterus paribus*, the throughput lags behind circular flow, then inflation ensues. If inflation becomes too onerous, then the circular flow must be slowed down, giving rise to unemployment, or a technological imperative manifests itself in our search for overcoming the bottleneck that constrains growth in throughput. And in this connection national accountancy is incapable of signaling the point at which the conventional priority and imperative of economic growth become counterproductive.

The market by itself has no criterion by which to limit its scale of operation vis-à-vis the physical and social environments. Its basic thrust, amplified by Keynesian policies, is toward continuous growth in GNP, which, under the present conventions of national accounting, implies a growing throughput.[96]

The self-equilibrating circular-flow theory is seriously incomplete, not only from its Natural Philosophy heritage, but also because it focuses on the flow of exchange-values (i.e., money), rather than throughput of low-entropy natural resources from which all goods and services are ultimately derived. We should count only service as income and that which renders service is capital.[97] In so doing we recognize that physical capital always depreciates (from entropy) and that its continual maintenance and replacement is a cost. The cost of maintaining capital intact must not be counted as a part of the net national dividend. Fisher's basic magnitudes (the capital stock, the service it renders, and the throughput it requires for maintenance) involve no circular flows. Stock, by definition, does not flow (though it does degrade entropically); service is a nontransferrable psychic experience and cannot flow; and low-entropy throughput is a flow, but is unidirectional, not circular.

Service is the satisfaction experienced when wants are filled. It corresponds to "psychic income" in Fisher's sense in which service is yielded by the stock. The quantity and quality of the stock determine the intensity of service. Service is yielded over a period of time and, thus, appears to be a flow magnitude. However, unlike physical flows, service, being a psychic flux, cannot be accumulated. And, according to Georgescu-Roegen, it is this psychic flux that is the ultimate economic output. Service (net psychic income) is the final benefit of economic activity, whereas, throughput (an entropic physical flow) is the final cost. The throughput flow does not yield services directly; it must first be accumulated and fashioned into a stock of useful artifacts (capital). All services are yielded by stocks, not flows—a fact that is sometimes obscured, according to Daly, because some stocks are short-lived and their services seem to stem from their destruction (but this is an illusion).[98]

Bernstein notes that Daly's net psychic income is the final benefit of economic activity, and that this is yielded by stocks of capital maintained by material flows.[99] The capacity of the natural environment to provide these flows without serious degradation is limited; that is, certain natural goods and services are scarce as well as essential and irreplaceable. A distributive mechanism based on consumer's willingness to pay does not recognize this. It treats natural goods and services as it does all other economic goods—as relatively scarce. It assumes that, as the price of scarce resources increases, it is always possible to substitute other more abundant resources. This method of valuing environmental goods and services can lead to an efficient allocation of ever-declining resources, but it displays no awareness of nonlinear phenomena, of ecological thresholds of viability of intergenerational distribution. "Current market prices do not necessarily reflect strategic lines of economic development."[100]

"Nature imposes particular scarcities, not an inescapable general scarcity."[101] Thus, only relative scarcity is of concern, and even that is in the process of being overcome:

> Advances in fundamental science have made it possible to take advantage of the uniformity of matter/energy—a uniformity that makes it feasible, without

> preassignable limit, to escape the quantitative constraints imposed by the character of the Earth's crust. . . . Science, by making the resource base more homogeneous, erases the restrictions once thought to reside in the lack of homogeneity. In a neo-Ricardian world, it seems, the particular resources with which one starts increasingly become a matter of indifference. The reservation of particular resources for later use, therefore, may contribute little to the welfare of future generations.[102]

Unfortunately for the economic analysis of growth, it is not the homogeneity of matter-energy that makes for usefulness, but precisely the opposite. If all materials and all energy were uniformly distributed in thermodynamic equilibrium, the resulting "resource base" would be no resource at all. It is precisely the nonuniformity, or differences in concentration and temperature, which constitutes a so-called gradient, that makes for usefulness. The mere fact that all matter-energy may ultimately consist of the same basic building blocks is of little significance if it is the potential for ordering those blocks that is ultimately scarce, as the entropy law tells us is the case. Only Maxwell's "Sorting Demon" could turn a lukewarm soup of electrons, protons, neutrons, quarks, and whatnot into a resource. And the entropy law tells us that Maxwell's Demon cannot exist. In other words, nature really does impose "an inescapable general scarcity of use values." It is a serious delusion to believe otherwise.

Ribald statements such as the one above are not exceptional in learned journals. We might reflect on the first sentence of the 1976 *Journal of Economic Literature* survey of contributions to environmental economics which reads: "Man has probably always worried about his environment because he was once totally dependent on it." Contrary to the implication, man's dependence on the Biosphere is still quite total, and is overwhelmingly likely to remain so.[103] Nevertheless, Robert Solow assures us that, thanks to "the productivity of natural resources increasing more or less exponentially over time," it is to be expected that "the world can, in effect, get along without natural resources."[104]

In view of Solow's sophomoric statement it is evidently impossible to insist too strongly that, in Soddy's words,

> life derives the whole of its physical energy or power, not from anything self-contained in living matter, and still less from an external deity, but solely from the inanimate world. It is dependent for all the necessities of its physical continuance primarily on the principles of the steam-engine. The principles and ethics of human convention must not run counter to those of thermodynamics.[105]

A fetishistic theory of economic analysis and a price mechanism based on relative scarcity ignores the crucial facts that ecosystems are nonlinear systems that differ in resilience to stress and have thresholds of disturbance beyond which radical changes occur. As these thresholds are approached, the alleged continuity upon which marginal analysis is grounded becomes meaningless, and

Alfred Marshall's erroneous motto that "nature does not make jumps" and most of neoclassical marginalist economics becomes inapplicable. The "marginal" cost of one more step may be to fall over the precipice. As many of the interactions between ecological and economic systems display these same characteristics, any economic approach to the natural environment that fails to recognize this will continue to be surprised by the sudden disappearance of natural goods and services.[106]

Living Systems and Economic Systems:
Political Economy in the Broad Sense

While Sraffa and other theorists sought to reconstruct production theory on the basis of classical models, a number of other economists have tried to explicitly reframe economic issues around general evolutionary and organizational principles as referred to by Bogdanov and Bertalanffy. The concept of the steady state of "living systems" is present not only in the work of general system theorists such as Bertalanffy, but also increasingly among economists such as Boulding, Daly, Norgaard, Passet, and Tamanoi. For instance, the French economist René Passet notes that the task is not to project living systems as the model of social organization, but to seek those principles of organization that make it possible for living systems to reproduce and evolve within a changing environment. In this connection, even Marshall alluded that biology is an advance on mechanicalism in exploring that approach.[107]

Imploring economists to adopt a broader understanding of the rich integration of the Biosphere and the livelihood of man, Passet states:

> We find ourselves at the intersection of several disciplines. The economist acquires tools that will permit him to enter into dialogues with ecologists, physicists and biologists, and to benefit from the knowledge that each can bring from his own discipline. Otherwise he condemns himself to be unable to take into account any of the consequences that economic activity brings to its environment. This dialogue is a prerequisite of survival.[108]

Few would now deny that the *economy* of any life-process is fundamentally constrained, not only by the laws of mechanics, but also by the second law of thermodynamics. However, if the economy is a living system, as Bogdanov, and more recently H. Daly, R. Passet, and Y. Tamanoi, maintained, then the economic process is entropic and not perpetual; its reference image should be the digestive system and not the circular flow. Herman Daly, consistent with René Passet and together with Y. Tamanoi, has commented that it is appropriate to refer to the economic process as a living process. The concept of the economy as an entropic open system is far removed from Lionel Robbins's concept of "economic."

Metabolism and the Economic Process

While both ecology and economics derived from the same Greek root, *oikos*, meaning household, these sciences have shared little with respect to methodology and their scope of analysis. From the root word one would suspect that each science is devoted to the study of households, one to the household of nature, the other to the household of man; both deal with the study of the laws of interactions among different species of our respective households. One of the central concerns of ecology is the way in which natural species earn their living— that is, attain the throughput necessary for their survival. Economic science similarly is concerned with how man earns his living. Both ecology and economic science go far beyond this initial concept and devote themselves to a study of how the interaction of individuals and species constitutes a total system. The network of material, energy, and information transformations that constitutes the livelihood of man (i.e., the econosphere), and the global complex of ecological interactions (i.e., the Biosphere), are ultimately interconnected subsystems of the Biosphere. Nonetheless, ecology and economic science have had relatively little contact; with but a few exceptions, these two life sciences have shared little.

Both ecology and economic science are life sciences and deal with production and distribution among a complex of producers and consumers. Underlying both ecological and economic processes is the transformation of energy and matter that is fundamental to all natural and social events; in effect nothing happens without some energy potential to explain its occurrence.

Energy from the sun drives all natural cycles and has provided the very conditions from which life itself sprang. Through evolution, the Biosphere has developed complex paths to tap the sun's energy, principally through photosynthesis. In turn, the energy stored by plants has allowed for the evolution of more complex and varied organisms. Today, human societies have become increasingly dependent upon this photosynthetic storage-energy in the form of fossil fuels, which are the lifeline to modern industrial societies. Insofar as energy and material transformations underlie these processes, both ecology and the economy must comply with the fundamental energy constraints imposed by the Biosphere. Clearly, energy use, natural resource availability, and global ecology have become critical issues in the life of modern societies. The laws of the transformation of energy and matter, as well as the principles of ecosystems, are fundamental constraints to the economy. They delineate the boundaries to economic processes and set the basis for a view of economic activity more closely integrated to other natural processes in the Biosphere.

Through eons of evolution, the Biosphere has developed complex energy webs based primarily on photosynthesis to tap the sun's energy. The energy stored by the plants has allowed for more complex and varied organisms to evolve. In biology, metabolism is presented as a physical and chemical transformation process, whereby energy is employed to assimilate materials through anabolism and breaks them down through catabolism releasing degraded energy (high entropy) in the process. The corresponding reference image (see Figure 3.2) is in marked contrast to the circular flow.

The close similarity of the life-process of metabolism (anabolism and catabolism) with that of the economic process (production and consumption) was present in the analysis of Marx[109] and made explicit by N.I. Bukharin.[110] It has more recently been reasserted by Passet.[111]

Bukharin, borrowing the concept of the open system from A.A. Bogdanov, and the concept of metabolism from Marx, wrote in his *Historical Materialism* of 1925 that "the . . . contact between society and nature, i.e., the abstraction of energy from nature is a material process. . . . This material process of 'metabolism' between society and nature is the fundamental relation between environment and system, between 'external conditions' and human society."[112] He went on to further clarify his analogy by asserting that

> the metabolism between man and nature consists . . . in the transfer of material energy from external nature to society; the expenditure of human energy (production) is an extraction of energy from nature, energy which is to be added to society (distribution of products between the members of society) and appropriated by society (consumption); this appropriation is the basis for further expenditure, etc., the wheel of reproduction is constantly in motion.[113]

Presenting an argument apparent in the earlier work of Bukharin and conspicuous in Bertalanffy's concept of the open system, Herman Daly has observed that

> from a strictly physical point of view, the maintenance of . . . stocks is accomplished by . . . the importation of low-entropy matter-energy from the environment and the exportation of high-entropy matter-energy (wastes) back to the environment. Both people and commodities are entropy converters, capable of mutually dependent self-renewal as long as the supply of low-entropy holds out.[114]

The economy is an open living system in which degraded matter-energy must be expelled from the economic process into the environment, from which new, useful matter and energy must be appropriated. The ecosystem recycles many human and industrial waste materials through biogeochemical cycles powered by the sun, so some waste materials eventually do get returned as fresh inputs. Replenishment of the physical basis of life is not a circular affair, it is vitally dependent upon a continuous flow of low entropy. This constitutes an environmental service external to the economic process, transient to the circular flow of money in the economy.

In this connection, Kenneth Boulding has attempted to provide a synthesis of selected elements of both classical and neoclassical economic theory with Ludwig von Bertalanffy's concept of *Fleissgleichgewicht* and its corresponding ana-

Figure 3.2. **Metabolic Model of the Economic Process**

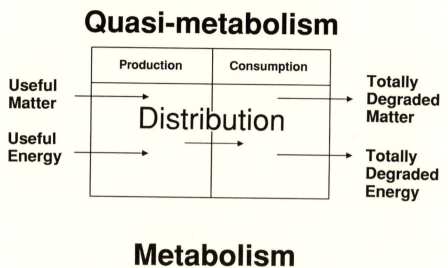

Quasi-metabolism

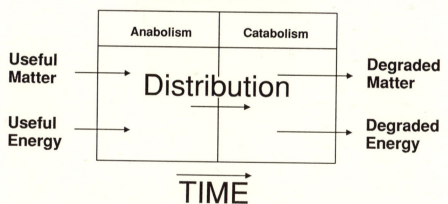

lytical categories.[115] Arguably, Boulding's adaptation of Bertalanffy's concept of open systems is analytically comparable to a number of his contemporaries. It at once delineates the locus of economic relations from Biospheric ones and yet situates the economy within the Biosphere. Moreover, consistent with the image present in the earlier analyses of Ostwald and Soddy, Boulding extrapolates the proposition that "it is throughput of energy in the earth that made evolution itself possible,"[116] and asserts that energy throughput is also fundamental to economic development. Moreover,

> from the point of view of the energy system, the econosphere involves inputs of available energy ... which are necessary in order to create the material throughput and to move matter from the non-economic set into the economic

set or even out of it again; and energy itself is given off by the system in a less available form, mostly in the form of heat.[117]

Consistent with the earlier propositions of Soddy, Boulding suggests a broader view and precisely locates the livelihood of man as embedded within a network of material balances that transcends institutional variants.[118] Though Boulding situates the economy within the Biosphere, the extent to which the economy is embedded within society is a different matter. He writes:

> Thus we see the econosphere as a material process involving the discovery and mining of fossil fuels, ores, etc., and at the other end a process by which the effluents of the system are passed out into noneconomic reservoirs—for instance, the atmosphere and the oceans—which are not appropriated and do not enter in the exchange system.[119]

Alfred Lotka obscurely refers to anabolic structuring processes as predominant over catabolic destructuring of organized matter.[120] "Organisms subject the elements that they borrow from the environment to an intense chemical activity—metabolism—that transforms them into assimilable forms adapted to the requirements of its survival, and of its development."[121] The question arises: How do economic and metabolic processes fit together? Clearly metabolism is partly contained within the economic subprocess of consumption. Whereas the material inputs that enter into metabolic processes generally are not totally degraded and, thus, can be further consumed, the ultimate physical output of the economic process is totally degraded matter-energy; in Marx's term, "devil's dust." Natural metabolic processes are adapted to the imperatives of life itself, whereas the structuring role and "metabolics" of artificially animated systems serve detached technological imperatives.[122] And, it is for this reason that we refer to techno-economic systems as being "quasi-metabolic." The total economic process may be viewed as a subprocess of the consuming side of the total ecological life process. The producing side of the latter consists mainly of photosynthesis carried on by green plants, which draw their inputs from the physical environment of air, soil, and sunlight.

The metabolic process, as identified by Bukharin in the livelihood of man, is illustrated in Figure 3.2.

This conceptual reference image has been reinforced by Norgaard, who writes that sociosystems and ecosystems are maintained through numerous feedback mechanisms, and that the two systems coevolve when at least one feedback is changed and an ongoing reciprocal process of change is initiated. One of the perversions of this process, according to Norgaard, is that feedbacks that previously sustained the stability of the ecosystem are subsumed by, or internalized by, the social system and the economic system in particular.[123] This may be viewed as a manifestation of the totalizing logic of capital.

For instance, the ecologist E. Odum and the biologist H. Laborit characterize technified agricultural development as a transformation of a natural ecosystem to one of reduced numbers of species characterized by a lower efficiency of nutrient recycling, higher, but less stable rates of production, and lower biomass stocks relative to natural conditions.[124] And as man adapts an ecosystem to suit his own needs, as Vernadsky indicated, he intervenes in some of the nutrient and biogeochemical cycles and disturbs some of the equilibrating mechanisms that had evolved with the natural systems.

Both ecological and economic systems involve a system of material exchanges among their various individuals and species. That economic principles are relevant to the study of ecology is by no means a new idea. H.G. Wells, G.P. Wells, and Julian Huxley, in their treatise *The Science of Life*, defined ecology as biological economics or an extension of economics to the whole world of life. For these authors, economics is "the science of social substance, of needs and their satisfactions of work and wealth. It tries to elucidate the relations of producers, dealer, and consumer in the human community and shows how the whole system carries on."[125]

In the converse case of economics, this system of exchange may be symbolized, according to Boulding and Daly, in the price-making market system.[126]

Boulding describes economic development in evolutionary terms by identifying isomorphisms and ecological systems along the lines suggested by Bertalanffy.[127] In other words, Boulding's understanding of evolutionary economics is that it is analogous to the dynamics of ecological systems. This amounts to saying that the dynamics of economic systems are formally consistent with those of ecosystems.

Taking a page from Bertalanffy's *Problems of Life*, and apparently disregarding institutionalism, Boulding notes that the market establishes the set of rates of exchange of different commodities with each other and the system resolves itself into a state of general equilibrium. In the case of ecological systems, the exchange locates itself within the metabolic systems and trophic chains—that is, the network of inputs and outputs of different individuals, organisms, or species.[128]

A Substantive Open-System Model

For those who adhere to the open-systems perspective and locate economic activity within the confines of the sociosphere and the Biosphere, their analysis embodies elements of a Neo-Physiocratic mode of thought characterized by a return to an ethos long forsaken by economic theorists.

Y. Tamanoi, a student of the Japanese Marxist Uno, has advocated the study of "the economy in the broad sense." This point of view is convergent both with a socio-cybernetic model and with the concept of the economy as a living system. In a manner familiar to us through the evolution of A.A. Bogdanov's thought, and following N. Georgescu-Roegen, Tamanoi and his coauthors have taken as their point of departure a critique of neoclassical, Marxian, and Keynesian economic theories,[129] which are alleged to address economic activities "narrowly defined." Tamanoi has remarked that

> the purpose of Marx's critique of political economy is to reveal the historically specific nature of the capitalist society in the light of the dialectic of capital. In doing this, Marx presupposes a purely capitalist society in which human activities follow the economizing principle of man (Homo oeconomicus) and in which natural phenomena abide by Newtonian physics which postulates the uniform and reversible pure-space. In such a society which, in actuality, is the premise for both Marxian political economy and neoclassical economics, market economy operates with little regard for [the category of] "life." ... By concentrating on the study of market economy, therefore, economists have viewed nature as a mechanical object . . . and human beings as abstract.[130]

Tamanoi's substantive economic thought was influenced in particular ways by Karl Polanyi's earlier institutional analysis.[131] That Polanyi was an inspiration is evident in Tamanoi's comment that in contrast to the economistic perspective, human economy is merely a name for our living activities. The substantive distinction makes it imperative for the development of a methodology of "the economy in the broad sense which clearly sheds light on [the] much neglected category of life."[132] But, here too, we find a similarity with A.A. Bogdanov who, in his 1902 article *The Development of Life in Nature and Society*, attempted to reformulate Marxism on the basis of open-systems thinking.[133]

Whereas Bogdanov reached his conclusions on the basis of theoretical studies, Tamanoi understood only too well the empirical evidence before him. In this connection it is worth noting that the classical economists, i.e., Ricardo, thought that the steady state economy would encounter limits on the depletion side (the law of increasing cost or decreasing returns), but, in fact, the main limits seem to be occurring on the pollution side. In effect, pollution provides another foundation for the law of increasing costs, but it has received little attention in this regard, since pollution costs are social, whereas depletion costs are usually private. On the input side, and within particular contexts, the environment may be partitioned into spheres of private ownership. Depletion of the environment coincides, to some degree, with depletion of the owner's wealth and inspires at least a minimum of stewardship. On the output side, however, the waste absorption capacity of the environment is not subject to partitioning and private ownership. However, beginning in the middle of the 1960s, a number of analysts recognized that it was impossible to disregard the aspect of production as the generator of disutilities (i.e., wastes), insofar as they began to undermine the very condition of use-value production and threaten life itself. To a certain extent this understanding was apparent in J.K. Galbraith's speculation that the limit of economic growth may well lie, not in the physical scarcity of resources, but in spatial scarcity of places to dispose of the waste by-products of the economic process.[134] Kenneth Boulding arrived at a similar conclusion, noting that

> every living organism and every social organization has a "throughput" of both energy and materials. In a total closed system the input of one part, such as an organism, has to be the output of other parts. A developed economy . . . involves a linear movement from fossil fuels and ores to pollution and dumps, but this is something that obviously cannot go on for very long.[135]

While Galbraith declined to elaborate on this reference image, and, though Boulding referred to it in a general sense,[136] Tamanoi understood that the production of use-values had changed into the annihilation of living nature and the alienation of labor. Having described this situation in Hegelian terms as "the phase of the object's self-negation,"[137] Tamanoi noted: "[The] production of products presupposes the production of wastes. In other words, the repeatability of production, or reproduction, is absolutely dependent on the irreversible process of waste generation. [It is from this realization that we are] brought to the entropy problem."[138]

Tamanoi's search for the "economy in the broad sense" began, like Bogdanov's, Soddy's, and Georgescu-Roegen's analyses, with a criticism of mechanistic economic theory. Tamanoi noted that

> while the Walrasian general equilibrium approach has its own merit within a certain limit, it is blind to the entropy generation during the process in which the economy gropes for the said equilibrium, for it is based on the Newtonian mechanics only applicable to the analysis of lifeless things. Now that the entire world faces severe environmental disruptions to the unprecedented extent, we cannot dwell on such a mechanistic utopia.[139]

Having rejected mechanicalism, Tamanoi sought a redefinition of the concept of production. He remarked that in both Marxian and neoclassical economic theory production has been interpreted as a benign process between inputs and outputs. In particular, Walras's production theory is a heroic simplification which reduces production to a benign and economically effective use of inputs. Omitting a broader analysis it reduces production to a mere technical expression of the cost-and-profit calculus. Joseph Schumpeter regarded it as nothing less than a theory presenting the mechanism of pure competition, allocating the "services" of different kinds and qualities of natural agents, labor power, and produced means of production. This theory of allocation is formally identical to price theory.[140]

Walrasian models occupy an extreme in assuming the existence of some arbitrary large list of resources of different qualities which are somehow combined together to yield an output. This approach says almost nothing about the constraints on production except to assume economic scarcity, convexity, and constant returns to scale in the combinations of inputs and techniques. No attention is paid to the conservation of mass and energy, the entropic nature of energy use, or specific features of particular production processes. Robert Solow, a neo-Walrasian, has defended growth by directly appealing to increasing resource productivity. Solow concludes that "there is really no reason why we should not think of the productivity of natural resources as increasing more or less exponentially over time."[141] This remarkable conclusion, if true, would be a boon to those who advocate limiting the throughput of resources, because it would mean that such a limit is totally consistent with continued exponential growth in GNP.

Atsushi Tsuchida, a physicist and associate of Tamanoi, notes that

> what makes it possible for a living organism to maintain a low-entropy state is, in fact, that it has the ability to discard into the outside of its body the entropy increment which it produces by living. A system which has the ability to discard the entropy increase into its environment is called an open system. Hence, the necessary condition for a living system is that it has to constitute an open system.[142]

This concept was derived from E. Schrödinger's definition of a living system.[143] It achieves a unity with Bertalanffy's general systems concept and with Bogdanov's Tektology.

According to Bertalanffy and Schrödinger, the reproduction of living systems requires that dissipated energy eventually leave the system. Passet notes that it may do this in three different ways:

> (1) if it is fully consumed in non-productive expenditures or rechanneled towards the outside, the system, which could then neither grow nor diversify itself, maintains itself in a state of stagnation;
> (2) if it feeds a simple quantitative increase in the magnitude of variables without any perceptible action on the system's structure, it maintains a process of growth; and
> (3) if it is utilized in order to bring about a quantitative growth of significant variables, and at the same time create new activities, that is, diversify and complexify the system, it will feed a process that is described as development.[144]

Consistent with Bertalanffy's and Schrödinger's concept of an open living system, Tamanoi, according to Murota, noted that "for an open system to be a living system, it has to be co-existent with other open-systems."[145] This is a specific instance of what Kamarýt considers to be a more general condition, which we shall address in Chapter 4.

Once again paralleling Bertalanffy, Tamanoi defines life as the subjective and active process of discarding low entropy outside the boundaries of the system. He defined a living system as independent and subjective and based on an ecosystem. Locating the livelihood of man within ecosystems, Tamanoi effectively incorporated the economy's artificial metabolism within that of ecosystems. His reference image was not the alienation of nature, but the promotion of a coevolutionary interdependence of the economy with nature.[146]

Tamanoi's quasi-metabolic argument focuses on the output side of the process. In so doing he notes that "no work would be done for lack of available energy. In order, therefore, to sustain production processes, the system must be kept open. This requires that high-entropy objects must be somehow carried away from the system. In other words, a sustainable production-process presupposes the disposal of entropy."[147]

Similar to F. Soddy's charge that the economy may be likened to a heat engine, Tamanoi asserts that production is fundamentally a thermal phenomenon, and the closely related concept of entropy explains production as a process of generating negative outputs. But Soddy merely referred to the economy as a heat engine and did not examine the thermodynamic implications at the level of the Biosphere.[148] This task fell to other analysts. The release of heat, i.e., dissipated energy, through living was addressed by Tamanoi, who, together with Tsuchida, identified the water cycle as a global and interlocking external feedback which further assures the existence of living systems. Earth's mechanism of entropy disposal "is the low temperature radiation from the upper layer of the atmosphere to the outer space. Associated with the heat transfer, the global water cycle and air's convection transfer the entropy from the Earth's surface to the upper layer of the atmosphere. The combination of these cycles on the Earth constitutes a heat engine."[149]

Contrary to the image related by K. Boulding of the "spaceship earth" as a closed system, Murota, on the basis of Tsuchida's analysis, asserts that the earth is an open system, a "heat engine" disposing entropy to space through the global water cycle. It is this feature that according to Murota, accounts for the earth being an open self-reproducing system.[150]

Having postulated the critical importance of the water cycle, Murota then argues that regional interruptions in that cycle jeopardize the fundamental basis of all living systems, including the economy of man. Indeed, Kawamiya effectively claims that Bertalanffy's notion of flowing open systems is a condition applying not only to "individual organisms but to their aggregates at all levels."[151] Consequently, the Bertalanffy–Schrödinger–Tsuchida concept of a living system enables us to distinguish more clearly between the two broad categories of production: agriculture and industry.

Marx allegedly committed an oversight by indiscriminately extending the laws of a capitalist society to the economy of a rural, agricultural society—an understanding that Tamanoi sought to avoid.

> The fundamental defect of conventional theories ... can be found in the total disregard of primary industry and of the original meaning of the latter. Primary industry is engaged in the maintenance and the renewal of human life. And from this point of view, agriculture, forestry, livestock farming and fishing are to be clearly distinguished from other industries. They should be considered as primary industry in the literal sense.[152]

As philosophically stimulating and analytically interesting as Tamanoi's contribution to the broadening of economic thought is, his is but one of a number of continuing attempts to provide a biophysical basis to economic analysis.

**Models of the Biophysical Approach
to the Economic Process**

The overwhelming diversity and the interconnectedness of socioeconomic and physicochemical relationships in Biospheric modeling raises a methodological problem for analysts. Since those analysts engaged in modeling economy–energy–environment interfaces are drawn from social sciences, engineering, and mathematical and physical sciences, a variety of approaches flourish. They reflect the different perspectives and frameworks of the various disciplines.

Lakshmanan and Ratick remark that the analytical view of conventional economic thought generally depends on regarding the price-making market and occasionally technology as dynamic self-correcting forces.[153] The analysts of the ecological processes emphasize the environmental processes of emission, transport, and abatement of pollutants. The energy technologists focus their attention (in an Ostwaldian fashion) on the description of energy flows, conversion efficiencies of different energy forms, and occasionally on engineering studies of different technologies. The distinctions suggested above shall become apparent in the following presentations.

The diagrams presented in Figure 3.3 attempt to illustrate the emergent interactive view of social and economic activity with nature. The central image related by such models is that our "econosphere" is not merely one of distribution of exchange-values among men, but one of elliptical orbits through interdependent Biospheric and energy sectors.

It is of interest to note that the diagrams are used by the different scientists working in diverse fields, yet all are concerned with global problems in a biophysical "post-Ricardian" context.

W. Stumm, a chemist interested in biogeochemical cycles and aquatic chemistry, emphasizes this aspect, but includes energy inputs and transformations as well as economic and political elements. Herman Daly aims to show the need to maintain an adequate stock of productive assets by means of a low rate of maintenance throughput from the ecosystem. He further argues for a balance between the damage done to ecosystems by productive activity and residual pollutants, and the benefits of additional production. Barry Commoner, a biologist, uses resources and energy flow from the ecosystem to the production system, where they are combined with labor and capital from the economic system. Resources are taken from the environment and pollution and heat are returned. The economic system distributes the output of production, and provides signals of how much to produce. The trouble, Commoner argues, is that the relationship is the wrong way about. It is the economic system that imposes requirements on the ecosystems, and not the other way around. The diagrams of Howard Odum, with their linkage of energy flows, material flows, and monetary counter flows, indicate that economic transactions cover only a small part of the total life process.[154]

Generally, the more inclusive assessment present in energy environmental modeling is traceable to the basic structure of economy–energy–environment interactions. Encompassed within the physical processes of the Biosphere are a large number of interesting interactions. Examples of such processes, apparent in the diagrams of Figure 3.3, are the emissions of pollutants and their spatial diffusion in the environmental media, the flow of low-entropy matter energy, as well as alternative technological processes.

According to the American engineer and systems analyst Herman Koenig man's history may be described as a series of self-inflicted divorces from his perceived dependence on those natural ecosystems that supply his material needs. During the agricultural revolution, man was divorced from a dependence on natural ecosystems for food. The industrial revolution, tapping ancient ecosystems as a source of energy, separated man in particular ways from a dependence on living ecosystems for energy. By sheer weight of numbers and his technological power, technified society is affecting the rhythms of the Biosphere. No longer merely responding to Biospheric patterns, the techno-economic system is instrumental in the processes that are reshaping them. "The problem of determining what these patterns shall be and how to regulate them may be the most crucial test ever faced by industrialized society."[155]

Consistent with W.S. Jevon's investigation of 1865 into the singular role of coal in England's historic and institutional development, Frederick Cottrell, a sociologist, sought to trace man's use of energy from low-yield organic sources to more complicated but high-yield non-organic (artificial) forms. His central synthetic proposition was that the amounts and types of energy employed are ubiquitous in conditioning man's material, ethical, psychological, political, and social existence.[156]

While Cottrell's perspective parallels in a number of ways the earlier analysis of Frederick Soddy and Alfred Lotka, it is more closely related to that of the anthropologist L.A. White.[157] White's analysis of the role of energy in the development of culture was in turn influenced not only by Wilhelm Ostwald, but also by Schrödinger. Ostwald expressed the opinion that "culture advances as the amount of energy harnessed per capita per year increases, or as the efficiency or economy of the means of controlling energy is increased, or both."[158] While Schrödinger noted that: "[This] law [i.e., the second law of thermodynamics] governs all physical and chemical processes, even if they result in the most intricate and tangled phenomena, such as organic life, the genesis of a complicated world of organisms from primitive beginnings [and] the rise and growth of human cultures."[159]

On the basis of Ostwald's and Schrödinger's analysis, L.A. White asserted that "the principles and laws of thermodynamics are applicable to cultural systems as they are to other material systems." Several pages later we read that "cultural systems operate by transforming [energy] in the production of human need-serving goods and services."[160] White insisted that a social system might well be defined as the way in which a society makes use of its particular technology in various life-sustaining processes. Nonetheless,

the effect of technology upon social organization is ... exercised directly

Figure 3.3. **Integrated Biospheric–Socioeconomic Models**

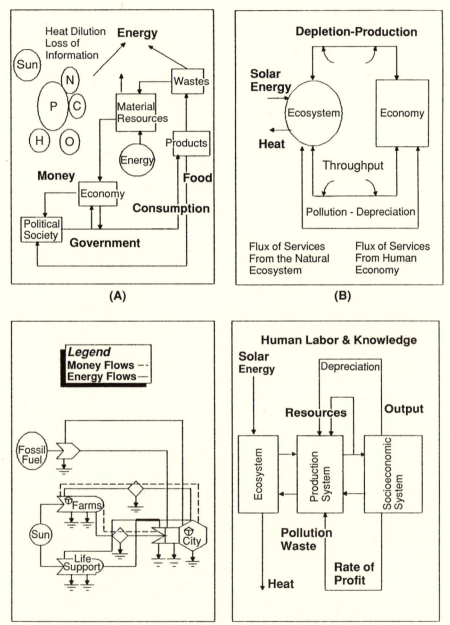

through the use of tools . . . and indirectly in the process of interrelating the social patterns formed directly by the technology.

Mechanical instruments are indeed essential. But they are merely the vehicle, the scaffolding, the skeleton; energy is the dynamic, living force that animates cultural systems and develops them into higher levels and forms.[161]

While Cottrell's analysis followed White's, it also parallels, in novel ways, Karl Polanyi's analysis in *The Great Transformation*.[162] Whereas in Polanyi's analysis technological mutation was a fundamental stimulus for institutional change, Cottrell asserts that the technological development of artificial converters of energy led to further significant changes in political and socioeconomic organization. It favored those regions possessing high quality low-entropy energy (i.e., coal, oil, gas, and falling water), over those areas confined to the use of energy gained primarily from organic sources.

The autocatalytic processes that pertain to energy conversion in ecological systems, according to Cottrell, manifest themselves historically in social systems as well. He writes:

[If] a social structure is successful in functioning under changed conditions it also gives direction to the new flow of energy, with more or less permanent effects. A slight initial push early in the development of a social structure that subsequently succeeds in converting a large amount of energy gives direction to that much greater force, which in turn continues to magnify the effects of the initial influence.[163]

In his analysis of the Ricardian framework, Cottrell, like F. Soddy, notes that there was a fundamental failure on the part of economic theorists to account for non-organic sources of energy. He reaches this conclusion in the following manner: The law of comparative advantage was developed to prove that differentials in the cost of production, based on the productivity of labor, justify nothing less than a world market, where labor subdivision could be carried out extensively. Thus, values measured in the market must not be made subordinate to any other values, lest labor's productivity thereby be reduced.

Briefly, Cottrell, following Polanyi, infers that the process of disembedding finalities was instituted. For instance, according to Cottrell, under the influence of Malthusian pressure workers were forced to compete within the newly institutionalized context of the price-making market until their wages just equaled subsistence costs. Additionally, differential richness of land in producing food established the alleged basis for "rent," thereby securing the cooperation of the landowner. Cottrell further notes that the system, though complete, was flawed, for it was based on man's historic experience with the exploitation of organic sources of energy. The amount of physical power available to archaic societies was expressed in multiples of the average man's working time and metabolic energy.[164] Though endowed with little physical power, man, nonetheless, built temples, moved mountains, wove cloth, and waged wars. Power was limited and was proportional to population.

Whereas, historically man and nature were the principal "converters" of energy, with the Industrial Revolution complex machinery progressively assumed the dominant role of accelerating the process of change. Conventional economic theory (i.e., Ricardian), failed to account adequately for non-organic or artificial forms of energy. This shortcoming in Ricardian analysis is alleged to be present in Marxian theory, and arose from the indiscriminate attribution of the marked increase in productivity, not to non-organic forms of energy sources, but to "labor."

While L.A. White and Fred Cottrell have extended Ostwald's original insight into socioeconomic energetics, and while these efforts are of continuing interest, other analysts are concerned with formulating models of the cybernetics of technico-ecological processes.

Technico-Ecological Engineering

The more recent view expressed by Herman Koenig is consistent with that of earlier analysts (see Figure 3.4).

Consistent with Bertalanffy's general system theory and Y. Tamanoi's substantive perspective, Koenig comments that until this point in history the industrial, agricultural, and energy-generating sectors of the economy have not been designed as integral parts of the total ecosystem with any particular ecosystem design objective or mass-energy equilibrium state in mind. To the contrary, the physical and technological designs, and the economic rewards that allegedly motivate them, were based on a concept of the environment both as an infinite source and as an infinite "sink." Moreover, the overall system of economic-ecological interaction has evolved into an "once-through" system whose mass-energy equilibrium state is at best socially undesirable and at worst ecologically disastrous.[165] Such systems are not ecologically viable in the long term. It is precisely their contradictions with the laws of material and energy balance under the pressures of an expanding human population that are generating the environmental crisis.

With Herman Koenig's analysis there emerges a spatial dimension not explicitly present in earlier analysis. He infers that in the first phase of industrialization ecological consequences were relatively confined and consequently did not figure in economic calculations.[166] However, and as we have already noted, as the scale of production activities increased the "entropy problem" achieved a global scale, and, insofar as it impacts economic calculations, it is progressively being addressed by economic science.[167]

However, within the context of the price-making market, the monetary costs assigned to pollutants discharged into an ecosystem are all taken as zero, and costs assigned to materials extracted from the geosphere are based on short-term opportunities rather than long-term ecological considerations. To assign a zero value to material exchange rates with the natural environment is to assume implicitly that the environment has an unbounded capacity to process externali-

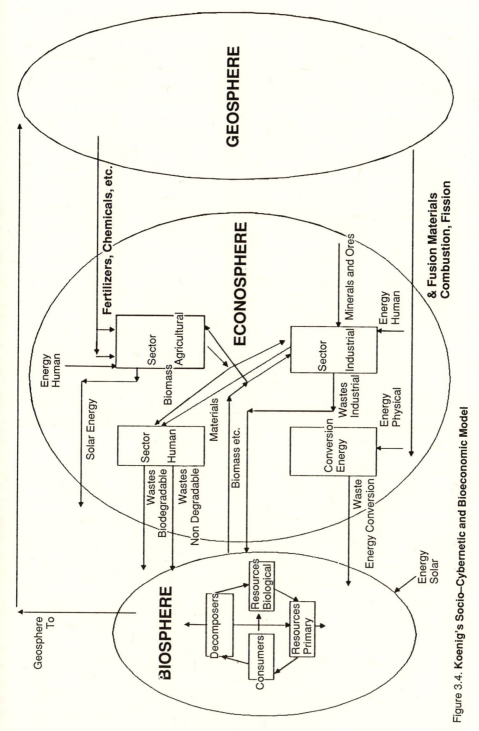

Figure 3.4. Koenig's Socio–Cybernetic and Bioeconomic Model

ties of industrial activities, or that we can safely disregard the dynamics of the Biosphere altogether.

Under these circumstances the economic equilibrium state of the ecosystem fails to correspond to desirable mass-energy equilibrium states. Unless special efforts are made to restructure the economy substantially, latent threats may manifest themselves in particularly harmful ways. Herein is the fundamental problem: the equilibrium states of an economy designed to operate in a finite environment must correspond to mass-energy equilibrium states that are ecologically feasible.[168]

Koenig's biophysical socioecological analysis precipitates from his thesis that the economy of man is fundamentally entropic. In his analysis of the thermodynamic economic process the mass-energy features of the industrialized ecosystem are conceptualized as a system of material transformation, transportation, and storage processes driven by solar and synthetic forms of energy. It is literally a thermodynamic "material processing machine."[169] In principle this material processing machine (Soddy and Tamanoi referred to it as a "heat engine") must obey the laws of material and energy balance, and, as such, it is subject to fundamentally the same design criterion that stands as the hallmark of engineering. Koenig, assuming a not unfamiliar Ostwaldian posture, is more specific. He writes that the livelihood of man is

> determined by the same basic laws of processing and interaction that determine the mass-energy characteristics, except that energy costs are measured in monetary value and aggregated with capital and other costs.
>
> The effectiveness of the life-support system in providing the physical needs and wants of man is determined ultimately by the mass-energy characteristics of the system, the availability of the requisite forms of energy to drive it, and the reliability of the functional system as a whole. Clearly man lives by materials and energy, not dollars.[170]

From this thesis, Koenig departs from vestiges of Ostwaldian logic. He argues for a "socio-cybernetic paradigm" which characterizes the essential processes by which industrialized man relates to his physical resources and natural environment, and in which the problems of technological planning and regional economic development are presented as fundamental in society's control of short-term mass-energy and long-term structural dynamics of the physical-biological (life-support) system. Short-term mass-energy has to do with temporal and spatial changes in the flow rates of material and energy for an essentially fixed physical structure, whereas long-term structural dynamics that are identified, for instance, with J.A. Schumpeter's analysis of business cycles, denote temporal changes in the technological form and physical structure.[171] From this cybernetic perspective the crucial questions for Koenig, as they were for Bogdanov, are: What family of states are to be avoided? And, given this information, what kind of social instruments are required to carry out the essential functions of control, and how shall they be deployed?

The socio-cybernetic model consists of two major subsystems:

(1) a life-support system with physical energy generation and material processing activities, and the associated material and energy exchange rates with the
geosphere and Biosphere; and
(2) a cybernetic regulatory and control system with its economic, political,
legislative, and religious institutions of social regulation.

In connection with what Koenig sees as a necessity for the planning of the
interaction of technico-economic and ecological systems, he writes that

> as a prerequisite to sound ecological planning we must know explicitly the
> time-space capacities of the various components of the environment (lakes,
> streams, airsheds, etc.) to process specific classes of materials (heavy metals,
> oxides of sulfur, organic compounds, etc.), as a function of the "quality"
> (ecological state) to be maintained in the environmental component. What, for
> example, are acceptable input rates of organic and inorganic nitrogen and
> phosphorus to particular lakes and streams, or the acceptable rate of applica-
> tion of urban wastes to terrestrial areas as a function of soil type? These
> mass-energy processing capacities stand as unremovable physical constraints
> on regional developments, population densities and distributions and techno-
> logical activity. The family of structural states that are not ecologically feasible
> in this sense must be avoided.[172]

The identification of appropriate "states" of the life-support system that are to
be avoided for reasons of long-term incompatibility with the environment, according to Koenig, is fundamentally a problem in the analysis of mass-energy
characteristics of alternative technological capacities. Such an analysis must
identify those technological capacities whose mass-energy transformations with
the natural environment are inconsistent with the broader Biospheric constraints.
The technico-ecological "engineering" approach of Herman Koenig's study of
elements of socioeconomic-ecological interactions is also apparent in the analytically interesting work of Professor Michel Grenon, project director of the multi-
criteria evaluation system known merely as "Water, Energy, Land, Manpower
and Materials" (WELMM).

Koenig's ecological focus is not exclusive for he recognizes the importance of
extrascientific categories as well. He writes that "social and cultural considerations in general impose additional constraints on the class of allowable structures
which may be more restrictive than ecological considerations."[173] Expressing a
perspective on technified society already present in Vernadsky's work of fifty
years earlier, Koenig writes that

> [with] the power of modern technology, the industrialized nations might develop
> national and international ecosystems that are not technically, economically, and
> politically controllable. The time delays in economic and political feedback loops,
> for example, may be too long in comparison to the response time of the
> mass-energy system and the "noise level" may mask the essential "signal."[174]

Articulating a view that gains global significance with N.N. Moiseev, Koenig remarks that "changes in technological and physical structure of the human life-support system can be constrained within an ecologically feasible class of structures."[175]

Not content to merely assert the need for the planning of technico-ecological systems, Koenig speculates on managerial possibilities. Departing from a price-making market analysis, he comments that classes of technico-ecologically viable interactions may be accommodated through monetary costs assigned to material exchange rates with the natural environment.[176] Locating his non-market "real costs" analysis within the context of a static economy, Koenig writes that

> as a general principle, the monetary costs assigned to these exchange rates must increase exponentially as the steady-state material processing capacity of the recipient environmental component is approached. Such costs in effect reflect environmental diseconomies as the assigned threshold of capacity is approached. Under such pricing mechanisms it can be shown that successional changes in the structure of the life-support system will theoretically approach an ecologically feasible climax state.[177]

Although Koenig's conception of ecological priorities and of mass-energy coordinates is both philosophically and analytically useful, his technical solution to the problem requires careful analysis.

> [As] a technologically sophisticated and dominating species on the surface of earth, man must learn how to engineer the developments in industry, agriculture, and human habitats as components of a life-support system (industrialized ecosystem) that obeys the laws of material and energy balance and operates within the limited mass-energy rate capacities of regionally specific natural environmental components. . . . Since [the price-making market] imputes a zero monetary value to mass-energy exchange rates with the natural environment, our present market economy cannot in principle function as a control mechanism for managing the development and operation of our life-support system. . . . To the extent that these fundamental malfunctions cannot be or are not corrected, very powerful and pervasive economic forces must be overridden by other instruments of social management.[178]

Integrated Ecological-Economic Interaction Models

Departing from the neoclassical modes of economic analysis, Peter Nijkamp questions the validity of economic decision making based on the scarcity definition of "economic." Nijkamp argues for a normative economic perspective in order to achieve a harmonious and balanced development of the Biosphere.[179]

Referring to the problems of market-driven technological innovation and the negative effects of advances in our material welfare, he calls for a reorientation of economic analysis with respect to prevailing economic tendencies. It is necessary to revise priorities and imperatives in order to safeguard the long-term continuities of the Biosphere. In particular, the protection of man's physical natural environment has to be pragmatically conceived—as an explicit aim in planning and political decision making.

Nijkamp calls for the use of materials-balance models present in Koenig's analysis as an effective method to obtain more insight into the relationship between economic-technological and ecological effects. A materials-balance model is a formal representation of the linkages among economic, technical, and ecological processes. The model arises from a basic law of physics concerning the conservation of matter, the first law of thermodynamics. In spite of numerous transformation processes in the course of production or consumption, no matter is destroyed—it is merely shuffled about. And apart from transformations of energy, there is a physical balance between inputs and outputs in all transformation processes of a given system. From a material point of view a transformation process does not generate matter or energy. In each transformation process matter and energy are absorbed, restructured, and discharged.[180] Materials-balance models render these relationships explicit. Figure 3.5 illustrates this interaction.

Scrutinizing the familiar image of an economic system in terms of a circular flow of exchange-values, Nijkamp maintains that the materials-balance model reveals that such a circular flow does not exist for material products.[181] Economic activities necessarily exert a claim on the environment both for the input sector (the resource base of the economy) and for the output sector (the emission of residuals from the economy). The first claim leads to exhaustion of natural resources, the second to pollution and environmental degradation. Insofar as the environment has a large, though finite, capacity to provide resources and to absorb waste residuals, we can deduce from the first law of thermodynamics that each increase in the levels of production of physical goods has two effects: (1) a corresponding increase in the amounts of natural inputs and energy from the Biosphere, and (2) a corresponding increase in waste loads on the absorptive capacity of the environment.

Like the work of Tamanoi and his associates, Nijkamp's material-balance model reveals the underlying trophic relation in the livelihood of man.[182] Integrated environmental-economic open-system models furnish us with a grasp of the intimacy of economic and environmental processes. For detailed sectoral models offer a compelling instrument to analyze direct and indirect effects of production processes, consumption patterns, and transportation flows. These models may also be useful for a selective development policy.

Referring to the contemporary literature, Nijkamp affirms that the analysis of the structure and development of the economic-ecological interaction demands an understanding of the concept of entropy. He writes that "one of the major links which connect economics to its biophysical and ecological foundations is the entropy law."[183]

It is evident that a continuation of ecological and economic-technical transformation processes is only possible if these processes are continuously fed by environmental low-entropy. At present, one is increasingly realizing that matter-energy with low-entropy is a scarce item, which can frequently be used only once. Owing to this particular kind of scarcity the economic process has generally an irrevocable development, as far as material flows are concerned.[184]

In a discussion of the evaluative appropriateness of cost-benefit analysis, Nijkamp notes that "the problem of spill-overs and intangibles (in other words, the problem of mutually irreducible elements or the multi-dimensionality), restricts the scope of cost-benefit analysis."[185]

From this critique Nijkamp asserts that particular attention must be paid to multi-objective decision methods and to multi-criteria analyses of complex ecological-economic interactions.

> Modern societies appear to become intricate and complex entities. Social, economic, environmental, technological and political-administrative systems within these societies demonstrate a dynamic interwoven pattern. Conflicts between these various systems do not only take place more frequently, but also more intensely. A balanced and harmonious development of modern societies is increasingly becoming problematic. In our opinion, the task of a social science is to develop a set of theories and operational methods so as to provide more insight into the complex and sometimes conflicting nature of societal processes, as well as to stimulate decision units . . . to take into account a whole series of relevant social norms. This plea for a so-called "steward-economy" in which man uses material goods in a responsible and harmonious manner [forms] the background of . . . [the] present study, in which an attempt has been made to concrete the above mentioned task of social science like economics.[186]

The quality of life, notes Nijkamp, is not the result of an uncontrollable or random process, but rather the projection of the ways in which man shapes his culture and his development. On the basis of a substantive perspective, also present in the work of Y. Tamanoi and H. Koenig, Nijkamp argues that it is critically important to include in economic analyses views and norms concerning man's task with regard to society and nature. He adds that an analysis of environmental problems also has a pragmatic and ethical aspect, in the sense that scientific theories and analyses should provide the means to place economic decisions in a broader social and ecological framework.

Presenting an argument for what constitutes a theory of the economy in the broad sense, Nijkamp stresses that

> economics as a social and ethical science should have a profound attention for an integrated economic evaluation of our present-day growth processes, technological developments and ecological repercussions. Welfare assessment, technology assessment and ecological assessment are necessary ingredients of a balanced societal development. External effects are not only a technical

Figure 3.5. **Nijkamp's Open-System Economic Model**

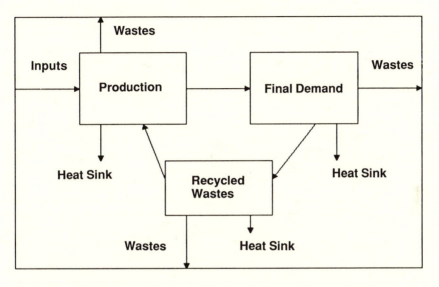

deficiency of a market mechanism, but reflect also the lack of a balanced and simultaneous integration of a wider variety of social norms and priorities.[187]

"Ecologized" Neoliberalism

Theorists of the open-systems paradigm are not without shortcomings, for there remains among some an unyielding market mentality. Counted among these theorists is Kenneth Boulding whose reductionism is evident in two respects.

In the first instance, on the basis of an ecological analogy, Boulding pursues a Darwinian line of discussion, arguing that the price-making market is inherently more stable, and, hence, preferable during a period of succession. In this connection, Boulding claims that the alleged stability-inducing qualities, which obtain from polymorphism in ecosystems, have an analogy in the price-making market economy. The ecological phenomenon of colonizing and succession or quasi-equilibrium has been conjectured by Boulding, following Bertalanffy, to be present in the economy.[188] He asserts that

> ecological interaction or selection follows rather different patterns in what has been called the "colonizing mode," in which organisms are expanding into a new and unutilized environment, and an "equilibrium mode," in which there are no new environments and everything settles down into at least an ecological quasi-equilibrium. In the colonizing mode, selection favors mobility, often increased size, efficiency, active competition, and so on. . . . In an equilibrium mode, mutations are fewer, or at least fewer are likely to succeed. The payoffs

are for adaptation, probably some small, high risk-aversion adaptation rather than an escape from an existing environment. . . . Thus, free competition beloved of economists may be a transient phenomenon of colonizing cultures, to be severely modified as colonization reaches its almost inevitable end.[189]

But whereas Adam Smith merely attributed a dreary "melancholy" to the stationary state, Boulding surpasses Smith's dismal analysis, threatening that

> in economic life [the advent of a climatic stage] may correspond to the development of imperfect competition, larger-scale organization, market intervention through selling costs, and even the development of the communist states in which there is a single, superdominant species in the shape of government and everything else has shelter under its thorny branches.[190]

In the second instance, and in the continuing development of Boulding's concept of evolutionary economics, he appears to be departing from his earlier hesitation, for he utters the sophomoric comment that an "ecosystem is a free enterprise system beyond the dreams of Milton Friedman." According to Boulding: "[Price] theory can be fitted into an evolutionary framework with great ease, for there is implicit in it an ecological interaction of commodities which continually exercises a strong selective process [and] Marshall's long-run equilibrium . . . is a concept virtually identical with that of a climactic ecosystem."[191] Not content with this utterance he continues, asserting that the "persistence of evolution and its whole course depends very much on the free enterprise aspects of it."[192] The unspoken Hayek-like corollary is that nonmarket institutions must inevitably spell the end of cultural development.

Boulding presents a Darwinian argument. He argues on the basis of observed "efficiencies" that attach to natural ecosystems and asserts that selection processes both in natural ecosystems and in the economy are phenotypical. And whereas mutability is the arrowhead of biogenesis, and while the economy of man may be conceptualized as an ecosystem, the mechanisms of mutation in man's economy are distinct. Employing as his point of departure Bertalanffy's concept of open systems, and while sharing an understanding on the structuring role of information in evolution, Boulding proceeds to develop an "ecologized" neoliberal point of view. Others advancing coevolutionary imperatives and logic argue for the role of structuring information in institutional terms. The former sanctifies the market where the latter seeks to broaden economic thought. It is prerequisite to consider that, whereas biogenetic development is guided by the imperatives of life itself, Boulding's naturalist concept of noögenetic development is guided by the narrower imperatives of the economic system whose dynamics he seeks to reduce to that of an ecosystem conflated as an ideal market.[193]

However, ecological interaction, particularly as it is spread out in space as in time, is extremely complex, displaying a nonlinear multidimensionality not present in Walrasian general equilibrium analysis, a conclusion Boulding heads toward when he remarks that: "The ecological interaction of populations of all different exchangeables is mediated through the structure of relative prices and profits in the market economy. This is something for which there is no close parallel in biological interaction."[194]

Despite a latent reductionist perspective, the ecological model provides a reference image analytically useful to the broadening of economic thought. I refer to "quasi-metabolic" qualities of the production process. Elements of this reference image appeared in the *Tableau Économique* of F. Quesnay some 200 years ago. Quesnay's Physiocratic insight is discernible in the thermodynamic analysis of N. Georgescu-Roegen and in the net-energy analysis of H. Odum and J. Zucchetto.[195]

Neosocial Energetics

The continuing investigation into the role of energy and ecological principles in economic analysis is not without lapses into the reductionism of social energetics. Although it is not without some compensating and important insights, neosocial energetics short-circuits the search for an understanding of the economy in the broad sense.

With the appearance and complexification of life there appeared new principles of stability among which is one identified with biological forms: Lotka's principle. Following the Darwinian model, one of the outstanding theoreticians of equilibrium thermodynamics, Boltzmann, said that "the struggle for existence is a struggle for free energy available for work."[196] This notion subsequently infused a number of analysts. Lotka's principle states that "whenever a group of organisms arises which is so constituted as to increase the rate of circulation of matter through the system . . . natural selection will operate to preserve such a group, provided always that there is a residue of untapped available energy."[197] This principle suggests that there is a natural process of selection operating at biotic levels of organization which effects a selection of those organizations that maximize the "throughput" of useful energy.[198] Systems that gain more power have more energy to maintain themselves to overcome stresses and predominate over competing units.[199] Bertrand Russell remarked euphemistically: "Every living thing is a sort of imperialist, seeking to transform as much as possible of its environment into itself and its needs."[200]

In his thermodynamic analyses of the economic process, Frederick Soddy chose, as his point of departure, the observation that human systems are subject to the same energy constraints as any other system. The American systems ecologist Howard Odum begins with a similar proposition: that energy, ecology, and economics form a single, unified whole.[201] He assumes an Ostwaldian conviction. For, according to Odum, energy is the primary, most universal measure of work. Consequently, the laws of energy apply to human processes and to processes in nature. This includes economics, culture, and aesthetics.[202] Societies, he writes, compete for economic survival according to Lotka's principle.

Echoing Ostwald's thesis in *Kulturwissenschaften*, Odum maintains that culture is formed by a process of trial and error selection and survival which produces a structure of information that tends to retain successful patterns.[203]

For Odum, Lotka's principle is an imperative. Attributing functional rationality to precognitive organisms, he notes that those systems that "win and dominate" do so by maximizing their total power from all sources and distribute that power toward needs affecting survival.

In Odum's Darwinian world, he observes:

> External sources of energy are the basis for a system; and the system gradually fits itself, its storages, its material cycles, its feedbacks, and its structure to the pattern which maximizes energy in the combination available to it. In the process of trial and error, there is a selection from among choices that develop as a result of random variations. Surviving systems are those that feedback their stored energy to stimulate the flow of energy.[204]

Odum's central thesis is that ecological and economic systems that survive and prosper have characteristic patterns adapted to the realities of energy laws and "ecological" principles. Combining Darwin's theory of natural selection and Lotka's theory, Odum hypothesizes a "general energy law" whereby maximization of useful work obtained from energy conversion is the principal criterion for natural selection.

According to Lotka's principle, those systems that appropriate the most energy and use it most effectively in competition with other systems will reproduce at a differentially higher rate. According to Odum, since economic resources are defined by technology, access to superior technologies gives a firm (or species) a competitive advantage in access to resources. Technology thus determines the size of the energy flow, which in turn permits a higher rate of reproduction. This sets up a positive feedback (autocatalytic) loop. A new technology generates a larger energy surplus which is "reinvested." As long as access to low entropy energy and material can be sustained, the system can grow at an exponential rate. The constraint of limited resources is, in turn, continually pushed back by technological change and the exploitation and depletion of new resources.[205]

Odum writes that "surviving systems are those that feedback their stored energy to stimulate the flow of energy."[206] He attests that external sources of energy are the basis for a system, and a system gradually fits itself, its storages, its material cycles, its feedbacks, and its design to the structure that maximizes energy in the combination available to it.[207]

We must hasten to note that while the observations and principles referred to above may be appropriate to levels of organization identified with ecological systems in a strictly Darwinian sense, Odum's insistence on the general applicability of the principle extending to the livelihood of man, while analytically useful, is imbued with market mentality and is, in fact, no less reductionist than

Cartesian economics. To speculate as Odum does on the universality of the maximum-power principle is a lapse into naturalism entirely inconsistent with the reality of the institutionalized economy.

While both man and nature have accelerated the entropic process through the increasingly effective use of energy, it is important to note that nature's "technology" has evolved consistent with the norms of the Biosphere, while *Homo faber's* innovations have been constrained by narrower institutional norms. This is a double-edged proposition; for, on the one hand, it provides fodder for reductionists like Odum who seek to correct the price-making market system with energy certificates. On the other hand, it argues for broader non-reductionist institutional modes. Among those pursuing the latter argument is M. Bookchin.

"In ecology the Newton of . . . thermodynamics, or more properly energetics, is Howard Odum," writes Bookchin.[208] He then pummels Odum for reducing the concept of an ecosystem to a mere analytical category for dealing with energy flow and for confusing life forms with mere reservoirs and conduits for calories, rather than the multifarious organisms that exist as ends in themselves and in vital developmental relationships with each other. Bookchin fails to see the more critical error—Odum's lapse into naturalism.

Much like Ostwald's argument of the last century, Odum argues that society is principally regulated by Lotka's maximum power principle.[209] For Ostwald, White, Cottrell, and Odum it has been difficult to comprehend the development of man in terms of less rather than more energy throughput. The reductionist Ostwaldian illusion that a "high culture" is one that maximizes the throughput energy must be overcome if we are to resolve problems of the Technosphere. However, this problem can only be clouded by further heroic attempts to salvage the myth that the market is metaphenomenal. In this connection we turn to the highly speculative energy theory of value.

Energy Theory of Value

In the tradition of Lotka and Schrödinger, Odum contends that the viability of any system depends on the energy inflow being at least as great as the outflow. If at any point a system's energy balance becomes negative, the process of death begins. It then becomes merely a matter of time, unless the balance is redressed, until a system depletes its internal energy stores and ceases to exist.[210]

Living systems cannot be separated from the energy that nourishes them, however technological systems merely stop and wait to be reactivated as soon as they are once again "nourished." As a result, notes Odum, it is possible for certain systems designed to concentrate energy from natural systems to have net negative balances without it being registered in a market economy. For example, Odum is adamant in his insistence that most nuclear power plants, as well as "exotic" energy projects, fall into this category. In seeking to redress the ensuing dilemma, he contends that monetary accounting and budgeting practices, insofar as they fail to reflect net energy efficiencies, are a central problem. Beginning with the proposition that monetized budgeting and accountancy fails to register the net energy efficiencies of capital, Odum pursues a search for a form of net energy accountancy.[211] A monetary unit, defined with such a scheme in mind, becomes a net energy certificate.

There is also a second level of analysis. For at the level of the economy the potential inconsistency of maximum-power behavior with environmental constraints—these may be resource limitations or the assimilative capacity of the environment—indicates that control mechanisms must be present in the system to keep the economic subsystem within environmental carrying capacity. In "primitive" economies, according to Rappoport, this mechanism was provided by social values and rituals which regulate and limit environmental exploitation.[212] In market economies this role is allegedly played by economic fluctuations: rapid price rises in the primary sector commodities provoking general price inflation, speculative bubbles, financial collapse, and depression. In the context of Odum's model, the price-making market mechanism is theorized not only to equilibrate psychological aspirations, but also to constrain the system to its niche in the global ecosystem. That it fails to do so warrants a revision of the monetary system but within the context of the price-making market system.

The classical and preclassical economists considered use-values as objective characteristics of goods—the tensile strength of steel, the pliability of cotton—for which no common quanta of value could be discovered nor rule of value magnitude prescribed. Centering on the subjective properties of these selfsame objective characteristics, the post-classicals focused on the varying "utilities" that could be derived from any fixed set of use-values. From this arose first the cardinal, then the ordinal, preference rankings which formed the bedrock on which could be grounded a systematic approach to supply and demand. But there is a circularity to the utility approach.

> The array of prices and quantities that emerges from the interaction of monads arises from the tastes and capacities of the actors. These in turn reflect their initial endowments of income and preference. Circularity enters insofar as the division of income into wages and profits, which certainly shapes the propensities of the actors, is itself the consequence of the functional division of income in the preceding period. This endless regress deprives the array of simultaneous equations of the very thing needed to establish order—namely, a knowable, objective starting point or premise.[213]

The recent rediscovery of "open" and "steady-state" system concepts emphasizing the role of energy flows—Bertalanffy's notion of *Fleissgleichgewicht*—has led to a new understanding of the principles of energy and the relation of these principles to value, to money, and, in addition, to a more quantitative understanding of the varying qualities of different energy sources in support of useful work.[214]

Perhaps seeking to avoid both the alleged "subversiveness" of Marxian analyses and the circularity of postclassical analyses, and in a renewed effort to discover the elusive quanta of value, a number of analysts formulated energy theories of value. In an effort to give his own views the gloss of respectability, Odum has invoked the name of Karl Marx.[215] He argues that Marx's labor theory of value represented an early attempt to use energy—in terms of that energy expended in the act of work—to measure value.[216] However, Odum notes that as Marxian thought originated prior to the clarification of either physical concepts of energy or the conventions of measurement, the concept failed to realize the significance of an energy theory of value. However, as we have already seen, Marx did make a rather prescient, if laconic and obscure, reference to use-value and energy.[217] Odum, nonetheless, exhorts us to speculate that had Marx been familiar with the principles of thermodynamics he would have revised the labor theory of value to an "energy theory of value." However, both from Engels's correspondence with Podolinsky and with Marx on the role of energy in agriculture, and from Engels's *Dialectics*, Marx and Engels disputed any such reduction that equates the expenditure of physical energy with value. In a brief note on the attempt by physicists to define work in energetic terms, Engels questioned whether work so defined can be adequately expressed.[218]

This lack of rigor is, of course, not unique to Odum. Frederick Soddy shared the same opinion, writing, in 1922, that

> had Karl Marx lived after instead of before the modern doctrine of energy there can be little doubt that his acute and erudite mind would easily have grasped its significance in the social sciences. As it was, in fairness to him it must be said that he did not attempt to solve the real nature of wealth, but concentrated entirely upon the problem of its monetary equivalent, that is, upon exchange-value rather than use-value.[219]

The reemergence of energy analysis, itself a by-product of the energy crisis, induced some energy analysts and even some economists to argue that energy equivalents are the true measure of money.[220] The root of the "energy costs theory of value," while it originates with analysts at the turn of the century, has recently been argued by energy analysts who, like M. Slesser, remark that "it makes sense to measure the cost of the things done, not in money, which is after all nothing more than a highly sophisticated value judgment, but in terms of thermodynamic potential."[221] This notion was adopted and expounded with additional arguments by Gilliland and Huettner.[222]

> An energy theory of value is based on embodied energy. If items and flows have value, it is because of the effects they can exert on a system, and, if their ability to act is in proportion to the energy used to develop them (after selective elimination of those that do not), the value is proportional to the embodied energy in systems emerging from selection processes.[223]

Odum makes the observation that "all systems that undergo natural selection maintain order through characteristic closed, autocatalytic loops of high-quality energy interacting with low-quality fuel energy. Such loops are accompanied by a circulation of money where human economic affairs are concerned."[224] In connection with the law of diminishing returns, Odum identifies it precisely with what is known as Liebig's principle.[225] With this principle in mind, Odum writes that "the limiting factor [attaches to] the law of diminishing returns in economics."[226] Adopting Pareto's analysis of marginal utility theory, Odum notes: "The marginal utility and prices rise with scarcity. [And] price is . . . proportional to the slope of the limiting-factor curve according to the theory of marginal utility."[227]

Robert Costanza has theorized the extension of market prices to the valuation of ecosystem services heretofore considered outside the domain of economic thought. Costanza, a representative of the Odum school, develops an energy theory of value using the earlier and more biophysical analysis of Soddy and Cottrell as a point of departure.[228]

Costanza's argument begins from a "costs theory of value" in which the principal issue is interdependence of factors of production, which he alleges has escaped conventional economists. Costanza notes that "Odum has pointed out that the currently defined primary factors are really interdependent by-products of our one observable net input—solar energy."[229] Following Odum, Costanza maintains that proposals to increase the "energy efficiency" of economic activity are ultimately grounded on the mutual independence of primary factors. At issue is whether the factors are really independent. Are the conventional primary factors—capital, labor, natural resources, and government services—free from indirect energy costs? Costanza contends that they are not.[230]

The concept of factor interdependence, notes Costanza, is summarily dismissed by neoclassical economists who contend that energy is qualitatively indistinguishable; that it is merely one of a number of primary inputs to the production process. This dismissal, remarks Costanza, is unwarranted if the traditional primary factors are, in reality, interdependent.[231]

The required perspective, notes Costanza, is an ecological or "systems" view that considers humans to be part of, and not apart from, their environment. Having located himself within this apparently "broadened" view, Costanza then asserts that an embodied energy theory of value is theoretically sensible and empirically accurate if the system boundaries are appropriately defined. Thoroughly mired in market mentality, he subscribes to the ideas that "market-determined dollar values and embodied energy values are proportional for all but the primary energy sectors."[232]

Costanza then concludes that

(1) Empiricism indicates that there is no inherent conflict between an embodied energy (or energy cost) theory of value and value theories based on utility.

(2) The empirical equivalence of these estimates . . . supports basic economic principles grounded in optimization while giving them a biophysical basis; and (3) Embodied energy values are accurate indicators of market values where markets exist. Because, as they are based on physical flows, they may also be used to determine "market values" where markets do not exist—for example, in ecological systems.[233]

On the basis of his analysis, Costanza argues for the "internalizing" of all factors external to the existing market system allegedly solving the natural resource valuation problem. Giving a new meaning to the expression market mentality, Costanza pronounces that from the ecological perspective, markets can be viewed as an efficient energy distribution mechanism. Not unlike K. Boulding, he contends that the development of the price-making market is merely a general form of the ecological system that every other species has developed. We might recall at this juncture Lenin's acerbic criticism of such social energetics as being "sterile, scholastic and lifeless."

Costanza maintains that "the flow of energy has not been the primary concern of mainstream economists" and yet he is led to conclude that "without realizing it, the flow of energy is the primary concern of economics."[234] Economists, it seems, are unwittingly led as if by an "invisible hand" tutored in energy principles to optimize the flow of energy. Costanza's proposition that market prices closely reflect embodied energy represents an extreme form of Ostwaldian "energetics," a positivist validation of market economics: a pious sanctification of the market within the framework of the energetic dogma. In denying the institutional dimensions of the economy, it fixes a naturalistic shroud over economic thought.

Bernstein criticizes Costanza principally on the basis of "the essential circularity involved in using current market values (GNP) to calculate a dollar/calorie ratio that is then used to derive the dollar value of goods and services now outside the market system."[235]

Following Schrödinger, Georgescu-Roegen asserts that we must accept it as an unambiguous fact of life that low entropy is a necessary condition for a thing to have use-value.[236] These utilities are scarce in the sense that available low entropy within our environment decreases continuously and inevitably with man's material progress. But, whereas the economic process is entropic in all its material coordinates, the idea that economic value can be reduced to a chemicophysical value through the concept of entropy must be rejected. Although low entropy is a necessary condition for something to have use-value, it is not a sufficient explanation of the exchange-value of commodities. Even Boulding cautions that it would be a great mistake to conceive of the economic process as a vast system of thermodynamic equations. However, a theory of value that ignores entropy is no more satisfactory than one that ignores labor.

The energetic dogma, though its theory of value sidesteps the problem of circularity, suffers from an even more severe case of one-sided mechanistic determinism than does neoclassical economic thought. When this fact is recognized, it is no longer so surprising that the energy theory of value results in the same laissez-faire conclusions.

Identifying the difficulty of intersystemic commensurability addressed in reductionist ways by Odum and Costanza, Passet notes that

> at the level of the Biosphere the monetary instrument is of no assistance: the rhythms of purification of waters or of the atmosphere, and their degree of purity cannot be translated into francs; without a reserve of energy expressed in kilocalories it does not correspond to any physical reality while if it is translated into a monetary value it loses all meaning.[237]

While the unorthodox economic concepts expounded by the energy optimizers reflect a reductionist attitude akin to the mechanical paradigm, one cannot disregard the valuable contribution they have made in identifying the biophysical dimensions of the livelihood of man. In particular, the contribution made by Odum's elaboration of Lotka's maximum power principle as an evolutionary selection mechanism raises an important, and, as yet, unresolved issue: that of the role of differentiated indebtedness and the phenomenon of money.[238]

Parenthetically, our critique is not merely with a chemicophysical theory of value, rather, any theory of value is suspect, whether it be Ricardo's labor theory or that of revealed preference in being invariably reductionist.

> The alternative is not to adopt an energy theory of value. . . . Nor is it to fall back on a theory of values = prices, since prices do not reflect energy costs now, nor can they reflect energy availability in time since this is not known. Besides, prices do reflect a very unequal distribution of income and therefore to guide production by prices means to accept this unequal distribution. The alternative is, perhaps to do without a general theory of value. This might not allow the world economy to be run in such a way that it produces the use values that people need, while at the same time destroying little non-renewable energy and sharing more equitably the burden of work. But at least it might permit people to think along such lines without feelings of guilt about their lack of economic (or chrēmatistikē rationality).[239]

Referring to the economy in the context of open-systems, Nijkamp observes that "one of the most important things occurring between the various levels of an ecosystem is the transfer of energy."[240] Consistent with the earlier analyses, Nijkamp writes that the behavior of "energy can be described in physical terms by means of the first and second laws of thermodynamics. . . . Energy can be thought of as the currency of ecological housekeeping, so that there seems to be a certain correspondence between money in economic systems and energy in ecological systems."[241] However, he hesitates at endorsing the systems ecologist's (Howard Odum) analysis, noting that the reduction of economic theories to energetic ones is a partial view of the working of an economic system. It reduces one's scope of analysis to reflecting merely those values derived from market-driven demand and supply coordinates.

Despite the one-sidedness of their analysis, Odum's and Costanza's "social energetic-ecological" model can be said to have reidentified a fundamental problem in economic thought; an issue albeit addressed at the turn of this century by Soddy and Ostwald.[242]

Optimization models such as the maximum power principle ignore the possibility of radical transformations—that is, transformations that change the definition of a problem and thus the kind of solution sought—and the inertial constraints that may eventually force a system into a pathological way of functioning. Similar doctrines and definitions of progress in terms of maximization or minimization criteria give an unfortunately reassuring representation of nature as an all-powerful and rational calculator, and of a coherent history characterized by global progress. To restore both inertia and the possibility of unanticipated events—that is, to restore the open character of history—it must be understood that development is fundamentally nonlinear in character. Here we could use a symbol—the apparently accidental character of the great Cretaceous extinction that cleared the path for the development of early mammals, a small group of ratlike creatures.

The application to social forms of organization of those selection principles—whether they be Onsager's principle, the principle of minimal dissipation, or the maximum power principle—raises the question, How justified is such an extension? For important though these contributions are to an understanding of lesser forms of organization, it is unlikely that an attempt to transfer such a theory to society is appropriate. While it is easy to understand a striving to identify some universal law, such as the second law of thermodynamics, that may serve as a basis for forecasting the course of social development, social structures are exceedingly more complex than simple thermodynamic systems, and it is probably objectively impossible to find a single law. The recognition of this fact led A.A. Bogdanov to a revision of his earlier focus on Ostwald's theory of energetics, and to a proposal of a more general theory of organization.

Moreover, Bogdanov maintained that the self-organization of matter (synergetics) displays a contradictory tendency toward the simultaneous destruction of organization and it coexists in a dialectical unity with structure conserving and elaborating principles. This dialectic describes a process by which new levels of organization appear and in turn create new irreducible modes of selection.[243] This progressive movement from one mode of stabilization to another, for instance, is recognizable in the progression from the principle of Le Chatelier in physical chemistry, to that of homeostasis in biology and, finally, to institutions in society.

That the principles of selection operating in the animate world may be reduced to the principles of conservation that select forms in the inanimate world is a possibility excluded by Bogdanov's dialectical theory of organization.[244]

At the present juncture in the development of science, the ecological approach and the systems approach once again have overlapped and share the same thrust toward a new synthesis and integration of scientific knowledge. It is, nonetheless, paradoxical that the reemergence of "systems thinking" has occasioned a reevaluation of the role of energy and the principles of thermodynamics. The paradox derives from the established fact that Bogdanov's original formulation of general principles of organization, or what he referred to as Tektology, was itself a consequence of his original interest in the role of energy in society.[245] To a significant degree the reductionism among modern energy theorists has duplicated the earlier analyses and has led to criticisms similar to those presented by Bogdanov. But, despite the one-sidedness of his ecological analysis, H. Odum's work contains a significant number of valuable ideas that have direct philosophical and theoretical significance.

Steady-State Economic Analysis

The systems ecologist argues that during times when there are opportunities to expand one's power inflows, the "survival premium," by Lotka's principle, is on rapid growth even though there may be waste. For instance, according to Odum's Darwinian interpretation, we observe

> a dog-eat-dog growth competition every time a new vegetation colonizes a bare field where the immediate survival premium is first placed on rapid expansion to cover the available energy receiving surfaces. . . . Most recently, modern communities of man have experienced two hundred years of colonizing growth, expanding to new energy sources such as fossil fuels, new agricultural lands, and other special energy sources. Western culture, and more recently, Eastern and Third World cultures, are locked into a mode of belief in growth as necessary to survival. "Growth or perish" is what Lotka's Principle requires, but only during periods when there are energy sources that are not yet tapped.[246]

As an ecosystem passes from succession to the steady state, its species are forced by the constraint imposed by the carrying capacity of the ecosystem to "explore" greater efficiency of energy flow-through.[247] The early stage of maximal flow-through is often referred to as the "colonizing phase"; the later stage of minimum flow-through is considered to be the climatic phase. In other words, during times when energy flows have been tapped and there are no new sources, Lotka's principle suggests that successful systems are those that do not attempt fruitless growth but seek the stabilizing properties of diversity.[248]

The colonizing phase, with its alleged emphasis on increasing flow-through, has the effect of hastening entropic processes. Odum notes that

> to survive—to avoid being excluded by competitors—when energy is available for expansion, a system must rapidly increase its use of energy. If the main

source of energy is already tapped to the maximum and if there is energy of production not required for pumping the primary source, then secondary sources of energy can be pumped even though they do not themselves yield net energy.[249]

However, when an ecosystem reaches its steady state, the rapid growth specialists are replaced by a new species of higher diversity, higher quality, longer living, and more stable components. Collectively, through a "division of labor" and specialization, the climax species secures more energy from the steady flow of available energy than do those species specialized in rapid growth.[250]

Herman Daly's assertions for a steady-state economy are bolstered by energy cybernetics of ecosystem analysis. Odum writes:

> High quality of life for humans and equitable economic distribution are more closely approximated in steady-state than in growth periods.
> During growth, emphasis is on competition, and large differences in economic and energetic welfare develop; competitive exclusion, instability, poverty, and unequal wealth are characteristic. During steady-state, competition is controlled and eliminated, being replaced with regulatory systems, high division and diversity of labour, uniform energy distributions, little change, and growth only for replacement purposes.[251]

Following the same ecological phases of succession and climax Odum maintains that our system of man and nature will soon be shifting from rapid growth as the criterion of economic survival to steady-state non-growth as the criterion of maximizing one's work for economic survival.[252] Absent from Odum's analysis is the institutional dimension of society, a dimension that was present in the earlier analysis of Cottrell. Cottrell theorized that trends in energy conditions within historic institutional settings brought out successive surges of growth of different species.

F. Soddy stated the so-called theory of energy determinants of the steady state: that the scale of living of any community is fixed by its rate of energy consumption. The last two centuries have seen a burst of temporary growth only because of fleeting use of artificial energy supplies that accumulated over long periods of geological time. "Once a community has accumulated possessions sufficient to enable it to consume its wealth in accordance with a scale of living fixed by its rate of consumption, more capital becomes a useless charge and a burden upon the possessors."[253]

More recently, ecologist Commoner has written:

> The total rate of exploitation of the earth's ecosystem has some upper limit, which reflects the intrinsic limit of the ecosystem's turnover rate. If this rate is exceeded, the system is eventually driven to collapse. This is firmly established by everything that we know about ecosystems. Hence, it follows that there is an upper limit to the rate of exploitation of the biological capital on which any productive system depends. Since the rate of use of this biological

capital cannot be exceeded without destroying it, it also follows that the actual rate of use of total capital (i.e., biological capital plus conventional capital, or means of production) is also limited. Thus, there must be some limit to the growth of total capital, and the productive system must eventually reach a "nongrowth" condition, at least with respect to the accumulation of capital goods designed to exploit the ecosystem and the products which they yield.[254]

The American environmental economist Herman Daly has reflected that ecologists are familiar with both growth states and steady state, and in their work routinely observe both in natural systems. However, the growth ethic has imbued economists to the extent that until recently they have been unaware of steady-state economics. Propositions central to this study originated in the Physiocrats' interest in reproduction, in the works of Adam Smith and John Stuart Mill, and later in Marx's concept of simple reproduction.

The steady-state economy, derided by Adam Smith, diagnosed by J.S. Mill, and, in more recent times, analyzed by physicists, ecologists, and economists alike, leads away from "growth-mania" and toward a new ethos for economic policy. This new ethos forces upon us the recognition of the intimate relationship between the Biosphere and the econosphere. According to Herman Daly, it shifts attention to stocks, the quality of the stocks, and to juridical rights and distributive issues.[255] It leads to impolite questions about inequalities in the distribution of wealth and to the realization that the thermodynamics of the economic process means that incessant and ill-conceived growth will encounter physical if not social limits. Consequently, redistribution presents itself as the only cure for poverty; growth simply cannot do the job.

The all-pervading ethos of "growth-mania" has enabled the foreclosure of two intimately related problems. On the one hand, growth is the cardinal policy to maintain full employment. And this introduces the issue of ethical distribution. Insofar as personal freedom enables one to be employed, the income-through-employment ethic of distribution is perceived as functional.[256] As the Great Depression in North America made manifest, it was not want of primal goods or industrial capacity to produce them that was at issue, but an inadequacy of purchasing power. The depression proved that there was more than sufficient capital stock to meet the basic requirements of the population, without requiring that each individual be a jobholder. However, conventional wisdom, expressed in Keynesian policy, precluded the understanding that a job might mean something other than a distributive mechanism. Indeed, the so-called Keynesian Revolution consisted in rescuing the discipline of economics and overcoming the market impasse by tapping through materially unsubstantiated spending the potential of the market to produce goods and services. This new situation empowered the market to again provide jobs and thus "legitimated" the necessary purchasing power. Keynesian policies, though they rescued and restimulated the market, represented only a postponement of the crisis foreshadowing the closure of the historical validity of the category of a "job" as a wealth distributive mechanism. On the other hand, growth is considered a method of harmonizing distributional conflicts. If everyone's absolute share of income is increasing, there is a tendency not to fight over relative shares, especially since such fights may interfere with growth and even lead to a lower absolute share for all. These problems cannot be kept at bay forever, because growth cannot continue indefinitely.

Earl Cook, author of *Man, Energy, Society*, was concerned with the dangers associated with the apparent incompatibility of our society's fervent, almost religious devotion to economic growth, and the fact that such growth was dependent upon a finite, nonrenewable stock of fossil fuel. Cook argued that industrial society, the United States in particular, is faced with a watershed unparalleled in history. With the quantity and quality of fossil fuels rapidly diminishing, industrial society has two options. The "progress option" is to go on believing that omnipotent technological change and so-called economic laws will rescue us from any resource-related problems. The "prudent option" is to accept the fact that physical limits to economic growth do exist and to adjust our values and life-styles commensurate with energy and resource realities.

Growth has become an axiomatic policy for promoting full employment coupled with the distributive ethic of income-through-jobs. However, in an economy constrained to steady-state growth in physical stocks, and a policy of using technological progress to either increase leisure or minimize costs, full employment and the income-through-jobs ethic eschew their distributive functionality. What happens when developed economies are confronted by large-scale structural unemployment, resulting from highly robotized processes, which adds merely another level of stress? For instance, Adam Schaff recently called attention to an emerging problem—that in the further "advancement" of technological systems the "robotization" of production in the OECD countries may well altogether deny (within the existing property-rights framework), workers of an income-through-jobs linkage.[257] If, with the prevailing distribution of wealth, income, and power, production governed by socially unjustified motives results in the output of great amounts of noxious junk, then something is wrong with the distribution of wealth and social power. We need some principle of income distribution independent of the income-through-jobs link. Our very understanding of a "job" must be reformed.

At another level of analysis, the steady-state economy humbles the Faustian covenant between science and technology and forces the view that not all things are possible through technology—that the global issues of territorially specific overpopulation and overconsumption may have no technical solution, but only moral solutions. As the consequences of growth-mania become more apparent and more costly, the steady-state open-systems paradigm will be taken ever more seriously.

A number of moral issues concerning distributive justice and intergenerational equity do not arise if one believes that continual economic growth is biophysically possible. Moreover, if one's field of moral consciousness excludes the indigent, future generations and subhuman life, then many biophysical constraints are of no concern. It is not enough to proselytize with moral arguments, because even among scientific opinion there is not yet a consensus. This encourages optimistic biophysical assumptions to cushion the blow with fanciful reference to space colonies, green revolutions, breeder reactors, etc. At the same time, popular "green movements" agitating bureaucracies from below with biophysical arguments leave too much room for elastic morality. The "grow or die" ethic is a time bomb that must be defused with a rigorous understanding of the biophysical realities together with philosophical and moral arguments. "Biophysically based conclusions about economic growth, or any other subject, should be in accord with morally based conclusions."[258] The problem of relative shares can no longer be avoided by appeals to growth. The overall problem is how to use ultimate means best to serve the "Ultimate End." We might call this an ultimate political economy, or stewardship.

Though the steady-state view is criticized by orthodoxy, it has also been criticized by one who is considered by some to be the founding father of the bioeconomic approach. Nicholas Georgescu-Roegen has written that J.S. Mill's "blissful world" has been resurrected as a "mythical" source of ecological salvation fraught with "various logical and factual snags."

> The crucial error consists in not seeing that not only growth, but also zero-growth state, nay even a declining state which does not converge toward annihilation, cannot exist forever in a finite environment. . . . And contrary to what some advocates of the stationary state claim, this state does not occupy a privileged position vis-à-vis physical laws.[259]

Economic theory is lagging behind the stability principles that attach to ecological succession. Concentrating on flows draws attention away from the thorny ethical issues of the distribution of wealth that is the real source of economic power. The income flow is unequally distributed also, but at least everyone gets some part of it within the context of the market. According to the myth of the market our fate is aligned to an immutable natural law. The market myth weakens the credibility of reformists and usurps the aspirations of the indigent. However, when the market is understood as an instituted process and not a natural phenomenon, those who institute it can be held responsible. Should that system produce results inconsistent with the public interest, those results do not have to be accepted as immutable. What was instituted in one way can be reinstituted in another way. Redistribution of income is liberal. Redistribution of wealth is radical.

Whereas in a growing economy, induced by Keynesian policy or otherwise, maximization of production and consumption is conjectured to be a desideratum, in the steady-state economy throughput loses such appeal. Rather, it is regarded as something to be minimized. In the steady[state economy focus is on stock maintenance, and any technological change that results in the maintenance of a given stock with a lessened throughput is clearly a gain. The minimization of production and consumption surely contradicts the growth-mania obsession of conventional economic thought.[260]

Conclusions

The biophysical dimensions of the livelihood of man have long been obscured by the closed-system mechanical paradigm that forms the basis of neoclassical economic thought. An alternative paradigm, based on the dynamics of open systems, is reemerging in the epoch of the Noösphere. In particular, the concept of the steady state of "living systems" is present in the work of general system theorists, and increasingly among economists. Their task is not to project living systems as the model of social organization; rather it is to seek those principles of organization that make it possible for the economy conceptualized as a living system to reproduce and to coevolve within changing Technospheric and Biospheric environments.

Indeed, the growing awareness of the thermodynamic and biophysical dimensions of the global Technosphere has led to a resurrection of a number of fundamental analytical issues first identified by the Physiocrats and subsequently addressed in the first quarter of this century. But it also marks a departure from economistic perspectives and symbolizes a return to substantive economic theory.

The reference image of the economic process as a circular flow is seriously incomplete because it focuses on the flow of exchange-values (i.e., money) to the exclusion of the throughput of low-entropy natural resources from which all goods and services are ultimately derived. Moreover, with a certain fetish, it has taken a characteristic of money and overgeneralized it into the analytical basis of the economic process. This, the fallacy of misplaced concreteness attaches to the conventional understanding of the circular flow.

The close similarity of the life-process as an open, metabolically interactive process with that of the economic process, was shown in the analysis of Quesnay and Marx. However, in both its Marxian and neoclassical variant, the economic theory of production was generally interpreted as a benign technological process between inputs and outputs. Neoclassical production theory, in particular, reduces production to merely a monetarily effective use of private inputs.

While a number of theorists sought to reconstruct production theory on the basis of classical models, others have tried to explicitly reframe economic analysis around general evolutionary and organizational principles. For having rejected mechanicalism and embraced an open-system model, a reconceptualization of production is required.

In this connection we come to the entropy law which is a principal determinant of all material transformations associated with life. Comprehending the economy as an open living system, low entropy must be appropriated from the environment and the degraded high-entropy matter-energy must be expelled. Thus, replenishment of the physical basis of life is not a self-sustaining circular affair. It is an environmental service integral to the economic process. Production is fundamentally a thermal phenomenon, and the closely related concept of entropy explains production as a process as one generating its own negativity.

While the concept of production was a central concern of classical theorists, so, too, were the issues of material wealth and the problem of development. These latter issues are also a fundamental problem in the maturing open-systems paradigm. In this connection, wealth, having a physical dimension, is subject to thermodynamic degradation; that is, its growth sooner or later encounters limits. The thermodynamic dimension of physical wealth is juxtaposed to its monetary representation.

On the basis of earlier analysis, it was asserted that the principles and laws of thermodynamics are applicable to cultural systems which operate by transforming energy in the production of goods and services. And, whereas, in Polanyi's analysis, technological change in general was a fundamental stimulus for institutional change, social energetics asserts that the technological development of artificial converters of energy, in particular, led to significant changes in political and socioeconomic organization. Moreover, it is theorized that economic development, rather than obtaining from a monetarily efficient division of labor, obtains from the surplus energy-generating attributes of the division of labor; that is, a system of division of labor is said to be effective because of its surplus energy efficiencies.

Theorists of the open-systems paradigm are not without shortcomings. There remains, among some, an unyielding market mentality which conflates the price-making market economy with ecosystems. For instance, the reemergence of energy analysis induced some analysts to argue for a "costs theory of value"—that energy equivalents are the true measure of money. Such assertions derive from distorted ecologism—that markets can be viewed as an efficient energy distribution mechanism.

The insistence on the general applicability of the ecological principles extending to the livelihood of man, while analytically useful, is no less reductionist than Cartesian economics. For important though these principles are to an understanding of lesser forms of organization, it is probably inappropriate to attempt to transfer such a theory to society. For social structures are exceedingly more complex than those simple thermodynamic systems analyzed, and it is probably objectively impossible to find a universal law by which to forecast their future course.

Departing from vestiges of Ostwaldian logic, some analysts argue for a normative economic perspective in order to achieve a harmonious and balanced development of the Biosphere. By subordinating the livelihood of man to biospheric constraints the economy's artificial metabolism is sustainably incorporated within that of ecosystems. This reference image refers to the promotion of an interdependence of the livelihood of man with nature. The economy, as an open living system, must coexist with other open systems. In other words, we must take a substantive view and precisely locate the livelihood of man as embedded within a network of material balances that transcends institutional variants. Some analysts assert that the human life-support system must be constrained within an ecologically feasible class of structures. They argue for a "socio-cybernetic paradigm" in which the problems of technological planning and regional economic development are presented as fundamental in the regulation of the long-term structural dynamics of the physical-biological system by society. From this cybernetic perspective the crucial questions are: What family of states are to be avoided? And what kind of social instruments are required to carry out the essential functions of control, and how shall they be deployed?

Though the "economy in the broad sense" has addressed itself to aspects of open systems made manifest by environmental issues, even broader issues remain. Economics as a social and ethical science should formulate a mode of integrated evaluation of our present-day growth processes, technological developments, and ecological repercussions. External effects are not only a technical deficiency of a market mechanism, but reflect also the lack of a balanced and simultaneous integration of a wider variety of social norms and priorities.

It is important to note that, aside from those indoctrinated by market mentality whose efforts only serve to distort the understanding of the economy in the broad sense, there remains an unexamined and yet critical dimension to the open-systems paradigm. It is to gain an understanding of the economy in an even broader sense that we now turn to Chapter 4 of this work.

Beyond Entropy and the Economic Process: Broadening Economic Analysis from a Systems Theoretical Approach

Introduction

The totalizing effects of the price-making market, together with the growing complexity of technified society, contravene the norms of the Biosphere and represent an inversion of finalities that normally attaches to open living systems. This necessitates a mode of analysis of wholes rather than isolated parts. And, in this connection, the formal categories of systems theory and cybernetics are of particular value.

While our understanding of political economy has been broadened by incorporating biophysical and thermodynamic categories of analysis which pertain to the concept of open systems, systems theory itself offers more penetrating insights. These are not gained by a narrowing of focus; for systems theory does not project a reductionist image. Rather it seeks to identify a hierarchy of levels of organization characterized by conservation principles, by dynamics, and by systemic finalities constrained by lower orders of organization.

Whereas we earlier addressed elements of production theory in open-systems contexts, from a systems perspective to the problem of technified society's coevolution with the Biosphere, we shall approach a "metagenetic" understanding of production situated within an institutional framework. It is contended that analytical categories of political economy in the broad sense must not only incorporate biophysical coordinates but also aspects of the general theory of organization, including the cybernetics of autopoiesis. In particular, principles underlying the general theory of organization are relevant to the issue of the genesis of institutions in the age of the global Technosphere. At this juncture in economic thought, the open-systems approach to the economic process attaches to a further elaboration of the moral and ethical concerns that first imbued Physiocracy.

While the Cartesian method has achieved unparalleled success in the physical sciences and has provided illuminating insights in the life sciences today, its limitations were increasingly apparent even in the early decades of this century.[1] In particular, the differences between forms of living processes pertain less to that which constitutes them and more to the problem of their organization. Furthermore, the finality of a living organism, for instance, can only be interpreted by beginning with an integrated conception which identifies the global dimensions from which we may comprehend the articulations of an organization's elements. We emphasize that it is precisely this fact that induces us to seek a broader substantive mode of economic analysis.

Our emphasis on the systems approach and the need for an integrative model of wholes is derived from a pragmatic issue: to identify those Biospheric norms that must be observed by man's economic activities in order not to compromise the natural reproductive mechanisms of the Biosphere. It is this that defines the Neo-Physiocratic approach to economic analysis—for to a certain extent it reaffirms a need for maintaining a natural order.[2] In this connection, it is only having once addressed the global issues that one can focus on the narrower methodological question. In other words, it is only within the context of the substantive (*Wertrational*) that the functional (*Zweckrational*) achieves relevance.

If in the course of our inquiry we first encounter biological or ecological metaphor, it is not because the very nature of the problems with which we are concerned (the organization of living systems maintaining the structure through the production of negentropy) has led us to follow this path before other disciplines, but, rather, as J. Piaget observes, it is because "we have finally come to conceive the concept of organization as the central concept."[3] Indeed, Bogdanov contended that "all the problems which confront mankind are problems of organization. Man must transform the world into an organized whole."[4]

General System Theory (GST), according to Bertalanffy, is a purely formal logico-mathematical discipline applicable to all sciences concerned with systems. Its position is similar to that, for example, of probability theory, which is itself a formal mathematical discipline but which can be applied to very different fields.[5] The systems approach is a means for perceiving facts. Its object is not to express the deep essence of things but to arrive at modes of representation that permit a better comprehension of reality and a more effective action with relation to phenomena. However, unlike mathematics, some analysts have distorted it into a politically charged ideology.

GST expresses a concern with organizational linkages and organizing principles, the hierarchization of levels and finalities, the self-organization, and the cybernetics that are common to all living systems. It does not relate to any specific doctrine. In other words, we are not specifically concerned with the organistic, but rather the "organizational." The task, therefore, is not to project living systems as isomorphic to social organization but to seek those principles of organization that make it possible for society as a living system to remain viable.

In the following we shall endeavor to present a theoretical elaboration of the open-systems framework. This facilitates yet a further broadening of the concept of the economy. The context of such an explication derives from the very concept of "system" or "organization," as a phenomenon whose dynamics are ontologically constrained and whose further evolution proceeds according to selective modes of behavior. It shall be argued, from an institutionalist perspective, that society may be analyzed in organizational or systemic terms and categories. In this connection we shall examine selected aspects of organizational dynamics and issues of systemic stability, complexity, dissonance, and differentiation. These categories of analysis provide a general systems perspective for a sociocybernetic analysis of institutions which includes the concept of autopoiesis. Contiguous to this line of discourse we shall argue for the primacy of information as a category of analysis for the economic process in the broad sense. At this juncture we are led to speculate on the problem of freedom in technified society as the leading issue in the epoch of the Noösphere.

Complexification through Differentiation

Organizational Dynamics: Stability and Complexity

According to Waddington, Darwin was right in emphasizing chance over strict causal determinism of the Newtonian kind, but Waddington argues that "in the sphere of evolution we are now finding ourselves confronted with the need for organismic thinking . . . the idea of organization, or cybernetic schemes of causation should be recognized as just as important as that of random chance, or stochastic causation."[6]

Recent developments in systems theory have seen a further elaboration of the paradigm of the whole and its parts revising the concept of "system" and "environment." This marks a return to theoretical developments of the early part of this century associated with A.A. Bogdanov and N.I. Bukharin. Following Bogdanov we may speak only of simple and more complex forms of organization. Organization is, like substance and energy, an integral part of things and processes. Embodying this concept of "organization" Geoffrey Vickers, the British cybernetician, noted that an organization is a set of specific internal and external relations. The internal ones enable the organization to maintain coherence even through change. The external ones regulate the organization's relation as a whole with its milieu. Vickers maintains that an organization is always exclusive in relation to a variety of possibilities.[7] In fact, any order by its very nature is exclusive and constrained from randomness. "Exclusive" means, in this context, selective of what is allowable and what is not allowable within the given order. In other words, any system or organization discriminates by its very nature against some of the available possibilities. Though one possibility is clearly randomness, the timeless paradox is that nature also discriminates in favor of an ever more complex organization.

"Order is more natural than chaos."[8] It was from an insight into the paradox that surrounds this expression that A.A. Bogdanov proposed his theory of organization, which identified the dialectical unity of the second law of thermodynamics, the laws of conservation and principles of stabilization, and the concept of open-systems. Organizational morphotransformation progresses through internal differentiation. "Differentiation" refers to the recursive construction of subsystems. The process is one of complexification. Through differentiation, subsystems come to treat each other as environments within the system and thus they can presuppose that the order achieved by the system appears in the structuring of their environments. This rather casual formulation should serve to clarify the concept of differentiation at least temporarily. Recursive differentiation refers to a system's ability to gain over time the advantages of internal systemic stability. This guarantees its subsystems and, in turn, their subsystems a variety-reduced environment within which complexification propagates even more improbable structures. Following G. Vickers, recursive system differentiation is a form of strengthening selectivity. Organizational differentiation, therefore, is conceived as the recursive reduplication of the difference between system and environment within systems. It is a form of system building characteristic of both reflexive and nonreflexive systems.

Internal differentiation fulfills one of the evolutionary functions since it provides a mechanism of stabilization. Systems within systems reproduce increasingly improbable behavior patterns and problem solutions and maintain evolutionary accomplishments (but also nonfunctional, or even dysfunctional, traits or residues) within an increasing zone of indifference to the fluctuations of outer and inner environments. Thus, functional differentiation increases and discriminates among the plethora of possibilities accessible to each subsystem. It stimulates variation and raises the requirements for selective operations to an extent that would be incompatible with any other form of retentive stabilization. It thereby accelerates evolution; and this again limits the range of possible innovations that can be retained.

On the basis of this preliminary analysis, general systems theory, as well as cybernetics, replaced the classical model of a whole that consists of parts and relations between parts by a model that focused on the difference between system and environment. This paradigm afforded the chance to relate system structures (including hierarchical forms of organizational differentiation) and system processes to the environment.

From the elementary molecules constituting cells to the entire cosmos, an infinity of systems integrate themselves into a coherent whole. In relation to the whole each constitutes a level of organization. However, to distinguish each of these levels is perhaps not as simple as one might be led to believe were we to refer merely to the simple image of successive inclusions. A number of criteria have been suggested in this regard. H. Laborit and the French information theorist Jean Voge emphasize the different levels of feedback of structural information in relation to the structure itself.[9]

Voge demonstrates what E.F. Schumacher asserted: that when industrial economies reach a certain limit of centralized, capital-intensive production, they will have to shift direction to more decentralized production technologies and decentralize economic activities and political configurations, using more laterally linked information networks, if they are to overcome the severe information bottlenecks of excessively hierarchical, bureaucratized institutions.[10]

Bogdanov's Tektology maintained that at all levels of organization, from the inanimate to social forms, principles of conservation work to stabilize organization. In this connection it is only at the level of inanimate matter that we observe stable forms of organization. Only unstable forms are apparent in living nature. Stable inanimate systems defy cybernetic regulation, for at this level the modes of regulation are dominated by the constancy of the physical laws—the principles of conservation, of minimum dissipation, and of entropy. The stability afforded by this constancy is theorized to have provided for the emergence of life itself.[11]

With the emergence of a qualitatively new level of organization of living matter we observe the appearance of new stabilizing principles—in particular, the principle of persistent non-equilibrium. In the case of living systems, changes in environmental conditions may require rapid changes in an organism's parameters. Accordingly, it must possess a significant capacity to adapt to new conditions. This in turn requires a principle of controllability; that is, the system must possess a high capacity for change. In other words, it must possess mutability. However, unlike the stabilization characterized, for instance, in physical chemistry with the principle of Le Chatelier,[12] the stabilization of living matter is achieved through the operation of specifically cybernetic mechanisms identified with reflexivity and nonreflexivity. Without these qualities it is impossible to refer to the functioning of biological or social systems insofar as these cybernetic mechanisms are characteristically nonenergetic. We might speculate that it was this realization that caused Bogdanov, who wrote of cybernetically automated processes, to move from Ostwaldian energetics to Tektology.[13]

Bogdanov's Tektology maintained that at all levels of organization, from the inanimate to social forms, principles of conservation work toward stability. This proposition was implicit in O. Lange's understanding and was also a focus of attention in Bukharin's general theory of equilibrium.

While at the inanimate level, for instance, with a crystal, the conservation of energy and matter together with minimal dissipation of energy dominate, at the biological and social level these principles are complemented by the stabilizing influence of specifically cybernetic properties.[14]

The Soviet academician N.N. Moiseev observes that

> stable systems are always difficult to control. Changes in the conditions may call for relatively rapid changes in the organism's parameters. It must possess a capacity for adapting to new conditions relatively quickly. Accordingly, its organizational structure must permit a substantial measure of controllability (possess a high capacity for change). This is why, unlike at the level of inanimate matter, we observe only unstable forms of organization at the biological level where stabilization was sought through the operation of feedback mechanisms. It is at this level of organization that we first meet the "principle of instability" that makes possible specific types of control.[15]

It bears repeating: Stable inanimate systems defy cybernetic regulation, for at this level the modes of regulation are dominated by the constancy of the physical laws—the principles of conservation, of minimum dissipation, and of entropy.[16]

Following Bogdanov and Bertalanffy, and according to Jacob, it then appears that open systems—and in particular all living systems—provide for their reproduction over time by combining three principles whose implications at the socio-economic level we will seek to describe more precisely:

(1)   a principle of interdependence (semi-autonomy);
(2)   a principle of hierarchization of norms, modes of action, and of finalities; and
(3)   the principle of persistent non-equilibrium, accompanied by a variety of cybernetic mechanisms that operate both from below upward as well as from the top downward.

Moreover, organizational differentiation expresses itself in transitions from instability to the three forms of stability that were studied by W. Ross Ashby,[17] namely: simple stability, ultrastability, and multistability.

(1)   Simple stability refers to a situation in which a system is able to respond to a limited perturbance through a compensatory feedback device that allows it to maintain its structure.
(2)   Ultrastability refers to the ability of a system to not only respond to perturbances, but also, when they become too strong, or too frequent, to change the type of response and to invoke new adjustment mechanisms. Ultrastable systems appear to be "equilibrium-seeking".[18] They are morphogenic insofar as they attempt to adjust their internal relationships so that the effect of the disturbance is offset by adjusting the microsystemic characteristics that marks Le Chatelier's principle. Its meaning may be interpreted from the point of view of maintaining organizational relations.[19]

(3)   However, even the term ultrastability is not sufficient for complex open-systems. Ashby, therefore, applied the term "multistability" to those cases where the partial functions of the system are themselves individually ultrastable and where they can therefore "search" relatively independently for those critical behaviors consistent with the maintenance of the system. Passet interprets multi-stability as a consequence of an assemblage of ultrastable systems that are rela-tively autonomous and are not activated simultaneously in response to a stimulus. The concept of multistability achieves particular importance when we encounter autopoiesis.[20]

While multistability may indeed be characteristic of systems possessing rela-tive autonomy, a more important quality attaches to discrete domains of attrac-tion. For instance, an examination of ecosystems indicates distinct but stable levels of prey–predator populations, some of which may be threatened with extinction.[21] Some ecologists interpret the transitions between levels to be trig-gered by exogenous fluctuations of a random character.

While biogenetic evolution depended on biological forms of stabilization identified with homeostasis, man's cultural development necessitated a con-scious and social mode of stabilization that attached to institutionalization, none-theless constrained by the thermodynamic qualities of life.[22] "Whereas at lower levels of organization the 'binding energies' as a force of integration are high, as one advances to higher levels of organization the binding energies decrease."[23] Following Laszlo's thesis one might speculate that in suprasystems, such as social systems, the "binding energies" are, in fact, replaced by variety-integrative and institutional forms. This suggests that there is in the evolutionary sequence a transcendence from reliance upon principles of energy-matter conservation to the critical role of genetic and "metagenetic" information in the stabilization of organization. But, it is first at the biological level of organization that we speak of the stabilizing properties that attach to the cybernetics of living systems.

Consistent with the hierarchically differentiated image that dates back to Au-guste Comte, Laszlo locates the organization of societies within institutional contexts. He writes that societies follow the program set by the general laws that govern the evolution of such systems within the limits and possibilities created by human beings, their values, beliefs, habits, and mores. Moreover, on their own societies follow institutionalized rules, modes of behavior, and so forth, which are not reducible to the biological level of their members.[24]

The hypothesis that the laws governing the evolution of natural systems also constrain the development of societies is intrinsically reasonable and formed the basis of Quesnay's *Maxims*. But we must be clear that such laws are not determi-nant. They do not strictly prescribe the course of societal development. They merely establish the boundary conditions—they define the degrees of freedom within which innovation may proceed. Whereas the rules for biological evolution have been set by evolution of the cosmos itself, sociocultural organizational dynamics are first and foremost determined by society. Parenthetically, it is for this reason as well that the broadening of economic thought must reach beyond the vestiges of natural law and the merely thermodynamic dimensions of the economic process. A central issue in organizational theory, therefore, is the explication of the underlying principle of organizational dynamics. The approach to be outlined below lends itself in particular to methods for analysis of the genesis of social institutions.

Institutional Implications

The social and institutional embeddedness of man has attracted the attention of social philosophers since Aristotle. The fact of society was interpreted in Adam Smith's analysis as a "spontaneous order" guided by the ubiquitous and eschatological "invisible hand." Among institutional economists and sociologists this issue has invited wide-ranging consideration. The analysis of social values and the problem of "embeddedness" emerged as a central theme. Values, as such, appear in the form of opinions, attitudes, orientations, norms of behavior, and rules of conduct. While these appear to shape individual behavior and motivation, they are a phenomenon often conjectured to be beyond the initiative and compass of individuals. It is only within the bounds of institutions that, for instance, individualism or individual motives acquire their meaning. Social interactions are rule-governed events, not motives. Motives lead people to engage in particular activities, but what and how they do it depends upon the structure of institutions. In other words, motives operate within those social structures we refer to as institutions. But the classical institutionalist approach of this century contrasts in fundamental ways with the position assumed by that tradition associated with David Ricardo.

The Ricardian theme of individualism bears a continuity to elements of the behaviorist approach to institutions. The corresponding literature extends from Carl Menger's *Problems of Economics and Sociology* of 1883 to Friedrich Hayek's *Rules & Order*. But whereas the traditional behaviorist image is presented as the "organic" (to use Menger's term) emergence of institutions from the maximizing actions of individuals, the approach introduced below embodies a substantive comprehension of rationality and diverges from the behaviorist predilection.

Social institutions comprehended as sets of rules that constrain the full potential of individualism emerge in a variety of ways. Some, like the International Monetary Fund, the United Nations, or central banking, are institutionalized through statute law, while others are designed *ex nihilo* by a planning agency. Still others, such as terms of implicit contracts and customary business practices, emerge in an unplanned manner, though within the context of broader, previously instituted norms which facilitate and legitimate them. If we examine the alleged "spontaneous emergence" of institutions, it becomes clear that for a given social institution the set of social constraints that evolves to "govern" the actions of "free agents" involves a subset of the feasible class of strategies available to the agents.

Consider the example of two players engaged in some interaction, a game, for instance. Though the game may permit a large number of possible strategies, the players defer from the set of strategies that knowingly results in mutually disadvantageous outcomes. This is especially the case where the game is repeated numerous times. It is contended that the players engage in strategies and game-forms that provide a steady-state or reproducible game to emerge.

That so-called free agents exist, of course, already presupposes a certain political power of disposition. Or, in other words, and in the case of price-making market economies, the stage has already been set for the development of economic integration on the basis of individuation. Moreover, the mutually agreed upon constraints involve a tacit agreement to limit interaction strategies and to exclude as prohibited some mutually destructive options. Players of such games may be said to employ "bounded rationality."[25]

Among the most influential discussions on the notion of "bounded rationality" is that presented by Herbert Simon. Simon's analysis involves the recognition that complexity may deter the players from selecting strategies identified with Pareto optimality—that which attaches to "unbounded" rationality. As a consequence, he recommends a reduced emphasis on Pareto optimality (formal rationality) and a greater emphasis on the effectiveness of the procedures in the choosing (procedural rationality).[26] It is worth noting at this juncture that if rationality consists in the optimal adjudication of means to ends, i.e., formal economic rationality or in Weberian terms *Zweckrationalität*, then rationality must presuppose some context of means and ends for the optimization, i.e., *Zweckrationalität* is context-sensitive.

Viewing, for the moment, a system as a linear network of cause–effect relationships, its efficiency may be assessed when one ultimate effect is chosen and each relationship can be judged for its contribution to that final effect. Herbert Simon's analysis views the organization as a decision-making structure whose context is a means–ends chain, where the decisions in the organizations are reduced to the selection of the best means for achieving the ends as defined higher up in the structure. And, parenthetically, this forms the basis of the concept of "management by objectives." However, Simon's analysis seems possible only where the ends of the organization can be made fairly clear at the highest level of organization. The idea that different individuals or different groups can have different or even mutually incompatible objectives does not fit within this framework. Moreover, the problem of nonlinearity that attaches to systems experiencing organizational dissonance invalidates the concept of "bounded rationality" as well as the dictum "management by objectives." This is not to contend that organizations are not purposeful. To the extent that they operate within certain domains and seek to guarantee their homeostasis, they display the purposefulness of substantive rationality—*Wertrationalität.* They are, in a sense, structures that try to remain viable in an environment that on the whole is not very encouraging to their existence.

Living Systems, Organizational Dissonance, and Cybernetics

Among the most formidable difficulties confronting nearly all aspects of socio-economic research is organizational dissonance. This phenomenon emerges when changes in the state variables of one contextual macro-system impact, through its shared elements, other systems, inducing the latter to adapt to a new internal state. The result of organizational dissonance is usually a complex, i.e., nonlinear, often counterintuitive feedback relationship, which may mature into a pattern of protracted dynamic change in which the reproduction of an element is not necessarily assured.[27]

Bogdanov and Bukharin theorized that the evolution of society seems to be guided by this multidimensional and multitemporal mechanism of shared subsystems and intersystemic resonance. Departing from conventional dialectical materialist implications, such a notion opposes determinant causality. The idea that organized forms evolve through a linear process of goal-oriented or instrumental adaptation to context is a myth fostered by functional rationality and the mechanistic mode of thought. This brings us to a historical note.

Alfred Russel Wallace, a young naturalist in 1856 (three years before the publication of Darwin's *Origin*) while in the rain forests of Ternatee, Indonesia, had an attack of malaria and, following delirium, a psychedelic experience in which he discovered the principle of natural selection. He wrote this out in a long letter to Darwin. In this letter he explained his discovery in the following words:

> The action of this principle, is exactly like that of the centrifugal governor of the steam engine, which checks and corrects any irregularities almost before they become evident; and in like manner no unbalanced deficiency in the animal kingdom can ever reach any conspicuous magnitude because it would make itself felt at the very first step, by rendering existence difficult and extinction almost sure to follow.[28]

It is amusing to speculate that had Wallace's insight received the attention due it, we might not only have had a theory of the cybernetics of self-regulating systems much sooner, but the coevolutionary theory might have penetrated economic analysis much earlier. Instead of adopting Wallace's cybernetic perspective for economic analysis, a number of economists embraced Darwin's mechanical analog.

Wallace's theory, and now cybernetics, reveals that organizations do not actively seek or orient themselves toward the achievement of a desired state.

Rather, they arrive at any given state through processes of adjustment which eliminate other possible system states. The existence of a particular form is necessarily dependent on the exclusion of other possible forms. This understanding, of course, has certain implications for economic or administrative rationality. However, a fuller explication of the nuances is beyond the domain of this work.

Maruyama contended that organizations evolve through deviation-amplifying mutual causal processes between some mutations and their environment, and continue to exist as species insofar as they establish deviation-counteracting processes which sustain a balance with their environment.[29] Wiener has characterized what we see in nature and in the social world as a "residual pattern," for these organized forms reflect what is left over after morphogenic and morphostatic influences within a system have worked themselves out.[30]

Cybernetics thus invites us to reframe our understanding of contexts in a number of ways. It invites us to understand the processes that shape and change the context in terms of the relationships that define the context itself. Such an understanding requires us to revise our traditional conceptions of causality and retreat from prescriptions based on functional rationality and to accede to substantive rationality. For similar conditions may not produce similar effects and a small initial disturbance within a system may be accompanied by improbable changes and trigger counterintuitive reorganizations of the system in question. Once again, this has particular consequences for that form of economic rationality that attaches to a means–ends adjudication.

It is conceivable that what appears to be a stable organization may, in fact, be a potentially pathological system—a disguised powder keg whose fate can be turned by the most insignificant event. One may, for instance, witness this phenomenon with frightening clarity in the global financial markets.

Whereas traditional conceptions of causality and rationality and, thus, of strategy, emphasize the importance of administrative rationality and of organizations striving toward the achievement of goals, i.e., *Zweckrationalität*, cybernetic epistemology suggests an alternative substantive strategy, *Wertrationalität*, in which the avoidance of hazardous modes of behavior becomes an imperative. This conception has a great deal in common with the notion that organizational goals are in themselves sets of constraints that place limitations on systemic behavior. We might, for instance, speculate that organizational goals, as behavioral constraints, are themselves situated within a broad system of norms that define institutions. In this context goal-oriented activity pertains to discovering courses of action that satisfy constraints. Rather than formulating goals in terms of fixed points of reference toward which an organization should orient itself, a substantive rational approach suggests specifying merely that which is to be avoided. The constraints that need to be placed upon such action would be seen as of top priority in the generating and testing of alternative action plans. Action would be geared toward avoiding threatening system states, thereby creating a residual pattern consistent with systemic viability.

Within the context of global coevolution of man and the Biosphere this raises the problem of identifying integral coevolutionary norms and interrelations that must be established between three spheres: the economic, the social, and the Biosphere. Moreover, it refers to the design of "metainstitutions," which we shall seek to address later.

The relatively recent development in the general theory of organization toward principles of self-organization and the analysis of self-organization in non-equilibrium systems presents interesting perspectives.[31] Insofar as this approach is concerned not only with structure, but also with the dynamics of structure (due to internal and external processes that influence it), it offers analytically interesting mechanisms of social evolution. Comprehending organizations as self-organizing within an environment fosters theories that explain the differentiation of organizations in complex environments. That is how they might develop various structural characteristics including a multilevel hierarchy and semi-autonomous unities.

It is with this understanding that we come to the cybernetic principle of requisite variety. It is worth noting at the outset that the following represents a further and explicit challenge to the formalist concept of economic rationality and traditional modes of strategic planning as well.

Requisite Variety and Regulation

The function of regulation, whether it attaches to reflexive biological forms or nonreflexive organizations, is to achieve a goal against a set of disturbances. The disturbances may be irregular, as are those that originate in an ecological system, actively hostile, or openly benevolent. These relations may be shown in a most general manner by the formalism well known in the theory of games.[32]

As illustrated in the matrix shown in Figure 4.1, a set D of disturbances d_j may be met by a set R of responses r_i. The outcomes provide a matrix in which each cell shows an element z_{ij} from the set Z of possible outcomes.

The form is general enough to include the case in which the events d_j and r_i are themselves vectors and have a complex internal structure. Thus, the disturbances D might be the moves made by one's chess opponent, and the responses R all the countermeasures that might be taken. What is required at this stage is that the sets should be sufficiently defined so that the facts determine a single-valued mapping of the product space $D \times R$ into the set of Z possible outcomes.

The outcomes are events, without any implication of desirability. However, in any real regulation, for the benefit of an individual, organism, or organization, the facts usually determine a further mapping of the set Z outcomes into a set E of values. The set of outcomes E may simply be a two-element set (Bad, Good), a commonly ordered set, representing preferences of the organization. Some subset of E is perhaps defined as a "goal." The set of values, with perhaps a preference scale, may or may not be obvious in human affairs; but generally, the

Figure 4.1. **Matrix A**

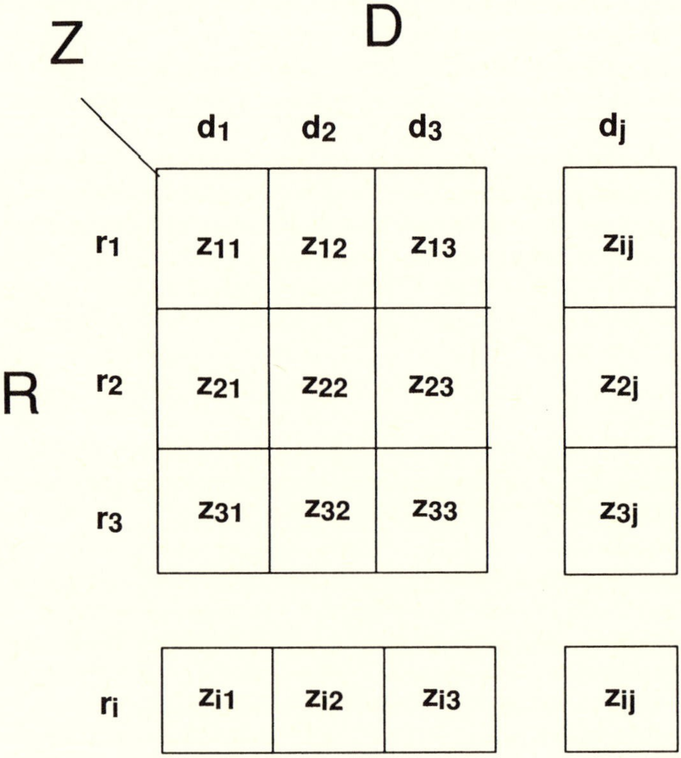

scale of values is related to "essential variables"—those fundamental variables that must be kept within, for instance, certain physiological limits. In an economic system, a firm may have a vector of such variables which include profit, market share, inventory, etc. which provide for the future viability of the firm.

Given the goal—the good or acceptable elements in $\mathbf{E}$—the inverse mapping of this subset will define, over $\mathbf{Z}$, the subset of acceptable outcomes. Their occurrence in the matrix will thus mark a subset of the product set $\mathbf{D} \times \mathbf{R}$.

Control

In the above formulation we considered the case in which the regulator acts to constrain the outcome to a particular subset, or to keep some variables within certain limits, or even to hold some variables constant. This reduction to constancy must be understood to include all those cases that can be reduced to this form. This same remark is clearly applicable to all those cases where an unchanging relation is to be maintained between one variable that is independent and another variable that is controlled by the regulator. We must at this juncture add a caveat. The concept of cybernetic "control" presented herein pertains to the cybernetics of linear systems. When one moves to systems characterized by nonlinearity, "control" loses its goal-oriented connotations. Rather than being identified with *Zweckrationalität*, its purposefulness assumes *Wertrationalität* dimensions.

Thus, if a variable **y** (which may be a vector) is to be controlled by a variable **a**, and if disturbance **D** intercedes in the system so that **y** is a function of both the control **a** and the value of the disturbance **D**, then a suitable regulator that can attenuate the disturbance may be able to counter its effects; that is, remove its effect from **y**, and thus leave **y** wholly under the control of **a**. In this case, successful regulation by **R** is the necessary and sufficient condition for successful control by **a**.

Requisite Variety

Now consider the case in which, given the table of outcomes (the payoff matrix), the regulator **R** has the best opportunities of achieving its goal. **R**'s opportunity is best if **R** can respond knowing **D**'s selection, **R** selects a countervailing value r_i, and thus selects a particular column. The outcome is the value of **Z** at the intersection. Such a payoff matrix might be as illustrated in Matrix B (Figure 4.2). If outcomes **a,b** count as Good and **c,d** as Bad, then if **D** selects d_1, **R** must select r_2, for only thus can **R** score a Good. If **D** selects d_2, **R** may chose r_1 or r_2. If **D** selects d_3, then **R** cannot avoid a Bad outcome; and so on.

Nature and other sources of payoff tables provide them in many forms, ranging from the extreme in which every one of **R**'s responses results in a Good (though these are undoubtedly rare!), to those hopeless situations in which every selection leads to a Bad. The more interesting case, however, is one in which each column has all its elements different. This implies that if the set **D** has a certain variety, the outcomes in any one column will have the same variety. In this case, if **R** is inactive in responding to **D**, i.e., if **R** adheres to one value of **r** for all values of **D**, then the variety of the outcomes will be as large as that in **D**. Thus, in this case, if **R** stays constant, **D** can be said to exert full control over the outcomes.

R's strategy, however, is based on confining the actual outcomes to some subset of the possible outcomes of **Z**. It is necessary, therefore, that **R** act so as to lessen the variety in the outcomes. If **R** conducts itself in this manner, then there is a quantitative relation between the variety in **D**, the variety in **R**, and the smallest variety that can be achieved in the set of actual outcomes; namely, the latter cannot be less than the quotient of the number of rows divided by the number of columns.

An approximate example of this is apparent in biology when an organism is

Figure 4.2. **Matrix B: Payoffs**

Z $\diagdown$ D		d_1	d_2	d_3
R	r_1	z_{11} (Bad)	z_{12} (Good)	z_{13} (Bad)
	r_2	z_{21} (Good)	z_{22} (Good)	z_{23} (Bad)

subject to attacks by bacteria (of species d_j) so that, if the organism is to survive, it must produce antitoxins r_i. If the bacterial species are all different, and if each species demands a different antitoxin, then, for survival, the organism must have at least as many antitoxins in its repertoire of responses as there are bacterial species.

While this example illustrates the principle for the trivial case in which responses r_i are continuously available, the situation is made more complex by making explicit the dynamics of each response i. This means dualities have to be mediated by time. Functionally differentiated technified societies need more time but in actuality have less time available than traditional societies. Their history, as well as their future, is much more complex and contingent than that of previous society. Nevertheless, time horizons relevant for orienting experience and action seem to shrink. As a consequence, we observe increasing time pressures in everyday life.[33] Thus, if we add the dimension of time to the problem, different selections r_i will have correspondingly different implementation times. Confronted with a disturbance d_j, whose effect is felt after time t, response r_i must be implemented in time $t_j < t$ if requisite variety is to be assured. That it may require a period of time for response r_i to be renovated from its previous selection against disturbance d_j may be interpreted as effectively removing it temporarily from the selection set Z_{ij}, if the periodicity of d_j is less that the renovation time of r_i.

The Cybernetics of the Error-Controlled Regulator

A case in which this limitation acts with peculiar force is the very common one in which the regulator is error-controlled. In this case the regulator's channel for information about a disturbance has to pass through an error-inducing variable which is kept as constant as possible (at zero) by the regulatory activity. Because of this route for the information, the more successful the regulator, the less will be the range of error, and therefore the less will be the capacity of the channel from **D** to **R**. In the extreme, if the regulator is totally successful, the error will be zero unvaryingly, and the regulator will be cut off totally from environmental information (about **D**'s value) that alone can make it successful—which, of course, is absurd. The error-controlled regulator is thus fundamentally incapable of being 100 percent efficient. Moreover, a controlled system is open to energy but comparatively closed to information. Consequently, although belonging to the universal scheme of things and intimately related to its environment, a system becomes semi-autonomous.[34]

Living organisms encountered this fact long ago, and natural selection and evolution have since forced the organization of channels of information through sensory organs that supply information about **D** before a chain of cause and effect goes so far as to cause actual error. As error-controlled regulation is often difficult to achieve in highly complex organizations, another higher-ordered means of regulation is called for. Regulation, which is excessively difficult to achieve when it is strictly error-controlled, may be more readily achieved if it is controlled, but not by what gives rise to the error. This is an application of the law of requisite variety and Shannon's tenth theorem. This rather benign comment assumes not-so-benign qualities in the context of autopoiesis and later in this chapter in the section on Freedom in Technified Society.

The cybernetician calls any situation in which a number of possible states might be realized a variety generator. Both that which is inclusive to a system, and that which is exclusive may be thought of as variety generators. In our game-theoretical context both **R** and **D** were variety generators. For instance, the quality of mutability, its degree and extensiveness, is a product of a system's inclusive variety generator **R**. With biogenesis this role is assumed by the DNA replicator molecule. **D**, on the other hand, refers to the environmental variety generator—anything outside the structure of **R**. This construction has broader implications which assume particular importance when we turn to address the institutional dimensions of socioeconomic systems theory, but it also pertains, more immediately, to organizational differentiation.

Complexity and Organizational Differentiation

Addressing himself to organization theory, Jan Koolhaas has written that

> organizing is the natural reaction to complex environments. In the sense of organization, another dimension is added to organizing; it is the rational solution to the problem of handling large complex tasks; tasks generated both inside and outside the organization. The concept of a task makes the organization necessarily purposeful with respect to the achievement of the results of the tasks.[35]

Whereas Herbert Simon views organization as a decision-making structure, Koolhaas argues that organization represents an attempt to find an answer to complex problems that need resolution.[36] Sir Stafford Beer regards the fundamental organizational problem as that of managing environmental variety. In this context organization is a structural device for reducing proliferating variety. He writes that when a large and complex system has been integrated into subsystems, "it loses the appropriate combinatorial power to become more complicated."[37] More specifically, the problem is that management processes require as much control variety as there is disturbance variety. Speaking abstractly, in a managerial situation, be it the multidimensional problem of cybernetic modes of regulation in human physiology or in the economy, as much controlling variety must be generated as there is variety in the system to be controlled. Consequently, we immediately have a criterion for systemic viability; a criterion, I might add, which escalates Ashby's principle of requisite variety to a preeminent role in the general theory of organization.[38]

The self-referential dimension of the Ashbian notion connotes an operation of self-closure, the perpetuation of which supposes that the viable system evolves ever more effective ways of interacting with its environment. Thus, enduring cybernetic systems are also open systems. However, the regulation of the flow of inputs and outputs requires, in turn, another kind of closure tending to isolate a system from the chaos of the external environment. No longer at the mercy of all the disturbances that affect it, a cybernetic system can persevere and seek to avoid the hazard of system breaks.[39]

The turn toward a theory of self-referential systems shifts the focus of systems theory from control to degrees of autonomy; from functional to substantive rationality. The guiding interest is no longer how to regulate systems, how to plan and implement changes, or how to overcome resistance. In other words, the praxis of control becomes nebulous. A controlled system escapes a wide range of environmental constraints and yet does not become, as a whole, fully autonomous.[40]

One interpretation we may now give to organizational differentiation is that it is a viability-seeking response which attaches to the principle of requisite variety. It is in this explication that Ashby's principle becomes not only a criterion of systemic viability, but represents a higher-ordered principle of conservation. Even Ashby recognized that his principle was analogous to the law of the conservation of energy.[41]

Thus, we may state that the "goal" of any viable system is to achieve requisite variety. Put abstractly, the system's objective function is the reduction of the overwhelming complexity of its environments to within manageable bounds. In the case of inanimate forms of organization, the operative mechanisms have been identified as the principles of conservation, the entropy law, and the principle of Le Chatelier. While in habitually reflexive forms, that mechanism for satisfying the criterion was provided by the principle of homeostasis.[42]

While biogenetic evolution depended on biological forms of stabilization identified with organic homeostasis, man's cultural development necessitated a conscious and necessarily social mode of stabilization that attaches to institutionalization. This, of course, does not divorce it from the open-systems analytical framework.[43]

The hierarchy created by organizational differentiation of systems is not only a structural and trophic hierarchy but also a control hierarchy, in which supra-systems seek to regulate selected aspects of the behavior of the subsystems. Thus, less complex systems on higher levels of organization can effectively control more complex systems on lower levels by virtue of a discriminating disregard of the dynamics and information of the lower-level units.

An organization's degree of hierarchical and/or functional differentiation is not only an expression of the structural complexity of the system, for the higher level is not necessarily more complex than its subsystems. Indeed, as paradoxical as it might seem, the emergence of a higher-level system is not a complexification but a simplification of system function. Any cognitive organization has limited feed-forward capacity. The cybernetics of feed-forward connotes the teleological proposition that the present state of a system may be an incarnation of an expected future system state. That capacity may be limited in its potential to gather and process information or to predict consequences of alternatives. To deal with situations of high complexity an organization must innovate processes for searching and learning as well as for decision-making. The full environmental complexity would annihilate the organization. It is confronted by an epistemic problem. It must restrict its knowledge and attach abbreviated meanings to phenomena; it must formulate decisions in "bounded *episteme*" and unavoidably employ "bounded rationality."[44]

Structural differentiation is fundamentally a vehicle by which organizations achieve "bounded *episteme*" and "bounded rationality." By delimiting responsibilities, control over resources, and other matters, organizations provide their participating members with boundaries within which efficiency may be a reasonable expectation.[45]

The age-old adage "time and tide stop for no man" is not without significance in technified society. Complex systems cannot afford to rely exclusively on one-to-one relations between external and internal events. The systems need time to process information and formulate viability-ensuring responses. As a consequence, they must include at least some structures or parts not directly embroiled in determining specific reactions. If external events require everything to be changed at once, even multistable complex systems would be eliminated. Organizational differentiation, in fact, is a structural technique for solving the time-consuming problems of systems situated in complex environments. Surrounded by "noise," organizations tend to stimulate morphotransformation processes and develop recursively structured systems.[46]

This is not to say that the variety "absorptive" capacity of a system is without limit. Some system break or a threshold exists beyond which there is too much "disorder" and "noise" and the system can then no longer be integrated. For example, ecologists have documented "threshold effects" which arise when a homeostasis is violated.[47] Once a critical threshold is transgressed in dissipative multistable systems, there may result the disruption of natural functions which threatens the survival of elements of the system. As soon as the impact of economic activities on the environment reaches critical thresholds the data are totally transformed.[48] Under such circumstances the environment can no longer be anticipated to provide for the system's own reproduction, and the realization of new forms of mutual interdependence, for instance, demolishes the image of man having been "liberated" from nature by technological evolution. The rediscovery of the dependence of man on natural phenomena cannot be perceived in terms of a return to a bucolic past with its blind submission to anarchic forces. The issue before us calls for a conscious harmonization to be effected in ways that respect the Biosphere, and of coherences without whose preservation human societies can have little prospect for the future.

A system cannot dispense with constraints, which are due as much to the physicochemical properties of its components as to the form of organization itself. But what is the limit of variety? A critical issue is to understand how a system can manage its own reproduction within an environment which is not in itself attuned to the requirements of the system; or, in other words, how a system can transform "noise" into that information that keeps in motion the self-referential network of internal processes.

In an expression of Gödel's theorem, functional differentiation leads to a condition in which the genesis of problems and their solution fall asunder.[49] Problems can no longer be solved by the system that produces them. They have to be consigned to the system that is best equipped to solve them. This is the role of the metasystem. There is, on the level of subsystems, less autarchy and self-sufficiency but higher levels of autonomy in applying specific rules and procedures to special problems.

A metasystem is structurally simpler than the subsystems that constitute it. And yet it possesses a metalogic and metalanguage with which to resolve problems and express itself. It might be said that it possesses a *"metaepisteme"*—a higher-ordered knowledge. The organizational hierarchy created by the evolution of systems is not only a structural hierarchy but also one of cybernetic metasystemic recursiveness. In a regulatory hierarchy, the metasystem exercises certain aspects of regulation on the behavior of the subsystems, but as Beer notes, it does so on the basis of authority rather than metalogically and metalinguistically. "The whole point about a metasystem is that it uses a metalanguage and while the point of a metalanguage is to be competent to decide propositions which are undecidable in the lower order languages of the systems concerned."[50] In short, Beer appeals to the logical transcendence at the metasystemic level of limitations imposed on the lower-ordered logics by Gödel's theorem. And it is precisely this that returns us to open-systems theory.

Jan Kamarýt asserts that every scientific and philosophical discipline appears to general system theorists as an "open system," that is, it cannot be completely understood in terms of its internal elements. Even the most logically consistent system must, at a certain level, that is, at the threshold of its *episteme*, step out of itself and cross its own boundaries.[51] Consequently, less complex metasystems can effectively regulate more complex systems on lower levels by virtue of the selective disregard of the dynamics of the lower-level constituents. This realization carries with it certain epistemological implications.

A Note on Complexity and Epistemology

Organizations may reduce the environmental variety in different ways consistent with Ashby's principle. Physical and organic systems proceed through natural structures and processes.[52] For instance, information is regarded as symbolization transposed from one type of signal to another by a source of information via selection. However, symbols are related not merely to other symbols, but also to the "meaning" of these symbols. Consequently, information achieves a semantic significance which thereby reduces environmental variety. In this sense Klaus, for instance, defines information as "an entity consisting of a semantic and a physical carrier."[53]

Following Shannon, Klaus contends that signals achieve "meaning" and semantic value by their receiver. In other words, a signal becomes information for its receiver only when it has been assigned clear "meaning" by the receiver.[54] In these terms "meaning" connotes a strategy of selective behavior in conditions of complexity consistent with Ashby's principle of requisite variety. This position achieves a unity with the arguments of Morgan, Maruyama, and Vickers—systemic viability refers to the avoidance of hazardous possibilities.[55]

Since variety and "meaning" converge on the fact of unavoidable selectivity, we are able to integrate both theoretical frameworks. Thus, variety and "meaning" may be comprehended as different expressions of the fundamental problem of order. Solving this problem requires a continuous organization of selective processes. "Meaning," as such, can be conceived as a representation of variety on the higher levels of recursion. It is this differentiation of meaning that attaches to the *metaepisteme* whereby each level of recursion possesses its own episteme—its own way of "knowing." Systems, like persons and social systems, which rely on "meaning" for coping with complexity, become, by this very fact, hypercomplex because they introduce into high-variety environments representations of their own variety.[56] By its very definition this infers that "meaning" is distinct from the "subject."[57] The problem of subject–object duality embodied in each *metaepisteme* assumes a phenomenological dimension—one that A.A. Bogdanov correctly sought to address at the level of a "metascience."

Among the implications that attach to cybernetic epistemology is the concept of misplaced concreteness. We may recall that Alfred North Whitehead referred to it, in the first instance, as "identifying abstract conceptions with reality" and, in the second instance, as "neglecting the degree of abstraction involved; when an actual entity is considered merely so far as it exemplifies certain categories of thought."[58] Cybernetic epistemology suggests that, in fact, all understanding is a form of misplaced concreteness of the first instance. The definitive issue, then attaches to Whitehead's second instance.

The essence of what comes to be experienced as "meaning" at a particular level of recursion consists of an actually given focus which radiates into further possibilities of experience and action. Only because of this can a difference make a difference and information processing, including cognitive processes, become possible. Ashbian cybernetics implies that we can never pursue all possibilities. We have to select what to think, what to see, and what to do next; irrelevancies, i.e., noise, must be attenuated. We can retain and reproduce actualized meaning only through selection.

The Problem of Wholes and Their Complexity

Aristotelian and later classical approaches to systems theory, using the paradigm of a whole and its parts, tended to discount the structural relevance of environments for systems. As we have already noted, such an understanding excluded, by these conceptual limitations, evolutionary perspectives. The result was a polarization of theories of order from theories of evolution, statics from dynamics, and interest in structure from interest in process. The respective theories generated controversies about whether structure or process was the fundamental reality of social life.

Moreover, traditional theory conceived complex systems as "wholes" synthesized of "parts." The basic idea was that the order of the whole accounts for qualities the isolated parts could never possess on their own. Beginning with the seminal contribution of A.A. Bogdanov, systems theory has departed from this traditional approach by introducing an explicit reference to the environment. The concept of an environment does not trivially imply that something exists outside the system being studied. Bogdanov's now-elaborated thesis was that the structures and processes of a system, including the economic system, are only possible in relation to an environment, and they can only be understood if considered in that relationship. This is the case since only by reference to an environment is it possible to distinguish between what functions as an element and what functions as a relation between elements.

Consequently, developments in systems theory increasingly focus on the environment of a system, attempting to understand systems as dependent upon and communicating with their environment. These developments, while differing among themselves, can be summarized in the fundamental idea that systems are reductions of the complexity of the world. They therefore inevitably sustain problematic relationships to environments that are not themselves reduced. Systems acquire an identity through their characteristic means of reducing complexity. However, if we refer to the Ashbian principle of requisite variety, then there is one fundamental mode of reducing environmental variety or complexity (the two terms being for our purposes synonymous). If we set out from this abstract formulation of the problem, we can functionally analyze and refer to all structures as selection processes. The means of comparison of structures could be grounded on Ashby's principle. Consequently, a theory of economy in the broad sense must concern itself with ideas such as the reduction of the extreme complexity and contingency of the world and with the creation of an ordered environment for societal subsystems. We might reinterpret this in the following manner: In order to comprehend the economy as an open communicative and coevolving system it is necessary to appreciate the principle of requisite variety.

Insofar as organization is interpreted as a dialectical response to complexity, which attaches to Ashby's principle, each successive resolution of polarities (within the system's renovation time) gives rise to a new "higher" level.[59] In this connection Oskar Lange posited that cybernetics explicates the mechanism behind the dynamic of dialectics.[60] Moreover, the very process of problem solving leads to the introduction of new elements or forces into a situation which engenders yet other problem situations. This dialectic is depicted in figure 4.3. For example, in order to promote coordination, organizational differentiation evolves along recursive if not hierarchical lines.

Yet, these processes often restrict communication critical to decision-making units. Consequently, the dialectics of problem and solution cumulatively generates a nonreduced environment which stimulates further organizational differentiation.

Organizational differentiation can be described as "intensifying selectivity." In the abstract, a critical function of the socioeconomic system, then, is to enlarge and reduce the variety of external and internal environments respectively to the effect that other systems will find enough structure to support boundaries and structures of higher selectivity. The process is recursive, repeating similar differentiation at the level of subsystems. The same mechanism thus facilitates organizations and interactions of high specificity and differentiation.[61]

The second law of dialectics, the transformation of quantity into quality, would also appear to be explicable in Ashbian cybernetic terms. Growth in complexity, i.e., variety, of a system implies informational and structural differentiation. The structural differentiation, along an organizational trajectory, embodies innovative properties and response capabilities in a system. The latter occasions qualitative changes of a basic nature. In terms of process, the operation of a positive feedback loop, if unchecked in its spiraling path, leads to collapse of a multistable system. The resultant state of affairs may represent a qualitatively different situation.

> The final stage of [the development systems theory] occurs when the relation
> between system and environment is understood in terms of a difference of

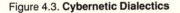

Figure 4.3. **Cybernetic Dialectics**

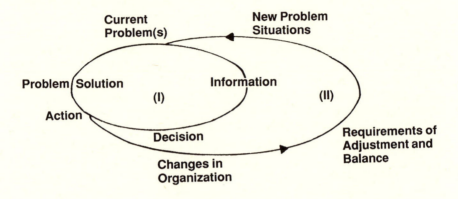

complexity. This is the cybernetic stage. It incorporates the findings of [Cannon and Bertalanffy] that is that systems, when open, maintain themselves through exchange with their environment. Only now the environment of any system is viewed as overwhelmingly complex which means that it always contains more possibilities than the system can utilize—incorporate into itself. This forces the system to make selections. They are aided in the process of making selections through the development of structures and processes which reduce the complexity of the environment and contribute to the system's own complexity. The system, therefore, at this stage of development, maintains itself by bringing its own complexity into a relation of correspondence—Ashby's law of requisite variety—with that of the environment.[62]

Systemic variety is manifest, insofar as a whole possesses qualities and properties that are not to be found in the parts in isolation and, conversely, that the parts possess qualities and properties that vanish as a result of the organizational constraints of the system. Systemic variety proliferates with the increase in the number and diversity of the component parts. With the increased flexibility and complication of the interrelations (interactions, feedback effects, interferences, etc.), in other words, as organizational dissonance rises, there is a decrease in that form of determinism suggested by the law of large numbers. A living system, for its part, possesses and combines to an exceptional degree the systemic variety of the "open" system and cybernetic complexity.[63] The cybernetic properties provide analytically interesting possibilities that pertain to the problem of order.[64]

Consistent with Ashbian cybernetics, with G. Vickers's dictum that "organization is always exclusive in relation to a variety of possibilities," and with Jan Koolhaas's and Stafford Beer's kindred insights, Nicklas Luhmann contends that systems are essentially "islands of lesser complexity in the world"; that a system is "anything actually existing . . . that maintains itself as identical to an extremely complex changing—as a whole unmanageable—environment."[65] In this sense every open system refers to the world as its ultimate environmental horizon because it can only maintain itself through metabolic interchange with that non-reduced environment. In order to maintain its stability, however, every system must reduce the variety of the world. Through "the grasping and reduction of complexity, Luhmann believes that social systems distinguish themselves significantly from all kinds of systems."[66]

Once having identified an organizational, i.e., managerial, principle, it is possible to conceptualize recursive organizational differentiation as "the reduplication of the difference between system and environment within systems."[67]

In organizations differentiated in this manner there are two kinds of environment: the outer environment common to all subsystems and the special bounded inner environment for each subsystem. For instance, J.K. Galbraith correctly argues that the corporation's organizational response to the so-called tyranny of the market is to retreat from its hazards; to seek refuge in a plan-guided alternative.[68] This implies that each subsystem constructs an abstraction of the whole system in the special form of a difference between system and environment. Differentiation performs the reproduction of the system in itself, replicating specialized versions of its own identity by a process of rationalization. This is, in fact, a process of growth by internal disjunction. The political subsystem, Luhmann argues, institutionalizes in a special way, conceiving society as an internal environment, and it tries to organize the political relevance of nonpolitical motives as the "public." Structural changes on the level of society, therefore, will have a selective impact on the whole; they do not necessarily affect the way the various subsystems (i.e., economic subsystem), in fact, interact.

The argument is that a general pattern emerges at the level of subsystems if functional differentiation is understood as the primary mode of the differentiation of society. Recursive functional differentiation maps onto a dialectical resolution and rationalization of problems from the level of society to the level of its subsystems. This is not simply a process of delegation or decentralization of responsibility, nor is it an expression of *Zweckrationalität*, that is, simply a factoring-out of "means for ends." The rationalization integrates each specific function into a new system/environment duality and produces types of problems and problem solutions that would not, and could not, arise at the level of the encompassing system.

In differentiated systems every subsystem has only three points of reference:

(1) its relation to the encompassing total system,
(2) its relation to other subsystems, and
(3) its relation to itself.[69]

The dialectic of differentiated systems emerges insofar as that in relation to their environment they function as a unity. However, at the same time they are internally apportioned into partial systems, none of which can delineate the unity of the total system. For, since everything within, be it a subsystem or an operational process, is only a part, according to Ashby's principle, it necessarily lacks the ability to encompass and reflect the totality, i.e., it lacks a universal episteme.

Might not this be an expression of the problem of a universal abstract? For instance, capitalism, as a totalizing system, seeks to internalize those systems with which it interacts, i.e., culture and nature. The internalization of externalities, according to the alleged efficiencies of market criteria, is symptomatic of market mentality. But it is also conceptually interesting to conjecture that it is on the basis of its natural philosophy predisposition that the market claims to be able to digest its own externalities, i.e., negativities that it itself generates. However, the paradox is that by its own logic it must fail; for it cannot reflect the logic of the other systems. We live in a society that cannot represent its unity in itself. Out of this dilemma, for instance, there emerges the problem of political legitimacy with its attendant implications, as well as the issue of global ecology.

An important aspect of system organization concerns the arrangement of processes at one or more levels. Within multilevel systems, the recursion of systems assumes particular importance. In such systems, each level includes all lower levels—there are systems within systems within systems.[70] This recursion attaches to a search for self-closure whereby a system evolves ever more effective (i.e., Ashbian variety-reducing) modes of interacting with its inclusive environment. Recursive systems reproduce increasingly improbable behavior patterns and problem solutions, and maintain evolutionary accomplishments within a zone of indifference against the environmental dissonances. This describes a situation for open systems in which "order is more natural than chaos."[71]

All concrete systems are based on a difference between system and environment. Therefore, organizational differentiation means the repetition of this difference within systems. The differentiated system becomes decomposed into a subsystem and an "internal" environment; for instance, as between the economic system and its environment. In this sense, organizational differentiation is equivalent to multiplication of the system by different internal epistemes. Complexification proceeds according to how the difference of systems and environments is realized.[72] The logic of capital is per force disembedding society and nature which are conceived as subservient subsystems. In turn, economic analysis itself has committed a series of self-induced divorces from substantive reality; first from nature and then from labor. This left capital, increasingly expressed only in its financial form, as the rarefied context within which calculation takes place.

Complexification by organizational differentiation means the progressive creation of internal environments. A multistable self-referential system replicates the difference between system and environment as part of the internal processes of self-reference. The system is continuously self-referential, distinguishing itself from the environment on the basis of its introspective episteme. This is accomplished by defining and maintaining boundaries which may be crossed occasionally, i.e., it is an open system. Such a system is a multistable "autopoietic" unit. It produces the elements that compose it, and, in turn, this necessitates the capacity to distinguish elements that belong to the system from elements that belong to the environment of the system. The distinction between system and environment is, therefore, constitutive for whatever functions as an element in a system.[73] Parenthetically, the recursiveness of systems–environment functional differentiation carries with it the denaturalizing threat which attaches to, for instance, extreme cases of bureaucratization of social institutions and its technocratic response.

Living Systems, Autopoietic and Allopoietic Systems

Systems on organizational levels, where life emerges, are too far from thermodynamic equilibrium to persist indefinitely in their milieu. Such systems can maintain themselves only if they evolve the capacity to replicate or reproduce their structure. Using a term introduced by Humberto Maturana in the 1960s, we can describe such relatively high organizational levels as "autopoietic" (from the Greek for "self-creating"). In the now-classic work of H. Maturana and Francisco Varela, an autopoietic system was defined as a multistable network of interrelated component-producing transformations whereby the components in the interaction replicate the network that produced them. The product is always the network itself, created and recreated in a flow of matter and energy. Thus, by definition, autopoietic systems are partially open systems.[74]

An autopoietic system is a distinguishable complex of component-producing processes, bounded as a semi-autonomous unity within its environment and characterized by organizational dissonance.[75] Autopoietic organization is further characterized by a partial closure of its constitutive processes. At least some of the products become necessary ingredients or conditions for their own reproduction. In this sense autopoietic systems seek closure from a complex environment whereby they define themselves as systems. Nonetheless, at various levels, they remain open with respect to their environment. It is this that confers upon them semi-autonomous organizational qualities. They are semi-autonomous in the sense that they subordinate changes to the maintenance of their own organization, independently of how profoundly they may otherwise be transformed in the process.

Autopoiesis is the holistic expression of a function that is primarily geared to self-renewal. Whereas in mechanical systems where the "solution" to Boltzmann's ordering principle is to delay the course of entropy and environmental variety by the high reliability of their component parts, the "solution" of living open systems is to accentuate and amplify disorder in order to find therein the means of renewing the order they evoke. Permanent reorganization and autopoiesis constitute categories applicable to the whole biological order and, we submit *a fortiori*, to the human socioeconomic order.

A cell is in a permanent state of self-production through the death of its molecules. An organism is in a permanent state of self-production through the death of its cells. A society and its economy, in the substantive sense, are in a permanent state of self-production through the death of their individual members, and through "metabolic" processes transforms low entropy into high entropy. And, from a Schumpeterian analysis capitalism is self-reproducing through its process of "creative destruction". It continually reorganizes itself through disorders, antagonisms, and conflicts, which undermine its existence and at the same time maintain its vitality.[76]

An autopoietic organization is a network of processes of production (transformation and destruction) of components that produces the components which, through their interactions and transformations, continuously regenerate and realize the network of processes (relations) that produced them. In biology a cell, for example, is autopoietic in its balanced self-renewal through the interplay of anabolic and catabolic reaction chains. Over extended periods, it does not consist of the same molecules. That the socioeconomic system is reproductive in an analogous manner is what we seek to demonstrate.

Living systems are autopoietic; they transform low-entropy matter and energy into themselves in a manner such that the product of their operation is their own organization. Thus, autopoiesis is necessary to characterize the organization of a living system. It follows that an autopoietic organization continuously generates and specifies its own organization through its operation as a system of production of its own components, and does this in a turnover of components under conditions of continuous perturbation and compensation for perturbation. It is a homeostat of high specificity; a device for holding critical systemic variables within physiological limits. In the case of autopoietic homeostasis, the critical variable is the system's own organization. Thus, an autopoietic unity may be understood as a "relations-static" homeostatic system which has its own organization (defining network of relations) as the variable that it seeks to maintain constant.[77]

We noted that the functional differentiation of systems is a response to environmental variety, i.e., complexity, wherefore the system seeks self-closure. It is within its self-imposed and self-composed boundaries that a system evolves toward a steady state characterized by minimum entropy production. In the case of an autopoietic system this is what contributes to its specificity. It does not matter, it seems, whether every measurable property of that organizational structure changes in the system's process of continuing adaptation. It survives as a steady-state non-equilibrium system; what matters are its relations.[78]

The product of an autopoietic system is the system itself; it maintains its own identity under a continuing turnover of its constituent components. Autopoietic systems have as their reference their own finality. From a global point of view it is possible to define levels of organization by elaborating the finalities of the whole, and the combinations and conditions for the appearance and existence of an autopoietic system. Indeed, we note that any living autopoietic system is inseparable from a finality that expresses itself through its function. However, such function or functions are simultaneously an outcome of combining a set of elementary tasks that may be located at an inferior level of organization, and when combined with others represent a means of accomplishing one or several responsibilities that are located at a metasystemic level.

Any motion, change, or transformation of any component results in a structural deformation of the field of components. The space in which the autopoietic system exists, i.e., the environment of its autopoiesis, is being continually perturbed and restructured by the autopoietic system itself. Yet, the autopoietic system is capable of maintaining its organization, its autonomy, and its overall structural pattern in spite of the changes of its components.[79]

Consequently, a change in any of the components must affect the interactions among all other components in such a way as to yield a net counterbalancing response of the system as a whole toward the maintenance of its integrity, i.e., its homeostasis. The whole and the parts reciprocally influence, coevolve, with each other.

Autopoietic organizations have individuality; that is, by keeping their organization invariant through their continuous production they actively maintain an identity that is independent of their interactions with an observer. Accordingly, the ontogeny of a living system is the history of maintenance of its identity through continuous autopoiesis.[80]

In fact, a living system is specified as an individual, as a unitary element of interactions, by its autopoietic organization. It is this that determines that any change in it should be subordinated to its maintenance. This stabilizes the boundary conditions that specify what does and does not pertain to it in the concreteness of its realization. If the subordination of all changes in a living system to the maintenance of its autopoietic organization did not take place, it would disintegrate; that is, it would lose that aspect of its organization that defines it as a whole.

Those organizations that have as the product of their functioning something other than themselves are called allopoietic organizations. Or, to put it another way, a system that only produces something other than itself, a different unity, is an allopoietic system. It is one that produces components which do not participate in its constitution as a semi-autonomous unity.[81] But, this definition is not yet rigorous enough, for it admits the possibility, for instance, of a fully robotized system producing components for its self-regeneration. Since the changes that allopoietic organizations may suffer without losing their definitive organization are necessarily subordinated to the production of something different than themselves, they are not semi-autonomous. Allopoietic organizations have an identity that depends on the observer and is not determined through their operation. Because their product is different than themselves, allopoietic organizations lack individuality. An autopoietic system refers, in the first instance, to its *being* and is therefore self-referential. In contrast, an allopoietic system, such as a technological system, refers to a function given from outside. For instance, the production of a specific output.[82]

Passet defines a system as "a finalized set of elements interacting with each other; whose set of finalities are decided within the system itself."[83] A corollary to this definition is that "a set whose finalities are decided outside of its limits is a false system, a subsystem of a larger reference within which other poles, i.e., nations or multi-national firms, decide its fate."[84] From this corollary, we may say that the organization that subordinates its own finality to that of another system is made *ersatz*. And, insofar as the price-making market seeks to subordinate the Biosphere to its finality, the Biosphere is made spurious to the finality of the sphere of market relations. Of course, it may also be argued forcefully that the market depreciates culture as well. But such a critique is beyond the compass of this work.

On the basis of this concept of system and finality, Passet mounts an argument counter to the Ricardian orthodoxy of international trade theory. He writes that

> to the extent that a nation exports its primary materials and its agricultural products in an untransformed state in order to import manufactured products it finds itself in a situation of a system that is crisscrossed by energy flows that it does not employ for developing its own structure. It permits others to utilize the same flows in order to develop their activities of transformation that is to diversify and grow at the expense of its own possibilities.[85]

For instance, the structure and development of a nation may be decided by transnational actors. Because they do not possess a capacity to define their own national finalities, they fail to constitute a system in the full meaning of that term and exist merely as a subsystem to transnational organizations within the context of a larger system of division of labor.

Autopoietic organizations are unities because of, and only because of, their autopoietic homeostasis. Their operations specify their own boundaries in the process of self-production. This is distinct from the allopoietic organization whose boundaries are defined by the observer, who by specifying its input and output, artificially specifies what pertains to its operations.[86]

Technological systems are allopoietic insofar as their objective finality is conferred upon them from without. And, it is in this connection that we may assert that technological systems are fundamentally disembedded systems. Autopoietic systems possess within themselves their *being*, their self-defined objective finality. They are, therefore, fundamentally embedded systems. Whereas a nexus of technological complexes is allopoietic and disembedded, naturally occurring ecosystems are embedded. It is on the basis of this distinction that the analysis, design, and management of these systems must differ.

For an organization to be autopoietic, its defining relations of production must be continuously regenerated by the components that it produces. Reproduction requires a system to be reproduced. That is why reproduction is operationally secondary to the establishment of the system, and it cannot enter as a defining feature of the organization of living systems. Furthermore, since living systems are characterized by their autopoietic organization, reproduction must necessarily have arisen as a complication of autopoiesis during autopoiesis, and its origin must be viewed and understood as secondary to, and independent from, the origin of the living organization. Sequential reproduction, with the possibility of change in each reproductive step, necessarily leads to evolution, and in particular, in autopoietic systems evolution is a consequence of self-reproduction.[87]

Components of each system, in the hierarchy of systems, are themselves differentiated systems whose ability to persist depends on their being part of the more comprehensive (higher-order) system. The more comprehensive systems themselves can maintain their existence only through the order-preserving behavior of their components.[88]

Subsystems, nested within larger systems as their components, are able to utilize the decay and disintegration products of the larger systems and organize such dispersed components into more complex structures, renewing their own existence. They are capable of autopoiesis—creating order from chaos and temporarily defying the second law of thermodynamics.

Biological phenomena depend on the autopoiesis of the individuals involved. Thus, there are biological systems that arise from the coupling of autopoietic unities, some of which may even constitute autopoietic systems of higher order. A living system is defined by its organization and, hence, it can be explained as any organization is explained, that is, in terms of relations, not of component properties. What about human societies we might ask? Or, to what extent do the relations that characterize a human society as a system constitutively depend on the autopoiesis of the individuals? If human societies are not biological systems, the social dynamics will depend on laws and relations that are independent of the autopoiesis of the individuals.[89]

The continuing developments of systems theory places a focus on the environment, attempting to comprehend systems as dependent upon and communicating with their environment. Such developments, as a whole, are consistent with the fundamental notion that systems are reductions of the complexity of the world. Consequently, they experience a sustained problematic relationship to a nonreduced environment. Systems, as such, may acquire their identity through the Ashbian principle of requisite variety by which they reduce environmental complexity to a level of manageability through selection, i.e., filtering, processes. On this basis, a theory of society, for instance, must concern itself with concepts such as the filtering of complexity of the environment and with the synthesis of an ordered environment for all the subsystems of society. This necessarily includes the economic subsystem.

Autopoiesis and Economic Production

The general emphasis on the cybernetics of autopoiesis is a very different perspective from that of either Alfred Lotka or Erwin Schrödinger, who were immersed in nineteenth-century mechanical materialism.[90] Schrödinger, following Boltzmann, in his definition of living systems, alluded to the so-called law of large numbers, referring to "the statistical mechanism which produces order from disorder." Schrödinger, in *What Is Life from the Point of Physics*, evaluated different processes in terms of their energy intensity. Schrödinger's analysis, for instance, indicated the operation of the principle of minimal dissipation of energy, while those of Boltzmann, and later A. Bogdanov, N. Bukharin, and Lotka, suggested the probable role of what Howard Odum refers to as the "maximum power principle" in the processes of living systems. Schrödinger, Boltzmann, and Lotka argued that the fundamental object of contention in the life struggle, indeed, in the evolution of the organic world, is available energy.[91]

Notwithstanding the relevance of the thermodynamic perspective, it is not singularly characteristic of autopoietic forms.[92] For while Boltzmann et al. maintain that the advantage in biological evolution must go to those organisms whose energy-capturing devices are most efficient in directing available energy, the origin of those efficiencies must lie with the reflexive and nonreflexive capacities of autopoietic forms.

It is the homeostatic perturbation avoidance-oriented activities of multistable autopoietic forms that activate new mechanisms of selection identified with feedback relations. It is important to emphasize that without accounting for feedback relations, which, I might add, are not produced by laws of physics, it is not possible to describe the functioning of living systems.

Substantiating this position, the physicist Ernest Hutten notes that the behavior of an organized system, the action of an organism or human activity, cannot be explained exclusively in terms of causal energy.[93] Information, rather than energy causality, describes processes in or between organized systems. Hutten maintains that the most general model of a natural process on which scientific explanation may be based pertains to the organization and the transmission of information within a system. The categories of energy and materials, though they are necessary for biological evolution, appear as limiting factors rather than determining ones; for with biogenesis it was the information system of genes that enabled evolution to accelerate away from simplicity.[94]

Of course, social systems distinguish themselves from biological systems through their capability of generating and bringing into play information (innovations) in negligible time spans compared with biogenetic morphotransformations. Cognition, insight, ideas, models, expectations: all introduce what, in biological terms, could be called extremely unstable chreods (organization lines) which interact and compete with each other. As John Calhoun puts it, the cybernetics of a deviance-controlling process is always slightly subordinate to the deviance-promoting processes—"man is a crisis provoker."[95] Calhoun's despairing comment, in fact, attaches to the issue of "complexity and organization differentiation," but also to the corresponding epistemological problem. The human capability of invention accelerates the evolutionary processes to such an extent that it is directly observable in the form of history.

We observe the appearance of a qualitatively new principle at the biological level of organization, namely, that of feedback, without which it is impossible to explain the functioning of autopoietic systems. Among the first to understand this was A.A. Bogdanov. Although his entire exposition did not use the term "feedback relation," his theory, as we have seen, is permeated with the spirit of the theory of feedback relationships. It is the homeostatic, hazard-avoiding activities of autopoietic forms that activate new mechanisms of selection and that attach to feedback relations.

Consequently, the description of autopoietic macrosystems refers to a system of relationships involving the circulation of matter and of energy together with behavior functions embodying feedback relations of reflexive and/or nonreflexive types. It is precisely this necessity that demands a further broadening of the theory of production beyond the merely thermodynamic qualities of open systems.

The Informational Dimension of Production

Traditionally, economic analysis resolved the production process in terms of a synthesis of three factors: land, labor, and capital. The Physiocratic perspective, in particular, focused on nature (land) as the origin of wealth. But with the advance of technological processes of production the center of attention shifted from the fertility of nature to the role of commodified labor.[96] And so William Petty's labor theory reemerged, theoretically elaborated by Smith and Ricardo and later, of course, by Marx.

However, the division of factors of production into land, labor, and capital has its origins not in the theory of production, where categories fit awkwardly as heterogeneous and "almost meaningless aggregates," but rather, in the theory of the price-making exchange economy, because these aggregates form units of exchange.[97]

In this context Walras's *Elements of Pure Economics* reduced circulating capital to the status of the services of fixed capital. Just as "a field will grow a crop for us year after year," he wrote, ". . . machines, instruments, tools . . . engender incomes in the same way."[98] But in treating machines and other capital goods as formally analogous to Ricardian land, Walras ignored the flows of materials and low-entropy energy without which there would be no physical flow of output whether from land or from industrial processes.

Moreover, despite numerous references in conventional economic literature to "capital," the essence of "capital" remains open to interpretation.[99] Following

Fisher,[100] Daly regards "capital" as representing "exosomatic organs," and conversely biological organs are interpreted as representing "endosomatic capital." Physical capital may be described as analogous to land, as matter that is capable of trapping artificial energy and channeling it to human purposes. And in this naturalistic sense it is said to bear a certain resemblance to the process of photosynthesis. It is in this sense that Daly regards "capital" as representing the "exosomatic organs" of man; prosthetic devices that may be described as artificial metabolizing agents.

This view of capital as the embodiment of nature holds a number of interesting insights. The first of these pertain to the fundamental difference between nature and artifice. And, whereas the photosynthetic processes of the leaf are a biochemical organization of matter and solar energy evolved by the complexification of autopoiesis, capital exists as a set of prostheses designed by the historical memory of mankind to artificially metabolize and restructure nature. And, whereas authentic autopoietic systems bear within themselves a self-defined finality, artificial systems have no concrete finality within themselves. They achieve their end only in connection with society at a certain stage in the historical development of capital.

In both autopoietic and allopoietic forms, external sources of energy are first disintegrated through natural anabolic processes and then directed to catabolic processes for the self-production and self-renovation of the system. Thus, both endosomatic and supporting exosomatic processes are said to have a physical bias (metabolism) which undergoes continual replacement over relatively short time periods (steady-state aspect), and which is capable of qualitative change and reorganization over long periods (evolutionary aspect). But authentic autopoietic systems cannot be separated from the energy that nourishes them. If separated from that source, they perish. The finality of the system is to protect itself from destruction, to renovate and reproduce, but above all to achieve the state of *being* that is the imperative of life itself.[101] Artificial allopoietic systems, i.e., machines, however, merely stop and wait to begin functioning anew as soon as they are once more "nourished." In the case of technological systems their finality is merely to renovate components of technological subsystems that they might serve as infrastructure to specific external functions, i.e., they pertain to a finality defined outside of themselves.

The foregoing infers that it is inappropriate to refer to technological design activities as negentropic. Nor is it the case that merely because external sources of low-entropy materials and energy are captured, whose net outputs are transmitted along a "trophic chain," is the production process analogous to an authentic autopoietic system, i.e., an ecosystem.[102] Consequently, any analysis of the technological dimensions of the economy in purportedly natural terms is distorting, conferring upon a dead allopoietic, i.e., mechanical, system the attributes of an authentic autopoietic system.

Whereas some economists have sought to broaden economic thought by reformulating our understanding of the economy and our concept of production consistent with the theory of open systems and have focused on its energy dimensions, others have supplemented that analysis by identifying the critical role of structuring information.

Organisms develop their informational activities with the help of the nervous systems with which they are endowed. Following G. Vickers's example we may say that there are two autopoietic feedback loops; one serves to regulate the internal relations of the system and the other seeks to partially isolate the autopoietic system from its ultimate environment while maintaining homeostasis.[103]

(1)   The internal feedback loop governs the overall set of internal responses and within relatively narrow limits keeps its own internal conditions constant. This may include central temperatures, arterial tension, contents of a variety of substances, excretions, etc. In this connection, the term homeostasis refers to the play of self-correcting mechanisms that tend to return each of these variables to its "normal" state as soon as it begins to deviate from it. For this to take place, all parts of the system continually exchange multiple relative indications of their state and of their needs. Consequently, we may refer to it as a message-conveying subsystem.

(2)   The external feedback loop links organisms to the environment from which they borrow those substances that they require for their existence and to which finally it returns the waste products of its metabolic activities; and that loop extends to the external world through the release of heat.

Though we have cautioned against confusing the methodological reductionism of mechanicalism, this is not to deny the analytical relevance of specific qualities of mechanical systems for living ones. And, though man's cultural development is not isomorphic to biological evolution, it is more than merely illustrative. There are significant differences between cultural and biological evolution on which sociobiologists equivocate. For instance, the genetic information that produced biological diversity is contained within the authentic autopoietic form itself, while the "genetic" information of allopoietic forms is disembodied—residing outside of the system itself. In this sense they are "metagenetic"; and it is this metagenetic quality that attaches to the production process within the concept of the economy as a open system.

Borrowing analytical concepts from general systems theorists, René Passet charges that a system's "organization leads it to oppose the entropic tendency by borrowing from the environments the elements that permit it to maintain its structure, and to develop and reproduce itself."[104] Parenthetically, it is worth noting that this phenomenon of "negentropy" is a manifestation of the cybernetics of autopoiesis, i.e., Ashby's law. However, in order to achieve viability it must, on the one hand, borrow low entropy from its environment. On the other hand, that borrowed low entropy must be structured through information. While this suffices to introduce the role of information, it already represents a departure from the concept of information embraced by conventional economic theorists.

To the neoclassical economist there is no distinction between "information" and "knowledge." The concepts are interchangeable and are loosely used to describe a category of boundary conditions that prevent economic actors from achieving functional rationality—from performances that may achieve some optimum in the allocation of resources. Moreover, conventional theorizing tends to either assume "perfect knowledge" or to argue that the price system itself conveys the requisite information for decision making. However, the underlying axiomatic abstractions in no sense capture the richness of socioeconomic autopoiesis.

The alternative mode of perceiving this problem, as we have already suggested, pertains to the analytical category of information theory, that is, defining information in a way that is logically independent of "meaning." Information theory conceptualizes "information" as a flow of "messages" having "news value," that is, they provide the receptive organization with some structuration. In this Aristotelian sense information is literally "in forming." This provides a basis for the general theory of socio-economic autopoiesis.

However, such a casual understanding has opened the theory up to some criticism. For instance, it may be asserted that the greater amount of information in any given system the smaller will be the entropy, or the greater will be the systems' negentropy. Moreover, the greater the flow of information, the greater the degree of information that has relevance to the process of economic production. It is precisely such an organizational feature that permits the conversion of information into useful knowledge and thence to technical process.

A. Tsuchida and T. Murota maintain that the notion that information or knowledge somehow possesses negentropic qualities is a delusion that attaches to the popular concept that post-industrialism refers to an "information society."[105] "We think that behind such anticipations there is a theorized myth that increasing the amount of information may decrease entropy. Such a myth could be derived from the view which puts the information in the sense of communication engineering measured by [binary units] on the same dimension as . . . [the] peculiar concept of negative entropy or negentropy."[106]

Insofar as Tsuchida and Murota's critique is directed to those closed-systems theorists who equate technological innovation with information and then speculate on the infinite substitutability of technological innovations for physical scarcities, their analysis is well founded. However, their argument does not categorically invalidate an informational approach to the economic process.

Indeed, the complexity of technified society may well demand an "information society." For insofar as a principal activity of the individual in a technified, functionally differentiated organization is to solve problems and to make decisions and their execution possible, his or her ability to do so can be seen as an important variable. However, by conceptualizing the individual as a problem solver, where the problems are posed by the complexity of the environment, for instance, by other operational groups within the organization, information becomes the critical "commodity." Instead of raw materials and the consumers of transformed raw materials, available information and the ability to process it are elevated to a preeminent role. Knowledge, in this context, is essentially a specific form of information. This understanding serves to reinforce the argument for a broader definition of the economic process.

Consequently, it is analytically useful to identify the factors of production as structuring information, energy, and materials. All processes of production are in a limited sense temporarily negentropic, involving the direction of energy by some structuring information toward the selection, transportation, and transformation of low-entropy energy and materials into a use-value. Thus, a theory of production in the broad sense is conceptually analogous to that expressed by the Aristotelian St. Thomas Aquinas, for whom the crafting of use-values was one of the sorting and shuffling of use-values appropriated by man from nature. Moreover, the economy may be conceptualized as a temporary negentropic structuring and restructuring activity whose effect is to incorporate structuring information into use-values.[107] Inert matter is transformed into a use-value together with the energy expenditure that must be supplied by networks of technological systems.

Clearly, it is the "informing" process that plays the critical role in the genetics of biological evolution and "metagenetics" in man's livelihood. It is the "structuring information" that is activated in economic activities. "The more a system is structured, the less it is probable, the more it is distant from a situation of entropy and the more it contains free energy. There exists a positive relation between structural information and free energy, and therefore a negative relation between structural information and entropy."[108]

Following Schrödinger's definition of open systems, J. Robin writes that "the essential characteristic of living systems is the production of order and movement against the stream of entropy."[109] However, autopoietic systems reorganize themselves and subject themselves to "self-reorganization" under the influence of the information that is communicated to them and that they carry. As such, dissipative autopoietic systems form "oases" in a general state of increasing entropy.

> Neither the existence of a machine nor its mode of functioning is inscribed in the species' genetic code. It is the written and oral traditions, as well as relevant forms of gesticulation, that continue the work of that code. Because they do assume its functions it has been possible to justifiably refer to them as a genuine cultural code. More flexible than the genetic code, not bound to invariably reproduce the same patterns, and possessing a capacity to diversify and evolve over time periods that are extremely brief by comparison with organic evolution, it, nevertheless, possesses the disadvantage of a greater instability. Acquired biological characteristics recorded in the genome are transmitted from generation to generation through the invariance of DNA, but

the cultural acquisitions of each person vanish with his death. The development of societies thus rests on a continuing effort to conserve, enrich and transmit the information that is contained in the cultural code. The societal structures that perform that function appear as networks of relations and of communications that make possible the continuity and survival of social groups. Like any organized system they first tend to provide for their own reproduction and develop for that purpose norms, values, and hierarchies that appear as a set of corresponding information systems pertaining to regulation: they regulate, in the proper sense of that term, the group's metabolism.[110]

"Metagenetic" or structuring information directs energy toward the transportation and transformation of materials into a use-value. These production processes involve a definite technologically determined sequence. And, as in the biological case, production may be constrained by an operational insufficiency of any one of three primal factors—information, energy, or materials. Systems may be open or closed in respect to the factors. The economy is open in regard to all three.[111]

Each of Alfred Marshall's three factors of production consists of varying combinations of structuring information, energy, and materials; and, as such, the role of entropy assumes critical import. The throughputs of information are elusive. Nonetheless, they exemplify an open system, supraordinate to and contingent upon transformations of matter and energy. It is fundamentally the structuring role of information that dominates. For it is the element of information that provides the adaptivity and diversity necessary for autopoiesis, i.e., it is the information that animates cybernetic systems and that facilitates adaptive responses.

The production of human artifacts is also multiparental, in the sense that the metagenetic information that organizes production is contained in a variety of cultural artifacts. And, it is this highly polymorphic phenomenon that is undoubtedly responsible for the accelerated pace of cultural development and for the evolution of the Technosphere.

The process by which a fertilized egg becomes a living system, while it is analogous to the process by which knowledge embodied in the minds of engineers is ultimately transformed into a use-value, is, nonetheless, distinct. The distinction lies in the finalities of the two. The ultimate finality of an authentic autopoietic system is simply "to be," whereas the finality of the technological production process is sharply divorced from the finality of the engineer. The imperative of the autopoietic system is life itself, whereas that of an engineer's services is increasingly motivated by a technological imperative which now assumes global dimensions. Within this framework a central problem is that release mechanisms identified with the generalized monetization of international pressures induce innovations whose constraint is imposed by monetary accountancy. In other words, the danger is that the normative conditions and constraints which guide technological development are divorced from those of the Biosphere. They are neither coevolutionary nor do they embrace the filtering principle embodied in the second cybernetics whereby socially irresponsible and undesirable forms are avoided.[112] These distinctions separate the conventional Ricardian mode of analysis from post-Ricardian plan-guided forms of coevolution analysis.[113]

A Note on Autopoiesis and Economic Reproduction

At this juncture it is worth noting that that which purports to be the science of the livelihood of man, with its doctrine of irresponsible individualism, cannot even show that it is necessary to provide for autopoiesis in the sense of social reproduction. Nor, of course, does it comprehensively address intergenerational resource distribution. And yet the self-evident finality of any autopoietic system, including society, is to maintain and reproduce its structure; that is, to be. It is only in relation to that finality that *Homo oeconomicus's* search for *having* acquires meaning.[114]

Whereas Quesnay, Ricardo, and Marx affirmed in various forms the need to devote a part of the flows to reproduction, except for Quesnay, for whom the economic sphere coincided with the Biosphere, that problem was conceived within the narrow confines of an included system (which possesses its own logic) and not of a wider whole, whose reproduction sustains its subsystems.[115]

Political economy in the narrow sense, i.e., economism, is situated within a reductionist and diametrically opposed perspective to that expressed above. Its postulate is mythic—that the coevolution of man and the Biosphere may be harmoniously regulated by a totalizing subsystem, namely, the price-making market system.

Increasingly fitted into a narrow logic of price-making markets that are thought to be self-sufficient, economic thought has made an inward turn.[116] This represents a departure from the first school of thought which appeared at a time when the sphere of economic relations conformed to the contours of the Biosphere. The Physiocrats could not envisage a reproduction of the livelihood of man—the economy—independent of the Biosphere. It was only a short time later that reproduction was limited to market factors and then, with Walras et al., was replaced by a theory of atemporal general equilibrium.[117] This represented an inversion of finalities, whereby substantive perspectives of the economy vanished from view to be replaced by a form of functionalist economic rationality that accorded priority to a logic of maximization of market values. It is within this inverted attitude that contemporary schools pretend to integrate natural phenomena by projecting upon them the truncated logic of a subsystem to which they do not belong.

When all major schools of economic analysis turn explicitly or implicitly to the problem of reproduction, they reduce it to the dimensions of market resources. But the limitation of economic science to the merely functionally rational dimensions of the livelihood of man condemns it to develop a logic and inspires a course of action that explicitly contradicts the norms of the Biosphere. This represents the analytical context for conflict. For the multidimensional phenomenon of the unregulated expansion of the Technosphere confronts the narrowing scope of economic thought which addresses the merely economistic dimensions of social reality.

Moreover, in the context of the foregoing discussion, the economic process, conceptualized as an open autopoietic system, is itself generating its own negativity. In the context of our analysis this constitutes an additional level of complexity. For instance, in producing nondisposable inorganic wastes and thereby overloading local and global ecosystems, the production process is generating for itself a heightened level of complexity—a complexity to which it must respond. Of course, how it responds is problematic. More generally, we might speculate that societal differentiation is itself a manifestation of man's adaptation to technology. For if functional differentiation is an organizational phenomenon, that is, a response to complexity, is technology not a primary source of that complexity? And, is it not also, then, a phenomenon that transcends the historic capitalist and socialist modes of adapting to technology?

It is relevant, at this juncture, to recall the propositions of Polanyi and Schumpeter. Karl Polanyi, for instance, asserted that capitalism and socialism were merely alternative social responses to technology.[118] Schumpeter, in *Capitalism, Socialism, and Democracy*, noted that: "Between socialism . . . and capitalism there is no necessary relation; the one can exist without the other. At the same time there is no incompatibility; in appropriate states of social environment, the socialist engine can be run on democratic principles."[119] From an Ashbian perspective this then defines capitalism and socialism as merely different variety-absorbing institutions. These speculations aside, the general problem of technified society is what new forms of institutional differentiation will ensue?[120]

Hierarchy of Finalities and the General Principle of Descending Constraints

The view that the laws of the higher forms of being cannot be completely reduced to those of the lower is widely prevalent in philosophy[121] and is found in Comte's positivism and in German philosophy. It is connected with the theories that the higher stages are based upon the lower but are qualitatively distinct. In English philosophy it takes the form of the theory of "emergent evolution," i.e., of a creative evolution that builds up new stages of being, the qualities of which are not merely due to the qualities of their components.

The hypothesis that the laws governing the evolution of natural systems also constrain the development of human societies is intrinsically defensible. Such laws do not prescribe the course of evolutionary development but merely define the boundary conditions: the limits and possibilities that the actors themselves exploit.

This is not a Spencerian lapse; for this does not mean that societies are biologically determined. It means only that societies are autopoietic systems emerging and persisting within the multilevel structure of other Biospheric systems. Societies follow the program set by the general laws that govern the evolution of such systems within the institutionalized limits and possibilities created by societies, their values, beliefs, habits, and mores.

In a differentiated autopoietic system, either a cell or an individual, the finalities of all subsystems express themselves in a harmonious manner. In the coherent state of a complex system of constraints operating from the top downward there are limits to the possible modes of behavior. They are restricted to a subset of those modes that do not contradict the metasystem's normative conditions. Were it otherwise it may interfere with the emergence of the finalities that assures the autopoietic homeostasis of the system as a whole.

This acumen did not escape the probing mind of Claude Bernard, the great French contemporary of Darwin, who wrote:

> It is not by struggling against cosmic conditions that the organism develops and maintains its place; on the contrary, it is by an adaptation to, and agreement with, these conditions. So, the living being does not form an exception to the great natural harmony which makes things adapt themselves to one another; it breaks no concord; it is neither in contradiction to nor struggling against general cosmic forces; far from that, it forms a member of the universal concert of things, and the life of the animal, for example, is only a fragment of the total life of the universe.[122]

Situated within an episteme, it is impossible, according to the principle of organizational dissonance, to perceive a level of organization only partially independent of all others. Their very definition, on the basis of an elaboration of their perspective semi-autonomous finalities, expresses their interdependence. The autopoietic hierarchization of finalities and progressive supraordination of subsystem homeostasis to the normative conditions of corresponding metasystems ensures global coherence. While a level of organization cannot be understood independently of others, it is, nevertheless, at its own level that its specific finalities manifest themselves. This is as true of living systems as it is of socioeconomic systems. Thus, the economic sphere achieves the satisfaction of human needs only through an autopoietic transformation of the environment to which the by-products of production and consumption, in fact, return. The state of the physical environment (i.e., climate, resources, etc.) in turn partially defines the conditions that bear on the existence, the nature, and the level of these activities.

While ascribing to the hierarchy of finalities, both in living systems and in the economy of man, there is also the organizational dissonance of interdependent autopoietic systems "that exists between the reproduction of the whole and that of its sub-systems."[123] Each level of the organization corresponds to systems that are partially open in relation to those to which they belong. Their metabolization of low entropy affords them temporary "negentropic" qualities, enabling them to temporarily resist the environment's entropic forces. In the case of systems characterized by reflexivity, information necessary for homeostatic responses enables them to be informed (in the Aristotelian sense) and facilitates the adjustment of their behaviors to that information.

A homeostatic or cybernetic mechanism involves a knowledge structure that is capable of perceiving, presumably through structural changes in the knowledge structure itself, divergences between some actual state of affairs and some desired state of affairs, and is capable of selecting and directing energy and matter toward diminishing this divergence. Such a prescription is consistent with Bernard's conviction and with Maruyama's second cybernetics, the cardinal objective of which is the avoidance of hazardous modes of behavior.[124] This attaches to the teleological dimensions of feed-forward capacities coupled with stabilization through "deviation-diminishing feedback." If these capacities and processes do not exist, then, the possibilities exist for the emergence of an unregulated and pathological development.

Two subsequent implications follow from these observations:

(1)   The laws of autopoietic organization, of living systems, are not laws of equilibrium, but of persistent non-equilibrium that are compensated or reestablished; to maintain the structure of each subsystem presupposes an appropriation of energy effected in relation to the environment, and that its subsequent organization will counterbalance the effects of entropy; the development of, and complexification of structures calls for the existence of an energy surplus that is utilized to effect this function; and

(2)   the reproduction of a system, at all levels of organization, can therefore be assured only through the totality of its interrelations with its environment.

Thus, each cell and each organ can maintain its organization only to the extent that the entire organism is able to preserve its structure. And, conversely, the latter can arrive at that result only through the functioning of its own organs. Should the organism integrate the overall structure of its components, it will dissolve; and should an important function effected by one subsystem attempt to subordinate the vital role of others, the organism would cease to exist.[125]

We submit that this phenomenon applies to the reproduction of the economy comprehended as an institutionalized autopoietic system. As a system that is open, in relation to both its human and natural environment, it draws from the latter the energy that animates it and experiences in turn the consequences of its own negativity. Its reproduction, however, must be grounded on a coevolutionary harmonization of the homeostasis of the social sphere and that of the Biosphere. The livelihood of man cannot, therefore, be assured by a rational (i.e., functional) management of only those forces that express themselves at the level of markets.[126]

The homeostatic qualities and finality of a whole (i.e., the Biosphere) encompass the homeostasis of, and exceed the finalities of, each of its constituents. It is, therefore, not through the latter that one could expect to provide for the continuity of the former. The emphasis that is habitually placed on the internally cohesive totalizing logic of the price-making market is unable to encompass the "logic" of the Biosphere. The price-making market may be analyzed as an autopoietic system whose totalizing internal logic (the logic of capital) in seeking self-closure theoretically dissociates itself from the substantive elements that ultimately sustain it. And when it is forced to come to terms with the substantive elements, for instance, with ecology, it merely seeks to extend the market mentality.

On the basis of its economizing rationality, the market presumes that what is good for the market must be good for the Biosphere. But the reproduction of capital does not assure that of the Biosphere, and it is at the level of the latter that we must place ourselves in order to achieve an authentic coevolutionary autopoiesis. It is the illusion of reductionist economism that the whole may be governed by the market subsystem.

At the level of inanimate organization, the principles of conservation of energy and matter, together with minimal dissipation, are formative. Whereas at the level of economy, structure-conserving and structure-differentiating cybernetic properties consistent with the concept of autopoietic homeostasis manifest themselves in terms of institutional constraints.[127]

Insofar as "all economic systems are subsystems within the biophysical system of ecological interdependence the ecosystem provides a set of physical constraints to which all economic systems must conform."[128] It is on the basis of these principles that it is asserted that there exists interdependence of the whole and its parts and that the reproduction of the economic sphere is inseparable from that of the Biosphere. The economic sphere is immersed in the social one and constitutes merely a subset that is itself open in relation to the Biosphere. It is therefore the latter that we are now considering as "the whole" within which human societies locate themselves, and within which the sphere of economic activity constitutes merely a subsystem. This nesting of system and subsystem, of the economy within society within the Biosphere, is illustrated in figure 4.4.

While an institutionalization of the hierarchy of finalities is imperative for the reembedding of economy in society and the Biosphere, there is an alleged positivist and technocratic threat implicit in according priority to the whole over constituent parts, subordinating the individual to the collective. The Aristotelian, "the whole is before the parts," or the Hegelian, "the truth is the whole," carries with it the specter of totalitarianism. In contrast to that form of functionalism whereby priority is given to the whole over the parts, within the autopoietic perspective the whole becomes inextricably interwoven, achieving an inter-organizational resonance so that reference to one dimension necessitates refer-

Figure 4.4. **The Embeddedness of Socioeconomic Relations within the Noösphere**

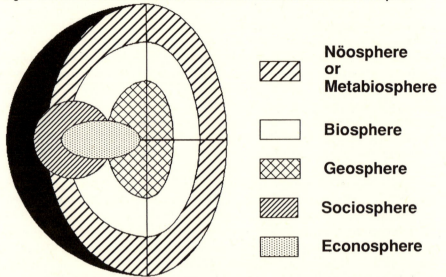

Nöosphere or Metabiosphere

Biosphere

Geosphere

Sociosphere

Econosphere

ence to another. Central to this perspective are the notions of interdependence and the total interrelationship of all things: indeed, a web of interconnections of sublime complexity.

Bertalanffy stresses that it is a widespread concept to view the state of a nation as an organism at a super-organizational level. Such a theory might constitute the foundation of a Fordist totalitarian state within which the individual would appear as an insignificant cell within the organism, a worker without importance within a beehive. Seeking to allay paranoia, Bertalanffy notes that one of two things follow:

> Either it will be necessary to entirely eliminate him and replace him by the hardware of computers and a mechanism that regulates itself, or he must be made as reliable as possible, that is mechanized, made to conform, controlled and normalized. More bluntly within the grand system man must become and in a certain measure he is already a button-pushing idiot, or else a trained idiot who is narrowly specialized or else simply a part of a machine. This conforms to a well known principle of systems: that of progressive mechanization; the individual is transformed into a wheel dominated by a small number of privileged leaders who are mediocre and rely on mystification and follow their own interests under the cover of ideology.[129]

Second, it has been alleged that socioeconomic systems theory has a hidden sociohistorical basis that attaches to post-modernist discussions of "endism"— the "end of reason," "the end of history" or the "end of the individual."[130] This is a misplaced criticism, for socioeconomic systems theory does not infer the deviation of society from substantive rationality, though it does question administrative rationality. From an observance of the hierarchy of finalities, socially responsible individualism, while it is accorded a place in the whole, is not construed to contribute to a narrow behaviorism. For clearly what is good for individual parts may be a mixed blessing for the total system.

Nonetheless, cybernetics has also been alleged to possess totalitarian and technocratic tendencies. Such a claim exhibits a narrow understanding of the concept of freedom that attaches to the liberal tradition, whereby any hint, methodological or otherwise, of the expansion of political "intervention" is viewed as necessarily detrimental to individual freedom.

Moreover, cybernetic theory pays no attention to the question of "knowing" how the goals that control systems are designed to achieve were generated in the first place. It conveys a neutrality to "meaning" and as such is devoid of the technocratic strain with which it is frequently labeled.

To rely on the neutrality of cybernetics as a pretext for rejection of the organizational approach is a distortion that renders sterile any discussion of purposefulness. The unique value of general organization theory is that it does not presuppose an arbitrarily defined threshold of purposefulness, but takes that dimension into account at the level at which it emerges. Thus, organization theory establishes a bridge between the objective and the subjective.

In a related issue Jürgen Habermas argues, not without some justification, that systems theory conceptualizes every social system from the point of view of a control center.[131] Thus, he notes, in functionally differentiated societies the political system assumes a superordinate role vis-à-vis the sociocultural and economic systems. Formally consistent with aspects of our concept of autopoietic differentiation, Habermas claims that "the reproduction of highly complex societies depends on the differentiated steering system and on the political subsystem. By increasing its capacity to process information and its indifference to other social subsystems, the political system acquires a unique autonomy within society."[132] Such an appreciation of systems theory is not inconsistent with the imagery, for instance, present in aspects of Norbert Wiener's cybernetics. However, as we have noted, the earlier emphasis on functional or administrative rationality that attaches to "control" is being replaced. Maruyama's second cybernetics deemphasizes "control." From both an epistemological and methodological perspective this reformulation constitutes a departure from functional rationality. It refers to viability-ensuring strategies which maintain many degrees of freedom. This approach, in deemphasizing "control," encourages degrees of autonomy within a hierarchy of finalities. Such an understanding defuses, on the one hand, Habermas's concern for the technocratic implications of systems theory, and, on the other hand, transcends Luhmann's approach.

Moreover, the second cybernetics, the cybernetics of avoidance, presents an image of more, not fewer, degrees of freedom, in spite of the problem of complexity. In addition, the functional modes of regulation, i.e., Habermas's steering, with the allegedly inevitable technocratic bureaucratization of decision making, demands that institutions subject themselves to rapid reconfigurations. We shall later return to elements of the theme briefly introduced here in the section entitled Freedom in Technified Society.

Describing society as being differentiated with respect to functions includes an awareness, to a certain extent, of continuing crises; for one of the consequences of functional differentiation, which attaches to organizational dissonance, is the expectation of more or less recurrent crises within and among subsystems. Insofar as technified society has attained a functional differentiation of high complexity, the phenomenon of organizational dissonance manifests itself in a spectrum of forms, which attach, for instance, to the phenomenon of alienation. This is the result of structural preconditions which prescribe semi-autonomy, autopoietic self-organization, and even self-reproduction of elements of subsystems and, at the same time, tangled interdependencies between systems and environments.

Lest society itself be destroyed, the hierarchization of finalities must accord primacy to what Karl Polanyi referred to as the reality of society.[133] Moreover, it signifies that collective projects in the epoch of the Noösphere cannot be reduced to their market dimensions alone. A Cartesian science, which necessarily views things from a specific point of view, cannot pretend to demonstrate the validity or superiority of a vision that concerns and engages man in all his dimensions.

Political Economy for the Epoch of the Noösphere

V.I. Vernadsky maintained that once life emerged from the Geosphere the appearance and reproduction of the Biosphere, together with the complexification of living forms, represented a diversity of phenomena corresponding to specific principles governing evolutionary processes. In particular, the era of biogenesis was identified with the capacity of organisms to progressively internalize programs for stability.[134] So there evolved genetic forms of memory.

The genetic program that underlies the organization of every organism includes a closed part, which is formulated in a strictly defined way, and an open part, which leaves the individual several degrees of freedom of organization. The closed part determines certain structures, functions, and properties, while the open part defines the possibilities. The closed part imposes constraints, whereas the open part leaves options. The trend in evolution has been to increase the importance of the open part. In the case of man, that part plays such an important role that we may speak about "free will."[135]

Both Vernadsky and Salk have asserted that the phase of social forms of memory marked the next major phase in the evolution of the Biosphere. Jacob emphasizes that in the process of the liberation of living beings from the rigors of the rule of genetic code (a liberation that accompanied the evolution of these beings), an important stage was marked by the emergence, at the mammalian level, of symbols which functioned as sui generis filters in the interaction between animals and their environment.[136] Further evolution in the same direction accounts for the fact that integration at the level of organisms and the relationship between organisms consist in an exchange of encoded information and not in interaction of molecules. According to Jacob, culture forms a second and superior "genetic code." That is why the "code" of these new integrating units goes beyond the schema of biological explanations.[137]

The emergence of human society marked a third stage in the evolution of the Biosphere. The socialization of man has greatly accelerated all evolutionary processes within the Biosphere and has brought it to a threshold beyond which its further development can only be secured by human reason. This is the epoch of the Noösphere. The development of the Biosphere into the Noösphere is a phenomenon more profound and powerful in essence than all of human history. The evolving Noösphere marks yet a fourth qualitative development in programming.

But, flourishing at its apogee, mankind is confronting a vital challenge that will be registered as one of the most profound in its history. For mankind has now obtained to a crucial phase in its conscious evolution at which mankind will either realize or destroy itself. For the present period in the history of both the human race and the planet, as a whole, is marked by an intense acceleration of all evolutionary processes, by the consolidation of a highly interdependent world system, and by an erosion of the boundaries between human evolution and human ecology. The growth of both human and machine populations, material and energy consumption, and the expansion of scientific knowledge and technological capabilities have forced upon mankind a new set of problems that focus on the interactions between natural and social environments.[138]

Rethinking man's place in nature, and critically reviewing the basis of legitimation for the form of life that scientific rationality imposes on technified society, is perhaps the greatest intellectual challenge confronting us today.[139] It is a challenge that calls for a global multidisciplinary perspective.

As we have sought to demonstrate, such a program collides with the doctrine of traditional economic science. For while the focus of post-classical economic analysis is on the cybernetic properties of self-regulating market systems, conceptualizing the socio-technico-Biospheric system as autopoietic calls for a more general conceptual basis appropriate for analyzing the coevolutionary cybernetics of Technospheric and ecological processes. Many research scientists share the view that such a platform could be based on V.I. Vernadsky's general image of the evolution of the earth and his proposition that in the next biogeological age more advanced forms of human consciousness, embodied in a Noösphere, will increasingly influence all forms of evolution.[140]

August Comte penned the epithet: ". . . the living are ever, and ever more, dominated by the dead." The quintessential message for us is that coevolution cannot be an anarchic process. It must become a conscious process. For man can now easily overstep the "permissible thresholds" beyond which irreversible changes in the conditions of his existence will begin. Therefore, mankind must equip itself to foresee the results of its actions and know where the fatal lines lay that separate the possibility of civilization's further development from its precipitant extinction.[141]

The human species represents the current culmination of the evolution of the Biosphere. By virtue of its very livelihood, humanity disrupts the very environment that sustains it. However, the quality of nonreflexivity, expressed by a species possessing the faculty of thinking and anticipating the consequences of its actions, characterizes a situation of interdependence which calls for the consideration of subordinating narrowly defined norms of science, technology, and the economy to those of autopoietic living processes.[142] In particular, the cybernetics of teleological control are needed, i.e., the cybernetics of feed-forward implies that "the present change of state is determined by an anticipated future state computed in accordance with some . . . model of the world."[143] Human systems capable of planning and defining their purposes and goals are obviously using feed-forward to guide their survival and development. Consequently, priority now attaches to evaluations of alternative "reinverted" institutional modes of human activity that will not disrupt the homeostasis of mankind as a species, and that instead of destroying man's coevolution with the Biosphere will enhance it. This is the problem of the epoch of the Noösphere.

The Coevolution of Man and the Biosphere

It is a patent fact of life that neither specifically economic nor non-economic human activities poses any reality without the support of nature. While Karl Marx, in *Capital*, observed that the reproduction of economic activity is contingent upon the reproduction of the social relations, so too does the reproduction of society require the reproduction of the Biosphere. It is this relationship that Marx noted in *Grundrisse*.

While all elements of the Econosphere are contained within the Sociosphere, and necessarily the Biosphere, not all elements of the Biosphere are observed in either the Sociosphere or Econosphere. Thus, while the dynamics of the Econosphere, by definition, belong to the Biosphere, the full dynamics of the Biosphere are not represented in the Econosphere (see figure 4.4).[144]

The appropriation of materials, to which useful forms are given, and the return of residual waste products represent the two classes of man's economic activity that most obviously merge with the Biosphere. The first refers to a temporary order-creating and structuring process that outwardly appears negentropic. The second appears as a destructuring process that is destructive of order. In this sense economic activity is manifestly entropic.[145]

It is with this understanding that we may claim that while lying outside of the economic system proper the Biosphere enters into the sphere of economic activity. Just as there is no aspect of the Biosphere that is immune from man's intrusions, neither is the livelihood of man divorced from his physical environment. On these grounds, far from being viewed in isolation, economic activities must be reevaluated in terms of their insertion into Biospheric norms, norms that it cannot perturb without, in turn, disrupting the global economy.[146]

The advance in technology has most profoundly affected man's relation with the Biosphere. The uncoordinated activity of man now often proves to be destructive on the scale of the entire Biosphere and limits the possibilities of further development. While until recently it was possible to speak of the evolution of man as an element of the Biosphere, due to his increasing alienation from the biotic environment and creation of an artificial "technological environment"—the Technosphere—we may address the coevolution of man and the Biosphere.

The concept of the Noösphere and the coevolutionary perspective has a historic tradition. Scientists of all times spoke extensively about harmony between man and nature. It was an important subject for ancient philosophers, the French Encyclopedists, and the Russian cosmists. The Physiocrats, for instance, contemplated this harmony in terms of man constraining his behavior to accord with the earth's natural development. It implied minimal interference with nature, a preservation of its pristine condition, and the greatest possible "closeness" of man and nature. In some respects these views were naive and lacked rigor. They reflected a bucolic image in their expression of an innate desire of people to be close to nature, to "remove" all the contradictions between man and nature.[147]

But the task of science and human action is not to preserve the world in its primordial condition but to find forms of man–Biosphere interaction that ensure the development of the Biosphere and of the human population as an inseparable component of the former.

The fundamental problems to be addressed in the corresponding institutional transition stem from the necessity to develop technico-economic systems that are compatible with broader norms. The issue before us calls for a conscious harmonization to be effected in ways that guarantee Biospheric norms and of coherences without whose preservation human societies can have little prospect for the future. In particular, it is imperative for economic science to develop a form of coevolutionary economic analysis.

Models of coevolutionary phenomena tend to highlight the differences between the points of view held by the various disciplines. On the one hand, geneticists are primarily concerned with the influence of the mechanism of inheritance on the coevolutionary process and with the influence of population interactions on the genetic structure of a population. On the other hand, ecologists and some economists are primarily concerned with the effect of coevolution on the phenotype, especially on traits that determine how populations interact, and with the effect of coevolution on the abundance and distribution of the interacting populations.[148]

Contrary to those analysts who, carrying the burden of market mentality, cavalierly equate the dynamics of ecosystems with the livelihood of man, it is necessary that the further socialization of mankind develop according to the transcendent *metaepisteme* and metalogic of the Noösphere. Whereas ecological coevolution theory focuses on the interface between population genetics and theoretical ecology, economic coevolution theory, following Vernadsky's reference image, centers on an evolutionary type of "quasi-demographic" and "metaecological" interaction among elements of the Sociosphere, the Technosphere, and the Biosphere.[149]

If social development is to be orderly and fit into the contours of the Biosphere, the quality of nonreflexivity at the level of society suggests that there must be some kind of institutionalized autopoietic homeostatic mechanism attached to the normative conditions. This is not a recent ethos. It hearkens back to the natural philosophic views expressed by François Quesnay on the positive laws, moral laws, and the natural order.

Expressing a commitment to Biospheric "homeostatic" norms comparable in their character to those asserted by the Physiocrats, Passet insists that in the preservation of resources both quantitative and qualitative norms must be observed.[150]

(1)   Quantitative norms refer to a respect for the rhythms of reconstitution of all renewable resources; the specification of rates of utilization that are compatible with prospects for shifts from one renewable resource to another; and

(2)   Qualitative norms refer to the environment's purity; the diversity that is required by the stability of ecosystems; the composition of nutrients required by an equilibrium in "feeding."

When seen from the point of view of an economic system, these norms constitute a set of positive laws; Biospheric constraints only within whose limits economic calculation may take place.[151]

Freedom in Technified Society

The continuing semi-autonomous evolution of the Technosphere is a problem of world complexity which has assumed a leading position.[152] How we address the conjoint problem of the complexity of technified society and democracy must assume a prominent place on our agenda for the epoch of the Noösphere.

Technified society is, by definition, one confronted with the manifest problems of the Technosphere. In other words, the Technosphere is an environment of technified society. It is a source of complexity, i.e., of perturbing variety, to which mankind and his institutions must respond. We have contended that through plan-guided approaches mankind can address related global issues. A coevolutionary approach to the problem, it has been maintained, must conform to the natural hierarchy of finalities and demands that society institute diverse design and operational constraints on technologies.

Paradoxically, the call for a "plan-guided" approach to the problem of the harmonious coevolution of man and the Biosphere comes at a time of a much-heralded convergence between plan and market types.[153] Operationally, it is a convergence that attaches to the process of bureaucratization; for bureaucracy operates in much the same way, whether it is capitalist or socialist.[154] This view was also expressed by J.K. Galbraith who noted: "The great corporation and the managerial revolutions have bureaucratized a large part of capitalist production, with the same ossification, the same hardening of the arteries that . . . have been identified in the socialist world."[155] However, the operational understanding is distinct from the ideological perception of "convergence." Moreover, secured against the realities of modern corporatism by a catholic and mythic doctrine of the market, the conclusion is trumpeted that the market has triumphed.[156]

Convergence theory assumes that the socialist (centrally planned economy), confronted by stultifying bureaucratic elements, is embracing the rhetoric, if not the ideology of the market. Indeed, "some of our economists," notes the Russian economist S. Menshikov, "have suggested that unemployment should be deliberately increased so as to strengthen discipline." The process of change in the former USSR and the remnants of the Eastern bloc is viewed as a case of "creeping capitalism." This image has its counterpart in the views expressed by some theorists of the "creeping socialism" of the West. An idea of some currency is that the socialist bloc's so-called deconstruction of its plan-guided economies and transition to mixed economies perforce means embracing a free market economy. Such views are clearly stated: "If we want to fight for democracy and freedom in communist countries, then we have to promote a market economy and private property."[157]

The popular concept of "convergence" not only conflates market modes of appropriation with free enterprise and personal freedom, but also misses the substantive issue of how the goals and objectives of society may be appropriately accommodated within the context of man's coevolution with the Biosphere. There is, of course, a real concern that the current reforms in the former USSR and the Eastern bloc may be diverted from their objective of social justice.[158] "The main thrust [of the reforms] is to relieve the economy from the grasp and burden of the bureaucracy and to do away with the shadow economy. The central point is to increase the freedom and responsibility of enterprises."[159] It may, nonetheless, become subordinated to a technocratically regulated regeneration of economic growth. For seeking to validate through other means Lenin's allegation that, when it reached higher productivity, socialism would decisively win in competition with capitalism, admits the possibility of technocratic options exasperated by international pressures that are conveyed by fully convertible currencies.[160] Quite aside from possible social dislocation, it could only further aggravate the problems of the Technosphere. One might say that there is a concern of replacing "plan fetishism" with "market fetishism."[161] The technocratic and market fetishism underlying the current rhetoric and proposals for economic liberalization, within both socialist and capitalist economies, ignores the historic incapacity of the price-making market to either integrate society in socially responsible ways, or to institutionalize a sustaining coevolution of man and the Biosphere; for "market prices do not necessarily reflect strategic lines of development."[162]

Market fetishism has its corollary in its concept of freedom. In this connection we must insist that it is crucial to understand that planning is not inimical to freedom. It is necessary to overcome the narrow view of freedom as the absence of political intervention in the market. Preoccupation with this devout concept has confined the liberal tradition to the conclusion that any expansion in the role of the state is necessarily to the detriment of individual freedom. This myopic perspective is rooted historically in the Ricardian and axiomatic conception of the market economy as a natural order that emerged *spontaneously*. The encyclopedists, Quesnay and Adam Smith, accorded harmonization of social interests to the social context, whereas the neoclassicals accorded priority to harmonization alleged to be achieved through the expression of individual interests and personal aspirations.

But how can we expect social institutions to emerge fully fledged from freely contracting individualistic interactions? At this juncture it is useful to provide a brief theoretical review.

In Smith's work there is no intimation that the economic interests of the capitalists laid down the law to society; no intimation that they were the secular spokesmen of divine providence which governed the economic world as a separate entity.[163] Despite the emphasis given to depoliticizing the economy, the economy remains subordinate to society's thinking because self-interest is guided by the fundamental dignity of man as a moral and social being seeking to gain the approval of his peers. Within this context individualism may present itself in socially responsible ways.

However, institutionalists are confronted with the alleged evidence of price formation. From the intellectual "gains" of the Ricardian methodological revolution we are unfailingly taught that prices are not separate facts unrelated to individual behavior. To the contrary, prices emerge, according to the pure theory, reducible to individualistic behavior. They derive from a process of specific social interaction among self-interested individuals little concerned with whether or how their actions contribute to the formation of clearing prices. This is a facile argument which the institutionalists counter with the observation that the institutionalization of the price-making market itself provides the necessary infrastructure, the context within which individuation emerges. In other words, the institutionalist approaches the problem and removes it to a deeper level of analysis.[164]

It is only within the bounds of institutions that, for instance, individualism or individual motives acquire their meaning. Social interactions are rule-governed events, not motives. Motives lead people to engage in particular activities, but what and how they do it depends upon the structure of institutions. In other words, motives operate within the social structures we refer to as institutions.

The liberal doctrine of individualism with its ideological concept of freedom commits the error of misplaced concreteness. For the economistic fallacy identifies an abstract model with reality. Thus, it considers empirical behavior only insofar as that behavior corresponds to the postulates of the formal model. This is very nearly what Schumpeter had in mind in his concept of the "Ricardian vice," i.e., jumping to policy conclusions from a highly abstract, near tautological basis.[165] Despite discarding much of Ricardo's theoretical system, conventional economics retains the Ricardian vice and fallacy of misplaced concreteness.

Adam Smith seized order from the apparent chaos by insisting that an "invisible hand" was at work. His followers, especially James Mill and David Ricardo, refined his themes on the self-regulating economy expunging societal views and further depoliticizing the economy. Indeed, it is probable that Mill and Ricardo, with their pathological contempt of government, implanted a much more stringent laissez-faire attitude into the self-regulating market disposition than ever crossed Smith's mind. The installation of the market economy required political action and ideological directive. This directive was, in the case of England, compellingly supplied by the classical economists.

It would seem to be undeniable that the free enterprise policy toward the competitive market framework was established in considerable part through the efforts of the classical economists, especially the elder Mill and Ricardo, and they did so with clarity of intent. T.W. Hutchinson argues that

> the main meaning and intention of the Millian-Ricardian theories and methods can be found in the nature of the policy conclusions derived from them. Ricardo's policy conclusions, which he went into Parliament to proclaim with all the authority of the new science behind him, followed from, and depended upon, with great exactness and rigidity, his "strongly" simplified assumptions or theories. The Millian-Ricardian abstract, deductive method started from starkly unqualified assumptions ... that led immediately and inevitably to sharply laissez-faire policy doctrines.[166]

And it is abundantly clear that nineteenth-century scholars were well aware of the ultimately experimental character of the price-making market economy. Walter Bagehot observed in 1895 that "it is difficult for a modern Englishman, to whom 'free trade' is an accepted maxim of tedious orthodoxy, to remember sufficiently that a hundred years ago it was a heresy and a paradox. The whole commercial legislation of the world was [then] formed on the doctrines of protection."[167]

The effective functioning of forms of economic integration depends upon the presence of definite institutional structures within which any number of degrees of freedom are possible. Nonetheless, it has long been tempting for some to assume that such structures are the result of certain kinds of personal attitudes. Adam Smith's "propensity to truck, barter and exchange" is without doubt the most famous example. It is not true, however, that freely contracting individuals simply add up to create the institutional structures that support the various forms of economic integration. Nonetheless, liberal society rests on the myth that the general interests of society arise from a spontaneous harmonization of private interests. Such an understanding is countered by the notion that the market economy itself resulted from political action, albeit a virtually suicidal action for the polity. This, the truism of the "double movement" demystifies the market fetishism and denies it the aura of inevitability which so often assumes ideological dimensions.[168]

"The institutional separation of politics and economics, which proved a deadly danger to the substance of society, almost automatically produced freedom at the cost of justice and security."[169] Moreover, a society whose freedoms are purchased at the cost of injustice and insecurity can be neither enduring nor beneficial. The challenge of democratic control of the economy is to protect society: to separate, on the one hand, the maleficent "freedoms" to exploit one's fellow, to make inordinate and nonlegitimated gain without commensurate service to the community, and the freedom to restrict access to property, from, on the other hand, the cherished freedoms (the freedom of conscience, speech, association, and the right to choose one's occupation). In other words, the problem is one of eliminating the former and preserving the latter. "On the institutional level, regulation both extends and restricts freedom; only the balance of the freedoms lost and won is significant."[170] In particular, constraint of the market-guided development of the Technosphere functions as a liberating freedom.

This is not to deny the value of the market economy in historically promulgating social and political freedoms—a view expressed even by Marx.[171] However, to infer from this that the demise of the market economy must necessarily extinguish those hard-won freedoms is to mystify the role of the economy in society. Nor should it be construed that the maleficent "freedoms" are somehow necessary costs of those we hold dear. The market economy is not the necessary condition for the cherished freedoms, nor is a planned economy the necessary abnegation of those freedoms. Institutional guarantees of personal freedom are compatible with any mode of economic integration.

Moreover, as the Fascist convulsion proved, the market economy does not even represent a sufficient condition for the continuity of personal freedoms. For the maleficent "freedoms" of the market economy pose a threat to those more cherished ones insofar as "it appears that the means of maintaining freedom are themselves adulterating and destroying it." Indeed, the freedoms championed by the liberal ethos threaten liberalism's overarching value. For liberalism has a narrow view of freedom insofar as its "idea of freedom degenerates into an advocacy of free enterprise."[172]

Such assertions are not confined to a bygone era. "Trade is the creature of liberty," asserts Lindblom.[173] Or, "liberty," writes Shaomin Li, "means that individuals have freedom to engage in trade and to establish enterprises to pursue gains of trade."[174] But, of course, it is precisely free enterprise, with its autonomous Technosphere, that is the very locus of the threatening and maleficent; for it is the freedoms of free enterprise that encourage irresponsible individuality and socially irresponsible actions. "Laissez-faire economics may well be characterized as the economics of irresponsibility, and the business system of free contract is also a system of irresponsibility when judged by the same standard. . . . Liberal economics [neglects the responsibility problem] by separating business sharply off from the rest of life."[175]

E.F. Schumacher has noted the irresponsibility of the market economy:

> The market . . . represents only the surface of society and its significance related to the momentary situation as it exists there and then. There is no probing into the depths of things, into the natural or social facts that lie behind them. In a sense, the market is the institutionalization of individualism and non-responsibility. Neither the buyer nor seller is responsible for anything but himself.[176]

Of course, what is astonishing is that it is also considered ethically virtuous to make maximum use of this freedom of irresponsibility. Irresponsible self-seeking is not merely present but expected and legitimated. As Thorstein Veblen argued, the freedom of free enterprise—the rule of "self-help and free bargaining"—is the right to wreck matters at large in the pursuit of one's self-interest.[177] For the essential power of private property in such a setting is not to hold for personal use but rather to withhold from social use if one is dissatisfied with the terms of the bargain. "Ownership of industrial equipment and natural resources confers . . . a right to legally force unemployment, and so to make the community's workmanship useless to that extent."[178] From this it follows that one's power to command an income in the normal operation of market capitalism is directly related to the mayhem one can wreak by refusing to cooperate, i.e., by the derangement of the social process of production that one can cause.

Karl Polanyi fervently believed that liberal capitalism was existentially incompatible with the nature of man as a social being. He considered capitalist society to be a form of "unfreedom" in the sense that interpersonal relations are veiled and appear as responses to depersonalized market forces forsaking any element of personal responsibility of man for man and man for his habitat.

We have inherited a political economy of irresponsibility which contrasts with the noble and humane elements of the Western intellectual heritage that is the Enlightenment.

The "liberty machine" we have invented is a self-defeating one. The freedoms of irresponsible, self-interested individuality threaten all freedoms because they threaten society. By creating injustice, insecurity, and disorder, they leave the way open to an authoritarian resolution. Without a viable resolution of the problem of freedom and order, in a free society the issue will be settled on the side of order. The fascistic regimes of the twentieth century arose from just such disorder created by a stalemate of irresponsible forces clashing in industry and government in a polarized political economy.

Viewing freedom simplistically, in other words, according to the ideology that conflates capitalism with free enterprise, the radical individualist attacks "planning and control . . . as a denial of freedom."[179] In so doing, the liberal neglects the primacy of society and the reality that power and compulsion are necessary for any functioning social order. The essential flaw in liberal logic is the eclipse of political thinking. It is, according to Polanyi, the key intellectual deficiency of the liberal era.[180] Politics and its role in society were obscured from view in the scramble to interpret social organization in a manner consistent with the needs of the market economy. Liberal democracy as a political system makes democracy synonymous with the limited choices involved in the election of leaders who then preside over bureaucratic and military apparatus. It is a form of democracy in which popular involvement and participation in political decision making is left to indirect extraparliamentary "pressures" operating under constraint. Democraticization or popular participation in the economic decision making of corporations, on the other hand, is virtually nonexistent, save in the narrow realm of collective bargaining. Liberal democracy gains its democratic legitimacy in the highly attenuated popular sovereignty expressed via political party elections and an amputated freedom of expression that corresponds to consumerism. The factual and vital role of polity in institutionalizing and controlling economic behavior and in upholding social ideals is neglected.

"The function of power is to ensure that measure of conformity which is needed for the survival of the group."[181] But by defining freedom as the absence of control, a control that is vitally necessary for the continuation of society, the liberal opens the way for the Fascist denial of freedom. Liberalism is defenseless against this conclusion because any "ideal that would ban power and compulsion from society is intrinsically invalid."[182] The task, then, is to institute the economy in such a way as to preserve the cherished freedoms of the market era and eliminate the maleficent ones, at the same time securing a harmonious coevolution of man and the Biosphere.

For all their limitations, the mechanisms of liberal democracy are not to be undervalued, for they make possible the cherished freedoms. Although considerable importance attaches to this acknowledgment and defense of those freedoms, the fact remains that decision making at the level of the economy is exceedingly undemocratic. It is exercised by state (bureaucratic) and corporate power which makes the popular notion of personal sovereignty a cruel joke. The liberal democratic values of fraternity, equality, and liberty are made into a parody.

Freedom within the context of the irresponsibility of the market and radical individualism cannot be condoned; nor is it a viable freedom because freedom cannot survive on the basis of a destruction of society. Indeed, the elevation of functional rationality to preeminence together with the effective institutionalization of radical individualism has disembedded the economy from society. De facto it meant the abandonment of the social contract and denial of societal responsibility in civil society. Its mythic dimensions have even inculcated social-ist economies seeking solutions to economic stagnation. However, the focus must shift from short-term material concerns to moral and ethical obligations; for life, in an era whose means of mass destruction and whose effective potential for influencing the environment are unprecedented invalidates the liberal myth. The Technospheric problems are of global dimension and the well-being of both present and future generations depends on whether ethically and morally sound ways are found to solve those problems.[183] The challenge of the Technosphere in the epoch of the Noösphere demands that we seek a substantive political economy, a political economy in the broad sense and a political economy of responsibility.

Industrialism makes possible an increase in freedom due to the tremendous advances it brings in mankind's substantive and technological power. But its imperatives and mass society also threaten freedom where "the danger to liberty lies in the subordination of belief to the needs of the industrial system."[184] To avert this peril the forces of the Technosphere must be humanized through a sound understanding of the place and function of the economy in the broad sense. This understanding necessitates plan-guidance for the further development of the Technosphere. "Regimentation of material and mechanical forces is the only way by which the mass of individuals can be released from regimentation and consequent suppression of their cultural possibilities."[185]

In this connection the further development of the classical branch of economic analysis is relevant. Fundamentally concerned with the social problem of avoiding disharmonies between forms of social organization, the classical branch, together with the analytical categories of cybernetics, identifies specific qualities that must be incorporated by institutions if they are to effect a "reinversion."

Social change is incessant: here dramatic, there imperceptible. Much of this change revolves around the interaction of technology and institutions, especially the adjustment of institutions to technological changes. Changes in the technical apparatus, organization, or knowledge of the social and material processes create tensions mandating adjustment in mores, laws, and guiding principles. This need not be simply a matter of one-sided adjustment to technological imperatives, but also includes the shaping or restricting of technology by norms that attach to life and culture. The subordination of the allopoietic to the autopoietic, the dis-embedded to the embedded, is the essence of substantive economic science.

A growing number of analysts assume as their point of departure the first principle of coevolutionary analysis: Whenever the objective principles and mechanisms that today govern the Technosphere's evolution are incompatible with the wider Biospheric and cultural norms, including economic reason, it is necessary to subordinate those Technospheric elements to appropriate institutional mechanisms in ways that limit the exercise of inappropriate forms of social power.

Thus, the first principle of coevolutionary economic thought is a principle of autopoietic viability. An allopoietic system must not impose its logic and dy-namic upon an autopoietic system without threatening the viability of the latter.

The creation of an artificial Technospheric environment is precisely an autopoietic response. One will recall that to maintain its stability an autopoietic system seeks partial closure, filtering "noise" from the environment—accepting the useful and rejecting the useless. Thus, it may be conjectured that "technified society" is an autopoietic response to complexity; a complexity that is self-induced. Such an autopoietic interpretation is logically consistent with Polanyi's assertion that capitalism and socialism are merely different ways of instituting technology.[186] Institutionalization is conceptually a form of societal autopoietic response. But, as an autopoietic system, capitalism seeks to transform itself; its logic and dynamic is inverted and it becomes disembedded.[187] In its disembedded state it behaves allopoietically. Pointedly, the inversion of economic thought is precisely the according of priority to allopoietic technological systems over autopoietic substantive systems that underlie the reality of society.

The general concept of an institution as an autopoietic system refers to the diversity of social arrangements (including specific forms of monetization) that eliminate undesirable or structurally inappropriate yet practically feasible and occasionally tempting uses of social power. Consequently, the role of the institution as an autopoietic system is the neutralization and harmonization of contradictions that would otherwise be a source of disruption.

While some institutions may be intended to favor particular social groupings, the basic role of institutions in general is simply to ensure specific types of homeostasis, that is, a joint viability of several rival participating groupings with regard to a limited and prioritized set of constraints. An example of the resulting efficiency of institutions is provided by automobile traffic regulations, which are also an example of a self-enforcing institution. By abandoning the possibility of driving on the "wrong" side of the road, all drivers achieve a vital liberation from the threat of continuous collisions.[188]

In this connection it should be noted that, whereas in biogenetic development there exist genotypical "filtering" mechanisms for suppressing pathological tendencies,[189] the absence of homeostatic mechanisms of the Ashbian type in the price-making market economy is a source of disruption.

> Error-correcting mechanisms prevent deterioration and self-destruction and are the basis for postponing the organism's aging and death. The inability of an organism or a system to correct its errors or defects leads to dissolution, rather than to survival and evolution. The error-correcting and error-preventing mechanisms in culture, in society, in the world, are necessary to inhibit the anti-evolutionary forces so as to allow development to proceed. What is needed particularly is to correct the accumulation of those errors that inhibit evolution: the unbalanced growth of population; excessive preparation for war; excessive utilization of energy; excesses leading to crime, violence, and terrorism; and excesses which have led to economic imbalance.[190]

The late French economist F. Perroux, in particular, stressed that in an age of powerful transnational technological organizations and of a multiplicity of territorial centers of social and political power, a leading problem is the identification of stabilizing capacities of social institutions.[191] It becomes necessary to design institutions whose socially legitimated right extends to new forms of property rights facilitating popular participation in the design, construction, and operational phases of technically feasible complexes by neutralizing potentially dangerous or undesirable possibilities. And in this connection the increasing threat of technological disasters is producing a greater awareness of the need for new and global forms of social control over major sectors of the Technosphere.

> Because of the immense potential for technological variety this implies a greater development of technological enclaves with fail-safe control systems. But it also implies the design of a specific class of flexible multilevel computer assisted institutions. Their social role is to help limit or replace particular obsolete forms of social power not only over the operation of networks of machines but also over their design and construction. Since many of the obsolete institutions have been made possible by historically novel forms of extensive monetization the new possibilities of differentiated electronic banking are especially relevant.[192]

Consequently, selection or filtering, in the epoch of the Noösphere, must, in technified society, become multidimensional, plan-regulated, and institutionalized.[193] It is from this metagenetic concept that we are lead to a concept of the Noösphere in keeping with Vernadsky's image.

The complex forms of analysis that the design and evaluation of corresponding institutions require call for an ultimate guiding principle in rejecting some modes of technological evolution while accepting and controlling others. Such a principle is implied in V.I. Vernadsky's and Jonas Salk's proposition that in the next biogeological age more advanced forms of human awareness, embodied in a "Noösphere," will increasingly influence all forms of evolution.

From an analysis of the crisis of the Technosphere, Jacques Robin, joined by René Passet, is led to propose that ultimately it is through institutional control over such activities that one may achieve a long-term subordination of an evolving Technosphere to "re-inverted" forms of dominance and finality. For Robin this infers the abandonment of market-driven futures for plan-guided ones.

In technified society new institutions must be developed that should, above all, avoid allopoietic modes of coevolution. In practical terms, this means that organizations entrusted, for instance, with design engineering should be prevented from creating artificial populations of robots and "megarobots" that may, in effect, be technological monsters from the social and political point of view. It is evident that the scope of relevant international institutions must eventually extend far beyond the dismantling of advanced weapons systems. When seen in the context of specific global Technospheric dilemmas this also identifies a central problem in the epoch of the Noösphere.

General Criterion for Institutional Design

In the further analysis of this problem we must refer once again to the analytical framework provided by the phenomena of organizational differentiation; for it bears directly upon the functionality of a plan-guided futures option. In this connection it is theorized that Ashby's principle of requisite variety provides a general principle of systemic viability by which institutional response may be guided. Practically, this infers two possible strategies of response: (1) to develop variety-absorbing apparatuses, i.e., institutions; and (2) to attenuate or otherwise constrain the generator of perturbing variety.

The first strategy suggests an incrementalist process, limiting itself to conditional planning. This reactive model, for instance, typically corresponds to forms of "crisis control" or "crisis management" rather than "crisis avoidance." In this case, the variety-generating capacity of the control system is as often as not of insufficient capacity.

A now patently critical problem is that social and technological systems evolve much faster than biological systems where changes occur over generations through genetic selection.[194] And, it is this last problem that points out the need for institutional modes of regulation consistent with the principle of requisite variety.[195] However, the relaxation time (that necessary for the operational unit to reconstitute itself) of the control center of traditional institutions is likely to be greater than the frequency of crises it seeks to manage. Consequently, its functionality may not meet the acid test of Ashbian requisite variety. In addition, the effective absorption of environmental perturbing variety may well correspond to the further bureaucratization of existing institutions and to the possibility of centralized technocratic and elitist approaches. Moreover, the planned creation of institutions in the traditional sense is unlikely to appreciably affect the underlying source of perturbing variety and may, in fact, exacerbate it. On these grounds it is argued that the selection of the first strategy demands rapidly adjusting institutional modes of variety absorption.

Complementary to the first strategy, but without doubt more disruptive, is the second strategy which refers to containment or attenuation of the sources of perturbing variety. In this instance the disruptive freedoms that attach to the free-market mandate of social irresponsibility are constrained. Within both the first and second strategy the role of the institution is recognizably that of a "variety absorber" or "variety attenuator."

Recall that the first principle of coevolutionary analysis is that: Whenever the objective principles and mechanisms that govern the Technosphere's evolution are incompatible with the wider Biospheric and cultural norms, including economic reason, it is necessary to subordinate those Technospheric elements to appropriate institutional mechanisms. It is, then, with this principle that the second "attenuating and absorbing" strategy gains its authority.[196]

In the foregoing we have noted that the complexification of the environment of an autopoietic system is selectively resolved through functional self-differentiation. This necessarily assumes a commanding position in the evolution of society conceived as an autopoietic system. Accordingly, the "steering" capacity of such a system, while it becomes dominant, also becomes ever more removed from concrete reality.[197] In the words of Stafford Beer, it becomes an "esoteric box."[198]

Perhaps the most threatening effect of the rapid evolution of perturbing variety of the Technosphere is that traditionally mandated institutions have a relaxation time less than that of the incidence of perturbing variety. Cybernetic epistemology seems to explain this phenomenon. For as functional differentiation proceeds, the epistemic models through which reality is interpreted and managed are inevitably and, we might add, necessarily, "surrogates of reality."[199] Such a conceptualization is in no way trivial; its implications strike at the very essence of freedom in technified society. However, before reconciling ourselves with the impossibility of freedom it is necessary to assess an underlying concept of rationality that in part informs this cheerless image.

The choice of a concept of rationality is definitive for the foundation of a planning theory. Planning theories crafted in formalist decision-theoretical terms are based on a concept of rationality of action that is taken from either the model of formalist rational choice of alternative means or from Simon's bounded-rationality model.[200] Such models of rational and bounded-rational action are suited to theories of rational choice and to planning techniques in areas of strategic action. The limits of the models can be seen at two levels in the attempt to formulate substantive theories of social systems:

(1) Both the formalist decision-theoretical concept of rationality and Simon's procedural-rationality of action imply a strategic action grounded largely on methodological individualism; and

(2) As we noted earlier the strategic action-oriented approach, "bounded" or "unbounded," has as its context a "bounded *episteme*"; a model of reality whose dynamics are conceived as being linear. However, and as we have noted already, the intersystemic dissonance of networks of autopoietic systems displays a nonlinearity which operationally abrogates the concept of strategic action.

Such a critique, however, does not invalidate the systems approach. Rather, it merely calls into question a particular concept of rationality and an approach to planning within the context of systems theory as it was formulated by Wiener's cybernetics. However, Maruyama's reformulation of cybernetics, the cybernetics of autopoietic systems, with its substantive conceptualization of rationality, forecloses such criticism.

Indeed, it is the cybernetics of autopoietic systems that informs Beer's conceptualization that planning is homologous to organization. In this sense,

> plans—which of their very nature ought to be syntheses of parts into a greater whole—become instead ever more detailed and localized sets of unrelated

minor decisions. That is because ... we [within the context of participative management] are trying to hold the level of decision at the lowest possible echelon as a matter of policy. But this ought to mean that small decisions made in appropriate locales are sucked upward, and reformulated into a master plan expressed metalinguistically.[201]

Beer argues for a metasystemic approach to planning in which the metasystem is not an authoritarian regime, but rather, equipped with a *metaepisteme*, it employs a metalogic and metalanguage in order to resolve systemic problems posed in vernacular epistemes, logics, and languages. Such an interpretation fits comfortably within the first principle of coevolutionary analysis.

In this connection, and according to Moiseev and Frolov,

[the] first step toward the age of the Noösphere is the establishment of [meta-institutions] capable of evaluating the ecological consequences of various activities, and the extent to which they correspond to the possibility of co-evolution of man and the Biosphere.[202] Today numerous projects are being carried out at national levels which lower the ecological stability and are gradually destroying the state of the Biosphere necessary for human existence. The lack of such institutions frequently leads to the implementation of evidently mistaken projects which meet purely institutional interests.[203]

The coevolutionary imperative, notes N.N. Moiseev, calls for international institutions capable of providing objective and systematic coevolutionary studies. For never before has mankind felt such a great need for objectivity and publicity on all questions affecting the problem of stability of the global Biosphere.

Institutional adjustment mechanisms form a focal point of substantive institutional analysis. Indeed, a central economic problem, in the substantive view, pertains to the reinstitutionalization of technological relations consistent with the broader imperatives of life, the Biosphere, and the harmonizing of social relations.

In meeting the challenge of the Technosphere, according to Medow, it is vitally necessary to have forms of socially legitimated power, including property rights and monetary power which attach to networks of metainstitutions. In such metainstitutions "there is a recognition of power and a corresponding constraint on liberty of subsystems, but it is not liberty that stands to be lost—merely license."[204] These "high touch" networks would seek to maintain the basic coevolutionary structure and balance of the system. The envisaged Noöspheric institutions must seek to regulate change in a way that preserves the integrity of the system itself and the relational value system upon which it rests. "It follows," observes Salk, "that the creation of rules to control and regulate human behaviour is a necessary and natural function and is merely an extension into the metabiological realm of biological reality."[205]

It is in this sense that the role of institutions is identified as one of neutralizing, absorbing environmental complexity, and "harmonizing" contradictions that would otherwise lead to disruptions. In the epoch of the Noösphere neither market nor technocratic plan fetishism are consistent with democratic aspirations. It is in the attempt to fashion and adapt institutions appropriate for man in the epoch of the Noösphere that mankind may well meet its ultimate test.[206]

Coevolution: Beyond Coexistence

Today it is widely acknowledged that fragmentary and uncoordinated actions both of individuals and regional groups of states can no longer overcome global contradictions. In spite of its economic, political, and cultural differences, a collective strategy must be developed to address the dualisms referred to above. According to some, such a strategy requires peaceful coexistence in solving global problems. However, the resolution of complex issues is based on the unconscious as well as conscious recognition and comprehension of the complementary elements of each dualism in a harmonized balance. Mere cooperation or coexistence, although necessary, is not sufficient, insofar as it denotes "independence" and not necessarily "interdependence." For "games" of cooperation or coexistence feasibly dissolve into competitive "win-lose" games. Consequently, in the epoch of the Noösphere cooperative or coexistence games must be transcended between elements of those dualisms to which we have been referring.

An internationalization of mankind's economic and cultural development guided by coevolutionary principles will provide a basis for the further development of human civilization. But in this development the greatest threat to freedom is the radical individualist's denial of the role of power in society, such as must exist so long as democratic industrial society labors under the influence of the market mentality. In practice, society must reject Hayek's call for submission to the organic process of uncontrolled market forces with its attendant windfall gains and losses, insecurity, instability, and unmanaged change.[207] The task ahead is to throw off the ideological remnant of the nineteenth-century market mentality, so to be able to construct a theory of the economy in the broad sense with which to inform and guide the practice to which democratic industrial society must commit itself.

Conclusions

At the zenith of its development mankind is challenged by a phenomenon that will be registered as one of epoch-forming dimension. For mankind has now attained to an era in which it becomes aware of its capacity to influence the further course of the evolution of the Biosphere. The present period in the history of both the human race and the planet is marked by an intense acceleration of all evolutionary processes, by the consolidation of a highly interdependent world system, and by an erosion of the boundaries between human evolution and human ecology. We are capriciously entering into an epoch in which the further socialization of man must be guided by reason. This inaugurates the epoch of the

Noösphere; a stage in which the power of technological systems must be restructured to renounce that form of rationality that has spawned the unthinking destruction of nature and debasing of cultures, in favor of that supporting the cultivation of the inner aspirations of life. But it is also in the attempt to fashion and adapt institutions appropriate for man in the epoch of the Noösphere that mankind may well meet its ultimate test. Where are we to turn for guidance?

Entrenched within a framework of functional rationality and market mentality conventional economic thought appears to have resigned itself to debate esoteria detached from the substantive issues now confronting mankind.[208] Political economy is ill-equipped to address the problem of the livelihood of man in the age of technified society, and must be elaborated in substantive ways. And although the understanding of the "economy in the broad sense" has addressed itself to the open-system and thermodynamic dimensions of the problem, in the foregoing our focus turned to an even broader cybernetic analysis.

We have argued that an analysis of political economy in the broad sense, whose context is exclusively provided by the principles of thermodynamics is inadequate. For, notwithstanding the relevance of the thermodynamic perspective, it cannot be identified with the reflexive character of living systems, nor with the quality of nonreflexivity in social organizations. While in the era of biogenesis it was the information system of genes that enabled evolution to accelerate away from simplicity, in the present era the astonishing developments of science and technology have been identified as an engine of social advancement. It is precisely this understanding that necessitates a reconceptualization of political economy beyond the merely thermodynamic dimensions of the economic process.

The econosphere, an open system, draws from the Biosphere the energy that animates it, and it experiences its own negativity—the consequence of its own thermodynamic properties. As the growing instances of pollution and resource exhaustion attest, the production process is generating for itself a heightened level of complexity—a complexity to which it must respond.

Seeking a broader analysis removed from rhetoric, doctrine, and dogma we turned to the general theory of organization and the cybernetics of autopoiesis. From the related categories of analysis we arrived at the understanding that those institutionalized modes of economic integration whose performances are allopoietically determined functionally describe an inversion of those finalities that normally provide for the continuity of living systems. Clearly, the analytical categories to which we refer facilitate an understanding of problems of technified society in ways that transcend earlier analyses.

At this juncture we entered into a substantive reconceptualization of the economy as an instituted process. For, from the cybernetic categories of analysis, the phenomena of organization, in abstract, and concretely realized in institutions, may be interpreted as a dialectical response to complexity. The dialectic of problem and solution cumulatively stimulates organizational differentiation.

Each rationalization integrates specific functions into a new set of system/environment coordinates and produces types of problems and problem solutions that could not arise at the level of the encompassing system. In this connection, organizational differentiation is an autopoietic viability-seeking response which attaches to the principle of requisite variety. Moreover, the institutional and functional differentiation of society may be understood as a manifestation of man's adaptive response to technology. For if differentiation is an organizational response to complexity, is not a fundamental source of complexity technology? From this perspective we are led to the apparently innocuous proposition that capitalism and socialism are merely different variety-absorbing institutions!

The cybernetics of open systems, moreover, carries with it an epistemological challenge. Whereas traditional conceptions of causality and rationality emphasize goal-oriented purposefulness, cybernetic epistemology suggests that the avoidance of hazardous modes of behavior is, in fact, the critical and substantive imperative. Within this context purposeful activity pertains to discovering courses of action that satisfy a hierarchy of constraints. Rather than formulating goals in terms of fixed points of reference the nonlinearities of organizational dissonance, which attaches to the dynamics of the Technosphere, suggest an alternate strategy. Action should be directed toward avoiding threatening system states, creating, in the process, a residual pattern consistent with society's autopoiesis. Such an epistemological reconceptualization issues a challenge in other directions beyond the scope of this work. Traditionally, sociological systems theory conceptualized social systems from the point of view of its control center. However, what might be termed "neosociological systems theory," in deemphasizing "control," complies with the hierarchization of finalities and progressive subordination of subsystem autopoiesis to the normative conditions of corresponding metasystems.

The institutionalization of semi-autonomous evolution of the Technosphere is a problem of world complexity which has assumed a leading position where neither market fetishism nor technocratic plan fetishism are consistent with democratic aspirations. How we address the conjoint problem of the complexity of technified society and democracy is problematic.

In addressing this issue, a growing number of analysts assume as their point of departure the first principle of coevolutionary analysis that attaches to autopoiesis: Whenever the objective principles and mechanisms that today govern the Technosphere's evolution are incompatible with the wider Biospheric and cultural norms including human reason, it is necessary to subordinate those Technospheric elements to appropriate institutional mechanisms in ways that limit the exercise of inappropriate forms of social power. In this connection, the functionality of institutions may be alternatively expressed as the neutralization and harmonization of contradictions that would otherwise be a source of disruption. This infers the abandonment of market-driven futures for plan-guided ones, and this also identifies a central problem of global coevolution.

Our central proposition has been that the forces of industrialism must be humanized through a sound understanding of the place and function of the economy in the broad sense. This understanding indicates the necessity of plan-guidance of the forces of industrialism. For the irresponsibility of the market and radical individualism is not a viable freedom because freedom cannot survive on the basis of a destruction of society. Surely as fascism proved, the market economy does not even represent a sufficient condition for the continuity of personal freedoms. The market economy is not a necessary condition for freedom, nor is a planned economy necessarily its abnegation. As the foregoing analysis has suggested, institutional guarantees of personal freedom are compatible with any mode of economic integration. "The function of power is to ensure that measure of conformity which is needed for the survival of the group."

In meeting the challenge of the Technosphere it is vitally necessary to have forms of socially legitimated power, including property rights and monetary forms, which attach to networks of metainstitutions. The envisaged Noöspheric metainstitutions must seek to regulate change in a way that preserves the autopoietic integrity of the system itself and the relational value system upon which it is based.

5

General Conclusions

The development of the Biosphere into the Noösphere is a phenomenon more profound and powerful in essence than all of human history. However, mankind is confronting a vital challenge that will be registered as one of the most crucial in its history. It has now reached a critical phase in the conscious evolution of the Noösphere at which mankind will either realize itself or destroy itself. For the present period in the history of both the human race and the planet, as a whole, is marked by an intense acceleration of all evolutionary processes, not only by the consolidation of a highly interdependent world system, but also by an erosion of the boundaries between human evolution and human ecology. Mankind's entry into the Noösphere epoch means that the earth's further evolution has also entered a new channel wherein its further flow should ensure the coevolution of man and the Biosphere as an indispensable condition of society's continued development.

The emergence of the Noösphere refers to a stage in the further evolution of the Biosphere in which man becomes aware of his capacity to influence the course of evolution. Moreover, it represents a stage in which the power of technological systems is restructured to renounce that form of rationality that has elicited the technological imperative, in favor of a rationalization of rationality supporting the cultivation of the inner aspirations of life. Consequently, priority now attaches to evaluations of alternative "re-inverted" institutional modes of human activity that will not disrupt the homeostasis of mankind as a species, and that instead of destroying man's coevolution with the Biosphere, will enhance it.

The well-being of both present and future generations depends on whether ethically and morally sound ways are found to solve these dilemmas. The challenge of the Technosphere in the epoch of the Noösphere demands that we seek a substantive political economy—a political economy in the broad sense. It is in the attempt to fashion and adapt institutions appropriate for man in the epoch of the Noösphere that mankind may well meet its ultimate test.

The emergence of the Noösphere calls for a reevaluation of the closed mechanical paradigm of economic thought. For it has become increasingly apparent that the role of market-oriented analysis may be appropriate for a select subset of problems confronting mankind in the epoch of the Noösphere. However, the abandonment of traditional forms of analysis for more substantive modes has raised the issue of the appropriate paradigm for economic thought. Some analysts are turning to energy analysis, while others seek broader terms of reference in general systems theory and find sustenance in selected aspects of classical economic analysis.

While this theme is maturing, a major obstacle to its development has been the orientation of economic analysis on the cybernetics of the self-regulating market conceptualized as a closed mechanical system. This understanding opposes that which informed the Physiocrats. Their materialist representation of the economic process was a holistic vision of reproduction of material wealth. It presented an image of the economy whose spirit we find again in emerging modern systemic approaches. For the reproduction of the economic sphere within the Biosphere, the Physiocrats' central preoccupation, is an emergent problem of coevolutionary economic analysis.

Marx also sought to give a materialist and systematic survey of the whole of economic science, whose scope extended beyond the analysis of Ricardo. His open-systems model departed from the artifice of naturalism in Quesnay's discourse and the linear causality present in Ricardo's work. Anticipating elements of open-systems theory, Marx referred to the complex interpenetrations of the nature–society nexus. The close similarity of the life process as an open metabolically interactive phenomenon with that of the economic process was present in the analyses of Quesnay and Marx. They, nonetheless, shared a, albeit flawed, view of the livelihood of man as an open metabolically interactive system which today is the hallmark of the economy in the broad sense.

In the first quarter of this century, and contiguous to Marx's totality theory and Engels's search for the unity of scientific knowledge, a number of seminal and rigorous contributions to the understanding of the economy in the broad sense were made. However, the corresponding philosophical and methodological concepts were not fated to endure. In particular, the promising advances of A.A. Bogdanov, who saw beyond the economistic and social energetic forms of reductionism, were obscured. When elements of these analyses reemerged, the analytical categories adopted were those of Ludwig von Bertalanffy rather than A.A. Bogdanov. But, whereas Bogdanov's analysis embodied dimensions of critical social theory, Bertalanffy's contribution was narrower in its scope.

The recent and growing awareness of the biophysical dimensions of the economic process has led to a resurrection of a number of fundamental ethical and moral issues identified by the Physiocrats and by Marx. This marks a departure from economistic perspectives and symbolizes a return to substantive economic thought. In particular, an alternative paradigm for economic thought based on the dynamics of open systems is reemerging.

But having rejected mechanicalism, and embraced an open-system model, a broad reconceptualization of production is required in which low entropy is appropriated from the environment and the degraded high-entropy matter-energy is expelled. Thus, replenishment of the physical basis of life is not a circular self-sustaining phenomena. In this reconceptualization production is conceived as a thermodynamic phenomenon. And, although it is analytically useful to refer to the production process as a thermodynamic phenomenon transforming low entropy into high entropy, yielding a service thereby, these categories appear as limiting factors rather than determining ones. The production process may be technically described as one of the "informing" of low-entropy matter-energy by some "structuring information" into a use-value.

But the thermodynamic qualities of the economic process are generating a heightened level of complexity—a complexity to which it must respond. In other words, the economic system is experiencing its own negativity. Indeed, the growing complexity of technified society, in contravening the norms of the Biosphere, represents an inversion of finalities that normally attaches to open living systems. In this connection the formal categories of systems theory and cybernetics are of particular value. For the analytical categories of political economy in the broad sense must not only incorporate biophysical coordinates but also aspects of the general theory of organization, including the cybernetics of autopoiesis. These analytical categories facilitate an understanding of problems of the organization of technified society in ways that transcend earlier analyses.

From the general theory of organization, the very phenomenon of organization is interpreted as a dialectical response to complexity. The dialectics of problem and solution cumulatively stimulates further organizational differentiation. Each rationalization integrates specific functions into a new set of system/environment coordinates and produces types of problems and problem solutions that would not, and could not, arise at the level of the encompassing system. In this connection, organizational differentiation is a viability-seeking response which attaches to the principle of requisite variety. In these terms the functional differentiation of society is a manifestation of society's adaptive response to technology. From an Ashbian perspective this defines capitalism and socialism as merely different variety-absorbing institutions.

Clearly the autonomous evolution of the Technosphere is a problem of world complexity which has assumed a leading position. However, neither market nor technocratic plan fetishistic responses are consistent with the vital integrity of the Biosphere and with democratic aspirations. Consistent with these aspirations a growing number of analysts assume as their point of departure the first principle of coevolution analysis: that it is necessary to subordinate Technospheric elements to appropriate institutional mechanisms in ways that limit the exercise of inappropriate forms of social power. How we address the coevolutionary problem of the complexity of technified society and democracy enters as the dilemma of the political economy in the epoch of the Noösphere.

In face of an uncertain future, the political economist must assume particular responsibility. For it has fallen to him to overcome misplaced concreteness and fetishisms in order to participate in the work of life that is carried through the human species and which alone may lend meaning to the coevolution of man in the Biosphere.

Notes

Chapter 1

1. The Industrial Revolution was more than merely a change in technics, it was also an institutional revolution. A condition for the profitable use of expensive, long-lived machinery was that entrepreneurs be assured of uninterrupted supplies of labor and other resource inputs to work machines. Moreover, internal and external markets were necessary to effectively demand the outputs of the new machine technology. For the merchant, this meant that all factors involved had to be on sale; that is, they had to be available in the required quantities to anybody who was prepared to pay for them. Unless this condition was fulfilled, production with the help of specialized machines was too risky to be undertaken—both from the point of view of the merchant, who stakes his money, and of the community as a whole, which comes to depend upon continuous production for incomes, employment, and provisions. In short, laissez-faire capitalism was created in response to the varied needs of machine technology. By acts of government, national labor, land, and other resource markets were decontrolled and financial markets were created and/or enlarged (Karl Polanyi, *Primitive, Archaic, and Modern Economies: Essays of Karl Polanyi*; Max Weber, *General Economic History*).

2. Joseph Needham, "Laud, the Levelers, and the Virtuosi," 175.

3. Karl Polanyi, *The Livelihood of Man*; Weber, *General Economic History*.

4. Polanyi, *The Livelihood of Man*.

5. Karl Menger, *Investigations into the Methods of the Social Sciences, with Special Reference to Economics*.

6. Guy Routh, *The Origin of Economic Ideas*.

7. Thorstein Veblen, "Why Is Economics Not an Evolutionary Science?" 373.

8. Rafal Serafin, "Noosphere, Gaia, and the Science of the Biosphere," 121.

9. Pierre Teilhard de Chardin, *The Phenomenon of Man*.

10. Erich Fromm, *Marx's Concept of Man*.

11. Pierre Teilhard de Chardin, *The Hymn of the Universe*, 31.

12. Serafin, "Noosphere, Gaia, and the Science of the Biosphere," 127.

13. Vladimir I. Vernadsky, "The Biosphere and the Noösphere," 9.

14. Vernadsky, as found in R.K. Balandin, *Vladimir Vernadsky*, 135.

15. Ivan Timofeyevich Frolov, ed., *Society and the Environment*, 8.

16. Paul I. Medow, "Protecting the Biosphere and Multiculturalism in the Age of Telematics-Assisted Institutions," 20, 56.

17. V.S. Lipitskii, "Social Ecology and Communist Education," 5, 18, 33–39.

18. Vere Gordon Childe, *What Happened in History?*

19. N.N. Moiseev, "Man's Coevolution with the Biosphere: Cybernetic Aspects."

20. Georg Henrik von Wright, "Images of Science and Forms of Rationality."

21. René Passet, *L'Économique et le Vivant.*

22. Elizabeth Fox-Genovese, *Origins of Physiocracy: Economic Revolution and Social Order in Eighteenth-Century France.*

23. Preindustrial mankind had no choice but to adapt itself to the cosmic order. The plan for Plato's City in reproducing that order was a submission to it (John Niemeyer Findlay, *Plato and Platonism*).

In the words of Francis Bacon: "It is only by submitting to nature that one commands it." Subjected to the laws of nature, man lived in a symbiosis with the Biosphere of which he is part.

24. Barry Commoner, *The Closing Circle: Nature, Man and Technology.*

25. Barry Commoner, *Ecology and Social Action.*

26. George Henrik von Wright, *Technology and the Legitimation Crisis of Industrialized Society.*

27. Polanyi, *The Livelihood of Man.*

28. Commoner, *The Closing Circle*; idem, *Poverty of Power: Energy and the Economic Crisis.*

29. Passet, *L'Économique et le Vivant.*

30. Atsushi Tsuchida and Takeshi Murota, "Fundamentals in the Entropic Theory of Water Cycle."

31. Routh, *The Origin of Economic Ideas.*

32. Joseph Needham commented that "the fundamental drawback of atomistic capitalism is that its parts have no organic connection with the whole" ("Laud, the Levelers, and the Virtuosi," 176).

33. Passet, *L'Économique et le Vivant.*

34. Ibid.

35. Ibid.

36. Joseph A. Schumpeter, *History of Economic Analysis*, 119.

37. Hannah Arendt, *Vita Activa*, 291.

38. Richard B. Norgaard, "Economics as Mechanics and the Demise of Biological Diversity," 108.

39. Adam Smith, *Wealth of Nations.*

40. Karl Brunner, "The Perception of Man and the Conception of Society: Two Approaches to Understanding Society," 367–88.

41. Translation of Quesnay's *The Dialogue on the Work of Artisans* can be found in Ronald L. Meek, *The Economics of Physiocracy: Essays and Translations.*

Bearing a similarity to Locke, Quesnay, in *Natural Right*, remarked: "In the state of nature, the things suitable for man's use are reduced to those which nature produces spontaneously and over which each man can exercise his indeterminate natural right only by procuring for himself a certain share through his labour, i.e., through his endeavors. When it follows: (1) that his right to everything is only ideal; (2) that the share of things which he enjoys in the state of pure nature is obtained through labour; (3) that his right to the things suitable for his use ought to be considered in the order of nature and in the order of justice" (ibid., 43).

42. Ibid., 211–12.

43. Cutler J. Cleveland, "Biophysical Economics: Historical Perspective and Current Research Trends," 49.

44. Lewis A. Maverick, "The Chinese and the Physiocrats: A Supplement," 312–18; George Weulersse, ed., *Manuscripts Économiques de François Quesnay.*

45. Adolf Reichwein, *China and Europe: Intellectual and Artistic Contacts in the Eighteenth Century.*

46. L.A. Maverick, *China, a Model for Europe*, 380.

47. Quesnay wrote: "One must conclude that ignorance is always the principal cause of the most disastrous errors of government, of the ruin of nations, and of the decadence of empires, from which China has always been so securely preserved by the ministry of the scholars, who occupy the foremost rank in the nation and who are as attentive in guiding the people by the light of reason, as in subjecting the government clearly to the natural and immutable laws which constitute the essential order of nations" (in ibid., 302–3).

Whereas Quesnay was substantially and, perhaps, over-optimistically influenced by Father Duhalde's accounts of China, Adam Smith, who in his *Wealth of Nations* casts dispersions upon the Chinese model of government so praised by Quesnay.

48. Meek, *The Economics of Physiocracy*, 46.

49. The concept of the "just society" is one of Aristotelian origin. It was a concept that informed the economic thought of the Physiocrats. For instance, the normative or socially determined adjudication of price and other economic (and of course political) activities is historically the oldest theory of value. It resolves itself into a search for order-bestowing principles. The normative commutative justice is an overt declaration of moral or political priority by which Aristotle's "just prices"—the absence of usurious or other improper mercantile practices—constituted an ideal for Aquinas and the medieval schoolmen, a system of remuneration devoid of "exploitation."

50. Lewis Mumford, *The Myth of the Machine*, 38.

51. It is of parenthetic interest to note that, according to Quesnay, this authority must not be left to an arbitrary despot, aristocrat, or aristocratic monarchy, nor should a government's authority be democratic, because the "ignorance and prejudices that are dominant among the common people, the unbridled passions and transitory furies to which the latter are susceptible," would expose the state to revolutions. (Cf. Reichwein, *China and Europe*.)

52. Maverick, *China*, 49. It was, of course, this naturalism to which Karl Marx was to later take strong exception. For Marx, the physiocratic emphasis on land obscured labor's alleged "real powers," and this only served to justify the aristocrat's source of wealth. Physiocracy, for Marx, was a clear instance of a mystification or ideology (Stephen Gudeman, "Physiocracy: a Natural Economics," 247).

53. Marquis de V.R. Mirabeau and François Quesnay, *Rural Philosophy*, 104–5.

54. Aristotle, *Aristotle's Politics*, Book I, Part 8, 13–15.

55. In fact, for the Physiocrats, this was the first principle of government in which, according to Quesnay: "If in that country [China] in which the speculative sciences have made little progress, those of the natural laws have reached the highest degree of perfection, and if, in other countries the former sciences are well cultivated and the latter neglected, it might seem that the one does not contribute to the other. . . . In China, where the speculative sciences are neglected, men are too much given to superstition; in other countries, where little study is given to the study of the natural law, the governments are deplorable; it is this which has made China to be preferred over those other countries" (Maverick, *China*, 190). From his adoration for Chinese despotism, Quesnay wrote that "[there] should be a single sovereign authority, standing above all the individuals in the society and all the unjust undertakings of private interests" (Meek, *The Economics of Physiocracy*, 231).

56. Maverick, *China*, 270.

57. Ibid., 272–73.

58. Ibid., 276, 274.

Quesnay further reasserted this theme in *Maxims*: "Neither men nor their governments make laws, nor can they recognize them as conforming to the supreme reason that governs the Universe and carry them into society. . . . This is why they are described as carriers of laws, legislators, and that we have never dared say makers of laws, legisfactors" (Meek, *The Economics of Physiocracy*, 390).

Maverick records that although Quesnay, in 1764, attributed his *Maxims* of government to Sully, the great financial minister of Henry IV (1589–1610), his maxims were, in reality, those expounded by Chinese mandarins and recorded by Father DuHalde and compose the edicts of the Emperor K'ang Hsi (*China*, 121, 129).

Quesnay reaffirmed this point, writing that "it is therefore self-evident that the natural right of each man is extended in proportion to the degree to which he strives to observe the best possible laws, which constitute the order most advantageous to men joined together in society" (Meek, *The Economics of Physiocracy*, 55).

59. Ibid., 293.

60. According to Huan-Chang Chen: "The equivalent of the English term 'economics' in Chinese is 'administering wealth.' . . . That which enables men to live collectively, is wealth. Administering wealth, formulating rules, and prohibiting people from doing wrong—this is called 'justice' " (*The Economic Principles of Confucius and His School*, 48).

61. Meek, *The Economics of Physiocracy*, 236.

62. Ibid.

63. M. Beer, *An Inquiry into Physiocracy*.

Li said that if prices of farm products were high, the consumers suffered; if prices were low, the farmers suffered. When consumers suffered, the nation was restless; and when farmers suffered, the nation was poor. Prices should be maintained at a moderate level (Maverick, *China*, 95).

64. Ibid., 276.

65. Ibid., 277–78.

66. Ibid., 279.

67. Ibid., 274–75.

68. Lewis A. Maverick, "Chinese Influences upon the Physiocrats," 65.

69. Maverick, *China*, 282.

70. Quesnay in Meek, *The Economics of Physiocracy*, 48.

71. Maverick, *China*; idem, "The Chinese and the Physiocrats"; idem, "Chinese Influences upon the Physiocrats."

72. The translation of François Quesnay's *Corn* [Graines] can be found in Meek, *The Economics of Physiocracy*.

73. Anne Robert Jacques Turgot, *Reflections on the Formation and Distribution of Riches*, 5.

74. Ibid., 252.

75. R.L. Meek, ed., *Mirabeau and Quesnay Precursors of Adam Smith*.

76. Meek, *The Economics of Physiocracy*, 60, 209, 223.

77. Turgot, *Reflections on Riches*, 9, 12, 13, 14, 51.

78. Quesnay addressed the issue of the maldistribution of wealth and the role of the single tax and noted:

[It may be said] that there is wealth everywhere . . . and that it is the inequality in the distribution of property that gives abundance to some and refuses necessaries to the others; that hence, the population of a kingdom would not exceed its wealth if the wealth of the nation were more equally distributed. This may be partly true in nations given to the plunder of irregular taxes or monopolies in commerce and agriculture authorized through bad administration of the government. For these disorders form sudden hoards of wealth that are not distributed, but cause a void in the circulation that can only be filled at the cost of suffering. (Maverick, *China*, 261).

Like Locke, Quesnay also held property rights as a significant factor. He wrote:

The proprietors, or the cultivators of the land, individually administer the farms that belong to them. This administration is necessary if they are to maintain and increase the value of the land and to assure themselves of the net proceeds or income that they may be able to obtain. If there were no possessors of the land, to whom the ownership was assured, and if the land were common, they would be neglected, for none would wish to assume the expense of improvement or maintenance, if his profit were not assured. Now, without these expenditures, the land would hardly repay the direct cost of cultivation which the cultivators, in constant uncertainty, might venture to undertake. The land would yield no net product or income which could provide for the support of the state. In this situation, neither nation nor government could exist; for the taxes themselves would be devastating if they took the money advanced to prepare the land for cultivation or from the current wage outlays for the labour of men. (Ibid., 291)

In reference to the securing of public revenues, Quesnay wrote:

One of the most terrible features in governments under the absolute authority of a prince, is the imposition upon the subjects of arbitrary taxes, which have appeared to have neither rules nor limits prescribed by the natural laws. However, the author of nature has decisively fixed the order of things in this respect, for it is manifest that the tax necessary for the fund to satisfy the needs of the state cannot have, in an agricultural nation, any other source or any other origin than that which produces the goods necessary to satisfy the needs of men, and this source is the soil itself, made fertile by outlays and labour. (Joseph A. Schumpeter, *Economic Doctrine and Method: An Historical Sketch*, 290)

79. Maverick, *China*, 294.
80. Turgot, *Reflections on Riches*, 4–5.
81. Expressing a patent disregard for merchants, as in the writings of the Chinese philosopher Hsu Kuang-ch'i, Quesnay cautioned:

Monopolies, the encroachments and usurpations of special interests upon the common interest, are naturally excluded by a good government. By the authority of a chief vested with superior power, this insidious robbery would surely be uncovered and suppressed, for in a good government the power of special communities, of special ranks, of special occupations, and the influence of specious pretexts, could not succeed in establishing such detrimental disorder. The trades-people, manufacturing entrepreneurs and artisan groups, always eager for profit and quite adept at finding expedients, are enemies of competition and forever ingenious in seizing exclusive privileges. (Maverick, *China*, 295).

Hsu Kuang-ch'i wrote: "The sages exhorted the people to provide clothes to wear and food to eat, to love their parents and respect the elders. These ends were to be accomplished by education and agriculture. To teach the people required scholars; to feed and clothe them required farmers. Therefore scholars ranked first and farmers second, while artisans and merchants stood last in importance" (ibid., 97).

Quesnay, espouses that "the natural policy with respect to commerce ... is free and extensive competition, which secures for every nation the greatest possible number of buyers and sellers, in order to assure to it the most advantageous price in its sales and purchases" (ibid., 296).

Quesnay opposed the mercantilist views then prevalent in Europe. He said that all wealth consumed in the nation originates within its borders, whether produced there or secured in exchange for things produced there (ibid., 99). Foreign commerce would decline in importance, because with proper management of agricultural resources, the country would produce practically all it needed for its own consumption. Here too, Quesnay's model was the Chinese economy. He wrote:

> [As] the Chinese find all the necessaries of life among themselves (and since the great population assures a market to consume all these commodities within the country itself), their foreign commerce is very limited in comparison with the size of the state. The principal trade is carried on within the empire, all of the parts of which are not equally provided with the same things. Inasmuch as each province has its needs and only its own particular products, all would lapse into poverty, were it not for the fact that they exchange with one another their useful products. An established circulation in a country eighteen hundred leagues in circumference obviously presents a very extensive commerce; moreover the historian says that the commerce carried on in the interior of China is so great that all Europe's commerce could be compared to it. A purely domestic commerce may seem quite inadequate to those who believe that nations must trade with foreigners in order to grow rich in money. They may not have noticed that the greatest opulence possible consists in the greatest consumption possible. . . . Moreover, the commerce of nations, which has no object other than consumption, is confused with the commerce of merchants, which is a service that they make very well, and all the more so when their commerce is extended afar. The more the nations can save the cost of this, even to the harm of the great fortunes of the merchants, the more they will gain for consumption and for the outlays necessary for the perpetual reproduction of the riches that spring from the earth and furnish the revenues of the nation and of the sovereign. (Ibid., 208)
>
> Foreign commerce is perhaps more injurious than favorable to the prosperity of the nations that devote themselves to it, aside from the merchants, who can make great fortunes from it, in large measure at the expense of their fellow citizens. The commodities that they go so far to seek are seldom more then expensive frivolities which support an injurious luxury. (Ibid., 211)

82. Schumpeter, *Economic Doctrine and Method*, 238.
83. Beer, *An Inquiry into Physiocracy*.

84. Schumpeter, *Economic Doctrine and Method*.

85. Ibid., 308.

86. Routh, *The Origin of Economic Ideas*.

87. Hobbes's approach was, according to Cutler Cleveland, successively developed by William Petty, Richard Cantillon, François Quesnay, Adam Smith, and their nineteenth-century successors, into a material-flow analysis of production and price ("natural" or production prices which covered the cost of raw materials, labor, amortization of instruments of production, plus profit at an average rate) (Cleveland, "Biophysical Economics."). A detailed diagram of this "circular-flow model" can be seen in Figure 3.1. Also see Maverick, "Chinese Influences upon the Physiocrats," 60.

88. Anne Robert Jacques Turgot, "Reflexion sur la formation et la distribution des richees," 20.

89. Meek, *The Economics of Physiocracy*, 232.

90. Ibid., 19.

91. Schumpeter, *Economic Doctrine and Method*, 238.

92. Meek, *The Economics of Physiocracy*.

93. Ibid., 347.

94. Whereas the Physiocrats considered land rent to be the only income in the nature of a surplus, the Smithian school afforded that status to profit as well as to rent (ibid.). To Smith himself it seemed clear that that portion of the annual produce that represented the social surplus over cost consisted of both rent and profit. One part of the produce, he wrote, is "destined for replacing capital, or for renewing the provisions, material and finished work which had been withdrawn from a capital; the other for constituting a revenue either to the owner of this capital, as the profit of his stock, or to some other person, as the rent of his land" (Smith, *Wealth of Nations*, 315).

95. Fox-Genovese, *Origins of Physiocracy*, 74.

96. Maverick, "The Chinese and the Physiocrats"; idem, "Chinese Influences upon the Physiocrats."

97. Cleveland, "Biophysical Economics," 50.

98. Fox-Genovese, *Origins of Physiocracy*, 76.

99. John Kenneth Galbraith, *Economics in Perspective*, 50.

100. Karl Marx, *Theories of Surplus Value: Part II*, 228.

101. Ricardo followed Adam Smith in giving greater emphasis to the universal role of capitalists in the social order. Because financial capital was mobile, or, rather was made commensurable, capitalists were involved in both agriculture and manufacturing, the rural and urban sectors. For Ricardo, productive agriculture was not opposed to capitalist-like trade, circulation, or artisanship. All three social functions—capital, labor, and landowning—were represented within agriculture. Ricardo's formulation, which presumed capital mobility, bridged the analogical divisions of use/exchange, productive/nonproductive, and rural/urban.

102. Alfred Marshall, *Principles of Economics: an Introductory Volume*.

103. See Samuel Hollander, *The Economics of David Ricardo*; idem, "Ricardo's Analysis of the Profit Rate, 1813–15."

104. Dieter Groh and Rolf-Peter Sieferle, "Experience of Nature in Bourgeois Society and Economic Theory: Outlines of an Interdisciplinary Research Project," 568.

It is striking that the debasement of nature in classical economic theory ran parallel to the debasement of a large part of humanity—the working class—in the course of industrialization (ibid., 569).

105. Ibid., 570.

106. Howard L. Parsons, ed., *Marx and Engels on Ecology*.

107. In his *Economic & Philosophical Manuscripts of 1844*, Marx wrote:

It is argued against physiocracy that agriculture, from the economic point of view ... does not differ from any other industry; and that the essence of wealth, therefore is not a specific form of labour bound to a particular element—a particular expression of labour—but labour in general (131)

Physiocracy denies particular, external, merely objective wealth by declaring labour to be the essence of wealth. But for physiocracy labour is from the outset only the subjective essence of landed property. It only turns landed property into alienated labour. It annuls its feudal character by declaring agriculture as its essence. But its attitude to the world of industry is one of denial; it acknowledges the feudal system by declaring agriculture to be the only industry (Ibid).

108. Parsons, *Marx and Engels on Ecology*, 29.

109. Immanual Kant, *Immanual Kant's Critique of Pure Reason*, Methodology, Part III.

110. Attila Àgh, "Totality Theory and System Theory," 120.

111. Ibid., 121.

112. Ibid., 122.

113. See "The Poverty of Philosophy" in Marx, *Manuscripts of 1844*.

114. Àgh, "Totality Theory and System Theory," 124.

115. Ibid.

116. Ibid., 125.

117. Karl Marx, *Grundrisse: Introduction to the Critique of Political Economy*, 163–64, 189, 365.

118. Donald McQuarie and Terry Amburgey, "Marx and Modern Systems Theory," 3.

119. See T.B. Bottomore, *Karl Marx: Selected Writings in Sociology and Social Philosophy*, 17.

120. See Engels to Starkenberg, 1894, in Karl Marx and Frederick Engels, *Selected Correspondence 1846–1895*, 466.

121. Karl Marx and Frederick Engels, *The German Ideology*, 42.

122. Marx, *Grundrisse*, 265.

123. Predeterminism claims that man is a puppet of World spirit (in the case of Hegel), of Fate, God, or economic forces which leads to the position of fatalism. The scientific determinism, to which Marx subscribed, argues that social and natural events are explainable on the basis of observed relationships. In this view, man makes his own history; that is, man can make decisions on the basis of his ideas but under the constraints imposed by nature and society. It argues that human beliefs and actions must be included as a dynamic determining factor of social analysis.

124. Howard Sherman, "Marx and Determinism." Among the German Social Democrats of the 1890s and later among Soviet Marxist theorists, Marx was interpreted in vulgar terms; that there was an inevitable, even predetermined, march of history; that socialism was inevitable because of the march of economic forces. It was this form of vulgar Marxism that became the strawman of many critics of his theories.

125. Karl Marx, *Capital: A Critique of Political Economy*, I:82n. In the first volume of *Capital*, Marx explored the relationship between technological means of production and society, and argued that social relations molded technology, rather than vice versa, as has often been assumed in discussions of Marxism. It was on this basis that Georg Lukács, for instance, challenged determinist claims about Marx's view of technology (Donald MacKenzie, "Marx and the Machines.").

126. Marx, *Theories of Surplus Value*, 228.

127. Marx, *Grundrisse*, 99–100.

128. Karl Marx and Frederick Engels, *Critique of the Gotha Programme: A Contribution to the Critique of the Social-Democratic Draft Programme of 1891*, 331.

129. See the following correspondence: Engels to Bloch 1890 and Engels to Schmidt 1890, found in Marx and Engels, *Selected Correspondence*.

130. The French philosopher Maurice Godelier notes that "Marx . . . in posing that the structure is not to be confused with the visible relationships, but that it explains their hidden logic, is clearly a forerunner of the modern structuralist movement" (Godelier, "Systems, Structure and Contradiction in *Das Kapital*"; see also McQuarie and Amburgey, "Marx and Modern Systems Theory," 12).

131. See correspondence of Engels to Bloch 1890 in Marx and Engels, *Selected Correspondence*, 417.

132. Marx and Engels, *The German Ideology*, 48.

133. See "The Process of Capitalist Production as a Whole," in Marx, *Capital*, 791–92.

134. See "Wage Labour and Capital," in Karl Marx and Frederick Engels, *Selected Works*, I:191.

135. J. Martinez-Alier and J.N. Naredo, "A Marxist Precursor of Energy Economics."

136. Karl Marx, *Pre-Capitalist Economic Formation*, 81.

137. See "The Power of Money in Bourgeois Society," as found in Marx, *Manuscripts of 1844*, 165.

138. Ibid., 207.

139. See "Private Property and Communism," in ibid., 132.

140. Marx, *Capital*, 177.

141. See "Critique of the Hegelian Dialectic and Philosophy as a Whole," in Marx, *Manuscripts of 1844*, 170.

142. Alfred Schmidt, *The Concept of Nature in Marx*, 78–79.

143. Marx, *Grundrisse*, 488. The discussion of nature as humanity's inorganic body appears in conjunction with precapitalist societies. It is clear, however, that the rupture between humanity and nature is another expression of the general phenomenon of capitalist reification and that the overcoming of capitalism means also the overcoming of fetishized nature. Max Horkheimer and Theodor Adorno, however, in their *Dialectic of the Enlightenment*, locate this process of dominating nature at the beginning of Western civilization—with Odysseus. But the question of the origin is somewhat scholastic, for what is clear is that such a relationship of domination has to end, which it can only if a qualitative change takes place in social relationships and in the quality of everyday life. (See also: Paul Piccone, "Reading *Grundrisse*: Beyond 'Orthodox' Marxism," 246.)

144. Marx, *Manuscripts of 1844*, 1226–27.

145. Schmidt, *The Concept of Nature in Marx*, 80.

146. Ibid., 81, 176.

147. Marx, *Grundrisse*, 397.

148. Marx, *Manuscripts of 1844*, 112; see also "Estranged Labour," ibid., 106.

149. Or, from the cybernetic perspective, organization is a response to complexity. Refer to Chapter 4.

150. Marx, *Capital*, I:186, 202.

151. Ibid., 177.

152. See "Critique of the Gotha Programme" in Marx and Engels, *Selected Works*, II:17.

153. See Marx's "Marginal Notes to the Programme of the German Worker's Party," in ibid.

154. Marx and Engels, *Critique of the Gotha Programme*, 112–13.

155. Marx and Engels, *Selected Works*, 18.

156. Marx, *Grundrisse*, 705.

157. See "Critique of the Hegelian Dialectic and Philosophy as a Whole," in Marx, *Manuscripts of 1844*.

158. Schmidt, *The Concept of Nature in Marx*, 61.

159. Frederick Engels, *Dialectics of Nature*, 180.

160. Ibid., 58.

161. Marx, *Grundrisse*, 188, 313.

162. Marx, *Capital*, III:745.

163. Ibid., I:603.

164. Ibid., I:144.

165. Marx, *Grundrisse*, 159.

166. Ibid., 313.

167. Ibid., III:250.

168. Donald C. Lee, "On the Marxist View of the Relationship between Man and Nature," 7. In this connection we shall, in Chapter 4, seek to mediate objectivity and subjectivity in the context of an analytical systems approach.

169. Val Routley, "On Karl Marx as an Environmental Hero," 237; Charles Tolman, "Marx and Nature," 72.

170. Groh and Sieferle, "Experience of Nature in Bourgeois Society," 575.

171. Marx, *Manuscripts of 1844*, 108.

172. Hegel generated the vocabulary that became central to Marx's theory of alienation. For example, Hegel employed the term Entaüsserung, in referring to man with Christ as his model "stripping himself of his finiteness" (Abraham Rotstein, "The Outer Man: Technology and Alienation"). Struik regards the Hegelian concept as pertaining to an "alienation from God" (see Marx, *Manuscripts of 1844*, 37).

173. Parsons, *Marx and Engels on Ecology*.

174. Karl Marx and Frederick Engels, *The Communist Manifesto*, 14.

175. Marx, *Capital*, 732–33.

176. Bozidar Debenjak, "Engels and the Problem of Alienation."

177. Marx, *Grundrisse*, 409–10.

178. Ibid., 410.

179. Groh and Sieferle, "Experience of Nature in Bourgeois Society."

180. Marx, *Capital*, I:71.

181. André Gorz, *Ecology as Politics*.

182. Thomas T. Sekine, "Socialism as a Living System."

183. "Nature becomes the body of man." This metaphor of nature as man's body is not further explained by Marx. One might ask: If nature is man's body, is man nature's "mind or spirit"? Extrapolating from the corpus of Marx's work, I suppose that he would answer in dialectic terms: prehistorical man did not know himself to be other than nature just as the infant does not distinguish himself as mind and body; but in a later stage of Western historical development he sees himself as separate from, and finally as conqueror of, nature. The next stage of development is a new harmony and unity, the overcoming of this separation, this alienation from nature.

184. Marx, *Grundrisse*, 542.

185. Marx wrote:

No longer does the worker insert a modified natural thing as middle link between the object and himself; rather, he inserts the process of nature, transformed into an industrial process, as a means between himself and inorganic nature, mastering it. He steps to the side of the production process instead of being its chief action. In this transformation, it is neither the direct human labour he himself performs, nor the time during which he works, but rather the appropriation of his own general productive power, his understanding of nature and his mastery over it by virtue of his presence as a social body—it is, in a word, the development of the social individual which appears as the great foundation stone of production and of wealth. (Ibid., 705)

186. Ibid., 706.
187. Engels, *Dialectics of Nature*, 239.
188. Ibid.
189. Tolman, "Marx and Nature," 73.
190. Gorz, *Ecology as Politics*.
191. Tolman, "Marx and Nature," 74.
192. Marx, *Grundrisse*, 706.
193. Parsons, *Marx and Engels on Ecology*.
194. This proposition is grounded both on Marx's and Engels's position on dialectics and metaphysics. Marx wrote: "When we reflect on Nature, or the history of mankind, or our own intellectual activity, the first picture presented to us is of an endless maze of relations and interactions, in which nothing remains what, where and as it was, but everything moves, changes, comes into being and passes out of existence. This primitive, naive yet intrinsically correct conception of the world was that of ancient Greek philosophy, and was first clearly formulated by Heraclitus: everything is and also is not, for everything is in flux, is constantly changing, constantly coming into being and passing away" (Marx, *Capital*, 177).
195. Ibid., I:183–84.
196. "Metabolism" is a rendering of *Stoffwechsel*, a term repeatedly used in *Capital*, and translated in the English edition as "material reaction" or "exchange of matter."
197. Marx was entirely familiar with the use of the concept of metabolism by Moleschott, the spokesman of the materialist movement. Moleschott was an investigator into nature and a physiological materialist with social leanings. From popular writings such as *Physiologie des Stoffwechsels in Pflanzen und Tieren* (1851) for instance, materialism put forward in such books, and supported with a mass of empirical material, portrays nature, on the model of human physiology, as a vast process of transformation and metabolism. In *Der Kreislauf des Lebens*, Moleschott elaborated his theory of metabolism. He wrote: ". . . just as trade is the soul of commerce, the eternal circulation of material is the soul of the world. . . . The quintessence of all activity on earth is the movement of the basic materials, combinations and division, assimilation and excretion" (p. 40).
In the Marx–Engels correspondence of November 18, 1864, from London Marx inquires if Engels lists among his collection of books Moleschott's *Lehre der Nahrungsmittel* [The Science of Foodstuffs]. It was this work that Feuerbach reviewed under the title "Natural Science and the Revolution" (Eugene Kamenka, *The Philosophy of Ludwig Feuerbach*, 110). In Moleschott's work Feuerbach understood nature as being literally incorporated into man through ingestion. "No phosphorous—no thought," quotes Feuerbach from Moleschott. From the pun "Der Mensch ist was er isst" [Man is what he eats], a social implication was given—that man creates himself in the labor of producing the means of his subsistence and in the social organization that assures this production and reproduction of species existence. Feuerbach approvingly referred to Moleschott's absurd proposition that a vegetarian has a vegetarian character, meateaters are strong-willed, and so on; the energy of the English workers is explained by their eating roast beef, and by contrast the laziness of the Italian lazzarone is the outcome of a vegetarian diet. From

these curiosities Feuerbach concludes that a German revolution will never be accomplished by cabbage eaters. Marx was less impressed with Moleschott categorizing him as a "vulgar materialist" precisely because the social and political contexts of the human production of sustenance were left out of his account, in the flat insistence on the physiological materialism of human existence (Max W. Wartofsky, *Feuerbach*, 413).

198. In 1885 Engels explained that "a knowledge of mathematics and natural science is essential to a conception of nature which is dialectical and at the same time materialist. Marx was well versed in mathematics, but we could only partially, intermittently and sporadically keep up with the natural sciences" (Saul K. Padover, *The Letters of Karl Marx*, 188).

Marx was aware of energy theory; in his correspondence with Lion Philips, dated London, August 17, 1864, he writes: "I have recently looked over a very important work on natural science, Grove's *Correlation of Physical Forces*. He demonstrates that all mechanical forces, heat, light, electricity, magnetism, and chemical affinity, are properly only a modification of the same force, and they mutually produce, replace and transform each other" (ibid.). (Also see: William Robert Grove, *Correlation of Physical Forces*.)

This approach, which in any case did not explicitly comprise the flow of energy, was not integrated into Marx's view of history, and this is why there has been no school of Marxist ecological historians or economists. Some early references to the flow of energy can be found in Engels, perhaps the first one in a letter to Marx of July 14, 1858, from Manchester, where Engels mentioned Joule and the law of conservation of energy. Writing thirty years later to Nicolai Danielson (October 15, 1888), Engels said that the nineteenth century would be remembered as the century of Darwin, Joule, and Clausius; it has been not only the century of the theory of evolution but also of the theory of the transformation of energy (J. Martinez-Alier, *Ecological Economics: Energy, Environment and Society*, 221).

199. Marx, *Capital*, I:505. Karl Marx noted that "capitalist production by collecting the population in great centres, and causing an ever increasing preponderance of town population, on the one hand concentrates the historical motive power of society; on the other hand, it disturbs the circulation of matter [metabolism] between man and the soil, i.e., prevents the return to soil of its elements consumed by man in the form of food and clothing; it therefore violates the conditions necessary for lasting fertility of the soil. By this action it at the same time destroys the health of the town labourer and the intellectual life of the rural labourer" (ibid., 474).

200. Ibid., I:42–43.

201. Ibid.

202. Schmidt, *The Concept of Nature in Marx*, 86–89. In ignoring the chemical basis of life, Feuerbach left all scientific advances behind, and thus he overlooked the metabolism of man with nature—the essence of man as a laboring being (Engels, *Dialectics of Nature*, 199).

203. Marx, *Capital*, 578.

204. Ibid. It is of more than passing interest to note that, though Marx expressed an interest in the chemo-physiological balances of the body, he and Engels dismissed out of hand the effort to understand the corresponding energy flows that was advanced by a contemporary Ukrainian socialist, Serhii Podolinsky.

205. Marx and Engels, *Selected Works*, 9; Karl Marx and Frederick Engels, *The Marx-Engels Reader*, 5.

206. Marx, *Grundrisse*, 137; and John L. Stanley and Ernst Zimmerman, "On the Alleged Differences Between Marx and Engels," 242.

207. In Schmidt, *The Concept of Nature in Marx*, 161.

208. Marx and Engels, *The German Ideology*, 41.

209. Edwin Alexander, "Consciousness, Necessity and Labor: A Discussion of Marx's 'Metabolic Interactivity'."

210. Marx in Vladimir Ilich Lenin, "The Economic Content of Narodism and the Criticism of It in Mr. Struve's Book," in *Collected Works*, 1:420.

211. Marx, *Capital*, I:43.

212. Thus, in his essay on Feuerbach, Engels found fault with the old materialism for its inability to "comprehend the universe as a process, as matter undergoing an uninterrupted historical development" (Marx and Engels, *Selected Works*, 374).

213. Marx, *Capital*, I:43, *n.1.*

214. Ibid., 177.

215. Ibid., 202.

216. Marx, *Capital*, 42–43.

217. Ibid., 513.

218. Ibid., 183.

219. Marx, *Manuscripts of 1844*, 137.

220. Schmidt, *The Concept of Nature in Marx*, 92. Marx described the exchange of commodities under bourgeois relations of production in the following manner: "The exchange of commodities is the process, in which the social metabolism takes place, i.e., the exchange of the particular products of private individuals, as well as the creation of definite social relations of production through which the individuals enter into this metabolism" (*Capital*, 55).

221. Karl Marx, *A Contribution to the Critique of Political Economy*, 109.

222. Marx, *Capital*, 168.

223. Ibid., I:177.

224. Ibid., 71.

225. Parsons, projecting from Engels's position, asserts that political economy, when it is sufficiently generalized, becomes ecology, and from time to time it was so generalized by Marx and Engels; for political economy pertains to the production and distribution of economic values and the social and governmental management of such values. At a deeper level it pertains to the basic laws that regulate individuals in human societies, as well as one society in its relations to other societies, so far as these relations implicate economic values. The original Aristotelian concept, *oikonomia* is the management of a household—familial, communal, national. While *oikologos* is the study of households of organisms in general—the mutual relations of organisms and their environments. The synthesis of the two terms in contemporary economic analysis has been referred to as "bioeconomics." Thus, political economy, according to Parsons, can be seen as a species of the generic science of ecology; or, we can reach ecology by tracing the most comprehensive, generic laws that underlie the transactions of human societies with their biophysical foundations in the context of totality theory (Parsons, *Marx and Engels on Ecology*).

226. Parsons, *Marx and Engels on Ecology*.

227. Marx's correspondence to Engels (December 7, 1867), in Karl Marx and Frederick Engels, *Collected Works*, 31:404.

228. Though Engels wrote *Anti-Dühring*, he never completed *Dialectics*. Written in 1885, when he had just set aside his work on the subject in order to complete *Capital* (Marx died in 1883 with only the first volume published), Engels's *Dialectics* remained an assortment of loose notes (David Joravsky, *Soviet Marxism and Natural Science: 1917–1932*, 10). (See Frederick Engels, *Herr Eugen Dühring's Revolution in Science* [hereafter, Anti-Dühring].)

229. Joravsky, *Soviet Marxism and Natural Science*.

230. Schmidt, *The Concept of Nature in Marx*, 51.

231. Frederick Engels, "Socialism: Utopian and Scientific," in Marx and Engels, *Selected Works*, I:143; see also Engels, *Anti-Dühring*, 29.

232. Georg W.F. Hegel, *The Phenomenology of the Mind*, 220.
233.

Modern natural science has had to take over from philosophy the principle of the indestructibility of motion, it cannot any longer exist without this principle. But the motion of matter is not merely crude mechanical motion, mere change of place, it is heat and light and magnetic stress, chemical combination and dissociation, life, and finally consciousness. The indestructibility of motion cannot be merely quantitative, it must also be conceived qualitatively; matter whose purely mechanical change of place includes indeed the possibility under favourable conditions of being transformed into heat, electricity, chemical action, of life, but which is not capable of producing these conditions from out of itself, such matter has forfeited motion; motion which has lost the capacity of being transformed into the various forms appropriate to it may indeed still have *dynamis* but no longer *energia*, and so has become partially destroyed. Both, however, are unthinkable. (Engels, *Dialectics of Nature*, 21)

234. Engels, *Anti-Dühring*, 133.
235. Engels, *Dialectics of Nature*, 38.
236. Engels, *Anti-Dühring*, 16, 62, 70.
237. The force of Engels's argument is apparent in the writings of the Soviet scientist and philosopher, V.I. Vernadsky, who, in 1945, wrote of man's biophysical and evolutionary linkage with nature.

In everyday life one used to speak of man as an individual, living and moving freely about our planet, freely building up his history. Until recently historians and the students of the humanities ... consciously failed to reckon with the natural laws of the Biosphere. Basically man cannot be separated from it; it is only now that this indissolubility begins to appear and in precise terms before us. He is geologically active connected with its material and energetic structure. Actually no living organism exists on earth in a state of freedom. All organisms are connected indissolubly and uninterruptedly, first of all through nutrition and respiration, with the circumambient material and energetic medium. ("The Biosphere and the Noösphere," 4)

Mankind taken as a whole is becoming a mighty geological force. There arises the problem of the reconstruction of the Biosphere in the interests of freely thinking humanity as a single totality. This new state of the Biosphere, which we approach without our noticing it, is the Noösphere. (Ibid., 9)

238. Engels, *Dialectics of Nature*, 26.
239. Ibid., 144.
240. Marx and Engels, *The Marx-Engels Reader*, 90–91.
241. In Richard Adamik, "Marx, Engels and Dühring."
242. See Engels's essays on Feuerbach in Engels, *Dialectics of Nature*, and Marx and Engels, *Selected Works*.
243. Jack Mendelson, "On Engels's Metaphysical Dialectics: A Foundation of Orthodox 'Marxism'," 69.
244. Engels, *Dialectics of Nature*, 205. By moving dialectics from mind to matter and by attempting to remove Hegelian mysticism from dialectics, Engels argued that the "dialectics of the mind is only a reflection of the forms of motion in the real world, both of nature and of history" (ibid., 203).

Once the distinction between natural and social regularities was blurred, Engels could no longer grasp the different relations of natural science and critical social theory to laws and practice. He developed a precritical epistemology in which the active role of subject was again lost sight of. In accord with his metaphysical presuppositions, Engels could only conceive of ideas in a naively realistic way—as "images" or "copies" derived from the true reality, nature, and society (Mendelson, "On Engels' Metaphysical Dialectics," 70).

Engels also spoke of dialectical thought as the "conscious reflex" of the dialectical movement of the "real world." This reflection or copy theory of knowledge was later elaborated by Lenin and then codified as the official epistemology of Soviet Marxism. It cuts off knowledge from its mediation through the synthetic activities of the subject and reduces it to a passive and uncritical reproduction of a separate object undergoing a law-governed evolutionary process (ibid). However, insofar as this accusation of a copy theory is true, Engels was not consistent in this attitude, an inconsistency he shared with Marx. Engels had already agreed with Marx on the profound difference between human and natural science, and the crucial difference between the two centered around production (Stanley and Zimmerman, "On the Alleged Differences Between Marx and Engels," 238).

For Engels motion was the binding element of nature. If this binding element consists in mere motion, and the mind merely reflects that motion (copy theory), both motion and mind would simply be randomly represented and history would be no more than a series of accidents or contingencies that simply change the direction and flow of motion in unpredictable ways. In such a case science could not overcome alienation but merely represent it in already discovered empirical phenomena; nature could not be brought under human control, but merely analyzed and depicted post facto. However, as Marx expressed it "all science would be superfluous if the outward appearance and essence of things directly coincided" (Marx, *Capital*, III:817). Therefore, some inner connection beyond mere motion must be sought, and Marx and Engels found that inner connection in dialectics (Stanley and Zimmerman, "On the Alleged Differences Between Marx and Engels," 239).

245. Engels in Schmidt, *The Concept of Nature in Marx*, 78.

246. Marx and Engels, *Collected Works*, 11:373–74.

247. Engels, *Anti-Dühring*.

248. Ibid., 77. This argument for the autodynamism of the social and material world was critical to Soviet arguments against Pareto's theory of equilibrium.

249. Ibid.

250. Engels, *Dialectics of Nature*, 43.

251. Marx, *Manuscripts of 1844*, 169.

252. Georg Lukács, *History and Class Consciousness*, 24.

253. In Joravsky, *Soviet Marxism and Natural Science*, 9.

254. Schmidt, *The Concept of Nature in Marx*, 195, 57.

255. See Stanley and Zimmerman, "On the Alleged Differences Between Marx and Engels."

256. Schmidt, *The Concept of Nature in Marx*, 60, 191.

257. See Engels's work titled "Die Lage Englands, I, Das 18 Jahrhundert," in Marx and Engels, *Collected Works*, 551.

258. Engels, *Dialectics of Nature*, 238.

259. See Engels's article "Ludwig Feuerbach and the End of Classical German Philosophy," in Marx and Engels, *Selected Works*; Norman Levine, "Marxism and Engelism: Two Differing Views of History," 225.

260. In other words, it displays general systems theoretical tendencies.

261. As quoted in Levine, "Marxism and Engelism," 228.

262. See Engels's article "Socialism: Utopian and Scientific," in Marx and Engels, *Selected Works*, 386.

263. Henri Lefebvre, *Dialectical Materialism*, 19.

264. Levine, "Marxism and Engelism," 228.

265. Terrel Carver, "Marx, Engels and Scholarship," 246. In the 1870s and 1880s, Engels was not merely responding to the revival of idealism. He was not merely trying to defend Marxism, or materialism in general, from the renaissance of subjectivist philosophy. Rather he was building on themes present in his 1858 correspondence (Levine, "Marxism and Engelism," 227).

266. On July 14, 1858, Engels wrote to Marx and reflected therein on Hegel's *Philosophy of Nature* (Marx and Engels, *Selected Correspondence*, 113). In that letter he noted that in the realm of physics there was the discovery of the correlation of forces, the law that under certain conditions mechanical motion would be changed into heat, and then heat into light, etc., as noted by Grove in 1838 (Levine, "Marxism and Engelism," 228).

267. Frederick Engels, *The Origin of the Family, Private Property, and the State*, 19.

268. It is, then, paradoxical that the Stalinists would also profess to be in favor of political struggle and revolution; for were socialism inevitable, or fated, why bother to struggle?

269. Karl Marx in E.K. Hunt, "The Importance of Veblen for Contemporary Marxists," 116.

270. See Marx and Engels, *Selected Correspondence*, 208, 496, 500, 503.

271. Engels's understanding of the second law of thermodynamics was clearly partial. He wrote: "the heat radiating in space must necessarily be able to convert itself into some other form of motion; and that in that new form it can immediately be reconcentrated and reactivated. In this way we are free of one main obstacle to dead suns being reconverted into incandescent nebulae" (*Dialectics of Nature*, 284). This argument implies that dialectical materialism with its immanent transformation of matter—the transformation of the quantitative into the qualitative—can contravene the second law.

272. This is not to say that Marx and Engels were unaware of the then emerging and speculative theory of social energetics, for in their personal correspondence they were sufficiently stimulated to note the contributions of the Ukrainian Serhii Podolinsky.

273. Vladimir I. Vernadsky, "Problems of Biogeochemistry: The Fundamental Matter-Energy Difference between the Living and the Inert Natural Bodies of the Biosphere," 489.

Chapter 2

1. Max Planck, "The Unity of the Physical Universe."

2. Sadi N.L. Carnot, *Memoir on the Motive Power of Heat*; Morris Kline, *Mathematics and the Search for Knowledge*; Pierre Simon de Laplace, *Celestial Mechanics*.

3. That the universe tends toward a final state of thermal equilibrium was Boltzmann's *Warmtod*. "Die Energie der Welt is konstant. Die Entropie der Welt strebt einen Maximum zu" (Ludwig Boltzmann, *Der zweite Hauptsatz der mechanischen Wärmtheorie*; idem, *Theoretical Physics and Philosophical Problems*).

4. As a possible direction of escaping from this gloomy image, discussions focused on the so-called Maxwell demon, which was said to be able to act as a sorter between high- and low-speed molecules so as to reduce entropy in isolated systems (David K.C. MacDonald, *Faraday, Maxwell, and Kelvin*). A variety of thought experiments of this concept were reviewed and concluded that the demon generated more entropy than it reduced. Though a number of variations of the story exist, the conclusions are unanimous—every effort to find an exception to the entropy law failed. Nonetheless, some obscurity remains, particularly in the apparent paradox of living systems.

5. Sir Arthur Eddington noted that "entropy is Time's arrow" (*The Expanding Universe*, 127).

6. Ilya Prigogine and Isabella Stengers, *Order Out of Chaos: Man's New Dialogue with Nature*.

7. Ludovico Geymonat, "Neopositivist Methodology and Dialectical Materialism," 178.

8. Ibid., 179.

9. Ibid.

10. Ibid., 180.

11. Ibid., 180–81.

12. Ibid., 182.

13. Kline, *Mathematics and the Search for Knowledge*, 199.

14. Anatol Rapoport, "Methodology in the Physical, Biological and Social Sciences."

15. Kline, *Mathematics and the Search for Knowledge*, 143.

16. C. Babbage, *On the Economy of Machinery and Manufactures*; see also J.R. McCulloch, "Philosophy of Manufacturers."

17. "From the indestructibility of matter, as the physical premise, it obviously follows that what we term production and consumption are mere transformations of substance. [The] phenomenon is alteration of matter in its quality, merely, without increase or diminution of its quantity. In every transition of matter from one condition to another, force is employed, or, as we say, consumed, and force is also evolved or produced. . . . Economic value is nothing but a kind of inertia; utility, an equivalent of mechanical momentum" (Henry C. Carey, *Principles of Social Science*, 61).

18. Indeed, he speculated that "[In] our Victorian age may we not owe indirectly to the lavish expenditure of our material energy far more than we readily conceive?" (William S. Jevons, *Coal Question: An Inquiry Concerning the Progress of the Nations*, 456).

19. Wilhelm Ostwald, *Energetische Grundlagen der Kulturwissenschaften*.

20. L. Winiarsky, "Essai sur la méchanique sociale: l'énergie sociales et ses mensurations"; idem, "La Method mathmatique dans la sociologie et dans l'économie."

21. Kline, *Mathematics and the Search for Knowledge*, 143.

22. Aleksandr A. Bogdanov, *The Philosophy of Living Experience*, 231–32.

23. Marx, *Manuscripts of 1844*, 143.

24. V.I. Ivanovsky, a contributor to *Pravda* under Bogdanov's editorship, wrote: "if anyone suggests that the connection of a scientific outlook with positivism undermines the recognition of matter as the ultimate basis of the world, he is sadly mistaken—simply because a scientific outlook does not demand such a recognition. The scientific outlook can be built not only on a materialist, but also on an energist, an agnostic, a phenomenalist or on various other bases" (V.I. Ivanovsky, "Chto takoe 'positivizm' i 'idealizm'."; and as found in James D. White, "The First Pravda and the Russian Marxist Tradition," 192).

25. The Austrian philosopher and member of the Vienna Circle, Ernst Mach, reduced phenomena to "experience," to sensations that are neither purely physical, nor purely mental, but neutral. Mach's subjective idealism expressed the "unknowability," indeed the nonexistence, the unthinkable nature of an objective reality independent of consciousness. This was the implicit Machian axiom. Knowledge, according to Mach, is progressive historically, as newer and more efficient ways of generalizing experience are demanded and discovered (ibid., 194).

Bogdanov, seeing in Mach's proposition an instrument for revising Marxist epistemology, reduced reality to experience.

26. Aleksandr A. Bogdanov, *Empiriomonism: Articles on Philosophy*, 7; Lenin, *Collected Works*, 14:50–51; Nikolay Valentinov, *Encounters with Lenin*, 258.

27. Lefebvre, *Dialectical Materialism*, 19.

28. Lenin, *Collected Works*, 14:22.

29. Ibid., 267.

30. Subscribing to a concept instrumental to the scientists and philosophers of the Vienna Circle, Lavróv held that beyond the realm of man the world was a meaningless chaos, "nothing but simultaneous concatenations of facts, so minute and fractional that man could scarcely even approach them in all their particularities" (Peter Lavróv, *Historical Letters*, 104).

31. K.M. Jensen, *Beyond Marx and Mach: Alexander Bogdanov's Philosophy of Living Experience*, 271.

32. Ibid., 209.

33. Karl G. Ballestrem, "Lenin and Bogdanov," 303.

34. Bogdanov acknowledged Hegel, Marx, and Spencer as precursors to what he called "today's formulation of the question." And that question was "What was the most expedient way to organize some complex of elements, real or ideal?" Bogdanov assumed there was a continuous process of organization–disorganization—indeed, that all human activities consisted of ordering, sorting, and organizing. The "task of tektology" was to systematize those activities (Zenovia A. Sochor, *Revolution and Culture: The Bogdanov-Lenin Controversy*, 44).

35. Ibid.; and Bogdanov as found in Alexander Vucinich, *Social Thought in Tsarist Russia: The Quest for a General Science of Society, 1861–1917*.

36. Aleksandr A. Bogdanov, *Revolution and Philosophy*, 51; see Vucinich, *Social Thought in Tsarist Russia*, 221.

37. I. Blauberg, "The History of Science and the Systems Approach," 91.

38. Ibid., 3.

39. Jensen, *Beyond Marx and Mach*, 89–90.

40. Bogdanov, *The Philosophy of Living Experience*, 24.

41. Ibid.

42. Ibid., 216f.

43. Vucinich, *Social Thought in Tsarist Russia*, 216.

44. Ibid.

45. Ballestrem, "Lenin and Bogdanov," 291.

46. Ibid., 292.

47. Frederick C. Copleston, *Philosophy in Russia: From Herzen to Lenin and Berdyaev*, 286.

48. Ibid.

49. Karl Kautsky, "Ein Brief über Marx und Mach," 452; also found in Joravsky, *Soviet Marxism and Natural Science*, 16.

50. Lenin as quoted in Ballestrem, "Lenin and Bogdanov," 288.

51. See V.V. Zenkovsky, *A History of Russian Philosophy*, 742.

52. Copleston, *Philosophy in Russia*, 286.

53. James D. White, "Bogdanov in Tula," 51.

54. Jensen, *Beyond Marx and Mach*, 268–69.

55. Ibid., 269.

56. Bogdanov, *The Philosophy of Living Experience*, 160, 186; Vucinich, *Social Thought in Tsarist Russia*, 212.

57. Aleksandr A. Bogdanov, *Sotsializm nauki: Nauchnye zadachi proletariata*, 54–56, 62–63; also found in Sochor, *Revolution and Culture*, 30.

58. "Class interests," wrote M.I. Tugan-Baranovsky, "are not a criterion of goodness, of truth or of beauty. Human history is something infinitely higher than a mere struggle by social groups for the means of life" (*The Theoretical Basis of Marxism*, 82).

59. Bogdanov, *Empiriomonism*, 15.

60. Aleksandr A. Bogdanov, "Ideal poznaniya," 1–2.

61. Bogdanov, *The Philosophy of Living Experience*, 242.

62. Bogdanov, *Empiriomonism*, 15; idem, "Ideal poznaniya"; idem, *Tektology: The Universal Science of Organization*.

63. Vucinich, *Social Thought in Tsarist Russia*, 225; White, "Bogdanov in Tula," 50.

64. Vucinich, *Social Thought in Tsarist Russia*, 219.

65. Bogdanov, *Revolution and Philosophy*, 77; Kenneth E. Boulding, *The Organizational Revolution*; Erwin Laszlo, *The Systems View of the World: The Natural Philosophy of the New Developments in the Sciences*.

66. N.F. Fyodorov, *The Philosophy of the Common Task*.

67. Sochor, *Revolution and Culture*, 20. Bogdanov drew a picture of a society heavily influenced by his systems thinking. To Bogdanov a socialist economy meant progressive rationalization of the parts and organization of the whole and was not to be equated with political intervention or state control. Ultimately, and in keeping with his systems thinking, he envisaged socialism as a "self-regulating system" (ibid., 87). Indeed, for Bogdanov a genuine socialist society was both self-regulating and harmonious. Although the organizational function in a system would remain, it would be substantially altered once it was founded on a "general and all-embracing organization of labour." That is, the regulating mechanism would not be the "old authoritarian centralism" but "scientific centralism." Most of the functions would be performed by a "gigantic statistical bureau based on exact calculation for the purpose of distributing labour power and instruments of labour" (Aleksandr A. Bogdanov, *A Short Course of Economic Science*, 383).

68. Aleksandr A. Bogdanov, *Red Star: The First Bolshevik Utopia*, 242, 243. For instance, Bogdanov anticipated that industries might become so threatening to man that they would have to be far removed from human habitat; a population outstripping its food stocks and consequent famines; the exhaustion of natural resources; nuclear energy as the primary source of energy; the degradation of ecosystems; and the biomedical knowledge that confronts ethical issues (ibid., 233).

69. Ibid., 243.

70. Martinez-Alier, *Ecological Economics*, 214.

71. See Bogdanov, *Red Star*.

72. Kari Polanyi-Levitt, "The Origins and Significance of 'The Great Transformation'," 10.

73. Jürgen Habermas, "The Place of Philosophy in Marxism"; idem, *Toward a Rational Society*; Herbert Marcuse, *One Dimensional Man*; idem, *Reason and Revolution*.

74. Sochor, *Revolution and Culture*, 209.

75. Habermas, *Toward a Rational Society*, 88.

76. Ibid., 88–89.

77. Jensen, *Beyond Marx and Mach*, 375.

78. Bogdanov, *The Philosophy of Living Experience*, 9.

79. Aleksandr A. Bogdanov, *Essays in Tektology: The Universal Organizational Science*, 87, 221; idem, *Red Star*, 245; George Gorelik, "Principal Ideas of Bogdanov's 'Tektology': The Universal Science of Organization; idem, "Reemergence of Bogdanov's Tektology in Soviet Studies of Organization."

80. Bogdanov, *The Philosophy of Living Experience*, 82.

81. Ilmari Susiluoto, *The Origins and Development of Systems Thinking in the Soviet Union: Political and Philosophical Controversies from Bogdanov and Bukharin to Present-Day Re-Evaluations*.

82. Bogdanov, *Tektology*, 211–19, 325; also quoted in Sochor, *Revolution and Culture*, 47.

83. W.S. Ashby's contribution is discussed in greater detail in Chapter 4.

84. Bogdanov, *Tektology*, 254.

85. Stephen F. Cohen, "Marxist Theory and Bolshevik Policy: the Case of Bukharin's Historical Materialism," 51.

86. Nikolai I. Bukharin, *Historical Materialism: a System of Sociology*, iv.

87. Susiluoto, *Origins and Development of Systems Thinking*, 73, 51, 81.

88. Bukharin, *Historical Materialism*, 72.

89. Cohen, "Marxist Theory and Bolshevik Policy," 51.

90. Bukharin, *Historical Materialism*, 74, 78, 79, 239–41.

91. Cohen, "Marxist Theory and Bolshevik Policy," 54.

92. Bukharin, *Historical Materialism*, 80.

93. Cohen, "Marxist Theory and Bolshevik Policy," 59. The view that perturbations are disequilibrating and necessarily pathological is a narrow view, as we shall see in Chapter 4. For the dynamics of non-equilibrium or dissipative systems, according to Hagen and Prigogine et al., is a principal source of structural innovation leading not merely to the dissolution of systems, but also to their further complexification.

94. Bukharin, *Historical Materialism*, 80.

95. Susiluoto remarks that such an interpretation tended to make his system of thinking devoid of concrete applications. Bogdanov's system, by contrast, was genuinely open. It had points of application in medicine, biology, technology, planning, and economics. Bogdanov's Tektology led to a social activism which emphasized human creativity. Bukharin was a mechanist, who saw human activity as being subject to the iron laws of equilibrium in nature (*Origins and Development of Systems Thinking*, 100).

96. Bukharin, *Historical Materialism*.

97. Ibid., 86. One might speculate that in the collaborative literature of Tamanoi et al. their analysis of the water cycle provides the "contradiction" Bukharin sought. See Yoshiro Tamanoi, Atsushi Tsuchida, and T. Murota, "Towards an entropic theory of economy and ecology: Beyond the mechanistic equilibrium approach."

98. Bukharin, *Historical Materialism*, 116, 123.

99. Ibid., 76.

100. Ibid., 74.

101. Cohen, "Marxist Theory and Bolshevik Policy," 42.

102. See ibid. Unlike Bogdanov's Tektological perspective, Bukharin's analysis of growth, equilibrium, and the breakdown of systems was a fetishistic one-sided mechanical interpretation in which they were presented as a function of the quantity of energy.

Cohen comments that Soviet critics accused Bukharin of having a naive understanding of dialectics. Lenin charged that Bukharin "did not understand dialectics at all," while Stalin pointed out that Bukharin's "theory of equilibrium had nothing to do with Marxism." Nonetheless, during the period 1924–1929 Bukharin played a central role in Soviet politics and became the leading Party theorist. In 1926 he was one of Stalin's collaborators in the struggle against Trotsky, Zinoviev, and Kamenev. However, within two years he was proclaimed a leader of the "rightist deviation" and a "falsifier of Marxism" and in 1929 was ejected from the Politburo. In March of 1937, then an editor of *Izvestia*, he was accused of being a Trotskyite and expelled from the Party. Finally, in March of 1938, at the last public trial of the Great Purge, together with twenty other prominent old Bolsheviks, he was tried, found guilty of high treason, condemned to death, and executed.

103. Stammler in Susiluoto, *Origins and Development of Systems Thinking*.

104. N.I. Bukharin, *Economic Theory of Leisure Class*, 26.

105. Passet, *L'Économique et le Vivant*; Yoshiro Tamanoi, "Living System as the Basis for Human Economy"; Norbert Wiener, *Cybernetics: or Control and Communication in the Animal and Machine*.

106. Rafael E. Bello, "The Systems Approach—A. Bogdanov and L. von Bertalanffy"; Bukharin, *Historical Materialism*.

107. Bukharin, *Historical Materialism*, 76–77.

108. Ibid., 77.

109. Ibid.

110. Nikolai I. Bukharin, *Attack*, 150.

111. Bukharin, *Historical Materialism*, 107.

112. Ibid., 76.

113. Susiluoto, *Origins and Development of Systems Thinking*, 80, 97.

114. Bukharin, *Historical Materialism*, chapters 5–6; also in Cohen, "Marxist Theory and Bolshevik Policy."

115. For a brief review of these dilettantes refer to Kenneth M. Stokes, "Heretical Philosophers of Social Energetics."

116. Frederick Soddy, *Dishonest Money: or why a larger pay-packet now buys less than it did*, 20.

117. Herman E. Daly, ed., *Economics, Ecology, and Ethics: Essays Toward a Steady-State*, 471, 187.

118. Frederick Soddy, *The Role of Money: What It Should Be, Contrasted with What It Has Become*, 8.

119. John Ruskin, "Unto This Last."

120. Frederick Soddy, *Matter and Energy*, 13.

121. Frederick Soddy, *Cartesian Economics: The Bearing of Physical Science upon State Stewardship*, 14.

122. Soddy, *Dishonest Money*, 16.

123. Soddy, *Cartesian Economics*, 70.

124. Ibid., 29.

125. Ibid.

126. Frederick Soddy, *Wealth, Virtual Wealth and Debt: The Solution of the Economic Paradox*.

127. Soddy, *Cartesian Economics*, 30.

128. Ibid., 27.

129. Ibid.

130. Marx and Engels, *The Marx-Engels Reader*, 33.

131. A.D. Cruickshank, "Soddy at Oxford," 284.

132. Soddy, *Wealth, Virtual Wealth and Debt*, 295.

Chapter 3

1. Ruskin, "Unto This Last," 98.

2. G. Voropaev and A. Kosarev, "The Fall and Rise of the Caspian Sea."

3. Economic Commission for Europe, "Economic Bulletin for Europe"; Organization for Economic Cooperation and Development, *Long-range Transport of Air Pollutants*; J.J. Stukel and B.L. Neimann, *Ohio River Energy Basin Study (ORBES): Air Quality and Relation Impacts*, 89.

4. B. Bolin and M. McElroy, "Biogeochemical Cycles"; T. Webb and J. Kutzbach, "20,000 Years of Global Change"; B. Bolin and R. Cook, eds., *The Major Biogeochemical Cycles and Their Interaction*; R.E. Dickinson, "The Impact of Human Activities on Climate."

5. Karl Polanyi, "On Belief in Economic Determinism," 97.

6. J. von Neumann, "Can We Survive Technology?"; V.V. Alexandrov, *Climatic Response to Global Injections*.

7. The specific attributes of life seemed to Descartes "not at all strange to those who are acquainted with the variety of mechanisms performed by different automata or moving machines fabricated by human industry." This superficial resemblance closed his eyes to

the immense gulf between man-made machines, composed of separate mechanical parts, and organisms, in which no cell, tissue, or organ has any existence or continuity except as a dynamic member of a unified self-renewing whole, most of whose essential characteristics vanish as life ceases (Mumford, *The Myth of the Machine*, 85). If nothing more, the understanding of life, attested to by Descartes (*Discourse*), which meant its dissection, should alert us to the nature of mechanical analogy in economic science.

8. "The stability of the internal milieu," wrote Bernard, "is the condition of free and independent life." The concept later came to be known as "homeostasis." He observed that an organism's internal environment was balanced or self-correcting. (See Eugene Debs Robin, ed., *Claude Bernard and the Internal Environment: a Memorial Symposium*.)

9. Jan Kamarýt, "From Science to Metascience and Philosophy: Dialectical Perspectives in the Development of Ludwig von Bertalanffy's Theoretical Work," 84.

10. The German term introduced by Bertalanffy was *Fleissgleichgewicht*.

11. L. von Bertalanffy, *Perspectives on General System Theory: Scientific-Philosophical Studies*, 128.

12. Milton D. Rubin, "Society for General Systems Research," 107.

13. Ibid.

14. L. von Bertalanffy, *Problems of Life: An Evaluation of Modern Biological and Scientific Thought*, 127.

15. Ibid., 125.

16. Ibid.

17. Erwin Schrödinger, *What is Life? and Other Scientific Essays*, 74.

18. It has been asserted that Bertalanffy formulated the open systems concept to counter the vitalist's assertion that living systems are fundamentally different from non-living systems (Stuart Umpleby, "Applying Systems Theory to the Conduct of Systems Research").

19. J.E. Lovelock, *Gaia: a new look at life on earth*, 4.

20. Tamanoi, "Living System as the Basis for Human Economy," 4.

21. "Living systems represent steady states of an extremely complicated kind, consisting of an enormous number of reaction components. The character of the organism, as being an open system, is at the basis of the phenomena in the living" (Bertalanffy, *Problems of Life*, 128).

22. Bertalanffy, *Perspectives on General System Theory*, 120.

23. This concept, which Bertalanffy associated with his concept of "equifinality," will be again encountered in the cybernetic concept of "autopoiesis."

24. A profound difference between most inanimate, or closed, systems and living systems is expressed by the concept of "equifinality." In an inanimate system the final state of the system is determined by its initial conditions. We may, for instance, interpret this as saying that determinism no longer applies. A change in the initial conditions produces a change in the final conditions. A different kind of behavior is shown among vital phenomena: under many conditions the same final state may be reached from different initial conditions and in different ways. Though equifinality is not a proof of vitalism, it can be shown that equifinality is not to be found in closed systems, which is why it is not generally found in inanimate systems (Robert Lilenfeld, *The Rise of Systems Theory*, 18).

25. L. von Bertalanffy, "The Theory of Open Systems in Physics and Biology."

26. Norbert Wiener offers a cautionary note, saying that "if we wish to use the word 'life' to cover all phenomena which locally swim upstream against the current of increasing entropy, we are at liberty to do so. However, we shall then include many astronomical phenomena which have only the shadiest resemblance to life as we ordinarily know it. It is my opinion therefore, best to avoid all questions begging epithets such as 'life,' 'soul,'

'vitalism and the like,' and say merely in connection with machines that there is no reason why they may not resemble human beings in representing pockets of decreasing entropy in a framework in which the large entropy tends to increase" (*Cybernetics: or Control and Communication in the Animal and Machine*, 32).

27. Even Erwin Schrödinger speculated that "[the second law of thermodynamics] governs all physical and chemical processes, even if they result in the most intricate and tangled phenomena, such as organic life, the genesis of a complicated world of organisms from primitive beginnings [and] the rise and growth of human cultures" (*Science and the Human Temperament*, 39).

28. Indeed, according to the theory of autopoietic systems, living systems may be conceptualized as a response to environmental complexity.

29. Baron Lionel C. Robbins, *An Essay on the Nature & Significance of Economic Science.*

30. Ibid., 78–9.

31. Ibid., 24.

32. The term economic, as commonly used to describe the livelihood of man, is a compound of two meanings. Though it is somewhat of a semantic exercise, the clarification of the place of the economy in society must begin with drawing the distinction between these two meanings. It is this crucial distinction that enables one to introduce the Biospheric foundations and the technological and institutional dimensions of the livelihood of man.

The formal meaning springs from the logical character of the means–ends relationship, as expressed by the terms "economizing" or "economical." Aristotelian efficient cause coupled with scientific rationality, economism becomes the science of choice, and its typical concern is the deductive exploration of the logic of maximizing under the constraint of scarcity (ibid.). In this view, calculated choice, oriented toward maximization, becomes the central economic problem, and the economy consists of a series of choices imposed by scarcity situations and informed by relative prices. It is in this context that the scarcity definition of the late Lionel Robbins surely arises.

The second and substantive meaning reflects the physical and social realities of the livelihood of man; that man, like all other living things, has no permanence outside the physical environment, which we know as the Biosphere. Peter Kropotkin, for instance, defined economics as substantively "a science devoted to the study of the needs of men and of the means of satisfying them with the least possible waste of energy" (*Fields, Factories, and Workshops Tomorrow*, 43).

The substantive definition of economic has, according to Polanyi, nothing in common with the formal economizing definition. The substantive meaning stems from man's patent dependence upon both his social and physical environment. His survival is ensured by virtue of an institutional interaction between himself and his natural surroundings. That institutionalized interaction describes a process that means the satisfying of his material wants. In this connotation "economic" denotes nothing more or less than bearing reference to the process of satisfying material wants. Whether useful objects are required to avert starvation or needed for educational, military, or religious purposes is irrelevant. Insofar as the wants depend for their fulfillment on material artifacts, the reference is economic (Robbins, *An Essay on Nature*). This interpretation of the term "economic" is not without an established tradition. J. Lloyd Hubenka writes that Ruskin defined "economic" precisely as "House-Law"—a literal translation from the Greek (*Four Essays on the First Principles of Political Economy*). With this definition, Ruskin attempted to convey the idea of stewardship, the administration, management, and regulation of the "house" to the best possible advantage. This was not unlike the definition of the Physiocrat, who referred to "economic" in connection with the husbanding of resources (Maverick, *China*). With its origin in the means–end relationship, the formal meaning of economic has an entirely different origin, whose referents are universal rather than being restricted merely to the material requirements of man (see "The Two Meanings of Economic," in Polanyi, *The Livelihood of Man*, 31–32). It is this interpretation that connotes the technical term "economizing" or "maximizing."

33. Nicholas Georgescu-Roegen, *Energy and Economic Myths: Institutional and Analytical Economic Essays*.

34. For Ricardo and his contemporaries (from Malthus to Mill) nature represented the limits of economic development. With *Principles* Ricardo defined labor as an abstract quantity which generates abstract social value, and regarded nature as an infinitely available and infinitely self-regenerating phenomenon. From assuming a central analytical category in *Essay*, in *Principles* nature is less worthy of analysis. "The inexhaustibility of nature is a logical consequence of the assumption of the unlimited generation of commodities through labour" (Hans Immler, *Natur in der Ökonomischen Theorie*, 187), which constituted a clean philosophical break with Quesnay. This is only partially true of those Marxian economic theorists who swear by the doctrine that nature offers man a spontaneous gift (for instance, refer to Kozo Uno, *Principles of Political Economy: Theory of a Purely Capitalist Society*, 54). There are ambiguities in *Capital*. For even while Marx's scheme of expanded reproduction, the economic process, is represented as a closed circular and self-sustaining affair, as we have seen, one finds numerous references in *Capital*, as well as among Marx's and Engels's correspondence, to contrary views.

35. Nobuo Kawamiya, "Analysis of Technological Progress, Resource Substitution and the Environment in Their Mutual Interaction: an Entropy Theoretical Approach."

36. Frederick Soddy, "Transmutation, the vital problem of the future," 200.

37. Thaddeus J. Trenn, "The Central Role of Energy in Soddy's Holistic and Critical Approach to Nuclear Science, Economics and Social Responsibility," 264.

38. Robert A. Solow, "Is the End of the World at Hand?" *Challenge* (March–April 1973)

39. Levi-Strauss, Claude, "Anthropology, History and Ideology" *Critique of Anthropology*.

40. Charles M.A. Clark, "Equilibrium for What? Reflections on Social Order in Economics," 598.

41. See Chapter 1 on Physiocracy.

42. Jon D. Wisman, "Legitimation, Ideology-Critique, and Economics," 291.

43. Passet, *L'Économique et le Vivant*; Tamanoi et al. "Towards an entropic theory."

44. Vivien C. Walsh and Harvey Gram, *Classical and Neoclassical Theories of General Equilibrium: Historical Origins and Mathematical Structure*.

45. G. Vaggi, "Profits in Physiocratic Economics," 3.

46. Soddy, *Wealth, Virtual Wealth and Debt*; Paul Christensen, "The Materials-Energy Foundations of Classical Theory."

47. Soddy, *Cartesian Economics*, 26.

48. Quesnay is said to have modeled his *Tableau Économique* after Harvey's representation of the circulation of blood. As such it was a closed system. To depict the economy as an open system would have required Quesnay to have supplemented his model with one depicting metabolism—that of the digestive tract.

49. MacDonald, *Faraday, Maxwell, and Kelvin*; Silvanus Phillips Thompson, *The Life of Lord Kelvin*.

50. Kline, *Mathematics and the Search for Knowledge*.

51. Marshall, *Principles of Economics*, 63–64.

52. Ibid., 238.

53. Christensen, "Materials-Energy Foundations"; Nicholas Georgescu-Roegen, *The Entropy Law and the Economic Process*; Thomas T. Sekine, " 'Entropy Problem' and the Future of Our Society."

54. Georgescu-Roegen, *Energy and Economic Myths*.

55. Georgescu-Roegen, *The Entropy Law*, 43.

56. Among those immersed in theorizing about the socio-ecological-economic issues is Herman Daly, whose "On Economics as a Life Science" offers a number of points of interest. Daly's effort has been to explore the similarities between biology and economics in the context of the open living system. Drawing on the early steady-state analysis of J.S. Mill and the later analysis of Ludwig von Bertalanffy, he focuses on what in essence is an evolutionary problem, that is, the challenge of integrating the world of commodities into the larger economy of nature.

57. Nicholas Georgescu-Roegen, *Analytical Economics: Issues and Problems*, 98.

58. Boulding, Martinez-Alier, Odum, Tamanoi, and Zucchetto count among the notable others who have contributed to the broadening of economic thought.

59. Marshall, *Principles of Economics*, 771.

60. Ibid.

61. Kawamiya, "Analysis of Technological Progress," 4.

62. Georgescu-Roegen, *Energy and Economic Myths*; Passet, *L'Économique et le Vivant*; Yoshiro Tamanoi, "Towards an Exodus from Market Mentality: On Marx and Polanyi"; idem, "Living System as the Basis for Human Economy"; also see Boulding, *Evolutionary Economics*, 154.

63. The economist John A. Hobson, famous for his theories of underconsumption and imperialism, had an appreciation for the concept of open systems when he noted in 1929:

> all serviceable organic activities consume tissue and expend energy, the biological costs of the services they render. Though this economy may not correspond in close quantitative fashion to the pleasure and pain economy or to any conscious evaluation, it must be taken as the groundwork for that conscious valuation. For most economic purposes we are well advised to prefer the organic test to any other test of welfare, bearing in mind that many organic costs do not register themselves easily or adequately in terms of conscious pain or disutility, while organic gains are not always interpretable in conscious enjoyment (*Economics and Ethics*, in Daly 1968:240).

See Georgescu-Roegen, *Energy and Economic Myths*, 9.

64. Boulding, however, cautions us on agitating for a new paradigm which rests narrowly on the concept of entropy. He writes:

> In effect what the 'entropy school' is saying is that all we can ever hope to do is to postpone the evil day when everything will be gone and all potential exhausted. . . . [If] they are right, however, the postponing of an evil day is a highly productive and desirable occupation, and the more postponement the better. In the wonderful phrase of Malthus, 'evil is in the world to move us not to despair, but to activity.' . . . There is a time's arrow which points in the opposite direction to the entropy law, although it does not violate it, toward the segregation of entropy, which is in a sense a higher law than the entropy law itself. The entropy school, therefore, takes too long a view, although what it has to say is important and must be listened to. It may indeed stir us to the right kind of activity. (*Evolutionary Economics*, 165)

65. Tamanoi et al., "Towards an entropic theory," 2.

66. William S. Jevons, *Lectures on Political Economy*.

67. Robert L. Heilbroner, "The Paradox of Progress: Decline and Decay in the Wealth of Nations," 243.

68. Smith, *Wealth of Nations*, 81.

69. Ibid., 94.

70. Boulding, *Evolutionary Economics*, 166.

71. Smith, *Wealth of Nations*, 734–35.

72. "It is otherwise the barbarous societies, as they are commonly called, of hunters, of shepherds, and even of husbandmen in that rude state of husbandry that precedes the improvement of manufactures, and the extension of foreign commerce. In such societies, the varied occupations of every man oblige every man to exert his capacity, and to invent expedients for removing difficulties that are continually recurring. Invention is kept alive and the mind is not suffered to fall into that drowsy stupidity, which, in a civilized society seems to benumb the understanding of almost all the inferior ranks of people. In those barbarous societies, as they are called, every man, it has already been observed, is a warrior. Every man too is in some measure a statesman and can form a tolerable judgment concerning the interest of the society, and the conduct of those who govern it" (Ibid., 734–35).

73. Ibid., 79.

74. Ibid., 736.

75. Adam Smith, *Lectures on Justice, Police, Revenue and Arms*, 259.

76. John Stuart Mill, *Principles of Political Economy*, 72–84.

The issue at hand is not the correctness of Mill's analysis of capitalism, an analysis disputed by Marx, rather it is merely that there is a historical continuity of analysis that attaches to the concept of steady-state economics (Marx, *Capital*, 25, 125, 483, 572).

77. John Stuart Mill, "On Liberty."

78. "By a stationary state . . . we mean . . . a certain state of the object of analysis, namely, an economic process that goes on at even rates or, more precisely, an economic process that merely reproduces itself. . . . [It] is nothing but a methodological fiction. Essentially, it is a simplifying device. . . . The term evolution may be used in a wider and in a narrower sense. In the wider sense it comprises all the phenomena that make an economic process non-stationary. In the narrower sense it comprises these phenomena minus those that may be described in terms of continuous variations of rates within an unchanging framework of institutions, tastes, or technological horizons, and will be included in the concept of growth" (Schumpeter, *Economic Doctrine and Method*, 964).

79. "Demand," wrote David Ricardo, "has no other limit but for the want of power of paying for the commodities demanded" (Piero Sraffa, ed., *The Works and Correspondence of David Ricardo*, 6:108).

80. Jevons, *Coal Question*, x, xxxi, 456.

81. Sraffa, *Works of David Ricardo*.

82. In this connection refer to the section on totality theory and systems theory in Chapter 1.

83. Marx, *Grundrisse*, 87.

84. Christensen, "Materials-Energy Foundations," 79.

85. Marx, *Capital*, Chap. 15:382.

86. Uno, *Principles of Political Economy*, 54.

87. Marx, *Grundrisse*, 705.

88. Fromm, *Marx's Concept of Man*, 19. See also Karl Marx's reference to socialism whereby "society is the unity of being of man and nature—the true resurrection of nature—the naturalism of man and the humanism of nature both brought forth to fulfillment" (*Manuscripts of 1844*, 137).

89. Marx, *Capital*, Chap. 7:184.

90. In this connection refer to the section on totality theory and systems theory in Chapter 1.

91. Arthur Cecil Pigou, *The Economics of Welfare*.

92. Soddy, *Wealth, Virtual Wealth and Debt*; idem, *The Role of Money*.

93. See Frederick Soddy, *Money Versus Man: a Statement of the World Problem from the Standpoint of the New Economics*; idem, *Wealth, Virtual Wealth and Debt*; idem, *The Role of Money*.

94. Indeed, Vilfredo Pareto overtly claimed that once we have determined the means at the disposal of the individual and obtained "a photograph of his tastes . . . the individual may disappear" (*Manual of Political Economy*, 120). See Kenneth M. Stokes, "The Problematique of Economic Externalities." *York Studies in Political Economy* vol. 7, (Winter 1988):102–14.

95. See "Introduction to the Steady-State Economy," in Daly, *Economics, Ecology, and Ethics*, 10.

96. Echoing the words of Soddy, M.K. Hubbert wrote: "One speaks of the rate of growth of GNP. I haven't the faintest idea what this means when I try to translate it into coal, oil, iron and other physical quantities which are required to run an industry . . . the quantity GNP is a monetary bookkeeping entity. It obeys the laws of money. It can be expanded or diminished, created or destroyed, but it does not obey the laws of physics" ("Man's Conquest of Energy: Its Ecological and Human Implications," 291).

97. Irving Fisher does not conflate income and capital. He proposed not adding up both the value of the item that renders a service and the value of the service itself. Arthur Cecil Pigou wrote: "Professor Fisher takes the position that the national dividend, or income, consists of services as received by ultimate consumers whether from their material or from the human environment. Thus a piano or an overcoat made for me this year is not a part of this year's income, but an addition to capital. Only the services rendered to me during this year by these things are income" (*The Economics of Welfare*, 35).

In his concept of capital, I. Fisher included the material and human environment. Human beings render services to other human beings, but we count only those services; we do not add in the capital value of the human being in the year he was born or was graduated. For the material environment, Fisher had in mind mainly artifacts, not the natural material environment (*The Nature of Capital and Income*).

98. Herman E. Daly, "Myths about Energy and Matter: Comment."

99. B.B. Bernstein, "Ecology and Economics: Complex Systems in Changing Environments."

100. S. Menshikov, "Dialogue Between Soviet and American Economists," 76.

101. Harold Barnett and Chandler Morse, *Scarcity and Growth: Resources for the Future*, 11.

102. Ibid.

103. "Environmental economics," writes Richard B. Norgaard, "is a contradiction in terms. . . . It is explicit to those who think of environmental systems in terms of complex, evolving interconnectedness and identify the economic model with the atomistic and mechanistic assumptions of classical mechanics" ("Environmental Economics: An Evolutionary Critique and a Plea for Pluralism," 382).

104. Solow, "Is the End of the World at Hand?"

105. Soddy, *Cartesian Economics*, 9.

106. Bernstein, "Ecology and Economics," 313.

107. Marshall, in his *Principles of Economics*, argued that economics is "a branch of biology broadly interpreted" (p. 50); and that "economics is a science of life that adjoins biology other than mechanics." Though he felt that it was, indeed, biology rather than Newtonian mechanics that should be the model of economic science, and claimed that

"The Mecca of the economist lies in economic biology," he was, however, reticent and noted that: "biological conceptions are more complex than those of mechanics; a volume on Foundations must therefore give a relatively large place to mechanical analogies" (ibid., xiv). Referring to the "marginalist revolution," he wrote:

> The new analysis is endeavoring gradually and tentatively to bring into economics, as far as the widely different nature of the material will allow, those methods of the science of small increments (commonly called the differential calculus) to which man owes directly or indirectly the greater part of the control that he has obtained in recent times over physical nature. It is still in its infancy; it has no dogmas, and no standard of orthodoxy . . . there is a remarkable harmony and agreement on essentials among those who are working constructively by the new method [marginalism]; and especially among such of them as have served an apprenticeship in the simple and more definite, and therefore more advanced, problem of physics. (ibid., xvi–xvii)

108. Passet, *L'Économique et le Vivant*, 166.

109. The concept of life-process, which is present in Marx's writings from the *German Ideology* onward, embodies the notion of external nature as the inorganic body of man. As it appears in the Paris *Manuscripts*, the description of the labor-process is that of the metabolism between man and nature. "The labour-process . . . is human action with a view to production of use-values, appropriation of natural substances to human requirements; it is the general condition for the metabolism between man and nature; it is the everlasting nature-imposed condition of human existence and therefore is independent of every social form of that existence or, rather, is common to every such form" (Marx, *Capital*, I:183–84).

110. Bukharin, *Historical Materialism*.

111. Passet, *L'Économique et le Vivant*.

112. Bukharin, *Historical Materialism*, 108.

113. Ibid., 110.

114. Herman E. Daly, *Steady State Economics*, 158.

115. Kenneth E. Boulding, *Beyond Economics*. Bertalanffy has written that

> it is . . . the throughput of energy in the earth that has made evolution possible. Any closed system very soon exhausts the potential within it and reaches an equilibrium. . . . This, of course, is the famous second law of thermodynamics. The earth, however, is an open system from the point of view of energy. All living systems, including man himself, are open systems. . . . All human societies have likewise been open systems. They receive inputs from the earth, the atmosphere, and the waters, and they give outputs into these reservoirs. ("Theory of Open Systems," 48, 24)

116. Boulding, *Beyond Economics*, 48.

117. Ibid., 277.

118. It becomes apparent that Boulding's definition of the term "economic" is inconsistent with the widely accepted economizing meaning. Indeed, contrary to Robbins, Boulding accords priority to a substantive concept of: "Economics [is that which] deals with that portion of human activity of commodities" (*Evolutionary Economics*, 16).

In so defining economic, Boulding distances himself from the neoclassical foundations, which he sought to buttress his ecological analogy. By so doing he advances his connection to the classical analysts.

119. Ibid.

120. Alfred J. Lotka, "Contribution to the Energetics of Evolution," 148.

121. Passet, *L'Économique et le Vivant*, 15–16.

122. While the inertia of the technological imperative is, of course, not the only force molding societal development in industrial countries, it is, nonetheless, inveterate and has attained a quasi-autonomous quality.

Lacking a justification in basic values, the ultimate nature of the ends we pursue have become obscured, and the metaphor of "technological imperative," an autojustified force that keeps the wheels of development turning, imposes itself upon us—displacing not only Bacon's "religious imperative" and Quesnay's ethic, but the last vestiges of Marshall's moral imperative. The essence of this dilemma of modern technified culture is crystallized in the distinction that "life as an end is qualitatively different from life as a means" (Marcuse, *One Dimensional Man*, 17). Refer to Chapter 4 herein where autopoiesis and allopoiesis provide a further analytical distinction.

123. Richard B. Norgaard, "Coevolutionary Agricultural Development," 529.

124. Howard T. Odum, *Systems Ecology: an Introduction*; Henri Laborit, *La Nouvelle Grille*.

125. D.J. Rapport and J.E. Turner, "Economic Models and Ecology," 368.

126. Boulding, *Evolutionary Economics*; Daly, *Steady State Economics*.

127. L. von Bertalanffy, *General Systems Theory: Foundations, Development, Applications*; K.E. Boulding, *Ecodynamics: A New Theory of Societal Evolution*.

128. However, while the quasi-trophic qualities apparent in input-output (I/O) analysis is an advance, I/O models are fundamentally static. In short, they do not admit evolution. The principal difficulty in analyzing the quasi-trophic qualities of production processes has been the absence of rigorous methods that include the evolutionary phenomenon of structural change. This problematique, while addressed by Boulding, has received a fuller examination in the work of Paul Medow, who has applied discrete event simulation techniques to the analysis of structural change in the international division of labor and corresponding material and energy flows (Medow, "Protecting the Biosphere").

129. Tamanoi et al., "Towards an entropic theory."

130. See Tamanoi, as found in Makoto Maruyama, "Economy and Living Systems," 1.

131. Yoshiro Tamanoi, "Review of *The Livelihood of Man* by Karl Polanyi," 821.

132. Tamanoi in Maruyama, "Economy and Living Systems," 1.

133. Ballestrem, "Lenin and Bogdanov."

134. John K. Galbraith, "Dialogues on Civilization between Boulding and Galbraith."

135. Boulding, *Ecodynamics*, 86.

136. Boulding remarks that "in the cowboy [i.e., growing] economy, consumption is regarded as a good thing and production likewise; and the success of the economy is measured by the amount of the throughput from the factors of production, a part of which, at any rate, is extracted from the reservoirs of raw materials and noneconomic objects, and another part of which is output into the reservoirs of pollution.... The gross national product is a rough measure of this total throughput" ("The Economics of the Coming Spaceship Earth," 281).

Indeed, Boulding has, for a number of years, petitioned that the concept of Gross National Product (GNP) is largely Gross National Cost (GNC). The economic historian Richard Wilkinson contends that not only is development historically and "primarily the result of attempts to increase the output from the environment rather than produce a given output more efficiently," but that "restraint on the growth of population and production seem to be an ecological necessity." And following Boulding he remarks that "the continuous expansion of gross national product ... should perhaps be regarded more as a reflection of the rising real cost of living rather than an indication of increasing welfare" (*Poverty and Progress: An Ecological Perspective on Economic Development*). "A policy of maximizing GNP," according to Herman Daly, "is practically equivalent to a policy of maximizing depletion and pollution" (*Steady State Economics*, 115–16).

137. Tamanoi in Maruyama, "Economy and Living Systems," 3.

138. Ibid.

139. Tamanoi et al., "Towards an entropic theory," 1.

140. Schumpeter, *History of Economic Analysis*, 1010.

141. Solow, "Is the End of the World at Hand?" 50.

142. Tamanoi et al., "Towards an entropic theory," 3.

143. E. Schrödinger, in his renowned description of living processes, noted :"That we give off heat is not accidental, but essential. For this is precisely the manner in which we dispose of the surplus entropy we continuously produce in our physical life process" (*What is Life from the Point of Physics*).

144. Passet, *L'Économique et le Vivant*, 141.

145. Takeshi Murota, "Environmental Economics of the Water Planet Earth," 2.

146. Tamanoi et al., "Towards an entropic theory," 14.

147. Tamanoi in Maruyama, "Economy and Living Systems," 3.

148. Soddy, *Cartesian Economics*; Tamanoi in Maruyama, "Economy and Living Systems," 3.

149. Tsuchida and Murota, "Fundamentals in the Entropic Theory," 1.

150. In this connection one might refer to the Gaia hypothesis of J.E. Lovelock (*Gaia*, 107). It has been noted that Lovelock's Gaia proposition is to some extent a reconstruction of the earlier work of V.I. Vernadsky.

In 1929 Vernadsky, author of the science of hydrogeochemistry, or the geochemistry of water, also made a study of the dynamic properties of water and referred to its role in the dissipation of energy. He wrote: "Of significant importance in the energetics of the Earth's crust is the transport by water of thermal energy from deep strata of the Earth's crust to the stratosphere and the Biosphere. . . . The thermal regime of the Earth's crust cannot be studied without proper regard for the colossal contribution of ground water because of the exceptional properties—high specific heat and mobility. This contribution is the transport of enormous quantities of heat and matter both vertically and horizontally" (Balandin, *Vladimir Vernadsky*, 174).

Reaffirming the critical role of water in the Biosphere, he wrote: "In the history of our planet . . . water enjoys a special, outstanding position. Though in the total composition of the planet water accounts for a fractional percent of the planet's mass, in the upper geospheres and particularly the Biosphere it predominates in terms of weight and predetermines their entire chemistry" (ibid., 172).

151. Kawamiya, "Analysis of Technological Progress," 4.

152. Tamanoi, "Living System as the Basis for Human Economy."

153. T.R. Lakshmanan and S. Ratick, "Integrated Models for Economic-Energy-Environmental Impact Analysis," 9.

154. Werner Stumm, ed., *Global Chemical Cycles and Their Alterations by Man*; Daly, *Steady State Economics*; Commoner, *Poverty of Power*; Odum, *Systems Ecology*.

155. Herman E. Koenig, W.E. Cooper, and J.M. Falvey, "Engineering for Ecological, Sociological and Economic Compatibility," 319.

156. Fred Cottrell, *Energy and Society: the Relation between Energy, Social Change and Economic Development*.

157. On Lotka's hypothesis that natural selection favors those who maximize the energy flux through their systems, Fred Cottrell stated: "The evidence for Lotka's position is not yet sufficient to make it clear that it should be formulated into a law" (*Technology,*

Man and Progress, 24). Also see: Leslie A. White, *The Evolution of Culture: The Development of Civilization to the Fall of Rome*.

158. Wilhelm Ostwald, "Efficiency," 870.

159. Schrödinger, *Science and the Human Temperament*, 39.

160. White, *The Evolution of Culture*, 39, 41.

161. Ibid., 21, 57.

162. Cottrell writes: "Polanyi's description of the way in which traders divested themselves of responsibility for the fate of those demoralized by the energy revolution they were carrying on provides thought-provoking evidence of the nature of economic liberalism. . . . Polanyi's evidence as to what was happening may well be used to supplement the simplified version of English history here presented. Polanyi does not deal at all extensively with the energy aspects of the shifts in power which he discusses" (*Energy and Society*, 174).

163. Ibid., 116, 115.

164. One might recall that Marx approached such an analysis. In this connection, and referring to Grove, Marx remarked on the chemical balances of the body within the context of the "normal working day."

165. Bertalanffy, *Problems of Life*; Koenig et al., "Engineering for Compatibility," 323.

166. H.E. Koenig, "Human Ecosystem Design and Management," 231.

167. Refer to the introductory remarks of Chapter 3.

168. Koenig et al., "Engineering for Compatibility," 326.

169. Ibid., 319.

170. Koenig, "Human Ecosystem Design," 224.

171. Joseph A. Schumpeter, *Business Cycles*.

172. Koenig, "Human Ecosystem Design," 228.

173. Koenig et al., "Engineering for Compatibility," 329.

174. Ibid., 326.

175. Koenig, "Human Ecosystem Design," 234; N.N. Moiseev, *Man, Nature and the Future of Civilization*.

176. Koenig, "Human Ecosystem Design," 234.

177. Ibid.

178. Koenig et al., "Engineering for Compatibility," 331.

179. Peter Nijkamp, *Theory and Application of Environmental Economics*, 2.

180. In consequence, there exists a continuous interaction between the economic process and the material environment (ibid., 10). For instance, Robert Ayres used a materials balance model to describe the inconsistency of the closed cyclic model of standard economics with the first law of thermodynamics (Cleveland, "Biophysical Economics," 61). (Also see Robert Ayers, *Resources, Environment and Economics: Applications of the Materials/Energy Balance Principle*).

181. Nijkamp, *Theory and Application*, 12.

182. Tamanoi, "Living System as the Basis for Human Economy." Nijkamp writes: "The materials balance model shows that each production or consumption activity constitutes a chain in the spatial dispersion of material products and, hence, of waste residuals" (*Theory and Application*, 12).

183. Ibid., 15.

184. Ibid., 16.

185. Ibid., 154.

186. Ibid., 326.

187. Ibid., 726–27.

188. On the one hand, variety appears to be correlated to energy throughput. On the other hand, the development of a high degree of diversity can favor the collection of

energy and the stability of a whole ecosystem (P. Corsson, "Patterns in agricultural development"; Laborit, *La Nouvelle Grille*). Development of diversity also provides flexibility in case there are changes in the relative availability of energy resources. It is in this sense that diversity stabilizes and increases the resilience of an ecosystem, insofar as there is introduced greater potential or genetic variability with different populations (C.S. Holling, "Resilience and Stability in Ecosystems"; idem, ed., *The Anatomy of Surprise*). One of the basic conditions for stability of ecosystems is their polymorphism (François Jacob, *La Logique du Vivant*; Laborit, *La Nouvelle Grille*).

Boulding, in *Evolutionary Economics*, writes that "an interesting but rather unsettled question in evolutionary theory, both biological and societal, is that of the optimum degree of variety in an ecosystem. Variety is a kind of insurance against the extinction of the evolutionary process itself . . . ecosystems are remarkably tough; they can survive all sorts of catastrophes and still continue the evolutionary process, simply because of the enormous variety involved in them" (Boulding, *Evolutionary Economics*, 108).

189. Ibid., 107.

190. Boulding, *Evolutionary Economics*, 106; see also Smith, *Wealth of Nations*.

191. Boulding, *Evolutionary Economics*, 87.

192. Ibid., 19.

193. K.E. Boulding, "Economics and Ecology"; idem, *Ecodynamics*.

194. Boulding, *Ecodynamics*, 170.

195. Georgescu-Roegen, *The Entropy Law*; Odum, *Systems Ecology*; James Zucchetto "Energy and the Future of Human Settlement Patterns: Theory, Models and Empirical Considerations."

196. Alfred J. Lotka, "Biased Evolution."

197. Lotka, "Contribution to Energetics," 148.

198. As A. Lotka and V.I. Vernadsky noted, the per unit power capacity of life generally must increase in the course of evolution. Organisms, for instance, have acquired the ability for absorbing a new portion of photons or for better utilizing the stored chemical energy in other organisms. They thereby gain an evolutionary advantage, and, in the course of evolution, gradually become involved in the biotic circulation, rationalizing it and increasing the summary flow of energy passing through the living system. (Lotka, "Contribution to Energetics"; Vernadsky, "Problems of Biogeochemistry").

199. Odum, *Systems Ecology*, 141.

200. Bertrand Russell, *Philosophy*, 27.

201. Howard T. Odum, "Energy, Ecology and Economics."

202. Howard T. Odum and Elisabeth C. Odum, *Energy Basis for Man and Nature*, 11.

203. Howard T. Odum, "Energy, Value & Money."

204. Odum and Odum, *Energy Basis for Man and Nature*, 115.

205. Ibid., 39. However, Lotka's formulation of a general design principle is but one of a number that have been offered: for instance, the maximization of biomass; reproduction rates, the minimum rate of entropy generation also known as the principle of minimum dissipation; minimum heat; maximum structural entropy, maximum profit, maximum efficiency, and so on. Odum, however, makes the claim that these are but special cases of the maximum power principle. He does not, unfortunately, elaborate. (See also Ramon Margalef, *Perspectives in Ecological Theory*.)

This dynamic feature of production systems is consistent with the Post-Keynesian emphasis on distribution and accumulation, but it is entirely missed by the efficiency emphasis of neoclassical theory. (See also Christensen, "Materials-Energy Foundations," 86; and Howard T. Odum, *Environment, Power, and Society*.)

206. Odum and Odum, *Energy Basis for Man and Nature*, 44.

207. Ibid.

208. Murray Bookchin, *Toward an Ecological Society*, 88.

209. Odum, *Systems Ecology*.

210. Odum, "Energy, Value & Money."

211. Odum, *Systems Ecology*; also see Malcolm Slesser, *Energy in the Economy*. Odum's proposition is not entirely unique, as Passet argues that

> All material goods may be expressed in terms of the quantity of energy that it contains; All forces engaged in work are an energy potential that may deliver energy and may be reconstituted by a delivery of energy; All productive capital, created by men, is a result of a work that may be expressed in energy units and its functioning is attributable to a delivery of energy and produces mechanical work that may be measured in energy units (*L'Économique et le Vivant*, 135).

212. R. Rappoport, *Pigs for the Ancestors*, postscript.

213. Robert L. Heilbroner, "The Problem of Value in the Constitution of Economic Thought," 273.

214. Bertalanffy, *Perspectives on General System Theory*.

215. Odum, *Systems Ecology*.

216. The notion of abstract labor, indispensable to Marx's theory, escapes Odum's analysis.

217. Parsons, *Marx and Engels on Ecology*.

218. Engels, *Dialectics of Nature*, 310.

219. Soddy, *Cartesian Economics*, 13.

220. Robert Costanza, "Embodied Energy and Economic Valuation."

221. Malcolm Slesser, "Accounting for Energy," 170.

222. Martha W. Gilliland, "Energy Analysis and Public Policy"; David A. Huettner, "Net Energy Analysis: An Economic Assessment."

223. Odum, "Energy, Value & Money," 252.

224. Ibid., 174.

225. The German Baron Justus von Liebig, an organic and agricultural chemist, formulated the "law of the minimum" which states that complex processes are constrained by scarce reactants, which become less important as their relative quantities increase (*The Natural Laws of Husbandry*).

226. Odum, *Systems Ecology*, 484.

227. Ibid.

228. Robert Costanza, "Embodied Energy, Energy Analysis, and Economics"; Cottrell, *Energy and Society*; Soddy, *Cartesian Economics*.

229. Costanza, "Embodied Energy and Economic Valuation," 1220.

230. Ibid., 1219.

231. Ibid., 1223.

232. Ibid., 1224.

233. Ibid.

234. Costanza, "Embodied Energy, Energy Analysis," 140.

235. Bernstein, "Ecology and Economics," 311.

236. Georgescu-Roegen, *Energy and Economic Myths*; Schrödinger, *What is Life?*

237. Passet, *L'Économique et le Vivant*, 166.

238. Odum, *Systems Ecology*.

239. Martinez-Alier and Nardeo, "Marxist Precursor," 219. Following Karl Polanyi

the Greek term chrematistike has been employed to refer to money-making aspects rather than providing merely for one's livelihood.

240. Nijkamp, *Theory and Application*, 4–6.

241. Ibid., 6.

242. Soddy, *Matter and Energy*; Wilhelm Ostwald, "The Modern Theory of Energetics."

243. N.N. Moiseev, "The Unity of Natural Scientific Knowledge."

244. Ibid.

245. Aleksandr A. Bogdanov, *Basic Elements of the Historical View of Nature*.

246. Odum, "Energy, Ecology and Economics," 222.

247. Bertalanffy, *Perspectives on General System Theory*, 128.

248. Odum, *Systems Ecology*, 216.

249. Odum and Odum, *Energy Basis for Man and Nature*, 1976.

250. Odum, *Systems Ecology*, 217.

251. Odum, "Energy, Ecology and Economics," 221.

252. Odum, *Systems Ecology*.

253. Soddy's position, though formulated in terms of open systems and energy throughput, is not unfamiliar to economists. For instance, following John Locke, J.S. Mill maintained that wealth or private property was legitimated as a bastion against exploitation, but only when a minimum amount was held ("Of Property"). "Private property, in every defense made of it, is supposed to mean the guarantee to individuals of the fruits of their own labour and abstinence. The guarantee to them of the fruits of the labour and abstinence of others, transmitted to them without any merit or exertion of their own, is not the essence of the institution, but a mere incidental consequence, which, when it reaches a certain height, does not promote, but conflicts with, the ends which render private property legitimate" (Mill in Daly, *Steady State Economics*, 54).

254. Commoner, *The Closing Circle*, 274.

255. Daly, *Steady State Economics*.

256. Of course, the supposition that "personal freedom" is enabling in the context of market economies carries with it certain doctrinaire perceptions shaped by the market myth that pertain to the concept of "freedom" itself. I wish to distance myself from such a narrow understanding; hence, the qualification "insofar." For a brief commentary on related issues refer to the section Freedom in Technified Society in Chapter 4.

257. See Adam Schaff's address to the International Conference on "Science and Technology at the Service of Development: The Role of Government and Social Institutions"; André Gorz, *Critique of Economic Reason*.

258. Herman E. Daly, 1980:11.

259. Georgescu-Roegen, *The Entropy Law*, 23.

260. Boulding, *Beyond Economics*, 281–82.

Chapter 4

1. E.J. Dijksterhuis, *The Mechanization of the World Picture*; Stephen H. Ford, *Imagination and Thought in Descartes*.

2. Let us be clear in that by a natural order we do not suggest a retreat to a free-will-denying Natural Philosophy.

3. Jean Piaget, *Biology and Knowledge: an Essay on the Relations Between Organic Regulations and Cognitive Processes*.

4. N.U. Lossky, *History of Russian Philosophy*, 379.

5. Bertalanffy, *Problems of Life*, 139.

6. Conrad H. Waddington, *The Nature of Life*.

7. Sir Geoffrey Vickers, "The Poverty of Problem Solving."

8. Stafford Beer, "Below the Twilight Art—a Mythology of Systems," 2.

9. Jean Voge, "Information and Information Technologies in Growth and Economic Crisis."

10. Ibid.; and regarding analogous biological dimensions of the underlying concept, refer to Jacques Ruffie, *Éléments de génétique générale et humaine*. We might speculate that the organizational restructuring of corporations from the so-called "U-form" to the "M-form" is indicative of that to which Voge refers (see Oliver W. Williamson, "The Modern Corporations: Origins, Evolution and Attributes"). Applying recent advances in information and telecommunication technology, a number of analysts have pointed to the development of "flattened" organizations (see Gareth Morgan, *Riding the Waves of Change*).

11. William R. Ashby, *An Introduction to Cybernetics*.

12. This principle has been discussed in Chapter 2.

13. Bogdanov, *Philosophy of Living Experience*, 382.

14. Moiseev, "The Unity of Natural Scientific Knowledge."

15. Ibid., 43.

16. Ashby, *Introduction to Cybernetics*.

17. Ibid.

18. Klaus, for instance, defined society, in terms of biological organism, as a "dynamic self-regulating system" which is "ultrastable." The concept of ultrastability implies that systems of this type can maintain their stability against multiple types of interference (Peter C. Ludz, "Marxism and Systems Theory in a Bureaucratic Society," 665).

19. Expressing similar ideas, within the context of his general theory of equilibrium, Bukharin also gave expression to a principle of persistent non-equilibrium.

20. See the section on Living Systems, Autopoietic, and Allopoietic Systems, in this chapter.

21. Holling, "Resilience and Stability in Ecosystems"; Daniel P. Loucks, "Evolution of Diversity, Efficiency and Community Stability."

22. See Jonas Salk, *Anatomy of Reality: Merging of Intuition and Reason*, 27.

23. Erwin Laszlo, *Evolution: The Grand Synthesis*, 24.

24. Expressing a view consistent with Bogdanov's Tektological dialectic, Laszlo infers that the principle of persistent non-equilibrium can be extended to higher levels of organization. Moreover, the problematique of systemic stability pertains not only to naturally occurring ecosystems but to social systems as well. (See Gregory Bateson, *Mind and Nature: a Necessary Unity*; Morton Kaplan, *System and Process in International Politics*; R.C. Lewontin, "The Meaning of Stability: Diversity and Stability of Ecological Systems.")

25. Herbert A. Simon's concept of rationality may be defined as "administrative." This is merely an organizational-specific representation of *Zweckrationalität* ("On the concept of organizational goals").

26. Simon's critique of Pareto optimality rests on what we might call the complexity argument. In the real world problems of economic decision making are frequently extremely complicated. The agent's difficulty in processing masses of information and computing an optimal solution will inevitably prevent him from taking the Pareto optimal strategy.

27. While organizational dissonance, i.e., intersystemic simultanity, is difficult to formalize at the societal level, less complex cases of this type of interdependence can be successfully analyzed through the use of computer-oriented simulation models.

That there is an urgency for modeling as a method of reducing the apparent complexity of reality to manageable levels is axiomatic. The fundamental theme, however, remains the lack of concreteness—the degree to which the process of abstraction from reality can be meaningfully nurtured without destroying the underlying validity of a particular model as an isomorphic representation of reality. A singular difficulty is that it is frequently impossible to increase the scope of inclusiveness of a particular model and still remain within the logic of the conceptual and methodological constructs being used to define the model.

In this connection, it is necessary to recognize that every methodology is an algorithmic structure which a priori imposes its own modalities on the type and quality of detail than can be intelligibly examined within its conceptualizations. The transition from paper and pencil solutions based on mathematical optimization methods, which has dominated science, to the multidimensional computer-resolved causal networks, while drastically increasing the permissible level of inclusiveness, does not eliminate the inherent limitations of algorithmic methodologies.

At present, however, we are in the midst of a number of developments that are reducing the scope of these limitations. One of the principal developments in the partial resolution of the limitativeness of analytical methodologies lies in the capability of increasing the concreteness of the structure of interacting hierarchies through discrete-event computer simulation techniques.

28. See Alfred Russel Wallace, "On the Tendency of Varieties to Depart Indefinitely from the Original Type."

29. Magoroh Maruyama has shown that these are processes of mutual causation characterized respectively by deviation-amplifying and deviation-counteracting interactions, i.e., positive and negative feedback relations ("The Second Cybernetics: Deviation amplifying mutual causal processes," 168; also see p. 173).

30. Norbert Wiener, *The Human Use of Human Beings.*

31. William R. Ashby, "Principles of Self-Organization"; G. Nicolis and I. Prigogine, *Self-Organization in Non-Equilibrium Systems: From Dissipative Structures to Order through Fluctuations.*

32. N.N. Moiseev notes that "by extending the framework of the Theory of Games to cover non-antagonistic games a language is provided for describing hierarchical control systems in economies. Its application in terms of the framework of the theory of optimal control to a simple two-level case with incomplete information indicates that it is possible not only to construct a mathematical theory of hierarchical systems but also to evaluate the control qualities of given hierarchical structures quantitatively. Because of the dimensions of the associated numerical problems, however, and also of the nonformal character of knowledge concerning objectives functions at individual levels, successful practical applications of such a theory will depend on the availability of appropriate man-machine simulation systems" ("The Theory of Games and Hierarchical Systems in Economies," i).

33. Niklas Luhmann, *The Differentiation of Society*, 249.

34. Laurent Dobuzinskis, "Autopoiesis in Nature and Politics: Some Reflections on the Epistemology of the New Cybernetics," 5.

35. Jan Koolhaas, *Organization, Dissonance and Change*, 76.

36. Ibid.; Simon, "On the concept."

37. Stafford Beer, *Brain of the Firm*; idem, *Platform for Change*, 313.

38. Throughout the balance of this book the term "Ashbian" or "Ashbian perspective" and the like shall be understood to symbolize Ross Ashby's principle of requisite variety.

39. Dobuzinskis, "Autopoiesis in Nature and Politics," 6.

40. Ibid., 8.

41. Ashby, "Principles of Self-Organization," 276.

42. The theory of equilibrium views the system as originating out of the unification of parts. A significant difference, however, resides in the functioning of the parts. Now the parts of a system are interpreted as a set of conditions that function or operate when something outside the system—in its environment—threatens. For Walter Cannon, to

whom this innovation may be traced, the "parts" are the coordinated physiological processes which maintain most of the steady states in the organism. He refers to the steady states, in general, as homeostasis and the constant conditions (physiological processes, "parts" of the organic system) as equilibria. Indeed, it is precisely the external disturbances—under this interpretation—that causes them to operate in order to preserve the organism. To assure the same degree of stability in the social organism that has been attained in the animal organism, the latter suggests such control of the fluid matrix that its constancy would be maintained. That would involve, in the first instance, the certainty of continuous delivery by the moving stream of the necessities of existence. But this is still a closed-system approach. Common to both Cannon's and Aristotle's interpretations is the belief that the whole can only exist through the conservation of its parts. Only at the next stage in the development of systems theory did the concept of an open system arise (Walter B. Cannon, *The Wisdom of the Body*).

43. Salk, *Anatomy of Reality*, 27.

44. The term "episteme" derives from the Greek for world view, theory, concept, or hypothesis. To call an episteme an epistemology, i.e., a theory about epistemes, as is often done, is an incorrect fusion of logical types. See Koolhaas, *Organization*, 41.

45. Ibid., 43.

46. Gottlieb Gutern, "Auto-organization in Human Systems," 328; Niklas Luhmann, "Insistence on Systems Theory: Perspectives from Germany," 993.

47. Holling, "Resilience and Stability in Ecosystems."

48. N.N. Moiseev, "Studying the Dynamics of the Noosphere."

49. Kurt Gödel, *On the Formally Undecidable Propositions in Principia Mathematica and Related Systems I.*

50. S. Beer, *Platform for Change*, 319.

51. Kamarýt, "From Science to Metascience and Philosophy," 84. Kamart notes that this, as was proved by the Vienna Circle mathematician Kurt Gödel in his now famous theorem, applies to axiomatizable systems in which at least one axiom is not provable on the basis of the system (ibid., 84). Gödel's theorem appears as Proposition VI in his 1931 paper "On the Formally Undecidable Propositions in Principia Mathematica and Related Systems I." According to Douglas R. Hofstadter, the essence of Gödel's theorem is that "provability is a weaker notion than truth, no matter what axiomatic system is involved" (*Gödel, Escher, Bach: an Eternal Golden Braid*, 19).

52. Recently obtained results show that under specific conditions the product of an interaction between two non-equilibrium structures may achieve regularity. The resulting dissipative structures, of which life is a general example, permit periodicity which attaches to contextual simultaneity, which in turn brings in intersystemic resonance as a general mode of communication. This attaches to Foerster's concept of "order from noise" (H.M. von Foerster, "On Self-Organizing Systems and their Environment").

53. Georg Klaus, *Cybernetics as Viewed by Philosophy*, 13.

54. Such a semantic interpretation assumes epistemological relevance in connection with reflection theory. The issue that emerges is: Can isomorphism be assumed where the reflective consciousness and the reflected being of the receiver of the signal has to transform the latter into information by giving it a content? (see Ludz, "Marxism and Systems Theory," 667).

55. Gareth Morgan, "Re-Thinking Corporate Strategy: a Cybernetic Perspective"; Maruyama, "The Second Cybernetics"; Sir Geoffrey Vickers, *Freedom in a Rocking Boat: Changing Values in an Unstable Society*.

56. Luhmann, "Insistence on Systems Theory," 994.

57. Josef Bleicher, "System and Meaning: Comments on the Work of Niklas Luhmann."

58. Alfred North Whitehead, *Process and Reality*, 11.

59. A.A. Bogdanov noted that "organizational activity is the predominant activity; that no other problems exist but organizational ones" (Bogdanov 1920). This statement is surprisingly close to that expressed above.

Both Ashby and Talcott Parsons note that for reasons of time, complex systems cannot afford to rely exclusively on one-to-one relations between external and internal events. Complex systems require time for processing information and selecting programs and reactions and, consequently, presuppose structures or other parts of the system that are not involved in working out specific relations. Outside events that would require a change in everything at once would amount to the devastation of the system. Organizational differentiation, then, is the structural technique for solving the temporal problem of complex (time-consuming) systems existing in complex environment (Talcott Parsons, *On Institutions and Social Evolution: Selected Writings*).

60. P.N. Rastogi, "Structure, Function and Process: A Cybernetic Approach to Social Phenomena," 316.

61. S. Beer, *Brain of the Firm*; idem, *Platform for Change*.

62. John Bednarz, "Complexity and Intersubjectivity: Towards the Theory of Niklaus Luhmann," 58.

63. Edgar Morin, "Complexity," 558.

Talcott Parsons analyzes decision making as a tool for reducing environmental variety and arriving at situational definitions; the sociopolitical system would depend on individual choices articulated through exchange or collective choice theory. The German perspective (espoused by Niklas Luhmann among others) treats the environmental definition as the independent variable, thus mapping some degree of individual dependence on the preexistent political system.

64. The works of Luhmann are alleged to bear a thematic similarity to those of Talcott Parsons. Both Luhmann and Parsons present concepts of society based on systems theory and start from the problem of order. Following Parsons, Luhmann adheres to a functional-structuralist theory of social systems. Luhmann, however, does not start from a monistic but from a pluralistic ground of order. Parsons views the social system as cybernetic controlling action, while Luhmann views it as constructed through action. (See Tannelie Blom, "Meaning and System"; Niklas Luhmann, *Trust and Power*; idem, *Differentiation of Society*).

Luhmann, for instance, tries to achieve a foundation of sociology on the basis of general organizational principles. This stands outside certain traditional patterns of fundamentalist and causal epistemology. His neofunctionalist sociology, based on Ashby's principle of requisite variety, foregoes any explanatory and predictive function.

65. Niklas Luhmann, *Soziologische Aufklärung I*, 7 and 116. Luhmann defines the term "complexity" as a measure of the incapacity of a system to relate each element to every other one, be it in the system itself (systemic complexity) or in its environment (environmental variety). The term complexity points to the internal selectivity of all relational combinations of elements. Complexity means the necessity of selective relations and, since relations specify what elements are possible within the system, complexity also means contingent elements. The analysis of complexity leads back to the notion of self-referential, self-organizing systems. Also see Koolhaas, *Organization*; Stafford Beer, *Cybernetics and Management*.

66. Bednarz, "Complexity and Intersubjectivity," 55.

67. Niklas Luhmann, "Differentiation of Society," 254.

68. John Kenneth Galbraith, *The Anatomy of Power*.

69. Luhmann, *Differentiation of Society*, 264.

70. Erich Jantsch, "The Unifying Paradigm Behind Autopoiesis, Dissipative Structures, Hyper- and Ultracycles," 83.

71. S. Beer, "Below the Twilight Art," 2.

72. Niklas Luhmann, "The Self-Description of Society: Crisis Fashion and Sociological Theory," 63.

73. Luhmann, "Insistence on Systems Theory," 992.

74. F.G. Varela, H.R. Maturana, and R. Uribe, "Autopoiesis: The Organization of Living Systems, Its Characterization and a Model."

75. Milan Zeleny, "A Paradigm Lost?" 4.

76. Morin, "Complexity," 563.

77. Humberto R. Maturana and Francisco Varela, *Autopoiesis: The Realization of the Living*, 82 and 79.

78. Stafford Beer, "Preface" to Maturana and Varela, *Autopoiesis*, 66.

79. Zeleny, "A Paradigm Lost?" 20.

80. Maturana and Varela, *Autopoiesis*, 98.

81. Zeleny, "A Paradigm Lost?" 7. Forty years ago the cybernetics elaborated by Norbert Wiener could only account for the performance of allopoietic systems, i.e., non–self-reproducing unities. It may now be applied to complex autopoietic unities which Prigogine describes as dissipative structures. (Wiener, *Cybernetics;. 1948 Prigogine, Introduction to Thermodynamics of Irreversible Processes,. 1968.*)

82. Jantsch, "Unifying Paradigm Behind Autopoiesis," 83. Passet's reference to finalities of living systems attaches to Jantsch's et al. understanding of autopoiesis. For Passet artificial machine systems have no finality; in Jantsch's terms they are described as being allopoietic (see Passet, *L'Économique et le Vivant*; E. Jantsch and C.H. Waddington, eds., *Evolution and Consciousness: Human Systems in Transition*).

83. Passet, *L'Économique et le Vivant*, 111, 153.

84. Ibid.

85. Ibid., 152.

86. Maturana and Varela, *Autopoiesis*, 81.

87. Ibid., 79, 100, 104.

88. Zeleny, "A Paradigm Lost?" 29.

89. Maturana and Varela, *Autopoiesis*, 76, 118.

90. Lotka, "Biased Evolution"; Schrödinger, *What Is Life?*; idem, *What Is Life from the Point of Physics*.

91. Boulding notes that the phenomena of "struggles are rare in the biological world. The struggle for existence . . . was a completely misleading metaphor" (*Beyond Economics*, 140). "In the ecological interaction of populations there is competition in the sense that the more there is of one species, the less there will be of another, but this is not the same thing as conflict . . . even mutually competitive relationships may produce an equilibrium for both species or they can also lead to the extinction of one species. . . . The "struggle for existence" as we have noted earlier, is an entirely inappropriate, anthropomorphic metaphor derived from human experience" (ibid., 254).

92. D. Elgin, *The Evolution of Consciousness and the Transformation of Society*.

93. E.H. Hutten, *Information, Explanation and Meaning*.

94. Lila L. Gatlin, "Conservation of Shannon's Redundancy for Proteins."

95. John Calhoun, in Ernest O. Attinger, *Global Systems Dynamics*; also see Rapoport, "Methodology in the Sciences."

96. In *Essay on the Influences of a Low Price of Corn on the Profit of Stock*, Ricardo sought to oppose capitalist's profits to landowners' rents. According to Ricardo, rent is "the remuneration given to the landlord for the use of the original and inherent power of the land." Alternatively, it is the portion paid for the "original power of the land." Adopting an image of Malthus, he also speaks of land as a "machine" with "original qualities and powers." (See Sraffa, *The Works of David Ricardo*.)

97. Passet, *L'Économique et le Vivant*; Leon Walras, *Elements of Pure Economics: or, The Theory of Social Wealth.*

Though some economists assert that labor and capital, as "factors of production," exist on an equal conceptual footing with one another, the uncontested ownership by capital of all value-added is surely evidence that the price-making market incorporates an asymmetry in the disposition of its product. It is a disposition reflecting a conveniently neglected social domination within its operation.

In this connection the ability of private property owners to organize and discipline social activities does not lie in the right of owners to dispose of their property as they will. Such a dangerous license never fully existed. (Agricultural land-use constraints in England existed until into the twentieth century. See Thomas T. Sekine, "'Entropy Problem and the Future of Our Society.'") Rather, the social right accorded to owners was the right to selectively withhold their property from generalized use by society. The social power of capital was one of refusal, not of assertion. The capitalist may deny others access to his resources, but he may not force them to work with them. Clearly, such power required circumstances that made the withholding of access an act of critical consequence. These circumstances could only arise if the populace was unable to secure its livelihood by other means—that is, unless it gained access to privately owned capital (see Karl Polanyi, *The Great Transformation*). It is precisely under these circumstances that capital becomes an instrument of power; for its owners are able to establish claims on output as their quid pro quo for permitting access to their property.

98. Walras, *Elements of Pure Economics*, 213.

99. "Capital," writes J.A. Schumpeter, "is nothing but the lever by which the entrepreneur subjects to his control the concrete goods which he needs, nothing but a means of diverting the factors of production to new uses, or of dictating a new direction to production" (*Essays*, 116).

100. Fisher's definition of capital may be thought of as the set of all physical things capable of satisfying human wants and subject to appropriation.

101. Passet, *L'Économique et le Vivant*, 111. Autopoiesis may be used to explain energy throughput rates of ecosystems moving from succession to steady state. System differentiation creates niches. Initially a system maximizes its growth and diversity is disregarded in an ecosystem maximizing throughput. With hierarchical differentiation diversification enables the tapping of what were hitherto wastes.

102. Ibid., 123, 124.

103. See Vickers, "The Poverty of Problem Solving."

104. Passet, *L'Économique et le Vivant*, 16–17; also see Schrödinger, *What Is Life from the Point of Physics*.

105. See Daniel Bell, *The Coming of the Post-Industrial Society*.

106. Tsuchida and Murota, "Fundamentals in Entropic Theory," 3:9.

107. Henri Laborit, "Societé Informationnelle," 29–30; also found in Passet, *L'Économique et le Vivant*, 139, 170.

108. Ibid., 170, 177.

109. See J. Robin's "La Logique du vivant," as found in ibid., 18.

110. Ibid., 157.

111. Kenneth E. Boulding, *A Primer on Social Dynamics*, 277.

112. Paul I. Medow, "Exploring the Technological Problematique of Global Coevolution"; Jacques Monod, *From Biology to Ethics*; Jacques Robin, "Culture and Technology: Fusion or Collision: an Extended Summary"; Salk, *Anatomy of Reality*.

113. The distinction here is between genotypical and phenotypical selection processes; that is, between design interventions at the planning stage and market-driven futures.

114. Passet, *L'Économique et le Vivant*, 111.
115. Ibid., 167, 121.
116. The concept of "inverted" logic expressed by Passet appears to be derived from Marx.

> The real barrier of capitalistic production is capital itself. It is that capital and its self-expression appear as the starting and closing point, the motive and the purpose of production; that production is only production for *capital* and not vice versa, the means of production are not mere means for a constant expansion of the living process of the society of producers. The limits within which the preservation and self-expression of the value of capital resting on the expropriation and pauperization of the great mass of producers can alone move—these limits come continually into conflict with the methods of production employed by capital for its purposes, which drive towards unlimited extension of production, towards production as an end in itself, towards unconditional development of the social productivity of labour. The means—unconditional development of the productive forces of society—comes continually into conflict with the limited purpose, the self-expansion of the existing capital. The capitalist mode of production is, for this reason, a historical mode of developing the material forces of production and creating an appropriate world market and is, at the same time, a continual conflict between this its historical task and its own corresponding relations of social production. (Marx, *Capital*, III:250).

117. Kozo Uno, the Japanese Marxist, writes:

> The intersector "equilibrium" observed in the reproduction schemes of a capitalist commodity-economy, even in the theoretically visualized model of a pure capitalist society, should be understood to hold only approximately as prices gravitate towards their central limits. Although the anarchistic production and accumulation of each individual capital are subject to the regulation of the law of value, no one need, either actually or theoretically, be trading at equilibrium prices. The theory merely demonstrates the necessity that the law of value asserts itself in the course of anarchistic production. Economic laws work quite different from the laws of nature, the working of which may be experimentally tested. The equilibrium of reproduction, therefore, does not suggest that a general economic norm which lies outside of a capitalist economy demands its compliance, nor that a capitalist economy because of its anarchism of production may from time to time deviate from this general norm. Each individual capital produces anarchistically indeed, but it must obey the regulation of the law of value, the global consequence of which is to realize the norm of reproduction common to all societies. In other words, the law of commodity-economy is not independent of a general economic norm, but rather contains the latter within its peculiar form of fluctuating prices. The law of value becomes an economic law because it has the power to realize a general economic norm on a society-wide scale. (*Principles of Political Economy*, 68–69)

118. Polanyi, *Primitive, Archaic, and Modern Economies*, 148.

119. Joseph A. Schumpeter, *Capitalism, Socialism, and Democracy*, 284.

120. The autopoietic approach is not without its methodological dimensions. For the concepts of autopoiesis and of general theory of organization should be applicable to the formulation of empirical models of policy analysis. From this we should expect much more than mere technical refinements. Complex organizations, i.e., those displaying the nonlinearities that attach to organizational dissonance, have no optimum. Consequently, the cybernetics of autopoietic organizations challenge the conventional notion of rationality and optimization (refer to Simon, "On the concept"). Insofar as the techniques of policy analysis rely upon optimization, alternative methods must be developed. In this connection there are tremendous potentialities in the continuing development of techniques of discrete-event simulation for the analysis of autopoietic systems (Dobuzinskis, "Autopoiesis in Nature and Politics," 16).

The development of cultural and ethical norms in a society depends on an original self-closure which discrete-event simulation methodologies can render explicit. While the cybernetic concepts of feedback and autonomy, which attach to autopoiesis, do not suffice to explore the normative, they are a vital link to further understanding. To disregard simulation techniques, to dispense with cybernetic concepts and systems theory merely because their neutrality lends them technocratic possibilities means renouncing the search for ways of escaping the positivistic separation of object and subject (ibid., 7).

121. Lossky, *History of Russian Philosophy*, 355.

122. Quoted in Frolov, *Society and the Environment*.

123. Passet, *L'Économique et le Vivant*, 217.

124. Refer to the foregoing Ashbian game-theoretical explication.

125. Schrödinger, *What Is Life from the Point of Physics*.

126. Passet, *L'Économique et le Vivant*, 219. This, for instance, explicates the "double movement" thesis of Karl Polanyi. What is essential for Polanyi is that the emergence of a self-regulating market as the primary mechanism for social reproduction simultaneously threatens the existence of society itself. Polanyi's central thesis "is that the self-regulating market was utopian since it could not exist for long 'without annulling the human and natural substance of society' by physically destroying humanity and transforming the environment into a desert. Inevitably 'society adopts measures to protect itself, it blocks the self-regulation of the market, disorganizes industrial life, and therefore threatens society in a different way. . . .' This dilemma encourages the development of the market system along a track which ends with the collapse of the social organization on which it was based" (Alberto Martinelli, "On the Relation of State and Market," 133). While Polanyi identified the "double movement" present in market-organized society, liberal theory and orthodox Marxism focus on the movement of self-regulating market forces, because their analytical frameworks eclipse the countermovement of the protective response. From Polanyi's analysis, Marxism appears as a "tendency," one mistaken for the essence of capitalism. Marx, in Volume I of *Capital*, presents an analysis (and a deterministic one at that), of the internal logic of capitalism which disregards the countermovement—the protective response which Polanyi understood.

Polanyi's "double movement" is antecedent to Marx's "class-bound" analysis of capitalism. Marx's paradigm assumes the existence of a fully constituted and completely disembedded economic sphere. However, capitalism never became the dichotomized class society in which the state became reduced, according to Brown, "to an epiphenomenon of the economic base," because the safeguarding countermovement prevented the complete disembedding of the economy from society (Douglas Brown, "Karl Polanyi's Influence on the Budapest School"). The proletariat was prevented from becoming a "class" in the Marxian sense, for it never reached the point of "having nothing to lose but its chains because the capitalist state never became the epiphenomenon of the base" (ibid., 13). The capitalist mixed economy is a result of the "double movement," the effect of which, according to Brown, was the denial of the democratization of capitalism's power structure. The contradictory tendencies, which sprang from the necessity of state intervention to mitigate the social evils caused by the dysfunctionalities of the market system, were regarded by Polanyi as a constituent element of capitalist development and not, as much current neo-Marxist theory will have it, as a distinctive feature of "late capitalism" in its state monopolistic stage. It is this image that is understood as the "double movement." And it is in the context of tension of this "double movement" that the corporatist form of capitalism emerged.

While projecting economic rationality to its zenith, and while simultaneously intervening to secure its citizens against the worst ravages of operationalized economic rationality, the tension of the "double movement" lead to the disintegration of individualism. In fascist ideology and practice Polanyi found an iconoclastic dogma which robs the human individual of his conscious will and purpose (Abraham Rotstein, "The Reality of Society: Karl Polanyi's Philosophical Perspective"). Polanyi's analysis conceives fascism as a perverse and opportunistic twisting of the social impulse to control the chaos of a capitalistic world and attributes its temporary success to the collapse of that world's regulative institutions.

127. Moiseev, "The Unity of Natural Scientific Knowledge." In this context, as well, one may refer to the Ashbian game-theoretical construct.

128. Daly, *Economics, Ecology, and Ethics*, 24.

129. Bertalanffy, *General Systems Theory*, 8.

130. Richard Wolin, "Modernism vs Postmodernism."

131. Jürgen Habermas, *Legitimation Crisis*, 5.

132. Ibid., 132.

133. Lee Congdon, "The Sovereignty of Society: Polanyi in Vienna"; Passet, *L'Économique et le Vivant*, 224; Polanyi, *The Livelihood of Man*.

134. N.P. Shchersak, *Vladimir Ivanovich Vernadsky*, 51; Bateson, *Mind and Nature*, 45.

135. I.I. Schmalhausen considered the stabilizing function of natural selection as a mechanism opposed to change, to mutability. A similar line of thought is stressed by Waddington. (See I.I. Schmalhausen, *The Organism as a Whole in Individual and Historical Development, Factors of Evolution*.) Adam Schaff, "Biology and the Social Sciences," 603.

136. Jonas Salk, *The Survival of the Wisest*; Vernadsky, "The Biosphere and the Noösphere"; Jacob, *La Logique du Vivant*.

137. Schaff, "Biology and the Social Sciences," 603.

138. Bernstein, "Ecology and Economics"; Herman E. Daly, *Toward a Steady-State Economy*; Stumm, *Global Chemical Cycles*.

139. Wright, *Technology and the Legitimation Crisis*.

140. Paul I. Medow, "Conversations on the Noosphere: the Context"; National Research Council, *Towards an International Geosphere-Biosphere Program: a Study of Global Change*; World Resources Institute (WRI), *The Global Possible: Resources, Development, and the New Century*.

141. Robin, "Culture and Technology," 2; Salk, *Anatomy of Reality*, 20.

142. See Lovelock, *Gaia*, 107; Elgin, *Evolution of Consciousness*.

143. R. Rosen, "Old Trends and New Trends in Systems Research," 28.

144. It is perhaps also useful to refer once again to Figure 4.1.

145. See Chapter 3 on the thermodynamics of the economic process.

146. OECD, *Economic and Ecological Interdependence*.

147. Salk, *Anatomy of Reality*, 20.

148. Douglas J. Futuyama and Montgomery Slatkin, eds., *Coevolution*, 33. It is im-

portant to distinguish, in a general way, between the prefixes "quasi" and "meta" as applied, for instance, to the terms "genetic" or "biological." The former refers to systems that are logically analogous to another, whereas the latter refers to systems, which, although they are analogous to other phenomena, are distinguished by possessing a distinct and transcendent logic. "Meta" conveys an image of a discrete system whose cybernetic qualities, internal logic, and modes of behavior are distinct both with their subsystems and supersystems. It is in this sense that Salk's concept of "metabiological" is analytically superior to "quasi-biological" which, for instance, attaches to Lotka's notion of "exosomatic" (*Anatomy of Reality*).

149. In this connection one also might refer to Koenig's and Nijkamp's energy-balance models of Chapter 3.

150. Passet, *L'Économique et le Vivant*, 228.

151. "Autonomy" is at heart a political or moral concept that brings together the ideas of freedom and control. To be autonomous is to be self-governing, independent, not ruled by an external law or force.

152. We need only refer to the emergence of multigenerational and global issues as addressed in the introduction to Chapter 4.

153. Milton Friedman and Rose Friedman, *Free to Choose*; Charles Lindblom, *Politics and Markets*.

154. John K. Galbraith and Stanislav Menshikov, *Capitalism, Communism and Coexistence: From a Bitter Past to a Better Prospect*, 78.

155. Ibid., 82.

156. A.M. Rosenthal has concluded that communism has failed and that Mikail Gorbachev is himself the result of a long deterioration of the Soviet economy. He concluded that Marxism–Leninism is no longer a political solution to any society (*The New York Times*, I:31:1).

157. Shaomin Li, "The Road to Freedom: Can Communist Societies Evolve into Democracy?" 186.

158. Mikhail Gorbachev, *Perestroika*, 66. The radical restructuring of the Soviet economy away from central planning and toward individual freedom and economic responsibilities has been interpreted as a retreat from socialism. However, significant elements of *perestroika* are consistent with concepts theorized and occasionally implemented within the context of the New Economic Plan of the 1920s. In contrast to the innovations theorized and introduced by Bukharin and Lenin, the centralization of the Soviet economy associated with Stalin (and which bore a resemblance to Trotsky's earlier-formulated plans) represented a departure from the orthodoxy of Marx.

159. Menshikov, "Dialogue between Economists," 79.

160. Ibid., 77. In an announcement former German Democratic Republic (GDR) economics ministry spokesperson, Christa Luft, remarked that "We must work toward the convertibility of the mark," and further noted that the GDR plans to discard all price controls by 1993. In an effort to adapt itself to the world market and attract foreign capital and expertise, the GDR has committed itself to discarding the subsidy system that undergirds its social welfare system ("East Germany plans to have convertible currency; scrap all price controls by 1993," *The Japan Times*).

161. Market fetishism and the technocratic style to which Kagarlistsky refers as more general phenomena. For instance, having neither provided continuous growth nor improved the general standard of living, economic reform in Hungary has betrayed its promise. It has replicated the worst aspects of contemporary capitalism by combining a fervent belief in the efficacy of the market with the entrenched bureaucracy intent on installing the free market to the detriment of social policy. (See Boris Kagarlistsky, "Perestroika: The Dialectic of Change.")

162. Menshikov, "Dialogue between Economists," 79.

163. Polanyi, *The Great Transformation*, 112.

164. See "Our Obsolete Market Mentality," as found in Polanyi, *Primitive, Archaic, and Modern Economies*, 59; and "Forms of Integration and Supporting Structures," as found in Polanyi, *The Livelihood of Man*, 35.

165. J.A. Schumpeter wrote: "It is very arguable that the science of political economy as studied in its first period after the death of Adam Smith (1790), did more harm than good. It destroyed many economic fallacies. . . . But it riveted on men a certain set of abstractions which were disastrous in their influence on modern mentality. It dehumanized industry . . . and fixed attention on a definite group of abstractions, neglected everything else, and elicited every scrap of information and theory which [was] relevant to what it . . . retained" (*Economic Doctrine and Method*, 473, 668, 1171).

166. See T.W. Hutchinson, *On Revolutions and Progress of Economic Knowledge*, 50, 60.

167. Ibid., 19.

168. J.R. Stanfield, *The Economic Thought of Karl Polanyi*, 139.

169. Polanyi, *The Great Transformation*, 245.

170. Ibid., 254.

171. Marx, *Grundrisse*, 188.

172. Polanyi, *The Great Transformation*, 254, 257.

173. Lindblom, *Politics and Markets*, 164.

174. Li, "The Road to Freedom," 184.

175. J.M. Clark, "The Changing of Economic Responsibility," 77.

176. Ernst F. Schumacher, *Small is Beautiful: a Study of Economics as if People Matter*, 42.

177. Thorstein Veblen, *The Theory of Business Enterprise*.

178. T. Veblen, *Absentee Ownership*, 65–66.

179. Polanyi, *The Great Transformation*, 257.

180. Polanyi, *The Livelihood of Man*, 15–17.

181. Polanyi, *The Great Transformation*, 258.

182. Polanyi, *Primitive, Archaic, and Modern Economies*, 74.

183. In this connection global simulation modeling provides a scientific basis for identifying and avoiding those possible futures that may not guarantee the further coevolution of man and the Biosphere. Moreover, it is producing an "Oedipus effect" in which simulated futures are exerting a perceptible influence on the present (Ivan T. Frolov, "The Global Peace Strategy and Nature Conservation," 59).

184. John K. Galbraith, *The New Industrial State*, 405.

185. John Dewey, *Liberalism and Social Action*, 20.

186. W. Brus wrote in a similar vein "Socialism does not abolish and will never abolish the economic problem; what it offers is a different way of dealing with the problem; conscious intervention by communal institutions, a 'visible hand' acting on behalf of the community" ("Socialism Feasible and Viable?" 48).

187. The institutionalized market pattern could not function unless society were somehow subordinated to its requirements. The reason for this assertion is that a market economy must comprise all elements of industry, including land (nature) and labor. The crucial point is that labor is only another name for a human activity that goes with life itself, which is produced not for sale but for other reasons—an activity that cannot be abstracted from the rest of life. Land is only another name for nature upon which society and, indeed, all of life exists. Land and labor are obviously not commodities; the postulate that anything that is bought and sold must have been produced for sale is emphatically untrue with regard to them. In other words, according to the empirical definition of commodities they are not commodities. To abstract them from the locus of their reality, to

include them in the market mechanism, requires nothing less than the subordination of society to the inconstancy of the market. Thus, Polanyi asserts that the description of labor and land is entirely fictitious. Nonetheless, the commodity fiction supplied a vital organizing principle in regard to the whole of society. It affected almost all of its institutions through the principle according to which no behavior could be permitted that might constrain the articulations of the market mechanism on the lines of the commodity fiction (Polanyi, *The Great Transformation*; idem, *Primitive, Archaic, and Modern Economies*).

188. The concepts embodied in the foregoing were made by P.I. Medow during private conversations in October 1988. Elements of this same analysis are also present in Karl Mannheim, *Man and Society: In an Age of Reconstruction*, 157.

189. Jacob, *La Logique du Vivant*.

190. Salk, *Anatomy of Reality*, 117–18.

191. François Perroux, *A New Concept of Development: Basic Tenets*.

192. Paul I. Medow, "Ecological and Genetic Approaches to the Exploration of Global Technological Scenarios," 1.

193. Medow, "Exploring Technological Problematique," 222, 224.

194. Norgaard, "Economics as Mechanics," 306.

195. S. Beer, *Brain of the Firm*; Medow, "Exploring Technological Problematique."

196. Parenthetically, the first principle of coevolution analysis attaches to the viability principle of autopoiesis. That is, priority of the first rank must attach to the structural relations within which subordinate units may express themselves. But the unities are temporary actors whose finalities are constrained to that of the whole within which they achieve their individuality. Moreover, the whole achieves its individuality, its "wholeness," through the synergy of its subordinate unities.

197. Habermas, *Legitimation Crisis*, 139.

198. S. Beer, *Platform for Change*, 407.

199. See "The Surrogate World We Manage," as found in ibid.

200. Simon, "On the concept."

201. S. Beer, *Platform for Change*, 315.

202. N.N. Moiseev's and I.T. Frolov's insistence on this achieves a unity with, for instance, Herman Koenig's socio-ecological cybernetic approach which refers to the identification of bifurcation points and the avoidance of modes of behavior detrimental to the long-run mass-energy balances between society and the Biosphere ("High Touch Technologies Society, Man and Nature in the Age of Microelectronics, Informatics and Biotechnologies").

203. Frolov, "Global Peace Strategy," 57.

204. S. Beer, *Platform for Change*, 399.

205. Ibid., 60. "The metabiological processes," notes Salk, "are not exempt from the laws of evolution nor from the process of natural selection even though they are somewhat removed from strict, direct genetic control. Since they are metabiological, they are also metagenetic and, therefore, in order to function they must possess a set of mechanisms that are analogous to other adaptive mechanisms" (*Anatomy of Reality*, 60).

206. A prototype of this kind of global institutional solution emerged from a three-day, forty country, U.N. Environment Program meeting to forge a global environmental protocol to save the ozone layer that surrounds the earth. The aim of the protocol is to take the first concrete step toward global protection of the ozone layer. The Canadian environment minister, Thomas McMillan, said of the protocol: "It is an historic first. On a global basis we will have a law of the atmosphere that deals with extremely important planetary problems." McMillan continued, saying, "The world is signaling to itself that certain kinds of chemicals are no longer acceptable; that they are lethal" (*Toronto Globe and Mail*).

Scientists estimate that overall as much as 7 percent of the ozone belt, which stretches six to thirty miles above the earth, has already been destroyed. As the world's ozone layer deteriorates, the sun's radiation could lead to a dramatic increase in skin cancer and cataracts, along with lower resistance to infection. It could damage plant life, both directly and as a result of a general warming trend; that warming could lead to a disastrous rise in sea levels (*Time*, 37).

The best computer models of the atmosphere must juggle with many gases in minute quantities, scores of chemical reactions, plus all the uncertainties of weather and climate. None of them predicted the Antarctic phenomenon that is deceptively known as the ozone hole. Each spring, the amount of ozone over the Antarctic decreases by ever-larger amounts and recovers by early summer. Most of the depletions occur in the Antarctic vortex, a vast, fast clockwise swirl of stratospheric air, and the latest evidence suggests that man-made chemicals are to blame (*The Economist*, 97).

207. Friedrich A. von Hayek, *The Road to Serfdom*; idem, *Studies in Philosophy, Politics and Economics*.

208. Wasily W. Leontief, "Letter to the Editor," 104.

Glossary

Aüsserung: Man's extension or externalization of himself including his consciousness. It embodies the notion of man expressing his life fully and coming to be through his own creative activities.

Autopoiesis: The process whereby (autopoietic) systems produce the elements of which they are composed. This necessitates a system capacity to distinguish between those elements belonging to the system itself from elements belonging to the system's environment. The distinction between system and environment is, therefore, constitutive for whatever functions as an element in a system. An autopoietic system is defined as a multistable network of interrelated component-producing transformations such that the components in the interaction replicate the network that produced them. The product is the network itself, created and recreated in a flow of matter and energy. It is this quality that enables us to describe autopoietic systems as being partially open. It is a distinguishable complex of component-producing processes and resulting components, bounded as a semi-autonomous unity within a highly interconnected environment of shared subsystems.

Closed System: According to the second law of thermodynamics, a time-independent equilibrium state, with maximum entropy and minimum free energy whose final, or any intermediate state, is determined by those forces and processes already within it at the moment of closure.

Communication: Not simply an act of utterance which "transfers" information but an independency of autopoietic operation that combines three different selections—information, operation, and understanding—into an emergent unity that can serve as the basis for further communication.

Complexity: Systemic complexity is said to be manifest when the whole possesses qualities and properties not to be found in the isolated parts, and conversely, the parts possess qualities and properties that disappear as a result of the organizational constraints of the system. Systemic complexity is said to increase with the increase in the number and diversity of the component parts and with the increased flexibility and complication of the interrelations (interactions, feedback, interferences, etc.) and the decrease in their determinism. A state of affairs is complex when it arises out of so many elements that they can only be related to one another selectively. An understanding of complexity necessarily involves a simplifying process; the construction of abstractions whereby there is elimination of empirical properties of the phenomenon as nonsignificant, irrelevant, or contingent.

***Cybernetics*:** The fundamental principles of control applicable to large systems, or alternatively, the science of management.

***Differentiation, functional*:** The formation of systems within systems. It does not necessarily designate the decomposition of an entire system into subsystems but rather the establishment of system/environment differences within the whole. The differentiation is functional insofar as the subsystem acquires and maintains an identity through the fulfillment of a function for the entire system. Functional subsystems tolerate an open fluctuating environment so long as other subsystems fulfill their function. This condition requires a constant selective adjustment by means of both influence on and adaptation to society's internal environment. Functional subsystems, therefore, are structurally required to process information about their environment.

***Empirio-monism*:** A philosophical system defined by A.A. Bogdanov as a synthesis of Mach's and Avenarius's theory of knowledge and Marx's theory of social history. Empirio-monism rejects the mechanistic orientation in science as an ideology rooted in the custom-bound organization of social labor in the seventeenth century. Like the philosophies of Mach and Avenarius, empirio-monism demands that both philosophers and scientists abandon their traditional concern with the "explanations" of mechanically intertwined phenomena and instead emphasize the "description" of pure forms of experience which are reducible to mathematical description.

Entropy: The measure of a system's inexorable tendency to move from a less to a more probable state. This entails an evening-out of the energy available to the system, which eventually reaches a standstill at unit entropy (equals maximum probability). For a living system, unit entropy equals death.

***Feedback*:** The return of part of a system's output to its input, which is thereby changed. Positive feedback takes an increase in output to increase the input; negative feedback takes back an output increase to decrease the input—and is therefore stabilizing in principle.

***Functionalism*:** A theory of society that takes as its point of departure an understanding of society as a totality, a whole within which survival, functioning, and evolution are key aspects supplemented by notions of adaptation, goal-attainment, integration, and pattern maintenance.

***Homeostasis*:** The capability of a system to hold its critical variables within physiological limits in the face of unexpected disturbance or perturbation.

Metasystem: A system over and beyond a system of lower logical order and therefore capable of deciding propositions, discussing criteria, or exercising regulation for systems that are themselves logically incapable of such decisions and discussions or of self-regulation (because the metalogic is inaccessible to the system's logic, or the metalanguage is capable of statements inexpressible in the system's language). Note that a metasystem is of a higher logical order than a system, but not necessarily of higher "seniority." For example: the school timetable is metasystemic to the timetable of a single class.

Negentropy: The measure of the negative entropy, equaling the active information content of a system (cf. entropy). Note that systems gaining entropy are analytically equivalent to those losing information, and vice versa.

Noösphere: The influence of living matter is being eclipsed by human activities that are causing increased biogenic migration through technology. For Vernadsky, this conscious influence signaled a new era in the evolution of the Biosphere—the Noösphere—an era in which biogenic migration is related not just to the quantity of living matter, but also to the influence of human reason. Teilhard de Chardin believed that the next evolutionary threshold would be the rise of a collective consciousness that would control the direction of future planetary evolution. He called this new evolutionary phase the Noösphere.

For Teilhard, the transition to the epoch of the Noösphere was a movement from biological to psychological and spiritual evolution. For Vernadsky the transformation of the Biosphere through human interference was the process of Noögenesis—the creation of the Noösphere. He considered the Noösphere to be the medium within which humanity could find fulfillment. He believed that humanity could achieve this through exercising deliberate and conscious control over its milieu. Whereas Teilhard's conception of the Noösphere tried to draw together material and spiritual interpretations of the development of the universe, Vernadsky maintained a materialist view. He saw the Noösphere in primarily materialist terms as a historically inevitable stage in the evolutionary development of the Biosphere. He believed that the growth of science and technology would transform inadvertent human interference in global biogeochemistry to more reasoned and purposeful intervention. This change would constitute the transition from Biosphere to Noösphere. According to Vernadsky, human development would be enhanced and sustained in the Noösphere through understanding and management of biogeochemical cycles—the limits of planetary life-support systems.

Objectification: In Marx's *Grundrisse,* "objectification" is defined as a historic universal process whereby man creates himself in his labor; he crystallizes himself in the objects on which he labors. Objectification, in other words, assumes an ontological dimension. Man interacts with nature, puts his labor into nature, and in the process transforms both himself and nature. In this sense, all labor objectifies. It is, moreover, the very essence of labor. It is only when the objectification is governed by needs and priorities other than the producer's that one can speak of alienated labor.

Ontogy: The history of the structural transformation of a system.

Open System: A system which, under certain conditions, may attain a time-independent steady state. That is, the system remains constant both as a whole and in its phases, though there is a continuous flow of component materials. It implies that, in the midst of throughput from inputs to outputs, some kind of structure is maintained whose final state, or any intermediate state, is determined both by the forces within it the moment it became open, and by the forces of the environment.

Organization: Like substance and energy, an integral part of things and processes. It is a set of specific internal and external relations. The internal ones enable the entity to maintain coherence even through change. The external ones regulate its relation as a whole with its milieu.

Paradigm: An exemplar or pattern; a basic way of doing something guided by principles or ideologies that may lie beneath hermetic levels of reasoning.

Self-reference: Every operation that refers to something beyond itself and through this back to itself. Pure self-reference that does not take this detour through what is external to itself would amount to tautology. Real operations or systems depend on an "unfolding" or deautologization because only then can they grasp that they are possible in a real environment.

Social Energetics: A reductionist monism that arose out of a growing appreciation of the role of energy in the economy. It tendered a biophysical basis of society and the economy, substituting the reductionism of mechanical materialism for a form of energy reductionism.

Social Systems: An organized pattern of social behavior ranging from whole societies to particular sets of institutions within a society, to particular institutions themselves, to particular patterns of behavior within an institution. At each level social systems always must be viewed in relation to their environments.

Society: That social system that includes all meaningful communication and is always formed when communication takes place in connection with earlier communication or in reference to subsequent communication. The collective consciousness.

Technified Society: One confronted with the problems of the Technosphere; that which is the environment of technified society. It is a source of complexity to which mankind and his institutions respond.

Technosphere: Populations and networks of machine systems. The Technosphere is the conjunction of subsystems—the energy system, the production system, and the distribution system—which constitute metabolically and managerially semi-autonomous infrastructural elements in support of the livelihood of man.

Tektology: A general science of organization which seeks to describe continuous processes of organization–disorganization. Its task was to systematize an understanding of self-realizing systems, as well as corresponding cybernetic categories of analysis raised by rapid scientific, technical, technological, and informational advances. It was a synthetic "universal science of organization," conceived as a science of sciences—a "metascience."

Ultrastability: The capacity of a system to return to an equilibrial state after perturbation by unknown or unanalyzed forces; that is against the intervention of which the system was not explicitly designed.

Use-value: Those substances appropriated by the labor-process from nature that are suitable to human requirements in a nature-imposed condition of human existence. Use-values are combinations of two elements: the stuff of nature and the labor that shapes it.

Variety: The total number of possible states of a system.

Bibliography

Adamik, Richard. "Marx, Engels, and Dühring," *Journal of the History of Ideas* 35 (1974).

Àgh, Attila. "Totality Theory and System Theory." *Problems of the Science of Sciences* 5 (1975–76): 119–30.

Albaum, M. "The Moral Defenses of the Physiocrats' laissez-faire." *Journal of the History of Ideas* 16 (1955): 179–97.

Alexander, Edwin. "Consciousness, Necessity and Labor: A Discussion of Marx's 'Metabolic Interactivity'." *Philosophy and Social Criticism* 7, no. 1 (Spring 1980): 71–97.

Alexandrov, V.V. *Climatic Response to Global Injections.* Moscow: Computer Center of the USSR Academy of Sciences, 1983.

Alexandrov, V.V., and Moiseev, N.N. "The Evolution of the Climate: Regional Consequences." Research Memorandum. Toronto: York Univ., Economic Research and System Planning Group, 20 March 1982.

Allen, Peter M. "The Evolutionary Paradigm of Dissipative Structures." In Jantsch, ed., *The Evolutionary Vision.*

Amin, Samir. "In Praise of Socialism." *Monthly Review: an Independent Socialist Magazine* 26, no. 4 (1974): 1–16.

Anderson; Kneese; Reed; Taylor; and Stevenson. "Environmental Improvement: The Economic Incentives." In Cameron, ed., *Resources for the Future.*

Anrep, G.V., ed. *Conditioned Reflexes: an Investigation of the Physiological Activity of the Cerebral Cortex.* New York: Dover, 1960.

Appleby, Joyce Oldham. *Capitalism and a New Social Order: the Republican Vision.* New York: New York Univ. Press, 1984.

————. *Economic Thought and Ideology in Seventeenth Century England.* Princeton, N.J.: Princeton Univ. Press, 1978.

Aquinas, Saint Thomas. *Summa Theologica.* 1st complete American ed. Literally translated by Fathers of the English Dominican Province. 3 volumes. New York: Benziger Bros., 1947–48.

Arato, Andrew. "Lukàcs Theory of Reification." *Telos* no. 11 (Spring 1972): 25.

Arendt, Hannah. *Vita Activa.* Stuttgart: N.p., 1960.

Aristotle. *Aristotle's Politics.* Trans. Benjamin Jowett, with an introduction by Max Lerner. New York: Modern Library, 1943.

Ashby, William Ross. *An Introduction to Cybernetics.* London: Chapman & Hall, 1956.

————. "Principles of Self-Organization." In Foerster, Park, and Zopf, eds., *Principles of Self-Organization.*

Attinger, Ernest O., ed. *Global Systems Dynamics.* Basel: S. Karger, 1970.

Averly, Edward. *The Student's Marx: an Introduction to the Study of Karl Marx.* London: Swann Sonnenschein, 1892.

Axelos, Kostas. *Alienation, Praxis and Techne in the Thought of Karl Marx.* Trans. Ronald Bruzina. Austin: Univ. of Texas Press, 1976.

Ayer, A.J. *Language, Truth, and Logic.* New York: V. Gollancz, 1946.

Ayres, Robert. *Resources, Environment and Economics: Applications of the Materials/Energy Balance Principle.* New York: Wiley-Interscience, 1978.

Babbage, C. *On the Economy of Machinery and Manufactures.* London: C. Knight, 1832.

Bacon, Francis. *Advancement of Learning and New Atlantis.* Oxford: Clarendon Press, 1974.

———. *Advancement of Learning and Novum Organum.* New York: Colonial Press, 1900.

———. *Bacon's Essays.* Ed. R. Whately. London: Longmans, Green, 1882.

———. "New Atlantis." In Dick, ed., *Selected Writings of Francis Bacon.*

Balandin, R.K. *Vladimir Vernadsky.* Moscow: MIR, 1982.

Ballestrem, Karl G. "Lenin and Bogdanov." *Studies in Soviet Thought* 9 (1969):283–310.

Barker, Sir Ernest. *Greek Political Theory: Plato and his Predecessors.* 5th ed. New York: Barnes and Noble, 1960.

Barnet, Richard J., and Müller, Ronald E. *Global Reach: The Power of the Multinational Corporations.* New York: Simon & Schuster, 1974.

Barnett, Harold, and Morse, Chandler. *Scarcity and Growth: Resources for the Future.* Baltimore: Johns Hopkins Univ. Press, 1963.

Bastiat, Frederic. *Harmonies of Political Economy.* Trans. from the French, with a notice on the life and writings of the author, by Patrick James Stirling. Ann Arbor, Mich.: Univ. Microfilms, 1967.

Bateson, Gregory. *Mind and Nature: a Necessary Unity.* New York: Dutton, 1980.

Beckerman, Wilfred. *In Defence of Economic Growth.* London: Jonathan Cape, 1972.

Bednarz, John. "Complexity and Intersubjectivity: Towards the Theory of Niklaus Luhmann." *Human Studies* 7 (1984): 55–69.

Beer, E.S. de, ed. *The Correspondence of John Locke.* Oxford: Clarendon, 1976.

Beer, M. *An Inquiry into Physiocracy.* New York: Russell and Russell, 1939.

Beer, Stafford. "Below the Twilight Art—a Mythology of Systems." *Proceedings of the First Systems Symposium of the Case Institute of Technology.* London: N.p., 1961.

———. *Brain of the Firm.* Toronto: John Wiley & Sons, 1972.

———. *Cybernetics and Management.* New York: Science Editions, 1964.

———. *Decision and Control.* Toronto: John Wiley & Sons, 1966.

———. *Platform for Change.* Toronto: John Wiley & Sons, 1975.

Behar, Nansen; Neikov, Vesselin; and Gerassimov, Peter, eds. *Ecoforum for Peace.* Sofia, Bulgaria: Sofia Press Publishing House, 1986.

Bell, Daniel. *The Coming of the Post-Industrial Society.* New York: Basic Books, 1976.

Bello, Rafael E. "The Systems Approach—A. Bogdanov and L. von Bertalanffy." *Studies in Soviet Thought* 30 (1985): 131–47.

Berndt, Ernst R. "From Technocracy to Net Energy Analysis: Engineers, Economists, and Recurring Energy Theories of Value." In Scott, ed., *Progress in Natural Resource Economics.*

Bernstein, B.B. "Ecology and Economics: Complex Systems in Changing Environments." *Annual Review of Ecological Systems* 12 (1981): 309–30.

Bertalanffy, L. von. *Biophysik de Fleissgleichgewichts.* Braunschweig: Vieweg, 1953.

———. *General Systems Theory: Foundations, Development, Applications.* New York: George Braziller, 1968.

————. *Perspectives on General System Theory: Scientific-Philosophical Studies.* Ed. Edgar Taschdjian. New York: George Braziller, 1975.

————. *Problems of Life: An Evaluation of Modern Biological and Scientific Thought.* New York: Harper & Bros., 1952.

————. "The Theory of Open Systems in Physics and Biology." *Science* 111 (1950): 23–29.

Berthoud, Gerald. "Toward a Comparative Approach: The Contribution of Karl Polanyi." Paper presented at the Karl Polanyi Commemorative Conference. October 27–29, 1986. Budapest: Hungarian Academy of Sciences, 1986.

Blauberg, I. "The History of Science and the Systems Approach." *Social Sciences* 8, no. 3 (1977):90–100.

Blaug, Mark. *The Methodology of Economics: or How Economists Explain.* Cambridge: Cambridge Univ. Press, 1980.

————. *Ricardian Economics: a Historical Study.* New Haven, Conn.: Yale Univ. Press, 1958.

Bleicher, Josef. "System and Meaning: Comments on the Work of Niklas Luhmann." *Theory, Culture and Society* 1, no. 1 (Spring 1982): 49–52.

Blom, Tannelie. "Meaning and System" [Zin en systeem]. *Tijdschrift voor Sociale Wetenschappen* 31, no. 1 (January/March 1986): 22–53.

Blyth, John, ed. *The Natural Laws of Husbandry.* London: Walton & Marberly, 1859.

Bogdanov, Aleksandr A. *Basic Elements of the Historical View of Nature* [Osnovnye elementy istoricheskogo vzgliada na prirodu]. St. Petersburg: N.p., 1899.

————. "Chto my svergli?" *Novaja zizn'* (17 May 1917).

————. *Cognition from an Historical Point of View* [Poznanie s istoricheskoi tochki zreniia]. St. Petersburg: N.p., 1901.

————. *Empiriomonism: Articles on Philosophy* [Empiriomonizm: stat'i po filosofii]. 3 vols. Moscow: N.p., 1904–7.

————. *Essays in Tektology: The Universal Organizational Science.* Trans. George Gorelik. Seaside, Calif.: InterSystems, 1980.

————. "Ideal poznaniya" *Voprosy Filosofi i Psikhologii.* kn. II. Moscow: N.p., 1913.

————. *Novyi mir.* Moscow: Stat'i, 1905.

————. *The Philosophy of Living Experience* [Filosofiia zhivogo optya]. Moscow: N.p., 1920.

————. *Red Star: The First Bolshevik Utopia.* Ed. L.R. Graham and R. Stites. Trans. Charles Rougle. Bloomington: Indiana Univ. Press, 1984.

————. *Revolution and Philosophy* [Izpsikhologii obshchestra]. Trans. from Russian. St. Petersburg: N.p., 1906.

————. *A Short Course of Economic Science* [Kratkij jurs ekonomicheskoj nauka]. Trans. from the Russian by J. Fineberg. London: The Labour Publishing Company, 1923.

————. *Sotsializm nauki: Nauchnye zadachi proletariata.* Moscow: N.p., 1918.

————. *Tektology: The Universal Science of Organization* [Tektologiia: vseobshchaia organizatsionnaia nauke]. 3 vols. Moscow: N.p., 1925–28.

Böhm-Bawerk, Eugen von. *Capital und Capitalzins.* 2 vols. Innsbruck: Wagner, 1900–02.

————. *Capital and Interest: a Critical History of Economical Theory.* Trans. William Smart. London: Macmillan & Co., 1890.

Bolin, B., and Cook, R., eds. *The Major Biogeochemical Cycles and Their Interaction.* SCOPE 21. New York: John Wiley & Sons, 1983.

Bolin, B., and McElroy, M. "Biogeochemical Cycles." In *Global Change: Proceedings of 1st ICSU Multidisciplinary Symposium.* Ottawa. September. Paris: International Council of Scientific Union, 1984.

Boltzmann, Ludwig. *Der zweite Hauptsatz der mechanischen Wärmtheorie.* Vienna: Gerold, 1886.

————. *Theoretical Physics and Philosophical Problems.* Ed. B. McGuinness. Dordrecht: D. Reidel, 1974.

Bookchin, Murray. *Toward an Ecological Society.* Montreal: Black Rose Books, 1980.

Bottomore, T.B. *Karl Marx: Selected Writings in Sociology and Social Philosophy.* New York: McGraw-Hill, 1956.

Boulding, Kenneth E. "The application of pure theory of population change." *Quarterly Journal of Economics* (August 1934): 645–66.

————. *Beyond Economics.* Ann Arbor: Univ. of Michigan Press, 1970.

————. *Ecodynamics: A New Theory of Societal Evolution.* London: Sage View, 1978.

————. "The Economics of the Coming Spaceship Earth." In Boulding, *Beyond Economics.*

————. "Economics and Ecology." In Darling and Milton, eds., *Future Environments of North America.*

————. *Evolutionary Economics.* London: Sage View, 1981.

————. *History as Dialectics and Development.* New York: Free Press, 1970.

————. *The Organizational Revolution.* New York: Harper & Bros., 1953.

————. *A Primer on Social Dynamics.* New York: Free Press, 1970.

————. "The Universe as a General System." *Behavioral Science* 22 (1977):299–306.

Bowley, Sir Arthur Lyon. *F.Y. Edgeworth's Contributions to Mathematical Statistics.* Clifton, N.J.: A.M. Kelley, 1972.

Bridgeman, Percy Williams. *The Nature of Thermodynamics.* Cambridge: Harvard Univ. Press, 1941.

Brooks, H. "Discontinuities in the interaction of development and the environment." In Clark and Munn, eds., *Sustainable Development of the Biosphere.*

Brown, Douglas. "Karl Polanyi's Influence on the Budapest School." Transaction from Karl Polanyi Memorial Session. Karl Polanyi Commemorative Conference. October 27–29, 1986. Budapest: Hungarian Academy of Sciences, 1986.

Brunner, Karl. "The Perception of Man and the Conception of Society: Two Approaches to Understanding Society," *Economic Inquiry* 25 (July 1987): 367–88.

Brus, W. "Socialism Feasible and Viable?" *New Left Review* no. 153 (July/August 1985): 43–62.

Bukharin, Nikolai I. *Attack* [Ataka]. 2d ed. Moscow: N.p., 1924.

————. *Economic Theory of Leisure Class.* New York: International, 1927.

————. *Historical Materialism: a System of Sociology.* New York: International, 1925.

————. "Organized Mismanagement in Modern Society." Trans. from the Russian by Valerie Rosen. In Howe, ed., *Essential Works of Socialism.* [Originally published in 1929.]

Bunge, Mario. "Technoethics." In Kranzberg, ed., *Ethics in an Age of Pervasive Technology.*

Burris, Beverly H. "Technocracy and the Transformation of Organizational Control." *The Social Science Journal* 26, no. 3 (1989): 313–33.

Cameron, Gordon C., ed. *Resources for the Future.* Baltimore: Johns Hopkins Press , 1970.

Campbell, Lewis, and Garnett, William. *The Life of James Clerk Maxwell: with a Selection from his Correspondence and Occasional Writings and a Sketch of his Contributions to Science.* London: Macmillan & Co., 1882.

Cannon, Walter B. *The Wisdom of the Body.* New York: W.W. Norton, 1950.

Carey, Henry C. *Principles of Social Science.* Philadelphia: Lippencott, 1858.

Carnot, Sadi N. L. *Memoir on the Motive Power of Heat.* Ed. B.P.E. Clapeyron. New York: Dover, 1960.

Carver, Terrel. "Marx, Engels and Scholarship." *Political Studies* 32 (1984): 249–56.

Carver, Thomas Nixon. *The Distribution of Wealth*. New York: Macmillan, 1904.

———. *The Economy of Human Energy*. New York: Macmillan, 1924.

Cassirer, Ernst. *An Essay on Man*. New Haven, Conn.: Yale Univ. Press, 1944.

Chadwick, Owen. *The Secularization of the European Mind in the Nineteenth Century*. Cambridge: Cambridge Univ. Press, 1975.

Chen, Huan-Chang. *The Economic Principles of Confucius and His School*. New York: Columbia Univ. Press, 1911.

Childe, Vere Gordon. *Piecing Together the Past*. London: Routledge and Kegan Paul, 1956.

———. *What Happened in History*? Harmondsworth, Eng.: Penguin Books, 1954.

Christensen, Paul. "The Materials-Energy Foundations of Classical Theory." In Costanza and Daly, eds., "Ecological Economics."

Clanchy, M.T. *From Memory to Written Record, England: 1066–1307*. Cambridge: Harvard Univ. Press, 1979.

Clark, Charles M.A. "Equilibrium for What? Reflections on Social Order in Economics." *Journal of Economic Issues* 23, no. 2 (March 1989):597–606.

Clark, J.M. "The Changing of Economic Responsibility." In J.M. Clark, ed., *Preface to Social Economics*. New York: A.M. Kelley, 1967.

Clark, Norman. "Some New Approaches to Evolutionary Economics." *Journal of Economic Sciences* 22, no. 2 (1988):511–31.

Clark, W.C., and Munn, R.E., eds. *Sustainable Development of the Biosphere*. Laxenburg, Austria: International Institute of Applied Systems Analysis (IIASA), 1985.

Clegg, Jerry S. *The Structure of Plato's Philosophy*. Lewisburg, Pa.: Bucknell Univ. Press, 1977.

Clerc, Nicolas-Gabreil Le. *Yu le Grande et Confucius*. Paris: Soissons, 1769.

Cleveland, Cutler J. "Biophysical Economics: Historical Perspective and Current Research Trends." In Costanza and Daly, eds., "Ecological Economics."

Cleveland, C.J.; Costanza, R.; Hall, C.A.S.; and Kaufmann, R. "Energy and the U.S. Economy: a Biophysical Perspective." *Science* 225 (1984): 890–97.

Coats, A.W. "Is There a 'Structure of Scientific Revolutions' in Economics?" *Kyklos* 22, no. 2 (1969).

Cohen, Stephen F. "Marxist Theory and Bolshevik Policy: the Case of Bukharin's Historical Materialism." *Political Science Quarterly* 85, no. 1 (1970): 40–60.

Cole, Charles Woolsey. *Colbert and a Century of French Mercantilism*. Hamden, Conn.: Archon Books, 1964.

Colp, Ralph. "The Contacts between Karl Marx and Charles Darwin." *Journal of the History of Ideas* 35 (1974): 332.

———. "The Myth of the Darwin-Marx Letter." *History of Political Economy* 14, no. 4 (1982): 461.

Commoner, Barry. *The Closing Circle: Nature, Man and Technology*. New York: Alfred Knopf, 1972.

———. *Ecology and Social Action*. Berkeley: Univ. of California, School of Forestry, 1973.

———. *Politics of Energy*. New York: Alfred Knopf, 1979.

———. *Poverty of Power: Energy and the Economic Crisis*. New York: Alfred Knopf, 1976.

Congdon, Lee. "The Sovereignty of Society: Polanyi in Vienna." Paper presented at the Karl Polanyi Commemorative Conference. October 27–29, 1986. Budapest: Hungarian Academy of Sciences, 1986.

Cook, Earl F. *Man, Energy, Society*. San Francisco: W.H. Freeman, 1976.

Copleston, Frederick C. *Philosophy in Russia: From Herzen to Lenin and Berdyaev*. Paris: Univ. of Notre Dame, Search Press, 1986.

Corsson, P. "Patterns in agricultural development." In Clark and Munn, eds., *Sustainable Development of the Biosphere*.

Costanza, Robert. "Embodied Energy and Economic Valuation." *Science* 210 (December 12, 1980): 1219–24.

———. "Embodied Energy, Energy Analysis, and Economics." In Daly and Umaña, eds., *Energy, Economics and the Environment*.

Costanza, Robert, and Daly, Herman, eds. "Ecological Economics." Special issue of the review *Ecological Modelling* 38 (1987).

Cottrell, Fred. *Energy and Society: the Relation between Energy, Social Change and Economic Development*. New York: McGraw-Hill, 1953.

———. *Technology, Man and Progress*. Columbus, Ohio: Merrill, 1972.

Cruickshank, A.D. "Soddy at Oxford." *The British Journal for History of Science* 12, no. 42 (1979):277–88.

Crump, Thomas. *The Phenomenon of Money*. London/Boston: Routledge and Kegan Paul, 1981.

Crutzen, P., and Graedel, T. "The Impact of Human Activities on the Chemistry of the Atmosphere." In Clark and Munn, eds., *Sustainable Development of the Biosphere*.

Daire, Eugene. *Physiocrates: Quesnay, Dupont de Nemours, Mercier de la Rivere*. Paris: Guillaumin, 1846.

Dalton, George. "A Note of Clarification on Economic Surplus." *American Anthropologist* 62 (1960):483–90.

———, ed. *Primitive, Archaic, and Modern Economies: Essays of Karl Polanyi*. Boston: Beacon Press, 1971.

Daly, Herman E. "The Circular Flow of Exchange Value and the Linear Throughput of Matter-Energy: a Case of Misplaced Concreteness." *Review of Social Economy* 43, no. 3 (December 1985): 270–97.

———. "Growth Economics and the Fallacy of Misplaced Concreteness." *American Behavioral Scientist* 24, no. 1 (September/October 1980): 79–105.

———. "Myths about Energy and Matter: Comment." *Growth and Change* 10, no. 1 (January 1979): 24–25.

———. "On Economics as a Life Science." *Journal of Political Economy* 76 (May/June 1968): 392–406.

———. *Steady State Economics*. San Francisco: W.H. Freeman, 1977.

———. *Toward a Steady-State Economy*. San Francisco: W.H. Freeman, 1973.

———, ed. *Economics, Ecology, and Ethics: Essays Toward a Steady-State*. San Francisco: W.H. Freeman, 1980.

Daly, H.E., and Umaña, A.F. "Toward a Biophysical Foundation for Economics." In Daly and Umaña, eds., *Energy, Economics and the Environment*.

———, eds. *Energy, Economics and the Environment*. Boulder, Colo.: Westview, 1981.

Darling, F. Frazer, and Milton, J.P., eds. *Future Environments of North America*. Garden City, N.Y.: Natural History Press, 1966.

Darwin, Charles Robert. *On the Origin of the Species*. Cambridge: Harvard Univ. Press, 1964.

Davidson, Julius, ed. "One of the Physical Foundations of Economics." *Quarterly Journal of Economics* 33 (1919):717–24. [Translation of "Lehrbuck der allgemeinen Chemie," vol 2., by W. Ostwald (1892).]

Debenjak, Bozidar. "Engels and the Problem of Alienation." *Social Praxis* 3, no. 1–2 (1975): 45–62.

DeGregori, Thomas R. *A Theory of Technocracy*. Ames, Iowa: State Press, 1985.

Descartes, René. *Discourse on Method and the Meditations of Descartes*. Trans. F.E. Sutcliffe. Harmondsworth: Penguin Books, 1968.

Dewey, John. *Liberalism and Social Action.* New York: Capricorn Books, 1963.

Dick, H.G., ed. *Selected Writings of Francis Bacon.* New York: Modern Library, 1955.

Dickinson, R.E. "The Impact of Human Activities on Climate." In Clark and Munn, eds., *Sustainable Development of the Biosphere.*

Diderot, D. *D'Alembert's Dream.* Harmondsworth, England: Penguin Books, 1976.

Dijksterhuis, E.J. *The Mechanization of the World Picture.* New York: Oxford Univ. Press, 1961.

Dobuzinskis, Laurent. "Autopoiesis in Nature and Politics: Some Reflections on the Epistemology of the New Cybernetics." Research Memorandum. Toronto, Ontario: Economic Research and Systems Planning Group, York Univ. Press, April 28, 1980.

Dodson, Edward O. *Phenomenon of Man Revisited: a Biological Viewpoint on Teil de Chardin.* New York: Columbia Univ. Press, 1984.

Dubos, René. "Man and the Man-Made." In Kranzberg, ed., *Ethics in an Age of Pervasive Technology.*

———. *So Human an Animal.* New York: Scribners, 1968.

Dufour, T., ed. *Correspondence Generale de J.-J. Rousseau.* 20 vols. Paris: A. Colin, 1924–34.

DuHalde, Jean Baptiste. *Description de l'Empire de la Chine et de la Tartarie chinoise.* 4 vols. Paris: N.p., 1735.

Dumont, Louis. *From Mandeville to Marx: the Genesis and Triumph of Economic Thought.* Chicago: Univ. of Chicago, 1977.

Dupont de Nemours. *Physiocrats.* Paris: N.p., 1786.

Economic Commission for Europe. "Economic Bulletin for Europe." *United Nations Economic Commission for Europe* 34 (March 1982): 34–37.

The Economist. "Can the air absolve man's sin of emmission?" 304, no.7516 (September 1987):89–90.

Eddington, Sir Arthur Stanley. *The Expanding Universe.* Ann Arbor: Univ. of Michigan, 1958.

———. *The Nature of the Physical World.* Ann Arbor: Univ. of Michigan, 1958.

Edel, Matthew. *Economics and the Environment.* Englewood Cliffs, N.J.: Prentice-Hall, 1973.

Edgeworth, Francis Ysidro. *Mathematical Psychics: an Essay on the Application of Mathematics to the Moral Sciences.* New York: A.M. Kelley, 1967.

Ehrlich, Paul R., and Raven, P.H. "Butterflies and Plants: a Study of Coevolution." *Evolution* 18 (1964): 586–608.

Elgin, D. *The Evolution of Consciousness and the Transformation of Society.* Report. Menlo Park, Calif.: Stanford Research Institute, 1974.

Ellul, Jacques. *Technological Society.* Trans. from the French by John Wilkinson. New York: Alfred Knopf, 1964.

Engels, Frederick. *Dialectics of Nature.* Trans. from the German by Clemens Dutt. 2d rev. ed. Moscow: Progress, 1954. [Originally published in 1934.]

———. *Herr Eugen Dühring's Revolution in Science* [*Anti-Dühring*]. Ed. C.P. Dutt and Trans. Emile Burns. New York: International, 1966. [Originally published in 1878.]

———. *The Origin of the Family, Private Property, and the State.* Ed. L.H. Morgan. New York: Pathfinder, 1972.

Epstein, Joel J. *Francis Bacon: a Political Biography.* Athens: Ohio Univ. Press, 1977.

Everitt, C.W. Francis. *James Clerk Maxwell: Physicist and Natural Philosopher.* New York: Scribner, 1975.

Fay, Margaret A. "Did Marx offer to Dedicate Capital to Darwin?" *Journal of the History of Ideas* 39 (January–March 1978): 140.

Ferguson. *An Essay on the History of Civil Society.* N.p., 1767.

Ferkiss, Victor C. "Ecological Humanism and Planetary Society." *The Humanist* 34, no. 3 (May/June 1974):24–27.

Findlay, John Niemeyer. *Plato and Platonism*. New York: Times Books, 1978.

Fisher, I. *The Nature of Capital and Income*. New York: A.M. Kelley, 1965.

Fisher, I., and Peterson, K. "The Environment in Economics: A Survey." *Journal of Economic Literature* (March 1976): 1–33.

Fleck, Alexander. "Frederick Soddy." *Biographical Memoirs of Fellows of the Royal Society* 3 (1957): 203–16.

Fleischer, Richard, ed. "The World Economy in Light of Physics" [Die Weltwirtschaft im Liche der Physik]. *Deutsche Revue* 22, no. 2 (April–June 1902): 29–38.

Florinsky, Michael T., ed. *Encyclopedia of Russia and the Soviet Union*. Toronto: McGraw Hill, 1961.

Foerster, H.M. von. "On Self-Organizing Systems and their Environment." In *Self-Organizing Systems*. New York: Pergamon, 1960.

Foerster, H.M. von; Park, R.A.; and Zopf, G., eds. *Principles of Self-Organization*. New York: Symposium Publications Division, Pergamon, 1962.

Foner, Philip Sheldon. *When Karl Marx Died*. New York: International, 1973.

Ford, Stephen H. *Imagination and Thought in Descartes*. N.p., 1977.

Forrester, Jay W. "Business Structure, Economic Cycles and National Policy." *Futures* (June 1976).

———. "Industrial Dynamics: A Major Breakthrough for Decision Makers." In Roberts, ed., *Managerial Applications of System Dynamics*.

Fosse, Peter J. de la, and Routh, G., eds. *Economics in Disarray*. Oxford/New York: B. Blackwell, 1984.

Fox-Genovese, Elizabeth. *Origins of Physiocracy: Economic Revolution and Social Order in Eighteenth-Century France*. Ithaca, N.Y.: Cornell Univ. Press, 1976.

Friedman, Milton, and Friedman, Rose. *Free to Choose*. New York: Harcourt Brace Jovanovich, 1979.

Frolov, Ivan T. "The Global Peace Strategy and Nature Conservation." In Behar, et al., eds., *Ecoforum for Peace*.

———. *Man Science Humanism: a New Synthesis*. Moscow: Progress, 1986.

———. "Modern Science and Humanism" [Sovremennaya Nauka i Gumanizm]. *Voprosy-filosofii* 27, 3 (March 1973): 3–15.

———, ed. *Society and the Environment*. Moscow: Progress, 1980.

Fromm, Erich. *Anatomy of Human Destructiveness*. Greenwich, Conn.: Fawcett, 1973.

———. *The Forgotten Language*. New York: Grove, 1951.

———. *Marx's Concept of Man*. New York: Fawcett Premier, 1961.

———. *The Sane Society*. New York: Ballantine Books, 1955.

———, ed. *Socialist Humanism*. Garden City, N.Y.: Doubleday, 1965.

Futuyama, Douglas J., and Slatkin, Montgomery, eds. *Coevolution*. With the assistance of B.R. Levin and J. Roughgarden. Sunderland, Mass.: Sinauer Associates, 1983.

Fyodorov, N.F. *The Philosophy of the Common Task* [Filosofiya obschechevo dela]. USSR: Harbin, 1930.

Galbraith, John Kenneth. *The Anatomy of Power*. Boston: Houghton Mifflin, 1983.

———. "Dialogues on Civilization between Boulding and Galbraith." *Mainichi Daily News* [Tokyo] (October 1, 1975):1.

———. *Economics in Perspective*. Boston, Mass.: Houghton Mifflin, 1987.

———. *The New Industrial State*. New York: New American Library, 1968.

Galbraith, John K., and Menshikov, Stanislav. *Capitalism, Communism and Coexistence: From a Bitter Past to a Better Prospect*. Boston: Houghton Mifflin, 1988.

Gantt, W. Horsley, ed. *Lectures on Conditioned Reflexes: Twenty-five Years of Objective*

Study of the Higher Nervous Activity (behavior) of Animals. New York: International, 1928.

Garelik, Glenn. "A Breath of Fresh Air." *Time* 130, no. 13 (September 28, 1987): 21.

Gatlin, Lila L. "Conservation of Shannon's Redundancy for Proteins." *Journal of Molecular Evolution* 3 (1974): 189–208.

———. *Information Theory and the Living System.* New York: Columbia Univ. Press, 1972.

Geddes, Patrick. *An Analysis of the Principles of Economics.* London: Williams and Norgate, 1884.

———. *John Ruskin, Economist.* Edinburgh: W. Brown, 1884.

Georgescu-Roegen, Nicholas. *Analytical Economics: Issues and Problems.* Cambridge: Harvard Univ. Press, 1966.

———. *Energy and Economic Myths: Institutional and Analytical Economic Essays.* New York/Toronto: Pergamon, 1976.

———. *The Entropy Law and the Economic Process.* Cambridge: Harvard Univ. Press, 1971.

———. *Evolution, Welfare, and Time in Economics: Essays in Honor.* Lexington, Mass.: Lexington Books, 1976.

———. "Inequality, Limits and Growth from a Bioeconomic Viewpoint." *Review of Social Economy* 35 (December 1977).

———. "The Steady State and Ecological Salvation: A Thermodynamic Analysis." *Bioscience* 27 (April 1977):266–70.

Gerasimov, I.P. *Man, Society and Environment.* Moscow: Progress, 1975.

Geymonat, Ludovico. "Neopositivist Methodology and Dialectical Materialism." *Science & Society* 37, no. 2 (Summer 1973):178–94.

Gilliland, Martha W. "Energy Analysis and Public Policy." *Science* 189 (September 26, 1975): 1051–56.

———, ed. *Energy Analysis: A New Public Policy Tool.* AAAS Selected Symposium Series 9. Boulder, Colo.: Westview, 1978.

Glansdorff, P., and Prigogine, Ilya. *Thermodynamic Theory of Structure, Stability, and Fluctuations.* New York: Wiley Interscience, 1971.

Godelier, Maurice. *Rationality and Irrationality in Economics.* Trans. from the French by Brian Pearce. New York: Monthly Review Press, 1973.

———. "Systems, Structure and Contradiction in *Das Kapital*." In Lane, ed., *Introduction to Structuralism.*

Gödel, Kurt. *On the Formally Undecidable Propositions in Principia Mathematica and Related Systems I.* Three vols. N.p., 1931.

Goldfrank, W.L. "Fascism and the Great Transformation." Paper presented at the Karl Polanyi Commemorative Conference. October 27–29, 1986. Budapest: Hungarian Academy of Sciences, 1986.

Goodwin, Richard M. "Oral Comments on *Theory of the Long Wave*." In G. Bianchi, et al., eds., *Long Waves, Depression and Innovation: Implications for National and Regional Economic Policy*, Proceedings of the Sienna/Florence Meeting. October 26–30, 1983. Laxenburg, Austria: IIASA, 1983.

Gorbachev, Mikhail. *Perestroika.* New York: Harper and Row, 1987.

Gorelik, George. "Bogdanov's Tektology: Its Nature, Development and Influence." *Studies in Soviet Thought* 26 (1983): 39–47.

———. "Principal Ideas of Bogdanov's 'Tektology', The Universal Science of Organization." *General Systems* 20 (1975): 3–13.

———. "Reemergence of Bogdanov's Tektology in Soviet Studies of Organization." *Academy of Management Journal* 18, no. 2 (June 1975):345–57.

Gorz, André. *Critique of Economic Reason*. London: Verso, 1989.

————. *Ecology as Politics* [Écologie et Politique]. Trans. Jonathan Cloud and Patsy Vigderman. Montreal: Black Rose Books, 1980.

Graham, Loren R., and Stites, Richard, eds. *Red Star: The First Bolshevik Utopia*. Trans. Charles Rougle. Bloomington: Indiana Univ. Press, 1984.

Gray, Andrew. *The Development of Economic Doctrine*. London: Longmans Green, 1948.

————. *Lord Kelvin: an Account of his Scientific Life and Work*. London: J.M. Dent, 1908.

Gray, William, and Rizzo, Nicholas D., eds. *Unity Through Diversity: A Festschrift for Ludwig von Bertalanffy*. Part I. New York: N.p., 1973.

Grenon, Michel. *Ce monde affamé d'énergie*. Rev. ed. Paris: Laffont, 1973.

————, ed. *Conference on Energy Resources*. First IIASA Conference on Energy Resources. Laxenburg, Austria: IIASA, 1975.

Grenon, M., and Lapillonne, B. *The WELMM Approach to Energy Strategies and Options*. #RR–76–19. Laxenburg, Austria: IIASA, 1976.

Groh, Dieter, and Sieferle, Rolf-Peter. "Experience of Nature in Bourgeois Society and Economic Theory: Outlines of an Interdisciplinary Research Project." *Social Research* (1980).

Grove, William Robert. *Correlation of Physical Forces*. London: N.p., 1855.

Gruber, H.E. "Darwin and *Das Kapital*." *ISiS* 52 (1961).

Gudeman, Stephen. *Economics as Culture*. London: Routledge and Kegan Paul, 1986.

————. "Physiocracy: a Natural Economics." *American Ethnologist* 7 (1980): 240–58.

Gutern, Gottlieb. "Auto-organization in Human Systems." *Behavioral Science* 27 (1982): 328.

Haavelmo, T. *A Study in the Theory of Economic Evolution*. Amsterdam: North-Holland, 1954.

Habermas, Jürgen. *Legitimation Crisis*. Trans. Thomas C. McCarthy. Boston: Beacon Press, 1975. [Originally published under the title *Legitimationsprobleme im Spätkapitalismus* in 1973.]

————. "The Place of Philosophy in Marxism." *Insurgent Sociologist* 5, no. 2 (Winter 1975): 41–48.

————. *Toward a Rational Society*. Trans. J.J. Shapiro. Boston: Beacon Press, 1970.

Haeckel, Ernst Heinrich Philipp August. "Our Monist: the Principles of a Consistent Unitary World View." *The Monist* 2, no. 4 (1892).

————. *The Riddle of the Universe at the Close of the Nineteenth Century*. Trans. Joseph McCabe. Grosse Pointe, Mich.: Scholarly Press, 1968.

Hahn, Roger. "Laplace as a Newtonian Scientist." A paper delivered at a seminar. Los Angeles: Univ. of California, William Andrews Clark Memorial Library, 1967.

Haken, Herman. *Synergetics: an Introduction*. 2d ed. New York: Berlin-Heidelberg, 1978.

————. "Synergetics: Is Self-Organisation Governed by Universal Principles?" In Jantsch, ed., *The Evolutionary Vision*.

Hall, C.A.S., and Day, J.W., eds. *Ecosystem Modeling in Theory and Practice*. New York: John Wiley & Sons, 1977.

Hall, C.A.S.; Cleveland, C.J.; and Kaufmann, R. *Energy and Resource Quality: The Ecology of the Economic Process*. New York: Wiley-Interscience, 1986.

Hamilton, Walton. *The Politics of Industry*. New York: Alfred Knopf, n.d.

Harris, M. "The Economy Has No Surplus." *American Anthroplogist* 61 (1959):185–99.

Harvey, William. *The Circulation of the Blood: and other Writings*. Trans. Kenneth J. Franklin. London: Dent; New York: Dutton, 1963. [Originally published in 1658.]

Hatfield, Mark. "Net Energy." *U.S. Congressional Record* 120, part 5, no. 11 (March 1974): 6053–76.

Hayek, Friedrich A. von. *The Counter Revolution of Science: Studies on the Abuse of Reason.* Glencoe, Ill.: Free Press, 1952.

———. "Laws, Legislation and Liberty." In *Rules and Order.* Vol. 1. Chicago: Univ. of Chicago Press, 1973.

———. *The Road to Serfdom.* Chicago: Univ. of Chicago, 1944.

———. *Studies in Philosophy, Politics and Economics.* Ed. F.A. Hay. Chicago: Univ. of Chicago Press, 1967.

Hecker, Julius F. *Russian Sociology: A Contribution to the History of Sociological Thought and Theory.* New York: Columbia Univ. Press, 1915.

Heckscher, Eli Filip. *Mercantilism.* Authorized translation by Mendel Shapiro. London: Allen & Unwin, 1935.

Hegel, Georg W. F. *The Phenomenology of the Mind.* Trans. U.B. Baille. New York: Harper & Row, 1967.

———. *The Philosophy of History.* Trans. J. Sibree, with an introduction by Prof. C.J. Friedrich. New York: Dover, 1956. [Original translation published by Colonial Press in 1899.]

Heilbroner, Robert L. *Behind the Veil of Economics: Essays in the Worldly Philosophy.* New York: W.W. Norton, 1988.

———. *Between Capitalism and Socialism: Essays in Political Economics.* New York: Random House, 1970.

———. "The Paradox of Progress: Decline and Decay in the Wealth of Nations." *Journal of the History of Ideas* (April–June 1973): 243–62.

———. "The Problem of Value in the Constitution of Economic Thought." *Social Research* 50, no. 2 (1983): 258.

Helm, George Ferdinand. *Die Lehre von der Energie.* Leipzig: Veit, 1887.

Henderson, Fred. *The Economic Consequences of Power Production.* London: George Allen and Unwin, 1931.

Henderson, Hazel. *The Politics of the Solar Age: Alternatives to Economics.* New York: Doubleday, 1981.

Henderson, J.M., and Quandt, R.E. *Microeconomic Theory.* 2d ed. Economics Handbook Series. Toronto: McGraw-Hill, 1971.

Herz, John H. "The Survival Problem." In Kranzberg, ed., *Ethics in an Age of Pervasive Technology.*

Hilferding, Rudolf. *Finance Capital: a Study of the Latest Phase of Capitalism.* London: Routledge and Kegan Paul, 1981.

———. "State Capitalism or Totalitarian State." In Howe, ed., *Essential Works of Socialism.*

———, ed. *Criticism of Marx.* Clifton, N.J.: A.M. Kelley, 1975.

Hilferding, Rudolf, and von Bortkiewicz, Ladislaus, eds. *Karl Marx and the Close of His System.* New York: A.M. Kelley, 1966.

Hill, Christopher. *The Intellectual Origins of the Industrial Revolution.* New York: Oxford Univ. Press, 1965.

Hirsch, Fred. *The Social Limits to Growth.* N.p., 1983.

Hisbin, John Grier. "The Theory of Energetics and Its Philosophical Bearings." *The Monist* 13, no. 3 (1903).

Hobbes, Thomas. *Behemoth.* London: Cass, 1969.

———. *Elements of Law, Natural and Political.* London: Cass, 1969.

———. *Leviathan, or the Matter, Form and Power of a Commonwealth.* Ed. C.B. Macpherson. Harmondsworth: Penguin Books, 1968. [Originally published in 1651.]

Hobson, John A. *Imperialism: a Study.* London: J. Nisbet, 1902.

Hofstadter, Douglas R. *Gödel, Escher, Bach: an Eternal Golden Braid.* New York: Basic Books, 1979.

Hollander, Samuel. *The Economics of David Ricardo*. Toronto: Univ. of Toronto Press, 1979.

———. "Ricardo's Analysis of the Profit Rate, 1813–15." *Economica* 42 (1975): 188–202.

Holling, C.S. "Resilience and Stability of Ecological Systems." *Annual Review of Ecological Systems* 4 (1973): 23.

———. "Resilience and Stability in Ecosystems." In Jantsch and Waddington, eds., *Evolution and Consciousness*.

———, ed. *The Anatomy of Surprise*. N.p., 1985.

Holling, C.S., and Timmerman, P. "Vulnerability, resilience and surprise in natural systems." In Clark and Munn, eds., *Sustainable Development of the Biosphere*.

Holt, T.; Kelly, P.M.; and Cherry, B.G. "Cyrospheric impacts of Soviety river diversion schemes." *Annals Glaciol* no. 5 (1984).

Hook, Sidney. *From Hegel to Marx: Studies in the Intellectual Development of Karl Marx*. Ann Arbor: Univ. of Michigan Press, 1950.

Horkheimer, Max. *Eclipse of Reason*. New York: Seabury, 1974.

Horkheimer, Max, and Adorno, Theodor. *The Dialectic of the Enlightenment*. New York: Seabury, 1972.

Howe, Irving, ed. *Essential Works of Socialism*. 3d ed. New Haven: Yale Univ. Press, 1986.

Hubbert, M.K. "Man's Conquest of Energy: Its Ecological and Human Implications." In Darling and Milton, eds., *Future Environments of North America*.

Hubenka, J. Lloyd, ed. *Four Essays on the First Principles of Political Economy*. Lincoln: Univ. of Nebraska Press, 1967.

Huettner, David A. "Net Energy Analysis: An Economic Assessment." *Science* 192 (April 9, 1976): 101–4.

Hume, David. *Dialogues Concerning Natural Religion*. Ed. N.K. Smith. Indianapolis: Bobbs-Merrill, 1970.

Hunt, E.K. "The Importance of Veblen for Contemporary Marxists." *Journal of Economic Issues* 13 (March 1979): 116–235.

Hutchinson, T.W. *On Revolutions and Progress of Economic Knowledge*. New York: Cambridge Univ. Press, 1978.

Hutten, E.H. *Information, Explanation and Meaning*. Rome: Ermando, 1975.

Illich, Ivan. *Shadow Work*. London: Marion Boyars, 1981.

———. *Tools for Conviviality*. New York: Harper & Row, 1973.

Immler, Hans. *Natur in der Ökonomischen Theorie*. Opladen, Federal Republic of Germany: Westdeutscher Verlag, 1985.

International Journal of General Systems 5, no. 1 (1979): 63–71.

Ivanovsky, V.I. "Chto takoe 'positivizm' i 'idealizm'." *Pravda* (March 1904).

Izrael, Y., and Munn, R.E. "A strategy for monitoring environment-development interactions." In Clark and Munn, eds., *Sustainable Development of the Biosphere*.

Jacob, François. *The Logic of Life: a History of Heredity*. New York: Vintage Books, 1976.

———. *La Logique du Vivant*. Paris: Gillimand, 1970.

Jantsch, Erich. *Technological Planning and Social Futures*. New York: Halsted, 1972.

———. "The Unifying Paradigm behind Autopoiesis, Dissipative Structures, Hyper- and Ultracycles." In Zeleny, ed., *Autopoiesis, Dissipative Structures and Spontaneous Social Orders*.

———. "Unifying Principles of Evolution." In Jantsch, ed., *The Evolutionary Vision*.

———, ed. *The Evolutionary Vision: Toward a Unifying Paradigm of Physical, Biological, and Sociocultural Evolution*. Boulder, Colo.: Westview, 1981.

Jantsch, E., and Waddington, C.H., eds. *Evolution and Consciousness: Human Systems in Transition*. Toronto: Addison-Wesley, 1976.

The Japan Times. "East Germany plans to have convertible currency; scrap all price controls by 1993." (February 4, 1980):8.

Jarret, H., ed. *Environmental Quality in a Growing Economy.* Baltimore: Johns Hopkins Univ. Press, 1966.

Jensen, K.M. *Beyond Marx and Mach: Alexander Bogdanov's Philosophy of Living Experience.* Boston: D. Reidel, 1978.

Jensen, Otto. *Marxismus und Naturwissenschaft: Gedenkschrifts zum 30. Todestage des Naturwissenschaftlers Friedrich Engels, mit Beitra, gen von F. Engels, Gustav Echstein und Friedrich Adler.* Berlin: Verlagess, des Allegemeinen Deutschen Gewerschaftbundes, 1925.

Jevons, W. S. *Coal Question: An Inquiry Concerning the Progress of the Nations.* Ed. A.W. Flux. New York: A.M. Kelley, 1965. [Originally published in 1865.]

―――. *Lectures on Political Economy.* Ed. R.D. Collison Black. London: Macmillan & Co., 1977.

―――. *The Theory of Political Economy.* Ed. R.D. Collison Black. 6th ed. Baltimore: Penguin, 1970. [Originally published in 1871.]

Jonas, Hans. "The Heuristics of Fear." In Kranzberg, ed., *Ethics in an Age of Pervasive Technology.*

Jones, Alwyn. "The Violence of Materialism in Advanced Industrial Society: an Ecosociological approach." *The Sociological Review* 35, no. 1 (1987): 19.

Joravsky, David. *Soviet Marxism and Natural Science: 1917–1932.* New York: Columbia Univ. Press, 1961.

Jordan, Zbigniew A. *The Evolution of Dialectical Materialism.* New York: St. Martin's, 1967.

Kagarlistsky, Boris. "Perestroika: The Dialectic of Change." *New Left Review* no. 169 (May/June 1988): 5–26, 69, 80–83.

Kamarýt, Jan. "From Science to Metascience and Philosophy: Dialectical Perspectives in the Development of Ludwig von Bertalanffy's Theoretical Work." In Gray and Rizzo, eds., *Unity Through Diversity: A Festschrift for Ludwig von Bertalanffy.*

Kamenka, Eugene. *The Philosophy of Ludwig Feuerbach.* New York: N.p., 1970.

Kamshilov, Mikhail Mikhailovich. *Evolution of the Biosphere.* Trans. from the Russian by Minna Brodskaya. Moscow: Mir, 1976.

Kant, Immanuel. *Immanuel Kant's Critique of Pure Reason.* Trans. Norman Kemp Smith. Unabridged ed. New York: St. Martin's, 1929.

Kaplan, Morton. *System and Process in Internâtional Politics.* New York: John Wiley & Sons, 1957.

Kapp, K.W. *The Social Costs of Private Enterprise.* N.p., 1963.

Karsten, Siegfried G. "Book Review." *History of Political Economy* 18, no. 3 (1986):531–33.

―――. "Dialectics and the Evolution of Economic Thought." *History of Political Economy* 12 (1971): 2.

―――. "Nature in Economic Theories: Hans Immler Traces Recognition of the Environment—and its Neglect—in Various Classics." *American Journal of Economics and Sociology* 46, no. 1 (January 1987): 61–70.

Kaufmann, George B., ed. *Frederick Soddy (1877–1956): Early Pioneer in Radiochemistry.* Dordrecht, Holland/Boston: D Reidel, 1986.

Kaufmann, R. "Biophysical and Marxist Economics: Learning from Each Other." In Costanza and Daly, eds., "Ecological Economics."

Kautsky, K. "Ein Brief über Marx und Mach." *Der Kampf* no. 10 (1909).

Kawamiya, Nobuo. "Analysis of Technological Progress, Resource Substitution and the

Environment in their Mutual Interaction: an Entropy Theoretical Approach." Working Paper. Nagoya, Japan: Department of Iron and Steel Engineering, Faculty of Engineering, Nagoya Univ. Press, January 24, 1985.

Kern, William. "Returning to the Aristotelian Paradigm." *History of Political Economy* 15, no. 4 (1983): 501–12.

Keynes, J.M. *The Economic Consequences of the Peace.* New York: Harcourt, Brace and Howe, 1920.

Klaus, Georg. *Cybernetics as Viewed by Philosophy* [Kybernetik in Philosophischer Sicht]. Berlin: Dietz Verlag, 1965.

Kline, G.L. "Bogdanov, Alexandr Aleksandrovich." In *The Encyclopedia of Philosophy.* New York: Macmillan, 1967.

Kline, Morris. *Mathematics and the Search for Knowledge.* New York: Oxford Univ. Press, 1985.

Knight, Frank H. "Review of *Wealth, Virtual Wealth and Debt.*" *Saturday Review of Literature* (April 16, 1927): 732.

Koenig, Herman E. "Human Ecosystem Design and Management." In Patten, ed., *Systems Analysis and Simulation in Ecology.*

Koenig, Herman E.; Cooper, W.E.; and Falvey, J.M. "Engineering for Ecological, Sociological and Economic Compatibility." *IEEE Transactions on Systems, Man, and Cybernetics* SMC–2, no. 3 (July 1972): 319–447.

Kondratiev, N.D. "Die Länge Wellen der Konjunktur." *Archiv für Sozialwissenschaft und Sozialpolitik* 56 (1926): 573–609.

Konstantinov, F.V. *The Fundamentals of Marxist-Leninist Philosophy.* Trans. R. Daglish. Moscow: N.p., 1982.

Koolhaas, Jan. *Organization, Dissonance and Change.* Toronto: John Wiley & Sons, 1982.

Koyre, Alexandre. *Galileo Studies.* Trans. from the French by John Mepham. Hassocks, England: Harvester, 1978.

Kranzberg, Melvin, ed. *Ethics in an Age of Pervasive Technology.* Boulder, Colo.: Westview, 1980.

Krivomazov, A.N. "The Reception of Soddy's Works in the U.S.S.R.." In Kaufmann, ed., *Frederick Soddy.*

Kropotkin, Peter. *Fields, Factories, and Workshops Tomorrow.* Ed. Colin Ward. New York: Harper & Row, 1987.

Kuhn, Thomas S. *The Structure of Scientific Revolutions.* 2d ed. Chicago: Univ. of Chicago Press, 1966.

Kupperman, Robert H. "The Threat of Technologies to Life." Unpublished paper, International Symposium on the Coevolution of Man and the Biosphere. Helsinki, Finland, September 7, 1983.

Laborit, Henri. *La Nouvelle Grille.* Paris: R. Laffont, 1974.

———. "Societé Informationnelle." *CERF* (1973).

Lakshmanan, T.R., and Nijkamp, P., eds. *Economic-Environmental-Energy Interactions: Modeling and Policy Analysis.* The Hague: Martinus Nijhoff, 1980.

Lakshmanan, T.R., and Ratick, S. "Integrated Models for Economic-Energy-Environmental Impact Analysis." In Lakshmanan, and Nijkamp, eds., *Economic-Environmental-Energy Interactions.*

Landes, Richard D. *The Unbound Prometheus: Technological Change and Industrial Development in Western Europe from 1750 to the Present.* Cambridge: Cambridge Univ. Press, 1969.

Lane, M., ed. *Introduction to Structuralism.* New York: Basic Books, 1970.

Lange, Oskar. *Wholes and Parts: A General Theory of System Behaviour.* New York: Pergamon, 1965.

Laplace, Pierre Simon de. *Celestial Mechanics.* Trans. Nathaniel Bowditch. Bronx, N.Y.: Chelsea, 1966.

————. *A Treatise Upon Analytical Mechanics: Being the First Book of the Mechanique Celeste of M. Le Comte Laplace.* Trans. and elucidated with explanatory notes by the Rev. John Toplis. Nottingham: H. Barnett, 1814.

Laszlo, Erwin. *Evolution: The Grand Synthesis.* Boston: Shambhala, 1987.

————. *Introduction to Systems Philosophy: Toward a New Paradigm of Contemporary Thought.* New York: Gordon & Breach, Harper Torchbooks, 1972.

————. *A Strategy for the Future.* New York: George Braziller, 1974.

————. *The Systems View of the World: The Natural Philosophy of the New Developments in the Sciences.* New York: George Braziller, 1972.

Laszlo, E., and Bierman, J., eds. *Goals in a Global Community.* Vol. 1. New York: Pergamon, 1977.

Lavine, M.J.; Butler, T.J.; and Meyburg, A.H. *Toward Environmental Benefit/Cost Analysis: Energy Analysis.* Draft Final Report for the National Coop. Highway Res. Cornell University. Ithaca, N.Y: Cornell Univ. Press, 1978.

Lavróv, Peter. *Historical Letters.* Trans. James P. Scanlon. California: N.p., 1967.

Lee, Donald C. "On the Marxist View of the Relationship between Man and Nature." *Environmental Ethics* 2 (Spring 1980): 3–16.

Lefebvre, Henri. *Dialectical Materialism.* Trans. John Sturrock. London: Jonathan Cape, 1968.

Lenin, Vladimir Ilich. *Collected Works.* 47 vols. Moscow: Foreign Languages Publishing House, 1960–80.

————. *État et la révolution: la doctrine marxiste de l'État.* Paris: Éditions Sociales, 1969.

————. *Imperialism, the Highest Stage of Capitalism.* Moscow: Progress, 1982. [Originally published in 1917 under the title of *Imperialism, the Latest Stage of Capitalism. Popular Outline.* This translation taken from Vol. 22 of Lenin's *Collected Works.*]

————. *Marx-Engels-Marxism.* 3d ed. Moscow: Foreign Languages Publishing House, 1947.

————. "The Question of Dialectics." *Under the Banner of Marxism.* Vols. 5–6. N.p., 1925.

Leontief, Wasily W. *The Economic System in an Age of Discontinuity: Long-range Planning or Market Reliance?* Ed. H. Stein. New York: New York Univ. Press, 1976.

————. "Letter to the Editor." *Science* 217 (1982): 104.

Levine, Norman. "Marxism and Engelism: Two Differing Views of History." *Journal of the History of the Behavioral Sciences* 9 (July 1973): 217–39.

Levi-Strauss, Claude. "Anthropology, History and Ideology." *Critique of Anthropology.* Vol. 6, 1979:44–45.

Lewis, John; Polanyi, Karl; and Kitchen, Donald, eds. *Christianity and the Social Revolution.* New York: Charles Scribner's Sons, 1935.

Lewontin, R.C. "The Meaning of Stability: Diversity and Stability of Ecological Systems." *Ecology* 36 (1969): 533–36.

Li, Shaomin. "The Road to Freedom: Can Communist Societies Evolve into Democracy?" *World Affairs* 150, no. 3 (Winter 1987–88):183–89.

Liebig, Baron Justus von. *The Natural Laws of Husbandry.* Ed. J. Blyth. London: Walton & Marberly, 1859.

Liebknecht, Wilhelm. *Briefwechsel mit Karl Marx und Friedrich Engels.* Ed. G. Eckert. The Hague: Mouton, 1963.

Lilenfeld, Robert. *The Rise of Systems Theory.* Toronto: Wiley-Interscience, 1978.

Lindblom, Charles. *Politics and Markets.* New York: Basic Books, 1977.

Lipitskii, V.S. "Social Ecology and Communist Education" [Sotsial'naia ekologiia i kommunisticheskoe vospitanie]. *Filosofskie-Nauki* 18, no. 5 (1975): 33–39.

Lisichkin, G. "Myths and Reality: is Marx Necessary for *Perestroika*?" [Mify i real'nost; nuzhen li Marks perestroika?]. *Novyi Mir* 42, no. 11 (November 1989): 160–87.

Locke, John. *The Correspondence of John Locke*. Ed. E.S. de Beer. Oxford: Clarendon, 1976.

———. *An Essay Concerning Human Understanding*. New York: Dover, 1959.

———. *Philosophical Works*. Ed. J.A. St. John. London: G. Bell, 1875.

Locke, John; Berkeley, George; and Hume, David. *Empiricists: John Locke: An essay concerning human understanding*. Garden City, N.Y.: Anchor Books, 1974.

Lossky, N.U. *History of Russian Philosophy*. New York: International, 1951.

Lotka, Alfred J. "Biased Evolution." *Harpers Monthly Magazine* (May 1924): 755–66.

———. "Contribution to the Energetics of Evolution." *Proceedings of the National Academy of Science* 8 (1922): 147–54.

———. *Elements of Mathematical Biology. Elements of Physical Biology*. New York: Dover, 1956.

———. "Evolution and Thermodynamics." *Science and Society* 8, no. 2 (1944): 161–71.

———. "The Law of Evolution as a Maximal Principle." *Human Biology* 17, no. 3 (September 1945).

———. "Note on the Economic Conversion Factors of Energy." *Proceedings of the National Academy of Sciences* 7 (1921): 192–97.

———. "An Objective Standard of Value Derived from the Principle of Evolution." *Washington Academy of Sciences Journal* 4 (1914): 409, 447, 499–500.

Loucks, Daniel P. "Evolution of Diversity, Efficiency and Community Stability." *American Zoology* 10 (1970): 17–25.

Lovelock, J.E. *Gaia: a new look at life on earth*. Oxford/New York: Oxford Univ. Press, 1979.

Lowe, Adolphe. "Is Economic Value Still a Problem?" *Social Research* 48, no. 4 (1981):786–815.

Lowenthal, David, ed. *Man and Nature*. Cambridge: Belknap Press of Harvard Univ. Press, 1965.

Ludz, Peter C. "Marxism and Systems Theory in a Bureaucratic Society." *Social Research* 42, no. 4 (Winter 1975): 661–74.

Luhmann, Niklas. "Differentiation of Society." *Canadian Journal of Sociology* 2 (1977).

———. *The Differentiation of Society*. Trans. Stephen Holmes and Charles Larmore. New York: Columbia Univ. Press, 1982.

———. "Insistence on Systems Theory: Perspectives from Germany." *Social Forces* 61, no. 4 (June 1983): 987–94.

———. "The Self-Description of Society: Crisis Fashion and Sociological Theory." *International Journal of Comparative Sociology* 25, no. 1–2 (1984): 59–64.

———. *Soziologische Aufklärung I*. Opladen: Westdeutscher Verlag, 1970.

———. *Trust and Power*. New York: John Wiley & Sons, 1978.

Lukács, Georg. *The Destruction of Reason*. Trans. Peter Palmer. London: Merlin, 1980.

———. *History and Class Consciousness*. Cambridge: MIT Press, 1971.

———. "Technology and Social Relations." *New Left Review* no. 39 (September/October 1966): 27–34.

Luke, Timothy W. "Social Ecology as Critical Political Economy." *The Social Science Journal* 24, no. 3 (1987): 303–15.

MacDonald, David K.C. *Faraday, Maxwell, and Kelvin*. Garden City, N.Y.: Anchor Books, 1964.

MacKenzie, Donald. "Marx and the Machines." *Technology and Culture* 25, no. 3 (July 1984): 473–503.

Macpherson, Crawford Brough, ed. *Leviathan, or the Matter, Form and Power of a Commonwealth*. Harmondsworth: Penguin Books, 1968.

Majone, G. "International institutions and the environment." In Clark and Munn, eds., *Sustainable Development of the Biosphere*.

Major, Jack. "Historical Development of the Ecosystem Concept." In G.M. van Dyne, ed., *The Ecosystem Concept in Natural Resource Management*. New York: Academic, 1969.

Malone, Thomas F., and Roederer, Juan G., eds. *Global Change: the Proceedings of a Symposium*. Sponsored by the International Council of Scientific Unions (ICSU) during its 20th General Assembly in Ottawa, Canada, September. New York: Cambridge Univ. Press, 1985.

Malynes, G. *The Ancient Law-Merchant* [Consuetudo, vel Lex Marcatoria]. London: N.p., 1629.

Mannheim, Karl. *Man and Society: In an Age of Reconstruction*. London: Routledge and Kegan Paul, 1980.

Marcuse, Herbert. *One Dimensional Man*. Boston: Beacon Press, 1964.

———. *Reason and Revolution*. Atlantic Highlands, N.J.: Humanities Press, 1954.

Margalef, Ramon. *Perspectives in Ecological Theory*. Chicago: Univ. of Chicago, 1968.

Marsh, George Perkins. *Man and Nature*. Ed. D. Lowenthal. Cambridge: Belknap Press of Harvard Univ. Press, 1965.

Marshall, Alfred. *Elements of Economics of Industry: Being the First Volume*. 3d ed. London and New York: Macmillan, 1964.

———. *Money, Credit & Commerce*. New York: A.M. Kelley, 1965.

———. *Principles of Economics: An Introductory Volume*. London: Macmillan & Co., 1920.

Martinelli, Alberto. "On the Relation of State and Market." *Telos* no. 73, (Fall 1987): 133–47.

Martinez-Alier, J. *Ecological Economics: Energy, Environment and Society*. New York: Basil Blackwell, 1987.

Martinez-Alier, J., and Naredo, J.N. "A Marxist Precursor of Energy Economics." *Journal of Peasant Studies* 9 (January 1982): 207–24.

Maruyama, Makoto. "Economy and Living Systems." Unpublished paper presented to the 4th World Conference of Social Economics. August 13. Toronto: N.p., 1986.

Maruyama, Magoroh. "The Second Cybernetics: Deviation amplifying mutual causal processes." *American Scientist* 51 (1963): 164–79.

Marx, Karl. *Capital: A Critique of Political Economy*. 3 vols. Moscow: Progress, 1977. [Originally published under the title *Das Kapital* in 1875.]

———. *A Contribution to the Critique of Political Economy*. Ed. Maurice Dobb and trans. from the German by S.W. Ryazanskaya. London: Lawrence & Wishart, 1971.

———. *The Economic & Philosophical Manuscripts of 1844*. Ed. D.J. Struik. New York: International, 1982.

———. *Grundrisse: Introduction to the Critique of Political Economy*. London: Pelican Books, 1973.

———. *The Poverty of Philosophy*. New York: International, 1963.

———. *Pre-Capitalist Economic Formation*. Trans. J. Cohen. New York: International, 1966.

———. *Theories of Surplus Value: Part II*. Moscow: Progress, 1963. [Originally published in 1905.]

———. "Theses on Feuerbach." In *Selected Works*. [Originally published in 1845.]

Marx, Karl, and Engels, Frederick. *Collected Works*. 40 vols. New York: International, 1975–87.

————. *The Communist Manifesto.* New York: Monthly Review Press, 1964.

————. *Critique of the Gotha Programme: A Contribution to the Critique of the Social-Democratic Draft Programme of 1891.* Moscow: Foreign Languages Publishing House, 1959.

————. *The German Ideology.* Ed. C.J. Arthur. New York: International, 1970.

————. *Marx and Engels on Ecology.* Ed. and comp. by H.L. Parsons. Westport, Conn.: Greenwood, 1977.

————. *The Marx-Engels Reader.* Ed. R.C. Tucker. New York: Norton, 1972.

————. *Selected Correspondence 1846–1895.* Trans. from the German by Dora Torr. New York: International, 1942.

————. *Selected Works.* Ed. I.B. Lasker. 2d English ed. 2 vols. Moscow: Foreign Languages Publishing House, 1946–1949.

Maturana, Humberto R. "Autopoiesis: Reproduction, Heredity and Evolution." In Zeleny, ed., *Autopoiesis, Dissipative Structures, and Spontaneous Social Orders.*

Maturana, Humberto R., and Varela, Francisco. *Autopoiesis: The Realization of the Living.* Dordrecht, Holland: Reidel, 1972.

Maverick, Lewis A. *China, a Model for Europe.* San Antonio, Tex.: Paul Anderson, 1946. [Contains the translation of François Quesnay's *Le despotisme de la Chine.*]

————. "The Chinese and the Physiocrats: A Supplement." *Economic History* 4, no. 15 (1940): 312–18.

————. "Chinese Influences upon the Physiocrats." *Economic History* 4, no. 13 (1938): 54–67.

May, R.M. "Will a large complex system be stable?" *Nature* 238 (1972): 413–14.

Mayhew, Leon H., ed. *On Institutions and Social Evolution: Selected Writings.* Chicago: Univ. of Chicago Press, 1982.

McCloskey, D.M. *The Rhetoric of Economics.* Madison: Univ. of Wisconsin, 1985.

McCulloch, J.R. "Philosophy of Manufacturers." *Edinburgh Rev.* 61 (1835): 453–72.

McLellan, David. *Karl Marx: His Life and Thought.* London: Macmillan & Co., 1973.

McLuhan, Marshall. *The Gutenberg Galaxy: the Making of Typographic Man.* Toronto: Univ. of Toronto Press, 1965.

McQuarie, Donald, and Amburgey, Terry. "Marx and Modern Systems Theory." *Social Science Quarterly* 50, no. 1 (1978):3–19.

Medow, Paul I. "Conversations on the Noösphere: the Context." Research Memorandum. Toronto, Canada: Economic Research and Systems Planning Group (E.R.S.P.G.), Stong College, York University, October 27, 1982.

————. "Ecological and Genetic Approaches to the Exploration of Global Technological Scenarios." Research Memorandum. Toronto: E.R.S.P.G., Stong College, York University, April 6, 1987.

————. "The Economic Problematique of Models of Global Coevolution: the Contribution of R. Passet." Research Memorandum. Toronto: E.R.S.P.G., Stong College, York University, January 13, 1982.

————. "Exploring the Technological Problematique of Global Coevolution." Research Memorandum. Toronto: E.R.S.P.G., Stong College, York Univ. Press, August 5, 1986.

————. "The Humanistic Ideals of the Enlightenment and Mathematical Economics." In Fromm, ed., *Socialist Humanism.*

————. "The Lasting Contributions of F. Perroux." Research Memorandum. Toronto: E.R.S.P.G., Stong College, York Univ. Press, October 26, 1987.

————. "Protecting the Biosphere and Multiculturalism in the Age of Telematics-Assisted Institutions." Research Memorandum. Toronto: E.R.S.P.G., Stong College, York University, September 13, 1983.

————. "Transnational Energy Infrastructures and the Neutralization of Counter-Productive

Innovation-Inducing Monetary Mechanisms: Elements of a Simulation Model." Research Memorandum. Toronto: E.R.S.P.G., Stong College, York University, November 14, 1973.

Meek, Ronald L. *The Economics of Physiocracy: Essays and Translations*. Cambridge: Harvard Univ. Press, 1963.

———, ed. *Mirabeau and Quesnay: Precursors of Adam Smith*. London: Dent, 1973.

Melman, Seymour. *Pentagon Capitalism: The Political Economy of War*. New York: McGraw Hill, 1970.

Mendelson, Jack. "On Engels' Metaphysical Dialectics: A Foundation of Orthodox 'Marxism'." *Dialectical Anthropology* 4, no. 1 (March 1979): 65–70.

Menger, Karl. *Investigations into the Methods of the Social Sciences, with Special Reference to Economics*. Ed. L. Schneider. New York: New York Univ. Press, 1963. [Formerly published under the title *Untersuchungen über die Methode der Socialwissenschaften und der politischen ökonomie insbesondere* in 1883.]

Menshikov, S. "Dialogue between Soviet and American Economists." *World Marxist Review* no. 1 (January 1988): 76–85.

Mill, John Stuart. "Of Property." In *Principles of Political Economy*. Book 2. New York: Appleton-Century-Crofts, 1881.

———. "On Liberty." Chicago: Encyclopedia Britannica Great Books, 1952. [Originally published in 1859.]

———. *Principles of Political Economy*. Ed., with an introduction, by D. Winch. Baltimore, MD.: Penguin Books, 1970. [Originally published in 1848.]

Miller, James Grier. "Jürgen Habermas, Legitimation Crisis." *Telos* no. 25, (Fall 1975):210–20.

Mirabeau, Marquis de V.R. "Tableau Économique avec ses elications par François Quesnay." *L'Ami de Hommes* 2 (1970): 6. [Reprinted from the edition of *Avignon*, 1758–60, Aalen.]

Mirabeau, Marquis de V.R., and Quesnay, François. *Mirabeau and Quesnay Precursors of Adam Smith*. Ed. R.L. Meek. London: Dent, 1973. [Original work published in 1763.]

———. *Rural Philosophy* [Philosophie Rurale]. Paris: N.p., 1763.

Mises, Ludwig von. *Planned Chaos*. Irvington-on-Hudson, N.Y.: Foundation for Economic Education, 1947.

Moiseev, N.N. "The Coevolution of Man and the Biosphere." Research Memorandum. Toronto: E.R.S.P.G., Stong College, York University, April 7, 1980.

———. "Coevolution: Some Propositions." Research Memorandum. Toronto: E.R.S.P.G., Stong College, York University, August 19, 1984.

———. "The Ecological Imperative." In Behar et al., eds., *Ecoforum for Peace*.

———. *Man, Nature and the Future of Civilization*. Moscow: Novosti Publishing House, 1986.

———. "Man's Coevolution with the Biosphere: Cybernetic Aspects." Research Memorandum. Toronto: E.R.S.P.G., Stong College, York Univ. Press, September 2, 1982.

———. "Noögenesis—Fundamental Problem of Our Time." Paper presented at the International Conference on "Science and Technology at the Service of Development: The Role of Government and Social Institutions." Kiev, Ukrainian SSR, June 28, 1989.

———. "Power and the Economy: a Coevolutionary Perspective." Research Memorandum. Toronto: E.R.S.P.G., Stong College, York Univ. Press, January 1, 1984.

———. "Studying the Dynamics of the Noösphere." Research Memorandum. Toronto: E.R.S.P.G., Stong College, York Univ. Press, September 18, 1978.

———. "The Theory of Games and Hierarchical Systems in Economies." Research Memorandum. Toronto: E.R.S.P.G., Stong College, York Univ. Press, January 5, 1973.

————. "The Unity of Natural Scientific Knowledge." Research Memorandum. Toronto: E.R.S.P.G., Stong College, York Univ. Press, September 1, 1977.

Moiseev, N.N., and Frolov, I.T. "High Touch Technologies Society, Man and Nature in the Age of Microelectronics, Informatics and Biotechnologies." Research Memorandum. Toronto: E.R.S.P.G., Stong College, York Univ. Press, October 22, 1984.

Moleschott, Jacob. *Der Kreislauf des Lebens*. Mainz: Von Zabern, 1852.

Monod, Jacques. *Chance and Necessity: an Essay on the Natural Philosophy of Modern Biology*. Trans. from the French by Austryn Wainhouse. New York: Vintage Books, 1972.

————. *Épistémologie et marxisme*. Paris: Union generale d'éditions, 1972.

————. *From Biology to Ethics*. San Diego, Calif.: Salk Institute for Biological Studies, 1969.

Montesquieu, Baron Charles-Louis de Secondat et de. *The Spirit of Laws: a compendium of the first English edition*. Ed., with an introduction, by D.W. Carrithers. Together with an English translation of "An essay on causes affecting minds and characters (1736–1743)." Berkeley: Univ. of California Press, 1977.

Mooney, Christopher F.J. "Teilhard de Chardin and Modern Philosophy." *Social Research: An International Quarterly* 34, no. 1 (Spring 1967):67–85.

Morgan, Gareth. "Re-Thinking Corporate Strategy: a Cybernetic Perspective." Research Memorandum. Toronto: E.R.S.P.G., Stong College, York Univ. Press, January 17, 1983.

————. *Riding the Waves of Change*. San Francisco: Jossey-Bass, 1988.

Morgenstern, Oskar. "Limits to the Use of Mathematics in Economics." In J.E. Charlesworth, ed., *Mathematics and the Social Sciences*. Transactions of a Symposium. June 12–29. Philadelphia: The American Academy of Political and Social Science, 1963.

Morin, Edgar. "Complexity." *International Social Science Journal* 26, no. 4 (1974): 555–82.

Mumford, Lewis. *The Myth of the Machine*. New York: Harcourt, 1964.

————. *Technics and Civilization*. New York: Harcourt, Brace & World, 1962. [Originally published in 1934.]

Murota, Takeshi. "Environmental Economics of the Water Planet Earth." In Pillet and Murota, eds., *Environmental Economics*.

Murota, T., and Tsuchida, T. "Fundamentals in the Entropy Theory of Watercycle, Ecocycle, and Human Economy." Unpublished document. August 25, 1986.

Murphy, John W. "Talcott Parsons and Niklas Luhmann: Two Versions of the Social 'System'." *International Review of Modern Sociology* 12, no. 2 (Autumn 1982): 291–301.

National Research Council (NRC). *Acid Deposition: Atmospheric Processes in Eastern North America*. Washington: National Academy Press, 1983.

————. *Changing Climate*. Washington: National Academy Press, 1983.

————. *Towards an International Geosphere-Biosphere Program: a Study of Global Change*. Washington: National Academy Press, 1983.

Naveh, Ze'ev. "Ecology and Ethics." In Kranzberg, ed., *Ethics in an Age of Pervasive Technology*.

Needham, Joseph. "Laud, the Levelers, and the Virtuosi." In Lewis et al., eds., *Christianity and the Social Revolution*.

Nelson, R., and Winter, S. *An Evolutionary Theory of Economic Change*. Cambridge: Cambridge Univ. Press, 1982.

Neumann, J. von. "Can We Survive Technology?" *Fortune* (June 1955): 32–41.

Neumann, J. von, and Morgenstern, Oskar. *A Theory of Games and Economic Behavior*. Princeton: Princeton Univ. Press, 1953.

Neurath, Otto. "Encyclopedia and Unified Science." In Neurath et al., eds., *International Encyclopedia of Unified Science.*

———. *Foundations of the Social Sciences.* Chicago: Univ. of Chicago Press, 1944.

Neurath, Otto.; Bohr, Niels; Dewey, John; Russell, Bertrand; Carnap, Rudolf; and Morris, Charles W., eds. *International Encyclopedia of Unified Science.* Chicago: Univ. of Chicago Press, 1938.

New York Times, June 24, 1988, Sec. I, p. 31, c. 1.

Nicolis, G., and Auchmuty, J.F.G. "Dissipative Structures, Catastrophes, and Pattern Formation: A Bifurcation Analysis." *Proceedings of the National Academy of Sciences* 71 (1974).

Nicolis, G., and Babloyantz, A. "Fluctuations in Open Systems." *Journal of Chemical Physics* 52, no. 6 (1969): 2632.

Nicolis, G., and Prigogine, I. "Fluctuations in Non-Equilibrium Systems." *Proceedings of the National Academy of Sciences* 68 (1974): 2102–07.

———. *Self-Organization in Non-Equilibrium Systems: From Dissipative Structures to Order through Fluctuations.* New York: Wiley-Interscience, 1968.

Niel, Mathilde. "The Phenomenon of Technology: Liberation or Alienation of Man?" In Fromm, ed., *Socialist Humanism.*

Nijkamp, Peter. *Theory and Application of Environmental Economics.* Amsterdam: North-Holland, 1977.

Norcia, Vincent di. "From Critical Theory to Critical Ecology." *Telos* no. 22 (Winter 1974–75):85–95.

Norgaard, Richard B. "Coevolutionary Agricultural Development." *Economic Development and Cultural Change* 32 (1984): 525–46.

———. "Coevolutionary Development Potential." *Land Economics* 60, no. 2 (May 1984):160–73.

———. "Economics as Mechanics and the Demise of Biological Diversity." In Costanza and Daly, eds., "Ecological Economics."

———. "Environmental Economics: An Evolutionary Critique and a Plea for Pluralism." *Journal of Environmental and Economic Management* 12 (1985): 382–93.

———. "Scarcity and Growth: How Does it Look Today?" *American Journal of Agricultural Economics* 57 (December 1975): 810–14.

O'Connor, D.J. *John Locke.* Harmondsworth, England: Penguin Books, 1952.

Odum, Howard T. "Energy, Ecology and Economics." *Ambio* 2, no. 6 (1973): 220–27.

———. "Energy, Value & Money." In Hall and Day, eds., *Ecosystem Modeling in Theory and Practice.*

———. *Environment, Power, and Society.* New York: Wiley-Interscience, 1971.

———. *Systems Ecology: an Introduction.* New York: John Wiley & Sons, 1983.

Odum, Howard T., and Odum, Elisabeth C. *Energy Basis for Man and Nature.* New York/Montreal: McGraw-Hill, 1976.

O'Manique, John. *Energy in Evolution.* London: Garnstone, 1969.

Oparin, Aleksandr Ivanovich. *Chemical Origin of Life.* Springfield, Ill.: C.C. Thomas, 1964.

———. *Life, its Nature, Origin and Development.* New York: Academic Press, 1964.

Organization for Economic Cooperation and Development. *Economic and Ecological Interdependence.* Paris: Organization for Economic Cooperation and Development, 1982.

———. *Long-range Transport of Air Pollutants.* Paris: Organization for Economic Cooperation and Development, 1979.

Ostwald, Wilhelm. "Efficiency." *The Independent* 71 (1911).

———. *Electrochemistry, History and Theory.* New Delhi: Published for the Smithsonian Institution, 1980.

————. *Energetische Grundlagen der Kulturwissenschaften.* Leipzig: N.p., 1909.

————. "Energetische Imperativ." *Annals of Natural Philosophy* 10 (n.d.).

————. "Lehrbuck der allgemeinen Chemie." *The Monist* 2 (1892): 37.

————. "The Modern Theory of Energetics." *The Monist* 17, no. 4, (1907):481–515.

————. "The Philosophical Meaning of Energy." *The International Quarterly* 7 (1903):300–15.

————. "The Relations of Biology and the Neighbouring Sciences," *Univ. of California Publications in Physiology* 1, no. 4 (1903).

Padover, Saul K. *The Letters of Karl Marx.* Englewood Cliffs, N.J.: Prentice-Hall, 1979.

Pareto, Vilfredo. *Manual of Political Economy.* Trans. A.S. Schwier. Ed. A.S. Schwier and A.N. Page. New York: A.M. Kelley, 1971.

————. *Mind and Society: a Treatise on General Sociology.* 4 vols. New York: Dover, 1935.

Parsons, Howard L., ed. *Marx and Engels on Ecology.* Westport, Conn.: Greenwood, 1977.

Parsons, Talcott. *On Institutions and Social Evolution: Selected Writings.* Ed., with an introduction, by L.H. Mayhew. Chicago: Univ. of Chicago Press, 1982.

Passet, René. *L'Économique et le Vivant.* Paris: Payot, 1979. [Unpublished English translation by P.I. Medow as *Economic Systems and Living Systems.* Toronto: York University, 1984.]

Patten, B.C., ed. *Systems Analysis and Simulation in Ecology.* San Francisco: Academic, 1976.

Pavlov, Ivan Petrovich. *Conditioned Reflexes: an Investigation of the Physiological Activity of the Cerebral Cortex.* Ed. and trans. by G.V. Anrep. New York: Dover, 1960.

————. *Lectures on Conditioned Reflexes: Twenty-five Years of Objective Study of the Higher Nervous Activity (behavior) of Animals.* Ed. and trans. by W.H. Gantt. New York: International, 1928.

Pearce, David. "Foundations of Ecological Economics." In Costanza and Daly, eds., "Ecological Economics."

Peccei, Aurelio. *Facing Unprecedented Challenges: Mankind in the Eighties.* Laxenburg, Austria: IIASA, 1980.

Perroux, François. *A New Concept of Development: Basic Tenets.* London: Croom Helm; Paris: UNESCO, 1938.

Pfaundler, Leopold. "The World Economy in Light of Physics" [Die Weltwirtschaft im Liche der Physik]. Ed. R. Fleischer. *Deutsche Revue* 22, no. 2 (April–June 1902): 29–38, 171–82.

Phillips, A. "The Tableau Économique as a Simple Leontief Model." *Quarterly Journal of Economics* (February 1955):137–44.

Piaget, Jean. *Biology and Knowledge: an Essay on the Relations Between Organic Regulations and Cognitive Processes.* Trans. Beatrix Walsh. Chicago: Univ. of Chicago Press, 1971.

Piccone, Paul. "Reading *Grundrisse*: Beyond 'Orthodox' Marxism." *Theory and Society.* 2, no. 2 (Summer 1975): 235–55.

Pigou, Arthur Cecil. *The Economics of Welfare.* 2d ed. London: Macmillan & Co., 1924.

Pillet, G., and Murota, Takeshi, eds. *Environmental Economics—the Analysis of a Major Interface.* Geneva: R. Leimgruber, 1986.

Pirenne, Henri. *Economic and Social History of Medieval Europe.* New York: Harcourt, Brace & World, 1937.

Planck, Max. "The Unity of the Physical Universe." In M. Planck, ed., *A Survey of Physics: A Collection of Essays and Lectures.* New York: E.P. Dutton, 1925.

Plekhanov, G.V. *Fundamental Problems of Marxism* [Izbrannye Filosofshie proizvedeniia]. 5 vols. New York: International, 1956. [Originally published in Moscow in 1929.

Podak, Klaus. "Without Subject, Without Reason: Reflections on Niklas Luhmann's Social Systems." *Thesis-Eleven* 13 (1986): 54–66.

Podolinsky, Serhii. "Human Labour and the Unity of Energy" [Le socialisme et la theorie de Darwin]. *Revue Socialiste* (March 1880). [Also published in German, "Menschliche Arbeit und Einheit der Kraft." *Die Neue Zeit* 1 (September 1883).]

Poincaré, Henri. *Value of Science.* New York: Dover, 1958.

Polanyi, Karl. *The Great Transformation.* Boston: Beacon Press, 1957.

———. "The Essence of Fascism." In Lewis et al., eds., *Christianity and the Social Revolution.*

———. *The Livelihood of Man.* Ed. H.W. Pearson. New York: Academic Press, 1977.

———. "On Belief in Economic Determinism." *The Sociological Review: Journal of the Institute of Sociology* 34 (1947):96–102.

———. *Primitive, Archaic, and Modern Economies: Essays of Karl Polanyi.* Ed. G. Dalton. Boston: Beacon Press, 1971.

———. *Trade and Market in the Early Empires: Economies in History.* Glencoe, Ill.: Free, 1957.

Polanyi-Levitt, Kari. "The Origins and Significance of 'The Great Transformation.'" Paper presented at Karl Polanyi Commemorative Conference. October 27–29, 1986. Budapest: Hungarian Academy of Science, 1986.

Popova, M.A. "The 'Humanistic Religion' of Erich Fromm and the Impasse of Bourgeois Humanism" ['Gumanisticheskaya religiya' Erikha Fromma i tupiki burzhuaznogo gumanizma]. *Vestnik-Moskovskogo-Universiteta, Filosofiya* 31, no. 5 (September–October 1976): 82–93.

Prigogine, Ilya. *Introduction to Thermodynamics of Irreversible Processes.* New York: Wiley-Interscience, 1968.

———. *Thermodynamics of Irreversible Processes.* 3d ed. New York: Wiley-Interscience, 1967.

Prigogine, I., and Stengers, Isabella. *Order out of Chaos: Man's New Dialogue with Nature.* New York: Bantam Books, 1984. [Trans. from the French edition "La Nouvelle Alliance."]

Prigogine, I.; Allen, P.M.; and Herman, R. "Long Run Trends and the Evolution of Complexity." In Laszlo and Bierman, eds., *Goals in a Global Community.*

Prigogine, I.; Nicolis, G.; and Babloyantz, A. "Thermodynamics of Evolution." *Physics Today* 25, no. 11 (1972): 12.

Prigogine, I.; Nicolis, G.; and Lam, T. "Stability, Fluctuations, and Complexity." *Cooperative Phenomena* 2 (1975): 103–9.

Quesnay, François. "Le Despotisme de la Chine." *Ephmides du Citoyen.* Paris (March, April, May, and June 1767). [English translation found in L.A. Maverick, *China, a Model for Europe.*]

———. *Dialogue on the Work of Artisans.* N.p., 1770.

———. "Graines." *Encyclopédie.* Paris: N.p., 1757.

———. "Observation sur la droit naturel des hommes réunis en société," *Journal of Agriculture, Commerce, and Finances* (September 1765): 17–38.

Rapoport, Anatol. "Methodology in the Physical, Biological and Social Sciences." In Attinger, ed., *Global Systems Dynamics.*

Rappoport, R. *Pigs for the Ancestors.* New Enlarged Edition. New Haven, Conn.: Univ. Press, 1984.

Rapport, D.J., and Turner, J.E. "Economic Models and Ecology." *Science* 195 (1977): 367–73.

Rasool, I. "Observational systems and techniques: remote sensing." In Malone and Roederer, eds., *Global Change.*

Rastogi, P.N. "Structure, Function and Process: A Cybernetic Approach to Social Phenomena." *Sociological Bulletin* 22, no. 2 (September 1973): 316.

Raymond, Allen. *What is Technocracy?* New York: McGraw-Hill, 1933.

Ree, Jonathan. *Descartes.* London: Allen Lane, 1974.

Regier, H., and Baskerville, G. "Global concepts—local actions: the problem of ecologically sustainable redevelopment." In Clark and Munn, eds., *Sustainable Development of the Biosphere.*

Reichwein, Adolf. *China and Europe: Intellectual and Artistic Contacts in the Eighteenth Century.* Trans. from the German by J.C. Powell. London: Routledge and Kegan Paul, 1968. [Originally published in 1925.]

Ricardo, David. *Letters of David Ricardo to Hutches Trower and Others.* Ed. J. Bonar. Oxford: Clarendon, 1899.

———. *On the Principles of Political Economy and Taxation.* Ed. Ronald Maxwell Hartwell. Harmondsworth: Penguin Books, 1971. [Original publication London: J. Murray, 1817.]

———. *The Works and Correspondence of David Ricardo.* Ed. P. Sraffa. 11 vols. Cambridge: Cambridge Univ. Press, 1951–73.

Richards, J.F. "World environmental history and economic development." In Clark and Munn, eds., *Sustainable Development of the Biosphere.*

Rifkin, Jeremy. *Entropy: a New World View.* Written with Ted Howard. Afterword by N. Georgescu-Roegen. New York: Bantam Books, 1980.

Riviere, Pierre F.J.H. Mercier de la. *L'Ordre naturel et essentiel des sociétés politiques.* Paris: N.p., 1767.

Robbins, Baron Lionel C. *An Essay on the Nature & Significance of Economic Science.* London: Macmillan & Co., 1935.

Roberts, Edward B., ed. *Managerial Applications of System Dynamics.* Cambridge: MIT Press, 1978.

Robin, Eugene Debs, ed. *Claude Bernard and the Internal Environment: a Memorial Symposium.* Proceedings of a symposium held at Stanford Univ. on February 10, 1978. New York: M. Dekker, 1979.

Robin, Jacques. "Culture and Technology: Fusion or Collision: an Extended Summary." Trans. and ed. by P.I. Medow. Research Memorandum. Toronto: E.R.S.P.G., Stong College, York Univ. Press, May 10, 1985.

Rogin, Leo. *The Meaning and Validity of Economic Theory.* New York: Harper & Bros., 1956.

Rosen, R. "Old Trends and New Trends in Systems Research." In *General Systems Research: A Science, a Methodology, a Technology.* Proceedings of the Twenty-Third North American Meeting of the Society for General Systems Research. N.p., 1979.

Rosenberg, Nathan. "Marx as a Student of Technology." *Monthly Review* 28, no. 3 (July–August 1976): 56–77.

Ross, Ian Simpson, and Mossne, Ernest Campbell, eds. *Correspondence of Adam Smith.* Oxford: Clarendon Press, 1977.

Rotstein, Abraham. "The Outer Man: Technology and Alienation." *The Canadian Forum* (August 1965): 104–5.

———. "The Reality of Society: Karl Polanyi's Philosophical Perspective." Paper presented at the Karl Polanyi Commemorative Conference. October 27–29, 1986. Budapest: Hungarian Academy of Sciences, 1986.

Roughgarden, Jonathan. *Theory of Population Genetics and Evolutionary Ecology.* New York: Macmillan, 1979.

Rousseau, Jean-Jacques. *Correspondance generale de J.-J. Rousseau.* Collationne sur les origineaux annotee et commentee par Theophile Dufour. Paris: A. Colin, 1924–34.

———. *Encyclopedia.* Vol. 5. N.p., 1755.

Routh, Guy. *The Origin of Economic Ideas.* London: Macmillan & Co., 1975.

Routley, Val. "On Karl Marx as an Environmental Hero." *Environmental Ethics* 3, no. 3 (Fall 1981): 237–44.

Rubin, Milton D. "Society for General Systems Research." In M.D. Rubin, ed., *Man in Systems.* New York: Gordon and Breach, 1971.

Ruffie, Jacques. *Éléments de génétique générale et humaine.* 2d rev. ed. Paris: Masson, 1974.

Ruskin, John. "Unto This Last." In Hubenka, ed., *Four Essays on the First Principles of Political Economy.* [Originally published in 1868.]

Russell, Bertrand. *Philosophy.* New York: W.W. Norton, 1927.

Sacher, Eduard. *Foundations of a Mechanics of Society.* N.p., 1881.

———. *Die Gesellschaftskunde als Naturwissenschaft.* Dresden and Leipzig: Piersons' Verlag, 1899.

Salk, Jonas. *Anatomy of Reality: Merging of Intuition and Reason.* New York: Columbia Univ. Press, 1983.

———. *The Survival of the Wisest.* New York: Harper & Row, 1973.

Schaff, Adam. Address to the International Conference on "Science and Technology at the Service of Development: The Role of Government and Social Institutions." Kiev, Ukrainian SSR, June 28, 1989.

———. "Biology and the Social Sciences." *International Social Science Journal* 26, no. 4 (1974): 598–610.

Schelling, T.C. "Climatic Change: implications for welfare and policy." National Research Council. *Changing Climate* (1983): 449–82.

Schmalhausen, I.I. *Cybernetic Questions in Biology.* N.p., n.d.

———. *The Organism as a Whole in Individual and Historical Development, Factors of Evolution.* N.p., n.d.

Schmidt, Alfred. *The Concept of Nature in Marx.* Trans. from the German by Ben Fowkes. London: NLB, 1971. [Originally published under the title *Der Begriff der Natur in der Lehre von Marx.*]

Schneider, Herbert Wallace, ed. *Adam Smith's Moral and Political Philosophy.* New York: Harper & Row, 1970.

Schrödinger, Erwin. *Science and the Human Temperament.* London: George Allen & Unwin, 1935.

———. *What Is life? and Other Scientific Essays.* Garden City, N.Y.: Doubleday, 1956.

———. *What Is Life from the Point of Physics.* Garden City, N.Y.: Doubleday, 1945.

Schumacher, Ernst Friedrich. *Small is Beautiful: a Study of Economics as If People Matter.* London: Abacus, 1974.

Schumpeter, Joseph Alois. *Business Cycles.* New York: McGraw-Hill, 1939.

———. *Capitalism, Socialism, and Democracy.* With an introduction by Tom Bottomore. New York: George Allen & Unwin/Harper & Row, 1976.

———. *Economic Doctrine and Method: An Historical Sketch.* New York: Oxford Univ. Press, 1954.

———. *Essays.* Ed. R.V. Clemence. Cambridge, Mass.: Addison-Wesley, 1951.

———. *History of Economic Analysis.* Ed. from manuscript by Elizabeth Boody Schumpeter. New York: Oxford Univ. Press, 1954.

———. *Imperialism and Social Classes.* Trans. Heinz Norden. New York: A.M. Kelley, 1951.

———. *Theory of Economic Development: An Inquiry into Profits.* Cambridge: Harvard Univ. Press, 1961.

Scott, Anthony, ed. *Progress in Natural Resource Economics.* Oxford: Clarendon, 1985.

Sekine, Thomas T. " 'Entropy Problem' and the Future of Our Society." Unpublished paper presented at the Conference on "Man's Coevolution with the Biosphere in the Age of Advanced Technologies." Toronto: L'Institut de la Vie, Stong College, York University, January, 1985.

―――. "General Economic Norms and Socialism—From Uno to Tamanoi." Paper. Toronto: Dept. of Economics, York UniversityPress, August, 1986.

―――. "Socialism as a Living System." Working Paper. Toronto: Department of Economics, York University, 1989.

Semtner, A.J. "The climatic response of the Arctic Ocean to Soviet River Diversions." *Climatic Change* 6 (1984): 109–30.

Senior, Nassau William. *An Outline of the Science of Political Economy*. New York: A.M. Kelley, 1965. [Originally published in 1836.]

Serafin, Rafal. "Noosphere, Gaia, and the Science of the Biosphere." *Environmental Ethics* 10 (Summer 1988):121–37.

Serbyn, Roman. "In Defense of an Independenet Ukrainian Socialist Movement: Three Letters from Serhii Podolinsky to Valerian Smirnov." *Journal of Ukranian Studies* 7, no. 2 (1982): 7.

Shchersak, N.P. *Vladimir Ivanovich Vernadsky*. Trans. from the Ukrainian by G.I. Gaivoron. Kiev: Naukova Dumka, 1981.

Sherman, Howard. "Marx and Determinism." *Journal of Economic Issues* 15, no. 1 (March 1981): 61–75.

Shinkaruk, V.I. "The Revolution in Science and Technology and the Formation of the New Human Being" [Nauchno Tekhnicheskaia Revoliutsiia i Formirovanie Novogo Cheloveka]. *Voprosy filosofii* 29, no. 7 (1975): 13–39.

Silverman, A.G. "Review of Wealth, Virtual Wealth, and Debt." *American Economic Review* (June 1927): 275–78.

Simon, Herbert A. "On the concept of organizational goals." *Administrative Science Quarterly* 9 (1964): 1–22.

Slesser, Malcolm. "Accounting for Energy." *Nature* 254 (March 20, 1975): 170–72.

―――. *Energy in the Economy*. London: Macmillan & Co., 1978.

Smith, Adam. *Adam Smith's Moral and Political Philosophy*. Ed. H.W. Schneider. New York: Harper & Row, 1970.

―――. *A Catalogue of the Library of Adam Smith, Author of the "Moral Sentiments" and "The Wealth of Nations."* 2d ed. Prepared for the Royal Economic Society by James Bonar, with an introduction and appendices. New York: A.M. Kelley, 1966.

―――. *Correspondence of Adam Smith*. Ed. I.S. Ross and E.C. Mossne. Oxford: Clarendon, 1977.

―――. *Lectures on Justice, Policy, Revenue and Arms*. New York: N.p., 1964.

―――. *The Theory of Moral Sentiments*. Prepared for the Royal Catalogue of the Library of Adam Smith by J. Bonar. New York: A.M. Kelley, 1966.

―――. *Wealth of Nations*. Books 1–3. With an introduction by A. Skinner. New York: Penguin Books, 1976.

Smith, Norman Kemp, ed. *Dialogues Concerning Natural Religion*. Indianapolis: Bobbs-Merrill, 1970.

Sochor, Zenovia A. *Revolution and Culture: The Bogdanov-Lenin Controversy*. Ithaca: Cornell Univ. Press, 1988.

Soddy, Frederick. *The Arch Enemy of Economic Freedom*. Pamphlet. Oxford: N.p., 1943.

―――. *Cartesian Economics: The Bearing of Physical Science upon State Stewardship*. London: Hendersons, 1922.

―――. *Dishonest Money: or why a larger pay-packet now buys less than it did*. London: N.p., 1950.

————. *The Inversion of Science: and a Scheme of Scientific Reformation.* London: Hendersons, 1924.

————. *Matter and Energy.* London: Williams and Norgate, 1912.

————. *Money Reform as a Preliminary to All Reform.* Birmingham: N.p., 1950.

————. *Money Versus Man: a Statement of the World Problem from the Standpoint of the New Economics.* London: N.p., 1931.

————. *The Role of Money: What It Should Be, Contrasted with What It Has Become.* London: G. Routledge and Sons, 1934.

————. *Science and Life.* London: N.p., 1920.

————. "Transmutation, the vital problem of the future." *Scientia* 2 (1912): 199–200.

————. *Wealth, Virtual Wealth and Debt: The Solution of the Economic Paradox.* New York: Dutton, 1933.

Solow, Robert A. "The Economics of Resources and the Resources of Economics." Richard T. Ely Lecture. *American Economic Review* 64 (May 1974): 1–14.

————. "Is the End of the World at Hand?" *Challenge* (March–April 1973): 39–50.

Solvay, E. "Formules d'introduction a' l'nergetique physio et psycho-sociologique." In *Questions d'nergetique sociale.* Bruxelles: Institut Solvay, 1919.

Spencer, Herbert. *Essays: moral, political and aesthetic.* New York: D. Appleton, 1882.

————. *The evolution of society: selections from Herbert Spencer's Principles of sociology.* Ed., with an introduction, by R.L. Carneiro. Chicago: Univ. of Chicago Press, 1967.

————. *First Principles.* New York: D. Appleton, 1880.

Spinoza, Benedictus (Baruch) de. *Correspondence of Spinoza.* Ed. A. Wolf. London: G. Allen and Unwin, 1928.

————. *Earlier Philosophical Writings: The Cartesian Principles.* Indianapolis: Bobbs-Merrill, 1963.

————. *Spinoza on Freedom of Thought: Selection from Tractatus.* Montreal: M. Casalini, 1962.

Sraffa, Piero. *Production of Commodities by Means of Commodities.* Cambridge: Cambridge Univ. Press, 1960.

————, ed. *The Works and Correspondence of David Ricardo.* 11 vols. Cambridge: Cambridge Univ. Press, 1951–73.

Stahl, G.E. "Véritable Distinction à établir entre le mixte et la vivant du corps humanin." *Oeuvres microphilosophique et pratiques.* Vol. 2. Montpelier: Pitrat et Fis, 1861.

Stanfield, J.R. *The Economic Thought of Karl Polanyi.* London: Macmillan & Co., 1986.

————. "The Institutional Economics of Karl Polanyi." *Journal of Economic Issues* 14, no. 3 (September 1980): 593–614.

————. "Karl Polanyi and Contemporary Economic Thought." Paper presented at the Karl Polanyi Commemorative Conference. October 27–29, 1986. Budapest: Hungarian Academy of Sciences, 1986.

————. "The Social Economics of Karl Polanyi." (n.d.)

————. "Toward an Ecological Economics." *IJSE* 10, no. 5 (1977): 27–37.

Stanley, John L., and Zimmerman, Ernst. "On the Alleged Differences Between Marx and Engels." *Political Studies* 32 (1984): 226–48.

Stokes, Kenneth M. "Concepts of Entropy and Work." Working Paper. Toronto: Stong College, York University, 1989.

————. "Confucian Ethics and the Origins of Economic Analysis." Working Paper. Toronto: Stong College, York University, 1989.

————. "Cybernetic Approach to Corporate Strategy." Working Paper. Toronto, Canada: E.R.S.P.G., Stong College, York University, 1989.

————. "Emergence of the Technosphere." Working Paper. Niigata, Japan: Graduate

School of International Relations (G.S.I.R.), International Univ. of Japan, 1989.

―――. "Freedom in a Technified Society." Working Paper. March. Niigata, Japan: G.S.I.R., International Univ. of Japan, 1990.

―――. "Heretical Philosophers of Social Energetics." Working Paper. Toronto: Stong College, York University, 1989.

―――. "The Marx-Engels Conception of Darwin's Theory." Working Paper. Toronto: Stong College, York University, 1989.

―――. "A Note on Feuerbach and Marx." Working Paper. Toronto: Stong College, York University, 1989.

―――. "Organizational Dissonance and Dissipative Systems." Working Paper. Niigata, Japan: G.S.I.R., International Univ. of Japan, 1989.

―――. "The Problematique of Economic Externalities." *York Journal of Political Economy, 7 (Winter 1988):102–14.*

―――. "The Social Energetics of Serhii Podolinsky." Working Paper. Toronto: Stong College, York University, 1989.

―――. "Technico-ecological Engineering: the WELMM Approach." Working Paper. Toronto: Stong College, York University, 1989.

―――. "Thermodynamics and the Problematique of Debt & Money." Working Paper. Toronto: Stong College, York University, 1989.

―――. "The Ubiquitous (and Unresolved) Problem of Value." Working Paper. Niigata, Japan: G.S.I.R., International Univ. of Japan, 1989.

Struik, D.J., ed. *The Economic & Philosophical Manuscripts of 1844*. New York: International, 1982.

Stukel, J.J., and Neimann, B.L. *Ohio River Energy Basin Study (ORBES): Air Quality and Relation Impacts.* Vol. 1. Washington: Environmental Protection Agency, Office of Research and Development, 1980.

Stumm, Werner, ed. *Global Chemical Cycles and Their Alterations by Man.* Berlin: Dahlem Konferenzen, 1977.

Suggett, Martin. *Galileo and the Birth of Modern Science.* Hove, Sussex: Wayland, 1981.

Susiluoto, Ilmari. *The Origins and Development of Systems Thinking in the Soviet Union: Political and Philosophical Controversies from Bogdanov and Bukharin to Present-Day Re-Evaluations.* Helsinki: Suomalinen Tiedeakatemia, Annales Academiae Scientiarium Fennicae, 1982.

Svirezhev, J.; Krapivin, V.F.; Tarko, A.M.; and Vilkova, L.P. *New Results in Modelling of the Global Biogeocenotic Processes.* Helsinki: International Symposium of the Coevolution of Man and the Biosphere, 1983.

Swaney, James A. "A Coevolutionary Model of Structural Change." *Journal of Economic Issues* 20, no. 2 (June 1986):393–401.

Szeci, Maria. "Looking Back on the Great Transformation." *Monthly Review: an Independent Socialist Magazine* 30, no. 7 (1978): 34–45.

Tamanoi, Yoshiro. "Living System as the Basis for Human Economy." *Japanese Economist* (March 27, 1984). [Trans. into English by M. Maruyama, 1987.]

―――. "Review of *The Livelihood of Man* by Karl Polanyi." In *Sociology and Social Research* 63, no. 4 (n.d.): 821.

―――. "Towards an Exodus from Market Mentality: On Marx and Polanyi." Paper. Emeritus Professor. Tokyo: Univ. of Tokyo, 1983.

Tamanoi, Yoshiro; Tsuchida, Atsushi; and Murota, Takeshi. "Towards an entropic theory of economy and ecology: Beyond the mechanistic equilibrium approach." *Économie Appliqué* 37, no. 2 (1984): 279–94.

Taschdjian, Edgar, ed. *Perspectives on General System Theory: Scientific-Philosophical Studies.* New York: George Braziller, 1975.

Teilhard de Chardin, Pierre. *Appearance of Man*. Trans. J.M. Cohen. New York: Harper & Row, 1965.
———. *The Hymn of the Universe*. New York: Harper & Row, 1965.
———. *The Phenomenon of Man*. New York: Harper & Row, 1959.
Teodor, Shanin, ed. "Late Marx and the Russian Road." In *History Workshop Series*. London: Routledge and Kegan Paul, 1983.
Thoben, H. "Mechanistic and Organistic Analogies in Economics Reconsidered." *Kyklos* 35 (1982):292–306.
Thompson, Silvanus Phillips. *The Life of Lord Kelvin*. 2 vols. New York: Chelsea, 1976.
Time, December 28, 1987, 37.
Toffler, Alvin. *Future Shock*. New York: Bantam Books, 1970.
———. *The Third Wave*. Toronto: Bantam Books, 1981.
Tolman, Charles. "Marx and Nature." *Environmental Ethics* 3 (Spring 1981): 63–74.
Tönnies, Ferdinand. *Community & Society* [Gemeinschaft und Gesellschaft]. Ed. and trans. by C.P. Loomis. New York: Harper & Bros., 1957.
The Toronto Globe & Mail. September 29, 1987.
Trenn, Thaddeus J. "The Central Role of Energy in Soddy's Holistic and Critical Approach to Nuclear Science, Economics and Social Responsibility." *British Journal for the History of Science* 12, no. 42 (1979): 261–64.
Tsuchida, Atsushi. "No Future in Store for Petroleum and Atomic Energy: An Investigation of Human-Oriented, Stabilized Technology in the Post-Petroleum Era." Unpublished article, 1976.
Tsuchida, Atsushi, and Murota, Takeshi. "Fundamentals in the Entropic Theory of Water Cycle." *Ecocycle and Human Economy* (January 16, 1985).
Tugan-Baranovsky, Mikhail I. *The Theoretical Basis of Marxism*. N.p., n.d.
Turgot, Anne Robert Jacques, baron de l'Aulne. *Reflections on the Formation and Distribution of Riches*. New York: Macmillan 1898. [Originally published in 1770.]
———. "Reflexion sur la formation et la distribution des richesses," (1776) cited by Gide et Rist, *Histoire de Doctrines Économiques* Sirey (1947): 20.
———. *Textes choisis et pref.* Paris: Librairie Dalloz, 1947.
Umaña, Alvari F. "Toward a Biophysical Foundation for Economics." In Daly and Umaña, eds., *Energy, Economics and the Environment*.
Umpleby, Stuart. "Applying Systems Theory to the Conduct of Systems Research." In *Information Science in Action: Systems Design*. Vol. 1. The Hague: Martinus Nijhoff, 1983.
Uno, Kozo. *Principles of Political Economy: Theory of a Purely Capitalist Society*. Sussex: Harvester, 1964.
Utechin, S.V. "Philosophy and Society: Alexandr Bogdanov." In L. Labedz, ed., *Revisionism: Essays on the History of Marxist Ideas*. New York: Praeger, 1962.
Vaggi, G. "Profits in Physiocratic Economics." *History of Political Economy* 17, no. 3 (1985):372–84.
Valentinov, Nikolay. *Encounters with Lenin*. London: Oxford Univ. Press, 1968.
Varela, F.G.; Maturana, H.R.; and Uribe, R. "Autopoiesis: The Organization of Living Systems, Its Characterization and a Model." *Bio-Systems* 5 (1974): 187–96.
Veblen, Thorstein. *Absentee Ownership*. Boston: Beacon Press, 1967.
———. *The Theory of Business Enterprise*. New York: Scribner, 1932.
———. "Why Is Economics Not an Evolutionary Science?" *Quarterly Journal of Economics* 13 (1898): 393–97.
Vernadsky, Vladimir I. *La Biosphere*. Paris: Librairie Felix Alcan, 1929.
———. "The Biosphere and the Noösphere." *American Science* 33 (1945): 1–12.
———. *Essays in Geochemistry* [zbrannye sochineniya]. 5 vols. Moscow: izdatelstvo AN USSR, 1958–60.

————. *L'Évolution des Espèces et la Matière Vivante.* Leningrad: N.p., 1928.

————. "Problems of Biogeochemistry: The Fundamental Matter-Energy Difference between the Living and the Inert Natural Bodies of the Biosphere." *Transactions of the Connecticut Academy of Arts and Sciences* 35 (June 1944): 483–517.

Vickers, Sir Geoffrey. *Freedom in a Rocking Boat: Changing Values in an Unstable Society.* London: Penguin, 1970.

————. *Human Systems are Different.* London: Harper & Row, 1983.

————. "The Poverty of Problem Solving." *Journal of Applied Systems Analysis* 8 (1981):15–21.

Vijoen, S. *Economic Systems in World History.* New York: Longmans, 1974.

Vodolazov, G. "The Choice of History and the History of Alternative." *World Marxist Review* 31, no. 10 (October 1988): 90–99.

Voge, Jean. "Information and Information Technologies in Growth and Economic Crisis." *Technological Forecasting and Social Change* (1979):1–14.

Voropaev, G., and Kosarev, A. "The Fall and Rise of the Caspian Sea." *New Science* (April 8, 1982): 78–80. [Trans. from the Russian publication *Priroda* 1981 (1) 61.]

Vucinich, Alexander. *Social Thought in Tsarist Russia: The Quest for a General Science of Society, 1861–1917.* Chicago: Univ. of Chicago Press , 1976.

Waddington, Conrad H. *The Nature of Life.* London: Allen & Unwin, 1961.

————. *The Strategy of Genes.* New York: Macmillan 1957.

Wallace, Alfred Russel. "On the Tendency of Varieties to Depart Indefinitely from the Original Type." In *Linnaean Society Papers.* London: N.p., 1858.

Walras, Auguste. *De la nature de la richesse et de l'origine de la valeur.* Ed. Jean Baptiste Say. Paris: Felix Alcan, 1938.

Walras, Leon. *Correspondence of Leon Walras and Related Papers.* Ed. W. Jaffe. 3 vol. Amsterdam: North-Holland, 1965.

————. *Elements of Pure Economics: or, The Theory of Social Wealth.* Trans. William Jaffe. Homewood, Ill.: Published for the American Economic Association and the Royal Economic Society by R. Irwin, 1965. [Orignally published under the title *Éléments d'économie politique pure: ou, Theorie de la riches.* Paris: Librairie générale de droit et de jurisprudence, 1956.]

Walsh, Vivien C., and Gram, Harvey. *Classical and Neoclassical Theories of General Equilibrium: Historical Origins and Mathematical Structure.* New York: Oxford Univ. Press, 1980.

Wartofsky, Max W. *Feuerbach.* Cambridge: Cambridge Univ. Press, 1977.

Webb, T., and Kutzbach, J. "20,000 Years of Global Change." In Malone and Roederer, eds., *Global Change.*

Weber, Max. *General Economic History.* Trans. Frank H. Knight. New York: Collier Books, 1961.

Weisskopf, Walter A. *Alienation and Economics.* New York: Dutton, 1971.

Wellmer, Albrecht. *Critical Theory of Society.* New York: Herder and Herder, 1971.

Wells, H.G. *A Modern Utopia.* Introduction by Mark R. Hillegas. Lincoln, Nebraska: Univ. of Nebraska Press, 1967. [Originally published in 1905.]

Wells, H.G.; Huxley, J.; and Wells, G.P. *The Science of Life.* Garden City, N.Y.: Doubleday, 1933.

Wetter, Gustav A. *Dialectical Materialism.* Trans. Peter Heath. London: Routledge and Kegan Paul, 1958.

Weulersse, George, ed. *Manuscripts Économiques de François Quesnay.* New York: B. Franklin, 1968.

Whately, Richard, ed. *Bacon's Essays.* London: Longmans, Green, 1882.

White, James D. "Bogdanov in Tula." *Studies in Soviet Thought* 22 (1981): 33–58.

————. "The First Pravda and the Russian Marxist Tradition." *Soviet Studies* [Univ. of Glasgow] 26 (1974): 181–204.

White, Leslie A. *The Evolution of Culture: The Development of Civilization to the Fall of Rome.* Toronto: McGraw-Hill, 1943.

————. "The Historical Roots of the Ecological Crisis." *Science* 155 (1967): 1203–7.

White, S. "Turning Russia's rivers round from north to south." *New Science* 8 (1982): 79.

Whitehead, Alfred North. *Process and Reality.* London: N.p., 1929.

————. *Process and Reality: an Essay in Cosmology.* New York: Free Press, 1969.

Wiener, Norbert. *Cybernetics: or Control and Communication in the Animal and Machine.* New York: John Wiley & Sons, 1948.

————. *The Human Use of Human Beings.* Boston, Mass.: Avon Books, Houghton Mifflin, 1967.

Williams, Bernard Arthur Owen. *Descartes: the Project of Pure Enquiry.* Hassocks, England.: Harvester, 1978.

Williamson, Oliver W. "The Modern Corporations: Origins, Evolution and Attributes." *Journal of Economic Literature* 19 (December 1981): 1537–68.

Wilkinson, Richard. *Poverty and Progress: An Ecological Perspective on Economic Development.* New York: Praeger, 1973.

Wilson, A.G. *Catastrophe Theory and Bifurcation: Applications to Urban and Regional Systems.* Berkeley: Univ. of California Press, 1981.

Winiarsky, L. "Essai sur la mécanique sociale: l'énergie sociales et ses mensurations." *Revue Philosophique* 49 (1900).

————. "La Method mathmatique dans la sociologie et dans l'économie." *La Revue Socialiste* 20 (1894).

Winner, Langdon. *Autonomous Technology.* Cambridge: MIT Press, 1977.

Wisman, Jon D. "Legitimation, Ideology-Critique, and Economics." *Social Research* 46 (Summer 1979): 291.

Wolf, Abraham, ed. *Correspondence of Spinoza.* London: G. Allen & Unwin, 1928.

Wolin, Richard. "Modernism vs Postmodernism." *Telos* no. 62 (Winter 1984–85): 9–29.

Woodwell, G.M. "Short-Circuiting the Cheap Power Fantasy." *Natural History* (October 1974).

World Resources Institute (WRI). *The Global Possible: Resources, Development, and the New Century.* Washington: WRI, 1984.

Wright, Georg Henrik von. "Images of Science and Forms of Rationality." Background Memorandum. Toronto: E.R.S.P.G., Stong College, York Univ. Press, October 25, 1985.

————. *Technology and the Legitimation Crisis of Industrialized Society.* Helsinki: N.p., 1983.

Zeleny, Milan. "Cybernetics and General Systems: A Unitary Science?" *Kybernetes* 7 (1978).

————. "A Paradigm Lost?" In Zeleny, ed., *Autopoisesis, Dissipative Structures and Spontaneous Social Orders.*

————, ed. *Autopoisesis, Dissipative Structures and Spontaneous Social Orders.* Boulder, Colo.: Westview, 1980.

Zenkovsky, V.V. *A History of Russian Philosophy.* Trans. George L. Kline. New York: Columbia Univ. Press, 1953.

Zolo, Danilo. "Reflexive Self-Foundation of Sociology and Autopoiesis. Epistemological Assumptions of Niklas Luhmann's 'General Theory of Social Systems' " [Reflexive Selbstbegrundung der Soziologie und Autopoiesis. über die epistemologischen Voraussetzungen der 'allgemeinen Theories sozialer Systeme' Niklas Luhmanns]. *Soziale Welt* 36, no. 4 (1985): 519–34.

Zucchetto, James. "Energy and the Future of Human Settlement Patterns: Theory, Models and Empirical Considerations." *Ecological Modelling* 20 (1983): 85–111.
———. *Energy-Economics Measured for Selected Economies of the World, 1960–1980.* Manuscript. Regional Science Department, Univ. of Pennsylvania, 1984.

Index

Agriculture, 22–27
Air pollution, 96–97
Alienation, 44–50
Allopoietic systems, 187–200
Anti-Düring (Engels), 57, 58
Aquinas, Thomas, 31, 197
Arendt, Hannah, 14
Aristotle, 18
"Arrow of time", 68
Artisans, 25
Ashby, W. Ross, 167–68, 178
Aüsserung, 46
Autopoietic systems, 187–200, 197
  and capitalism, 218
  differentiated, 201–2
  and economic production, 192–93
  and economic reproduction, 199–
    200
  and energy, 194
  price-making market as, 203
Avenarius, Richard, 72

Bagehot, Walter, 213
Beer, Stafford, 178, 221
Bernard, Claude, 201
Bernstein, B.B., 120–21, 151
Bertalanffy, Ludwig von, 99–103, 124, 130,
    163, 204, 228
Bioeconomic model, 137
Biogeochemical evolution, 97
Biosphere
  coevolution of man and, 208–10
  evolution of, 207
Bogdanov, Aleksander A., 71–73, 93–94, 128,
    182, 228
  revisionist Marxism of, 73–81
  and self-organization of matter, 153
  socialism of, 249n.67
  theory of organization, 165
Boltzmann, Ludwig, 68, 100, 145 .

Bookchin, Murray, 147
Boulding, Kenneth, 124–29, 255–56n.64
Bukharin, Nikolas I., 84–89, 94, 124, 250n.102
  cybernetics of, 87–88
  general theory of equilibrium of, 85–87
  metabolics of, 88–89, 125, 126
Bureaucratization, 211

Calhoun, John, 192–93
Cannon, Walter, 267n.42
Capital, 120, 194, 270n.97
Capital (Marx), 39, 43–44, 117, 208
Capitalism, 51, 200
  as autopoietic system, 218
  Engels on, 46–47
  functional rationality, 31
  Marx on, 43–44, 47–48, 115–17
  mastery of nature, 48–50
  Mill on, 115–16
  mode of production, 36
  Polanyi on, 215
Capitalism, Socialism, and Democracy
    (Schumpeter), 200
Carbon dioxide, 97
Carey, Henry C., 70
Carnot, Sadi N.L., 67
China, 16–17, 21, 233n.55
Christensen, Paul, 113, 117
Circular flow, 118–22
  misplaced concreteness of, 103–10
  model of, 107
  myth of perpetual motion and, 113–18
Class interests, 78
Class structure, 25
Clerc, Nicolas-Gabriel, 16
Coal Question (Jevons), 116
Coevolution, 208–10, 223
  first principles of, 225–26
  school of, 7
Commodification, of nature, 45

Commoner, Barry, 132, 155–56
Complexification, 164–71, 186–87
Complexity, 164–69
  and epistemology, 181–82
  and organizational differentiation, 177–81
  of wholes, 182–87
Comte, Auguste, 68–69, 207
Comtean positivism, 36
Confucianism, 16–17, 29
Constraints, descending, 200–206
Consumption, 110
Contra-differentiation, 83
Control, 174–75, 205, 216
Convergence theory, 211
Cook, Earl, 157
Copleston, Frederick C., 76
Corn (Quesnay), 23
Cosmotheoros (Huygens), 99
Costanza, Robert, 150–51
Cost-benefit analysis, 142
Cottrell, Frederick, 133, 135, 155
Critique of the Gotha Program (Marx), 36, 42
Critique of Political Economy (Marx), 33
Critique of Pure Reason (Kant), 32
Cybernetics, 87–88, 171–82
  of autopoiesis, 192, 195, 221–22
  of avoidance, 205–6
  dialectics of, 184
  and epistemology, 181–82
  of error-controlled regulator, 176–77
  and freedom, 205
  and organizational differentiation, 177–81
  socio-cybernetic model, 137, 138–39
  and stable systems, 167

Daly, Herman E., 119, 122, 124, 132, 155, 156, 194
Darwin, Charles, 56, 164
Debenjak, Bozidar, 47
Debt, 91–92, 118
Democracy, 216
Determinism, 62–63, 70
The Development of Life in Nature and Society (Bogdanov), 128
Dialectical materialism, 56, 68
  epistemology and, 71–72
  and motion, 59
  and progress of science, 69
Dialectics, 51, 58, 59, 60, 183, 245n.244
  and Bogdanov, 75, 78
  cybernetic, 184
  of differentiated systems, 186
  fundamental laws of, 57
  quasi-equilibrium and, 87
Dialectics of Nature (Engels), 60
The Dialogue on the Work of Artisans (Quesnay), 15, 24
Diamat. *See* Dialectical materialism
Differentiation, 164–71, 185

Differentiation *(continued)*
  see also Organizational differentiation;
    Structural differentiation
Distribution, 119–20, 156–59
Diversity, 262n.188
Düring, Eugene, 59
Dynamic equilibrium, 99–100

Ecological-economic interaction models, 140–47
  "ecologized" neoliberalism, 143–45
  neosocial energetics, 145–47
Economic process
  biophysical models of, 132–59
    energy theory of value, 147–59
    integrated ecological-economic
      interaction models, 140–47
    steady state analysis, 154–59
    technico-ecological engineering,
      136–40
  integrated biospheric-socioeconomic models,
    134
  metabolic model of, 125
  and metabolism, 123–27
  neo-physiocratic models of, 95–131
    generational concerns, 95–98
    living systems and economic systems,
      122–31
    living systems, open systems, and
      general systems, 99–122
  as open autopoietic system, 200
  thermodynamics and nature of, 110–12
Eddington, Arthur Stanley, 68
Elements of Pure Economics (Walras), 193
Empirio-monism, 72–73, 75
Empirio-monism (Bogdanov), 76
Employment. *See* Labor
Energetics, 68–69, 70–71
  heretical philosophers of social, 89–90
  neosocial, 145–47
Energy, 118, 133
  artificial sources, 12
  autopoietic and allopoietic forms, 194
  Bogdanov on, 73, 77, 86
  causality, 192
  conservation of, 67
  Cottrell on, 135
  dissipation of, 130–31
  and Industrial Revolution, 136
  and Lotka's principle, 146
  Soddy on, 91
  solar, 123–24
  and steady state analysis, 154–59
  theory of value, 147–59
Engels, Frederick
  and capitalism, 46–47
  diamat, 68
  and energy theory of value, 149

Engels, Frederick *(continued)*
  on labor, 53
  and Marxism, 32, 33, 36–37
  and metabolic interaction with nature, 8
  and natural unity of science, 56–64
  scientific socialism of, 74
  on technology, 43, 50
Engineer Menni (Bogdanov), 80
Enlightened despotism, 21
Entaüsserung, 46
Entropic degradation, 102
Entropy
  Daly on, 111
  low, 112, 151, 195–96, 229
  minimum, 100–101
  Nijkamp on, 141–42
  and philosophy of materialism, 68–69
  and production, 131, 229
Epistemology
  and complexity, 181–82
  and dialectical materialism, 71–72
Equifinality, 252*n.24*
Equilibrium, general theory of, 28, 85–87
Equilibrium analysis, 106
Ergosphy, 90
Essays on Tektology (Bogdanov), 74
Evolution, 61, 67, 85
  and functional differentiation, 165
  open part, 206
  see also Coevolution; Historical evolution
Exchange-value, 92, 118
  circular flow of, 108–9

Feedback, 193
  autopoietic loops, 195
Feudalism, 30
Finalities, hierarchy of, 200–206
First Principles (Spencer), 68
Fisher, Irving, 120, 257*n.97*
Fleissgleichgewicht, 124
Fox-Genovese, Elizabeth, 29
France, 24–27
Freedom, 205, 226
  in technified society, 210–19
Free will, 17–18, 206
Frolov, Ivan T., 222
Fyodorov, N.F., 79

Galbraith, John Kenneth, 185, 211
General equilibrium, 28
General systems, 99–122
General Systems Theory (GST), 163–64
Genetic code, 206–7
Georgescu-Roegen, Nicholas, 110–12, 151, 158
German Ideology (Marx), 37, 53
Gilliland, Martha W., 149
Gödel's theorem, 180
Graham, Loren R., 79

Gram, Harvey, 108
The Great Transformation (Polyani), 135
Grove, William, 53
Growth, 118–22, 156–59
Grundrisse (Marx), 41, 42, 44–45, 46, 208
GST. *See* General Systems Theory

Habermas, Jürgen, 80, 81, 205
Harvey, William, 27, 28
Hegel, Georg W.F., 32–33, 57
Historical evolution, 58–59
Historical materialism, 56, 58–59, 73
Historical Materialism (Bukharin), 84, 85, 124
History and Class Consciousness (Lukács), 60
History of Economic Analysis (Schumpeter), 13–14
Hobbes, Thomas, 14
Hobson, John A., 255*n.63*
Homeostasis, 178–79, 202–3
  autopoietic, 188, 190, 203
Homo oeconomicus, 11–13
Hsu' Kuang ch'i, 20, 235–36*n.81*
Huettner, David A., 149
Hutchinson, T.W., 213
Hutten, Ernest, 192
Huxley, Julian, 127
Huygens, Christian, 99

Individualism, 4, 115, 169, 204–5, 212–13, 216
Industrial Revolution, 12, 136, 231*n.1*
Information, 192
  and production, 193–99
Institutions, 169–71
  as autopoietic system, 218
  general criteria for design, 220–23
  and individualism, 212
  role of, 222–23
  stabilizing capacities, 219

Jacob, François, 207
Jensen, K.M., 77
Jevons, W.S., 70–71, 113, 116
Joravsky, David, 57

Kamart, Jan, 181
Kant, Immanuel, 32
Kautsky, Karl, 76
Kawamiya, Nobuo, 112, 131
Keynes, John Maynard, 91
Klaus, Georg, 181
Koenig, Herman, 133, 136–40
  socio-cybernetics and bioeconomic model of, 137
Koolhaas, Jan, 177–78
Kulturwissenschaften (Ostwald), 71

Labor, 38, 42–43
  employment, 156–57
  Marx on, 49, 117, 30

Labor *(continued)*
  matter as prerequisite to, 92
  as metabolic interaction, 52–56
  objectification, 46
  and Physiocrats, 25–26, 30
Laborit, Henri, 127, 166
Laissez-faire, 15, 20–21, 215
Lakshmanan, T.R., 132
Lange, Oskar, 183
Laplace, Pierre Simon de, 109
Laplacean prototype, 67–69
Laszlo, Erwin, 168
Lectures of Justice, Policy, Revenue and Arms (Smith), 115
Le Despotisme de la Chine (Quesnay), 16, 24, 29
Legal Marxists, 72–73
Lenin, Vladimir Ilich, 73, 250*n.102*
  monism of, 75–76
  reaction to *Empirio-monism*, 76
Levi-Strauss, Claude, 105
Lindblom, Charles, 214
Li, Shaomin, 214
Living systems, 99–122, 171–82
  and autopoietic and allopoietic systems, 187–200
  and economic systems, 122–31
  and energy theory of value, 147
  reproduction of, 130, 191
Locke, John, 4
Lotka, Alfred J., 97, 126, 145
Lovelock, J.E., 101
Ludwig Feuerbach and the End of Classical German Philosophy (Engels), 58, 62
Luhmann, Nicklas, 184–85, 268*n.65*
Lukács, Georg, 60

Mach, Ernst, 68–69, 72, 247*n.25*
Manufacturing, 25
Marcuse, Herbert, 80
"Marginal Notes to the Programme of the German Worker's Party" (Marx), 42
Market fetishism, 211–12
Market system
  as autopoietic system, 203
  as energy distribution mechanism, 151
  and freedom, 211–19
  irresponsibility of, 215
  origins, 11
Marshall, Alfred, 30, 111, 258*n.107*
Maruyama, Makoto, 172
Marx, Karl, 8, 92, 208, 258*n.109*
  and capitalism, 33–34, 43–44, 47–48, 115–17
  and Darwin, 56
  and dialectics, 57, 59–60, 62–63
  doctrine of nature, 40–51
  labor theory of value, 149
  Marxism's revisionism of Bogdanov, 73–81
  open-system concept, 35–37

Marx, Karl *(continued)*
  and overall economic system, 228
  and Physiocrats, 8, 30–31
  prevalence of class contradiction, 86
  process of nature, 51–56
  and production, 77
  and second law of thermodynamics, 64
  social theory of, 34
  and totality theory, 32
  see also specific writings
Marxism. *See* Marx, Karl
Materialism, philosophy of, 68–69
Materials-balance model, 141
Matter, conservation of, 141
Maturana, Humberto, 187
Maxims (Quesnay), 20, 27
Mechanical causation, 3
  adherence to, 109–10
Mechanical materialism, 59, 61
Mechanical systems, 100
Meditazioni sulla Economica Politica (Verri), 53–54
Medow, Paul I., 222
Meek, Ronald L., 28–29
Memory, 206
Menshikov, S., 211
Metabolic interaction, 51–56
  and Bukharin, 88–89, 125, 126
  and economic process, 123–27
Metasystems, 180
Methodenstreit, 4
Military, 97–98
Mill, James, 213
Mill, John Stuart, 115–16
Mirabeau, Marquis de V.R., 18, 23, 24
Misplaced concreteness, 181–82, 213
Moiseev, N.N., 167, 222, 266*n.32*
Moleschott, Jacob, 52
Money, 91–93, 149
Money fetishism, 118
Montesquieu, Baron Charles-Louis de Secondat et de, 19
Multistability, 168
Murota, Takeshi, 131, 196

National income, 108
Natural order, 16–23, 106
Natural Right (Quesnay), 17–24
Natural selection, 171
Natural theology, 13–14
Nature
  as aesthetic experience, 45
  capital as embodiment of, 194
  Marx's doctrine of, 40–51
  Marx's process of, 51–56
  and society, 10, 37
  and species-being of man, 37–40
  and totality theory, 31–65
Needham, Joseph, 3

Negative selection, 83–84
Neoliberalism, 143–45
Net product, 23–27, 28
Nijkamp, Peter, 140–43, 152
  open-system, economic model of, 143
Noösphere, 7, 37–38, 64–65
  defined, 5–6
  political economy for, 206–26
Norgaard, Richard B., 126
Norms, biospheric, 210
Nung Cheng Ch'an Shu (Hsu' Kuang-ch'i), 20

Objectification, 45, 46
Objectivity, 33
Odum, Elizabeth C., 127
Odum, Howard, 132, 145–50, 154–55
OECD. *See* Organization for Economic
  Cooperation and Development
Ohio River Basin Study, 96
On the Correlation of Physical Forces (Grove),
  53
Open-systems economic analysis, 99–122, 167
  according to Bertalanffy, 102
  in Marx's model, 35–37
  Nijkamp's model of, 143
  philosophical origins, 3–65
    historical background, 9–13
    political economy, 13–31
    totality theory, 31–65
  substantive model of, 127–31
  and Tektology, 83–84
Organic systems, 32
Organizational differentiation, 183, 186, 220
  cybernetics and, 177–81
Organizational dissonance, 171–82, 266n.27
Organizational dynamics, 164–69
Organization for Economic Cooperation and
  Development (OECD), 96
Organization, general theory of, 66–94, 173
  problem of wholes and their complexity,
    182–87
*The Origin of the Family, Private Property and
  the State* (Engels), 63
Ostwald, Wilhelm, 68–69, 71, 133
Ozone layer, 276–77n.206

Paris Manuscripts (Marx), 39, 40–41, 51, 53,
  258n.109
Parsons, Howard, 38, 46, 51, 243n.225
Passet, René, 112, 122, 130, 152, 190, 195, 210,
  219
Perpetual motion, 113–18
Perroux, François, 218–19
Persistence of Force, Law of, 67–68
Phenomenalism, 68
Phenomenology of the Spirit (Hegel), 32
The Philosophy of Living Experience
  (Bogdanov), 73, 77
Physiocrats, 8, 13–31, 90–93, 199, 228, 233n.55

Planck, Max, 67
Political economy, 13–31, 199
  in broad sense, 122–31
  for epoch of the Noösphere, 206–26
    coevolution, 223
    coevolution of man and Biosphere,
      208–10
    conclusions, 223–26
    institutional design, 220–23
  origins of, 13–31
    conclusion, 30–31
    natural order, 16–23
    produit net, 23–27
    Tableau Économique, 27–30
Politics (Aristotle), 18
Pollution, 133
  local, 96
  monetary costs of, 97, 136
Polyani, Karl, 80, 128, 135, 200, 215–16,
  272–73n.126
Population, 114, 209
Positive laws, 19, 21, 210
Positive selection, 83–84
Positivism, 69, 72
Power, 216
"Principle of Recursion" (Montesquieu), 19
Problems of Life (Bertalanffy), 99
Process, 182
Production, 113, 159–60, 229
  autopoiesis and economic, 192–93
  and circular flow, 110
  forces of, 77
  informational dimension of, 193–99
  relations of, 34–35, 38, 43
  Tamanoi's redefinition of, 129
*Production of Commodities by Means of
  Commodities* (Sraffa), 108
Produit net, 23–27
Psychic flux, 120

Quasi-equilibrium, 86–87
Quesnay, François, 8, 15–31, 145, 233n.55
  234–36nn.78, 81
  produit net, 23–27

Randomness, 163
Rappoport, R., 148
Ratick, S., 132
Rationality, 170, 205, 221
Recursion, 186
Regulation, 173–77
Reichwein, Adolf, 16
Rent, 29
Requisite variety, 173–77, 178, 183–84, 191,
  220
Resources, natural, 34, 55, 105, 112, 117, 121
Revolution, 85
Ricardo, David, 31, 114, 213

Riviere, Pierre F.J.H. Mercier de la, 20
Robbins, Lionel, 103–04
Robin, J., 197–98
Rubin, Milton D., 100
Rural Philosophy (Mirabeau and Quesnay), 18
Ruskin, John, 95

Salk, Jonas, 206
Scarcity, 104
Schaff, Adam, 157
Schmidt, Alfred, 37, 38, 52, 58, 60–61
Schrödinger, Erwin, 101–02, 130, 135, 192
Schumacher, E.F., 215
Schumpeter, Joseph A., 13–14, 26, 28, 129, 200
Science, 65
    natural unity of, 56–64, 69–84
    see also Technology
Science and Life (Soddy), 90
The Science of Life (Wells, Wells, and Huxley), 127
Self-interest, 15, 21
Senior, Nassau, 70
Service, 120
Simon, Herbert, 170, 178
Simple stability, 167
Smith, Adam, 4, 14–15, 29, 106, 113–15, 144, 212, 213
Social Darwinism, 36
Socialism, 200
Society
    four organizational modes of, 113–15
    relationship with nature, 10, 37
Socio-cybernetic model, 137, 138–39
Soddy, Frederick, 94, 105, 121, 145, 149
    and circular flow, 108–9
    Physiocracy, 90–93
    theory of energy determinants of steady state, 155
Solar energy, 123–24
Solow, Robert, 121, 129–30
Spencer, Herbert, 67–68
Spinoza, Baruch de, 4
Sraffa, Piero, 108
Stability, 164–69
Stalin, Joseph, 250*n.102*
Stammler, Rudolf, 87
Stationary state, 116, 144
Statistical laws, 70
Steady states, 100–101, 102
    economic analysis, 154
Stites, Richard, 79
Structural differentiation, 183
Structure, 182
Stumm, Werner, 132
Subjectivity, 33
Sulfur dioxide, 96–97
Surplus, 26–27, 29
Susiluoto, Ilmari, 86
Symbiosis, 31
Systemic variety, 184

Systems, general. *See* General systems
Systems theory, 32–35, 162, 182
    complexification through differentiation, 164–71
    institutional implications, 169–71
    organizational dynamics, 164–69
    see also General Systems Theory (GST)

Tableau Économique (Quesnay), 27–30, 108
Tamanoi, Yoshiro, 101, 112, 113, 127–31
Taxation, 24
Technico-ecological engineering, 136–40
Technological systems, 190
Technology, 10–11, 32, 65, 117
    and Biosphere, 209
    Bogdanov on, 79, 80
    Bukharin on, 87
    Engels on, 43
    freedom and, 49–50, 210–19
    Odum on, 146
    and steady state economy, 157
Teilhard de Chardin, Pierre, 5–6
Tektology, 74, 75, 81, 93, 154, 166
    empirio-monism to, 72–73
    and generalized metabolics, 82–83
    Hegelian dialectics of organization to, 81–84
    and open systems, 83–84
    and regulating mechanism, 82
The Theory of Open Systems in Physics and Biology (Bertalanffy), 100
Thermodynamics
    discovery of and collapse of Laplacean prototype, 67–69
    first law of, 141
    and nature of economic process, 110–12
    second law of, 61, 64
Threshold effects, 180
Tolman, Charles, 50
Totalitarianism, 203–4
Totality theory, 31–65
    conclusion, 54–65
    Marx's doctrine of nature, 40–51
    metabolic interaction, 51–56
    natural unity of science, 56–64
    nature and species-being of man, 37–40
    open system concept in Marx's model, 35–37
    and systems theory, 32–35
Transmutation: the Vital Problem of the Future (Soddy), 90
Tsuchida, Atsushi, 130, 196
Tugan-Baranovsky, Mikhail I., 78
Turgot, Anne Robert Jacques, 23–24, 26, 27

Ultrastability, 167
Use-values, 55, 92, 110, 129, 148, 149, 151, 197–98

Value, 13, 30, 52–53
    energy theory of, 147–59

Varela, Francisco, 187
Veblen, Thorstein, 4–5, 215
Vernadsky, Vladimir I., 5, 6, 7, 37, 49,
    64–65, 206, 244*n*.237
Verri, Pietro, 53–54
Vickers, Geoffrey, 164–65
Vucinich, Alexander, 79

Waddington, Conrad H., 164
Wallace, Alfred Russel, 171
Walrasian models, 129
Walras, Leon, 193
Walsh, Vivien C., 108
Warmtod, 68
Wastes, 12, 112
Water cycle, 131
Wealth, 18, 24–26
    circulation of, 27

Wealth *(continued)*
    maldistribution of, 234–35*n.78*
    and Soddy, 90–93
Wealth of Nations (Smith), 14, 113
Wells, G.P., 127
Wells, H.G., 127
What is Life? (Schrödinger), 101
What is Life from the Point of Physics
    (Schrödinger), 192
White, J.D., 76
White, L.A., 133, 135
Whitehead, Alfred North, 181–82
Wiener, Norbert, 172
Winiarsky, L., 71

Yu le Grand et Confucius (Clerc), 16

Zenkovsky, V.V., 79

About the author

Kenneth M. Stokes was formerly attached to the Economic Research and Systems Planning Group of York University. He is now teaching at the Graduate School of International Relations of the International University of Japan where he is finalizing a companion piece titled *Against Common Sense*.